Rioters and Citizens

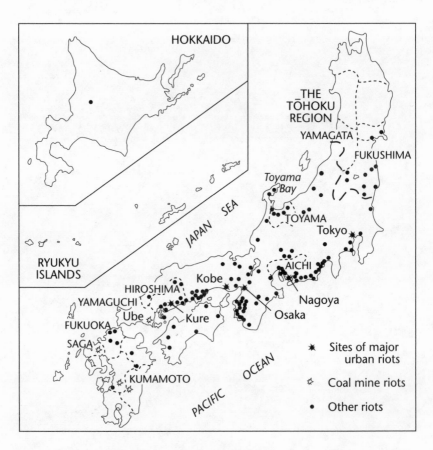

Map 1. Schematic Distribution of Rice Riots
This map does not include uprisings in agricultural villages or indicate multiple incidents in the same general vicinity. To include either category would require several hundred additional dots. Rural uprisings tended to be clustered around cities undergoing rapid industrialization. Although all cities reported unrest, the major urban riots occurred along the Inland Sea and Pacific coasts in a belt extending from Hiroshima prefecture to Fukushima prefecture. Coalfield protests occurred at Ube in Yamaguchi prefecture and at mines in Fukuoka, Saga, and Kumamoto. Unrest was also reported at the Jōban region pits in Fukushima. The Tōhoku region, with the exception of Fukushima (the region's most industrialized prefecture) was quiet during the weeks of protest.

Rioters
and Citizens

Mass Protest
in Imperial Japan

Michael Lewis

UNIVERSITY OF CALIFORNIA PRESS
Berkeley   Los Angeles   Oxford

University of California Press
Berkeley and Los Angeles, California

University of California Press, Ltd.
Oxford, England

Library of Congress Cataloging-in-Publication Data

Lewis, Michael Lawrence.
    Rioters and citizens : mass protest in imperial Japan / Michael Lewis.
      p.   cm.
    Bibliography: p.
    Includes index.
    ISBN 0-520-06642-1 (alk. paper)
    1. Rice Riots, Japan, 1918. 2. Rice—Prices—Social aspects—
Japan—History. 3. Japan—Politics and government—1912–1926.
I. Title.
DS888.L49   1990
952.03'2—dc20   89-32111
                                                        CIP

Printed in the United States of America

1 2 3 4 5 6 7 8 9

To my parents,
Lawrence F. and Odell Lewis

Contents

Illustrations follow page 134

Tables

Figures

Acknowledgments

The writing of this study owes much to many. At Stanford University, I am indebted to Jeffrey P. Mass for conveying an understanding of pre-Tokugawa Japan and to Hal Kahn who sparked my interest in the politics of popular protest. Peter Duus, my dissertation adviser, deserves special thanks. Over the long period from thesis to book, he has been a source of insightful criticism and constant encouragement. I am sure that he will welcome this study if for no other reason than its publication will at last free him from having to read yet another revised version.

I am grateful to Matsuo Takayoshi, Kinbara Samon, Kaneko Tadao, Ochiai Shigenobu, and Takeda Hōichi for sharing with me their extensive knowledge of modern Japanese history and of the 1918 rice riots, and for facilitating research conducted in Japan between 1981 and 1985. I am also thankful to Imoto Mitsuo, a historian of Toyama's local history, for organizing fieldwork conducted in his home prefecture. Professor Imoto was especially helpful in arranging interviews with participants in the 1918 riots who generously shared with me their recollections. Masuyama Kamee provided invaluable assistance in deciphering handwritten documents to supplement oral accounts. Thanks are also owed to Nimura Kazuo, the director of the Ōhara Social Problems Research Institute (Ōhara Shakai Mondai Kenkyūjo), for providing access to that institution's rich collection of Taishō documents and to Mitani Taichirō for hosting my stay as a visiting scholar at the

Faculty of Law, Tokyo University, during 1981 and 1982, and again from 1988 to 1989.

For granting permission to use illustrations that appear in the text I am grateful to Kaneko Tadao of the Namerikawa Historical Museum; Tazaki Yoshinobu, managing editor, Kobe Shinbun Company; Kawamura Zenjirō of the Nihon Kindaishi Kenkyū Kai; Hisamoto Santa, president, Ashi Shobō Publishing Company; Morimoto Masahiko, editor in chief, Chikuma Shobō Publishing Company; and Watanabe Miyoshi, curator, Ōmiya Municipal Cartoon Exhibition Hall.

Many colleagues have provided helpful criticisms of this monograph during its various stages of completion. In particular, I would like to thank Ann Waswo, Gail Lee Bernstein, Jeff Hanes, Jim McClain, Betsey Scheiner, Michael Malloch, and the late Sharon Nolte for their comments and advice. Ann Waswo and an anonymous reader at the University of California Press deserve special recognition for reading the entire manuscript and calling my attention to several problems of fact and interpretation. I am also grateful to Harold Marcus, Lisa Fine, and Justin Kestenbaum of the Department of History, Michigan State University; to Harold for his ever sharp editorial pencil, to Lisa for her insights into women's history, and to Justin for patiently conveying his considerable knowledge of computer arcana. Sheila Levine, sponsoring editor at the University of California Press, has been unflagging in her support since first reading this study in its dissertation form in 1984. She has worked long and hard in shepherding the manuscript toward publication.

The Stanford University Department of History, the Japan Foundation, Stanford's Center for Research in International Studies, and the Whiting Foundation provided financial support for completing the dissertation on which this monograph is based. Postgraduate research and writing have been made possible by a Japan Foundation Professional Fellowship, a summer research grant from the Northeast Asia Council of the Association for Asian Studies, and Michigan State University Research Grants.

Finally, I thank Junko and Mie, my wife and daughter, for bearing with me during what must have seemed an interminable period of research and writing. With warmth, patience, and a renewable supply of good humor they provided the conditions indispensible for completing this work. Support and advice have come from many quarters, but I am, of course, responsible for any remaining errors of fact or interpretation.

Japanese Measures
Used in the Text

Square Measures

1 tan = .245 acre
1 chō = 2.45 acres or 10 tan

Capacity

1 shō = 1.92 quarts
1 to = 4.8 gallons or 10 shō
1 koku = 44.8 gallons, 4.96 bushels, or 100 shō

Monetary Units

1 yen = 100 sen
1 mon = approx. 1 sen

Introduction

On 22 July 1918, a group of fishermen's wives in a small village on the coast of Toyama Bay gathered in the evening coolness to discuss what they could do to bring down the spiraling cost of rice. This first peaceful meeting around a community well marked the beginning of the 1918 rice riots, a series of mass demonstrations and armed clashes on a scale unprecedented in Japan's modern history. For eight weeks unrest continued from Hokkaido to Kyushu in fishing villages and rural hamlets, in city streets, and around coal pits. The central government resorted to drastic measures to contain what some political observers believed to be the beginning of a second Russian Revolution. Prefectural governors, finding local police incapable of controlling the massive unrest, requested that troops be mobilized. The central government speedily complied by dispatching more than 100,000 troops to 140 localities to suppress rioting. In restoring order, soldiers turned their guns on the crowd, killing more than thirty civilians and wounding scores of others.

Although of enormous scale, the riots seemed to end in utter failure for the protesters. Rice prices continued at high levels for nearly a year after the riots. The legitimacy of the imperial system, which the protesters never seriously challenged, remained intact and unaltered, as did the basic structure of the Meiji constitutional order. Indeed, the robust health of state authority appeared confirmed by the more than five thousand convicted rioters who accepted their sentences, quietly paid fines, and served prison terms with barely a murmur of dissent.

The riots seemed no more than ephemeral events that simply passed over the surface of Japanese society. They nevertheless tell much about the changing traditions of popular protest and Japan's modern political and economic development. Just as in Europe, the action of the unenfranchised crowd came to influence the course of politics and the formulation of social policy. A study of popular protest in Japan or the West reveals the political thinking of otherwise inarticulate sections of society that in historical inquiries often appear as the passive objects of state policies and sweeping economic changes.

The riots further demonstrate that the Meiji leadership's aim of creating a new citizenry, unified ideologically and consistently supportive of national goals, was still work in progress. Japanese political practice has been, for long historical stretches, more local than national in focus. Although the Meiji government had made tremendous strides in welding more than 250 "feudal" domains into a modern nation-state, local politics still preoccupied the citizens of greater Japan. As discussed in the following chapters, the 1918 riots manifest a variety of regional responses to the nationwide economic and social changes that followed the 1868 Restoration and reveal a public neither unified in outlook nor single-minded in action. The disunity, however, does not suggest that Japan had become a nation polarized into opposing camps, the people on one side, the state on the other. The rioters themselves acted out of mixed motives because their protests were part of a complex process that depended on preexisting beliefs and local social relations. Certain traditional factors appeared steady and enduring, such as popular assumptions about "moral" economic behavior and paternalistic assistance from landlords in northeastern rice-farming districts; others were in flux, as is seen in the relations between crowds and the police in Japan's rapidly industrializing cities.

This study tends to question rather than affirm standard historical interpretations of the riots. The protests were indeed massive, but the "masses" were not a unitary group acting out of a special "class consciousness" or inchoate popular yearning for leftist revolution. Although the riots possibly corresponded with the desires of several individual intellectual socialists and anarchists, the protesters' interpretations of their own actions usually differed from the analyses of postriot political commentators and political activists. In some cases, the local uprising could not even be called liberal, if that means an advocacy of natural political rights or principled opposition to autocracy. Although certain regions did indeed possess long traditions of resistance to authority, in the form of a samurai magistrate or the governor of a modern prefecture, the riots can be better understood by referring to Confucian benevolence and the responsibility of social "superiors" rather than to Lockean notions of inalienable rights to life, liberty, and property.

Nor were the protests the direct result of the accumulated grievances resulting from absolute deprivation. Had economic want supplied the only motivation, then popular protest would have been far more common, not just during the Taishō years but throughout Japan's modern history. In fact, riots and tumults would assuredly have been widespread in most of the years following the Meiji Restoration.

That the 1918 protests do not support general historical "laws" does not detract from their historical importance. A study of them tells much about the relationship of state authority and the public. It also provides insights into the varied conceptions of legitimate popular political participation and into the process by which segments of the unenfranchised public "bargained," sometimes forcibly, for preferred policies and against disliked programs. The diverse nature of Japanese popular protest also reveals the patently false stereotype of the bland uniformity of Japanese society. Finally, in the scope of changes they engendered, the riots altered the course of Japanese history, auguring a shift to new forms of political involvement by the public.

Despite the riots' historical importance, relatively little is known of the 1918 uprisings outside the Japanese academic community, which began immediately to analyze their significance. Not surprisingly, most contemporary observers interpreted the protests with an eye toward formulating policy changes that would serve to prevent a recurrence of widespread unrest. Many recommended that the Terauchi government accept responsibility for its mistaken policies regarding rice prices and immediately resign. A number of journalists and political pundits also wrote on the need to revise laws governing national food reserves and to strengthen local police forces. Others recommended measures to smooth relations between capital and labor or to bolster religious and educational institutions as a means of mending the national unity apparently shattered by the often violent protests.

Most analysts paid scant attention to the long-term causes of unrest. They were even less concerned with the varieties of protest evident in the nationwide uprising. In general, two views of the riots coexisted in 1918. The first suggested that the riots were a massive outburst of frustration over high prices for rice, a structurally simple protest reminiscent of the *ikki,* or peasant-led rural uprising. In the 1918 riots, however, the *ikki* was said to have broken out in city streets as well as farming villages. The second view described events as a violent, albeit unconscious, expression of class war in the making, one in which Toyama fishwives served as Japanese Charlotte Cordays in sparking a movement that threatened the existence of Japan's imperial system.

Two decades later, government researchers developed a deeper analysis of the causes and consequences of the 1918 riots. In 1938 Nagoya district prosecutor Yoshikawa Mitsusada presented a lengthy private report on the riots to Justice Ministry superiors. Using statements made by protesters at massive urban rallies and recorded by plainclothes police, Yoshikawa attempted to assess the rioters' objectives by studying what they had to say about their actions. In examining the political motivation for the riots and the protests' possible linkages with socialism, the prosecutor paid special attention to the activities of journalists, leftists, labor organizers, party politicians, and regional officials. He also relied on local police reports and district court records in attempting to understand better why rioting occurred and why it went out of control. The title of Yoshikawa's work, *Iwayuru kome sōdō jiken no kenkyū* (Research on the so-called rice riot incidents), indicates his view that the protests were less uniform than the term "rice riot" might suggest. His appraisal seems entirely valid, but his report was circumscribed by the purpose for which it had been drafted. Although comprehensive in its compilation of background information, the study was written for central-government officials keen on understanding the origins and consequences of unrest, particularly because Japan was now on a war footing and food shortages had become a worrisome future possibility. Not surprisingly, the report, which tended to investigate the riots as social pathology, was not made public until after World War II.[1]

Outside government circles, one Japanese scholar, Hosokawa Karoku, began an intensive study of the riots long before Yoshikawa started his work. In the early 1930s he published a portion of his "materials" (*shiryō*) on the Toyama and Wakayama protests. Yet, like the official government report, Hosokawa's work was not widely available until the immediate postwar period when scholars, freed from wartime restraints on studying politically sensitive subjects, turned their attention to modern Japan's single largest incident of civil unrest. In 1946, Hosokawa, a social-policy scholar at the Ōhara Social Problems Research Institute (Ōhara Shakai Mondai Kenkyūjo), recommended publishing material that he had been gathering since the late 1920s.[2] His understanding of the riots was strongly influenced by Katayama Sen, whom Hosokawa met in Moscow in the mid-1920s. Although the precise details of their conversations remain unclear, there is no doubt that Hosokawa was won over to a class-based analysis of the riots.[3]

Between 1927 and 1933 Hosokawa quietly carried out field research concerning rioting in Toyama and other regions throughout Japan. He also carefully collected reports of the riots published in central and regional newspapers and transcribed testimony given by suspected rioters at public trials. Owing to Hosokawa's efforts, a small but important sampling of county (*gun*) government records from Toyama, Wakayama, and Yamaguchi prefectures were saved after the district system was abolished in 1926. His efforts provided a dauntingly massive documentary base useful for understanding both the local causes of protest and the state's response.

During the 1950s and 1960s other scholars rapidly built on Hosokawa's prewar work, a collection of approximately sixty thousand draft pages in almost a hundred volumes. Researchers from Hōsei, Waseda, and Kyoto universities, often accompanied by teams of eager university students, descended upon scenes of the riots to interview actual participants, relatives of rioters who had died, and local officials. Members of Kyoto University's Social Science Research Institute (Jinbun Kagaku Kenkyūjo), with funding from the Ministry of Education, organized the Hosokawa materials and supplemented that work with new materials, including findings from their own fieldwork and case studies. The Kyoto University team produced the most thorough investigation of the protests. Led by Inoue Kiyoshi and Watanabe Tōru and including many historians active today, the researchers published the results of their work, *Kome sōdō no kenkyū*, in five volumes between 1959 and 1962. Without this massive collection of primary materials (including government reports, trial testimony, interviews, and statistical records), the present study would have been extremely difficult to undertake.[4]

Scholarship directed toward the riots during the 1950s and 1960s has been exhaustively thorough, but it has also tended to be skewed by some of the same preoccupations evident in prewar studies. In particular, class-based analysis has distorted the political significance of the riots. Postwar historical treatments have viewed the mass protests as indicative of a crisis of capitalism that pitted the rich against the poor and portended the possible onset of class warfare. Thus, the common image of the riots is one of failed revolution. Japanese scholars have argued that, although deteriorating economic and social conditions led to class mobilization that was especially marked from 1914 to 1918, class consciousness was insufficient to create class organization. Their work suggests that although conditions for sweeping change were present in uprisings like the rice riots, a counterpart to the Russian Bolshevik party was not. According to the long-prevailing view, the handful of Japanese socialist and anarchist thinkers had neither the organization nor the uniform ideology required to transform mass discontent into a fundamental social restructuring.

Studies written by local historians and regional research groups during the 1970s and 1980s have tended to modify slightly the class-based analysis of the protests. Scholars at central universities have also revised earlier interpretations. The work of Koyama Hitoshi, a historian at Kansai University, is representative of the changed view of the protests:

> The rice riots themselves were not an economic struggle based on fixed and clear class relationships, capitalist against labor, landlord against tenant farmer. Sharply higher rice prices directly worsened living conditions, suddenly causing a spontaneous explosion of discontent by the masses living in cities, farm villages, and fishing hamlets. From start to finish the overall incident was unplanned and unorganized. In concert with the rice riots, disputes mounted by industrial workers broke out one after another in August. But because the disputes were spontaneous economic struggles by groups still lacking union leadership, no links could be forged in any organized fashion with the rice riots. The socialist movement had not yet revived and, although individual leftists joined the protests, self-conscious socialist leadership was not to be seen.[5]

This interpretation, in its suggestion of opportunities missed and in its stress on the reflexive nature of protest, is not a significant break from the general postwar view of the riots.

Although neither Japanese nor Western studies use the term *Jacquerie*, they nonetheless suggest that something similar to a national Jacquerie took place in 1918. Like the Jacquerie, the riots have been described as spontaneous, violent, and politically unconscious. But those who rose up are identified not as peasants but as lower-order laborers (*saimin*). Despite this difference, the notion of a Jacquerie of enormous scale comes closest to characterizing the general historiographical interpretation of the 1918 uprisings. The riots have been described as spontaneous or naturally occurring (*shizen hassei-teki*), owing to the absence of identifiable plans and planners, spasmodic, because of the lack of any national-level organization, and apolitical, because the rioters' objectives appeared to begin and end with rice.

The aim of this study is to examine the variety of protests, that historians have heretofore tended to view as a single cataclysmic event. Throughout the following chapters, I attempt to answer four basic questions about the 1918 riots. First, what political significance did the riots have within the communities in which they occurred? Second, how and why did protest change in different regions or when carried out by divergent occupational groups? Third, how did officials, community leaders, and the heads of private enterprises cope with the unprecedented outbreak of unrest? And finally, what lasting effects did the riots have on local political relations, economic ties between groups such as landlords and farmers, and the development, or lack thereof, of trade unionism in the coal-mining industry?

With regard to the first question, the works of E. P. Thompson and others on the functioning of a "moral economy" have been especially helpful in understanding the significance of crowd protests. Thompson defines the moral economy in the following manner:

> It was grounded upon a consistent traditional view of social norms and obligations of the proper function of several parties within the community, which taken together, can be said to constitute the moral economy of the poor. An outrage to these moral assumptions, quite as much as actual deprivation was the usual occasion for direct action.[6]

Although Thompson's concept is valuable for an understanding of the protests in Toyama and rural regions, to be discussed in the following chapters, it is less pertinent to uprisings that occurred in Japanese cities or in coalfields during 1918. Protest changed when it took place in these areas. While traditional protest tended to overlap with more overtly political struggles in some regions, in city rioting or in protests between management and workers, "rational" collective bargaining by riot seemed to replace any popular desire to reinstate traditional social norms. Protest was transformed when carried out by the heterogeneous populations of growing Japanese cities. By destroying property and physically attacking the forces of order, city rioters seemed to go beyond the bounds of action deemed proper by rural protesters. Indeed, the sometimes violent struggle for freer political expression and economic rationality waged by city dwellers and coal miners appeared to deny the very paternalistic authority that rioters elsewhere sought to restore.

Throughout this study I also devote attention to the "official" reaction to the riots. This includes measures taken in response to rioting by those with leadership positions within local communities, even though they may not have held formal political office. The official reaction to rioting was often harshly repressive. Yet this generalization is not valid for all incidents of rioting. Just as the rioters' objectives and methods shifted regionally, with traditional food riots overlapping more modern forms of protest, so did the response of community leaders.

The approach taken in the following chapters has been to allow riot participants, to the greatest extent possible, to speak for themselves. Although rioters are not well known for writing down reflections of their activities, a variety of sources, including my own and previously published interviews, do contain the rioters' perspective on the 1918 protests. Firsthand accounts, of course, pose problems in ascertaining reliability. Riots are typically fast-moving, fluid events, which, like the incident in Akutagawa's *In a Bamboo Grove*, can be variously interpreted, depending on the observer's particular role in the occurrence. Events are also apt to become embroidered in the retelling. Nevertheless, the rioters' actions tended to confirm not only their words but in many cases the official record as well.

ONE

The 1918 Nationwide Riots
Mass Protest, Political Parties, and State Response

With the advent of World War I, Allied demand for textile and industrial goods enabled a small segment of Japan's population to become wealthy almost overnight. Journalists and politicians saw the rapid growth of a nouveau riche, or *narikin*, class as a worrisome problem. In 1919 the *Japan Year Book* included a new section, "Plutocracy in Japan." The yearbook's editors placed it squarely between discussions of "wages of laborers" and "recent labor troubles" so that no one could miss the relatedness of all three issues. In describing this group they noted that "millionaires" had increased by 115 percent between 1915 and 1919 and, with an unmistakably derisive tone, defined membership in this group by the newness of the fortunes. Of wealthy shipowners the yearbook writers observed that such men "have to thank the European war for their creation."[1] The wider population shared the journalists' disdain for the *narikin*. The word itself, borrowed from a Japanese chess move in which a pawn is suddenly transformed into a vastly more powerful piece, suggested unjustified gain. In the popular imagination, as well as in newspaper cartoons, the individual *narikin* was depicted, with a mixture of moral superiority and envy, as a Taishō-era fat cat, a jowly arriviste ever willing to burn yen notes instead of matches to impress an obliging geisha (see figs. 1 and 2).

In contrast to the *narikin*, the great majority of Japanese saw real spending power decline during the boom years 1914–1918. That conditions generally worsened for Japanese consumers during that period does not negate long-term improvement, which might have begun before (and undoubtedly continued long after) the Meiji Restoration.[2] Yet statistical improvement did not translate into real gains for Japanese workers or their families. Wage increases during the war years actually lagged far behind the doubling in the cost of food, fuel, cloth, and other consumer goods during this period. The erosion began gradually: real wages in 1915 declined by only 3 percent from the previous year, but by 1918 they had fallen by more than 30 percent from the 1914 level.[3] Although statistics inadequately reveal the human toll taken by inflation during 1914–1918, they nevertheless suggest a widespread decline in material well-being. Higher rates of contagious disease, including increased incidents of tuberculosis, were registered at the very time that factory output and trade nearly quadrupled.[4]

Inflation did not confine its toll to a single class or segment of the population. Newspaper reports flesh out the impression given by quantified evidence that the material quality of life was worsening, not only for the poor but also for the emerging "middle class" (*chūryū kaikyū*). Although neither the press nor politicians seemed surprised about continued poverty among traditionally impoverished social groups, the general decline in economic well-being gave cause for alarm. Newspapers reflected popular concern by regularly reporting on the plight of lower-level government officials such as policemen, teachers, and clerks, whom journalists occasionally referred to as "paupers in Western clothes" (*yōfuku saimin*; see fig. 3).[5] One estimate put the decline in the purchasing power of minor public servants in 1914–1918 at approximately 50 percent; that is, at a lower real-wage level than most of the working poor.[6] Indeed, the rapid rise in commodity prices hit the official and "salary man" classes harder than factory hands or craftsmen. Unlike craftsmen or industrial workers, who could put in overtime and take in piecework for themselves and family members, groups that were socially "middle-class" lacked the time and opportunity to supplement their wages. Even if they could find time, a wife's taking in sewing or a husband's moonlighting at a neighborhood workshop was beneath the dignity of officials and white-collar workers, however lowly their rank.

Consequently, policemen, teachers, and civilian workers engaged in an unprecedented number of wage disputes. Walkouts, such as that staged by 150 Osaka policemen in August 1918—the very month that urban rioting left major Japanese cities under virtual martial law—were familiar occurrences among public workers in 1918. Threatened or actual work stoppages were carried out by waterworks employees and sanitation workers in Sakai, city clerks in Amagasaki, mail handlers in Himeiji, as well as by 420 guards and other workers at Osaka Prison.[7] Even low-ranking employees within the Imperial Household Agency vowed to walk out if their wages were not increased. Editorial writers, shocked at the reduced circumstances of nominally white-collar workers, warned that the middle class, "the mainstay of the nation," was on the verge of toppling into real poverty.[8]

Before 1918 no protest on the scale of the rice riots occurred despite the doubling, and in some cases tripling, of prices for woven cloth, hardware, and other goods during the war years.[9] Nor did people take to the streets when average consumer prices during the first half of 1917 doubled over the same period in 1914. The number of industrial labor disputes, however, did increase dramatically during 1917 and 1918. Looking only at strikes and not taking into account other more diverse protests, we see an increase from 49 incidents with 5,763 participants in 1914 to 417 protests joined by 66,457 workers in 1918. Although the number of strikes declined following World War I, the number of total participants continued to grow.[10]

The trend toward greater labor militancy was not entirely new. Worker agitation had waxed and waned before the Taishō years. But during most of the Meiji period, the state and private enterprise had more easily dealt with the demands of labor. Many Taishō analysts, in observations strikingly similar to those made by many Western students of the post-1945 economic "miracle," credited unique cultural factors for the accord existing between Japanese labor and capital.[11] Yet not everyone agreed with this explanation. Kuwada Kumazō, a professor at Tokyo Imperial University, a member of the House of Peers, and the payer of the highest taxes in Tottori prefecture in 1917, took a more analytical view. In an article written toward the end of World War I, he observed that it was the level of Japanese industrialization and the force of law, rather than comfortable paternalistic traditions, that had contributed to labor peace. "Peculiar circumstances" in Japan—an industrial base not yet fully concentrated, the predominance of docile female workers, and strict laws against strikes—served to postpone the confrontation between labor and capital already occurring in the industrialized West. Kuwada warned, however, that current economic conditions could easily result in labor strife:

All sensible observers must admit that with rent and other necessary factors
of living rising out of proportion to increases of wages and with the unre-
laxed severity of employers in treating the employed, the voice of discontent
against capitalists and employers is growing in volume and intensity.[12]

Among the more vocal in expressing discontent were skilled workers.
Even before the rice riots, they used their increasingly strong bargaining
position in the expanding industrial economy to force management
concessions on wages, overtime, and benefits. But most Japanese had no
comparable leverage. The great majority of the labor force cultivated
the land or toiled in small workshops rather than large ones in city
factories. They consequently lacked a formal organizational base from
which to bring pressure on their employers or political representatives.

Despite warnings from the press and from observers like Kuwada,
Japan's leading political parties offered few concrete measures to re-
verse the growing gap between real wages and the cost of living. To
understand why this was so, it is necessary to consider two points: first,
the party men's general conception of their political role vis-à-vis the
"people"; and second, relations among the parties, the genro, or informal council of elder statesmen, and the Terauchi cabinet from 1917
through 1918.

We should remember that the leadership of the Seiyūkai, Kenseikai,
and Kokumintō, Japan's three major political parties in 1918, sought to
guide rather than follow public opinion. Katō Kōmei, the head of the
nominally antigovernment Kenseikai, "was neither egalitarian, pop-
ulist, nor even democratic" in his views on popular participation in
government.[13] Nor was his attitude exceptional. Hara Takashi, leader
of the Seiyūkai during most of the Taishō period, provided in his well-
kept diary multiple examples of attitudes that were proparty but clearly
antipopulist. Inukai Tsuyoshi, the avowedly uncompromising democratic leader of the Kokumintō, likewise seldom confused liberal theory
and lofty rhetoric with the actual practice of party politics. Although
historians have traditionally presented him as a symbol of statesman-
like integrity in an age of back-room deals, Inukai consistently attempted to broaden his party's influence by swinging its support between its two larger rivals. He slipped in and out of interparty alliances
with scant attention to hard principle but with keen concern for maintaining and enlarging party strength.[14]

As experts in Taishō political history have convincingly demonstrated, it would have been naive for party leaders to have acted otherwise. The most unbending proved the least successful in advancing their

party's aims, which, intended or not, broadened the base of representative government by removing central decision-making prerogatives
from the hands of a small and dwindling number of aging oligarchs to
the wider arena of party politics. Nevertheless, the champions of expanding the political prerogatives of faction-based parties, a group
perhaps more representative of Taishō republicanism than of Taishō
democracy, were *not* champions of the "masses." To understand the
parties' passive role in ameliorating the inflation-caused economic
crisis of the war years, we should keep in mind that men like Hara and
Katō, and arguably Inukai as well, in several respects had more in common with Count Terauchi Masatake, the prime minister of the "transcendent" cabinet of nonparty, genro-selected appointees, than with
liberal social reformers. In their educational backgrounds, elitist views,
and years of service in central-government bureaucracies, the party men
and genro spoke a mutually understood political language.

Incidents from Hara's career before and after becoming the "commoner" prime minister in 1918 illustrate this point. As home minister in
1914, Hara was quick to ban the publication of newspaper articles
critical of the Yamamoto cabinet's involvement in the Siemen's scandal
in which the German company paid kickbacks to Naval Ministry
officials to secure contracts. He also showed no hesitation in calling out
government troops to control crowds demanding the resignation of the
cabinet. Although Hara is known as Japan's first commoner prime
minister, his no-nonsense policies and actions led to campaigns by
petition to unseat the "despotic" home minister. These protests were
remarkably like those later waged against Terauchi cabinet officers for
their inability to control rice prices and for their forcible suppression of
rioting.[15] Hara's well-known and rigid opposition to universal male
suffrage is also indicative of his view that bureaucratic politicians
should lead and good citizens should follow.

The structure of the Japanese government bolstered attitudes similar
to Hara's. The Meiji Constitution, a gift from the emperor, was long on
duties and short on freedoms. It made no provision for cabinets formed
by any means other than imperial appointment and was absolutely silent on political parties. Party leaders realized that the security of their
organizations within the Meiji system rested upon the rather weak reed
of political practice and not upon constitutional provisions. They therefore did not see their fortunes tied to wide public support of their policies. True, party politicians had to be voted into office, and constituencies had grown larger with the 1902 revision regarding suffrage, which

increased the number of legally qualified voters by reducing property-holding qualifications. Yet only 2.5 percent of the population could vote in the 1917 elections.[16] On the eve of the riots, Japanese political parties were responsive, therefore, not to the general population's concern over the high cost of rice but to the less than 2 percent of the population with money or property requisite for the right to vote. Although violent nationwide demonstrations could contribute to the fall of a cabinet, the "masses" did not vote party men in or out of office. Nor did they provide the money essential for creating a local base of political support. That came increasingly from such major commercial concerns as Mitsui, Mitsubishi, and Suzuki Shōten, all of which had profited handsomely from the war boom.

Labels such as "liberal," "conservative," "Tory," or "Whig" were ill-suited to the Taishō political parties. Undeniably, the official public position of the three major parties in 1918 was one of opposition to Terauchi's nonparty government. Long before the Terauchi cabinet had even been formed, party politicians and political observers foresaw that genro-designed cabinets had become anachronistic and would, probably sooner rather than later, give way to party governments. Nevertheless, party leaders recognized the continuing need for compromise with the genro in creating effective cabinets. Genro support, however tacit, for one's party provided more concrete benefits than could be gained by championing the nonvoting citizen's right to fair wages or the consumer's demands for reasonably priced rice. In elections during the Taishō period a party leader willing to horse-trade with the genro and their protégés secured the governmental resources—money and bureaucratic cooperation—essential for strengthening his party in elections and in the Diet.

That Hara and other party leaders saw as vital some kind of modus vivendi with Yamagata Aritomo, Saionji Kinmochi, and the other elders is obvious if we keep in mind that the opposition parties were, on many issues, as much opposed to each other as they were to the genro. Moreover, interparty contention seldom grew from strong ideological differences; instead, it arose because similarly constituted parties competed for control of the lower house and aimed for dominance of the cabinet. Ironically, the parties that most effectively cooperated with the genro and in 1918 quietly supported the nonparty Terauchi government could come closer to the ultimate goal of throwing off genro interference in cabinet formation. In short, although the Seiyūkai, Kenseikai, and Kokumintō were in principle opposed to Terauchi's nonparty government, not one of them could indiscriminately attack it on the issue of its inability to control inflation or provide cheap rice.

Hara, perhaps more clearly than either Inukai or Katō, understood the "politics of compromise." When Terauchi's national-unity cabinet took office in 1916, Hara's Seiyūkai had suffered a serious defeat, losing to the Kenseikai the Diet majority it had held from 1908 to 1915. Hara and party leaders were intent on regaining lost ground, and although avowedly neutral, Seiyūkai Diet members generally supported the Terauchi government's stand in lower-house deliberations. Of course, a favor was expected in return and was not long in coming. In the 1917 elections, called to quiet opposition from the Kenseikai and Kokumintō nonbinding vote of no confidence in the Terauchi cabinet, the government extended covert support to Seiyūkai candidates. The elections benefited both Terauchi and Hara. After the ballots were counted, the Kenseikai had lost majority control in the lower house while Seiyūkai seats had increased from 111 to 160, a number sufficient for Hara's party to retake comand.[17] Although neither Yamagata nor Terauchi supported party politics, they nonetheless acted on the premise that the enemy of one's enemy can, temporarily at least, be an ally. Given the warm relationship between the Terauchi government and the "neutral" Seiyūkai, it is easy to understand why Hara's party was not overly critical of Terauchi's policies toward rice prices.

Less clear is why the Kenseikai and Kokumintō did not draw more tightly together in opposition to Terauchi's and Hara's maneuvering. Part of the explanation is found in Terauchi's strategy of divide and, if not conquer, at least scatter the opposition. In early 1916, opposition party leaders, including Hara and Katō, met and agreed to oppose the formation of nonparty cabinets.[18] But once the Terauchi ministry was installed, the verbal pact was immediately broken after the prime minister, in a move intended to soften party opposition, invited Hara, Inukai, and Katō to join the cabinet-level Investigative Committee of Foreign Affairs.

Katō refused, and while Inukai agreed, he took an independent course. Inukai had mixed feelings about Hara and Katō and their parties. His Kokumintō had narrowly escaped ruin by his rivals when, during the Taishō political crisis of 1912 and 1913, half of the Kokumintō deserted to join what later became Katō's Kenseikai. The Kokumintō's later opposition to the Hara government suggests that Inukai saw the Seiyūkai as more inimical to his party's interests than the Kenseikai. Nevertheless, he could not resist the spoils that might derive from accepting Terauchi's invitation to join the foreign affairs committee. Beyond the personal prestige of the post, cooperating with the government in power carried the more tangible benefit of gaining electoral strength. The Terauchi government, without a party constituency of its own, was free to help cooperative "opposition" parties. Inukai's Kokumintō thus benefited from Terauchi's support in the 1917 elections, although not to the extent of the Seiyūkai.

Electoral gains derived from government support did not mute Kokumintō criticism of the cabinet's rice policies to the extent that Terauchi's patronage compromised the Seiyūkai. Inukai's party had nominally supported the no-confidence vote, and as we shall see, the Kokumintō, especially its Osaka branch, took the strongest stand of any of the major political parties against the Terauchi government once rioting began. Yet, in the months of growing tension before the outbreak of the national crisis, Inukai's organization, instead of charging forward as the party of the people, took a cautious wait-and-see stance.

The Kenseikai, the closest thing to a genuine opposition party after the 1917 elections, acted similarly. With their numbers in the lower house severely reduced, party leaders were keen on exploiting any weakness in the Terauchi government. But Katō also had to consider the cost of any unrestrained attack on the transcendent government, given his desire to reestablish the Kenseikai as the majority party. Katō's alienation from Yamagata led to cooperation between Hara and Terauchi, with disastrous results for the Kenseikai in the 1917 elections. Moreover, even if the Terauchi cabinet collapsed because of some major policy blunder, hastening its fall would not necessarily benefit Katō's party as much as it would help his rivals. Terauchi might go, but the watchdog Yamagata would still be there. Further complicating the situation for Katō was the Kenseikai's future ties with the Seiyūkai. Although Hara's party enjoyed a cozy relationship with the nonparty government in 1917 and 1918, it was nevertheless committed to the goal of government by Diet men. Given the delicately balanced relationships among opposition parties and the possibility for a rapid change of fortune, Kenseikai leaders joined with those of the Seiyūkai and Kokumintō in biding their time as public protest began to build against the Terauchi government's economic policies.[19]

On 10 August, after rioting had broken out throughout the country, leaders from the Kokumintō, Kenseikai, and Seiyūkai met at their separate Tokyo headquarters to discuss the crisis. In these executive sessions, the Kokumintō rather than the Kenseikai took the most critical stand toward the government's policies for regulating the price of rice. The Kokumintō's Political Affairs Investigation Committee declared that Terauchi's ministers had refused to recognize that current grain reserves were inadaquate for public needs. In excoriating the government's economic policies, Kokumintō leaders aimed their strongest criticisms at the minister of agriculture and commerce, Nakakōji Ren. In their view, his attempts to control distribution with imperial ordinances had resulted in the state's ineffective interference in the private business of commodity exchanges and grain brokers. The authors of the committee's resolution on the rice crisis argued that ministerial attempts to rule by fiat had aroused the resentment of the private sector with consequences opposite to those desired by Nakakōji and his subordinates. In sum, the Kokumintō party executives concluded that the government's policies had resulted in greater confusion in the marketplace and ever-higher prices for rice.

The Osaka city branch of the Kokumintō took an even more critical stand. On 11 August, much to the dismay of the Osaka police department, Kansai party leaders sponsored an "Osaka Citizens' Rally" (*Ōsaka shimin taikai*) to discuss "rice price regulation" publicly. Although rioting had not yet been reported within the city, disturbances had sporadically broken out throughout the Kansai region. Osaka officials rightly feared that large crowds, inflammatory speeches, and summer heat were a volatile combination that might result in civil disobedience, property destruction, and the need for expanded police mobilization.

The principal organizer of the Osaka rally, Morishita Ryūtarō, a lawyer and local Kokumintō leader, assured the police that nothing untoward would come of the meeting, confidently asserting that if the crowd got out of hand, city officials "would never see his face again." His bravura quickly evaporated as it became obvious that rioting might spread throughout the country. On the day of the rally, after an overflow crowd of three thousand had already gathered in one of Osaka's public parks, Kokumintō leaders announced that the meeting was canceled. The crowd ignored the appeal to disband and proceeded on its own, cheering on a stream of speakers who, one after another, berated the Terauchi government. At the end of the rally self-appointed committeemen resolved in the name of the "Osaka Citizens' Meeting on Rice Price Regulation" that the minister of agriculture and commerce should resign immediately, that all duties on foreign rice should be lifted, and that *narikin* industrialists should provide funds for those impoverished by the war boom. Although the eventual outbreak of rioting was probably unavoidable, historians usually point to the Kokumintō-sponsored rally as the fuse sparking more violent protests in Osaka.[20]

Neither the Seiyūkai nor the Kenseikai sponsored rallies similar to those of the Kokumintō. This is not surprising given the Seiyūkai's leadership support from agricultural interests. The central office of the Imperial Agricultural Association (Teikoku Nōkai), which lobbied the government and parties for support of higher farm prices, contributed significantly to the Seiyūkai's landslide victory in the 1917 elections by directing county (*gun*) branches to support Seiyūkai candidates. The Seiyūkai garnered about the same number of votes in urban districts in the 1917 election as it had in the previous national balloting. But it was the party chosen before all others in rural voting. Seiyūkai members, intent on maintaining good relations with the farm lobby, also dominated the supposedly supraparty Agricultural Governance Research Association within the lower house.[21] Significantly, at the 10 August meeting of party executives called to discuss protests over rice prices, the grain issue was actually placed second on the agenda after a discussion of upcoming by-elections in Saitama prefecture. When the inflation issue was finally broached, Seiyūkai leaders did nothing more than request that the Terauchi government take "uniform and sincere" steps to resolve the crisis.

Similar suggestions emanated from the Kenseikai executive meeting. After a brief exchange over whether to call for the resignation of the Terauchi cabinet, Kenseikai officials expressed concern over skyrocketing rice prices. The party's resolution that the government step up grain imports was paired with the overtly political demand that the sitting cabinet take final responsibility for its policies on price regulation.[22]

None of the parties' recommendations contained serious or fresh proposals for dealing with the crisis. Indeed, they suggested steps that the Terauchi government was taking at long last. The timing of the executive meetings, at the onset of massive protests in Japan's major cities, also makes clear the party leaders' opportunistic intentions. After years of indifference to the decline in living standards, opposition party leaders now demanded that the sitting cabinet immediately resolve the problem of high rice prices. Nevertheless, when it became clear that the riots might bring down the transcendent government, clearing the way for a political party cabinet, opposition leaders felt little compulsion to be either consistent or even responsible in their criticism of Terauchi's policies—even if these policies at one time differed little from their own.[23]

While the politicians fiddled, the threat of a doubling or a tripling in retail rice prices spread the flames of unrest to all but the richest segments of the population. Commentators in newspapers and popular magazines discussed ways of coping with spiraling costs to the consumer. Before and after the riots, pundits recommended "rice-less" days, "two-meal-a-day-ism" (*nishoku shugi*), eating wheat or other substitutes instead of rice, and careful family budgeting.[24] Such advice was not really necessary. Inflation had already forced many Japanese to pare family spending to the bone. Newspapers published letters from poorer urban residents who could no longer afford to buy spare clothing and, in order to save a few sen, had given up riding city trolleys. In the countryside tenant farmers were reported to have economized by increasing the proportion of inferior grains in the their diets and by reducing purchases of the more expensive polished rice.[25]

Piecemeal economizing may have helped in getting by from one day to the next. But it did nothing to soothe the public's anger over the necessity of rice-less days or at being forced to fill the rice pot with barley or wild greens. As prices continued to rise, threatening to push domestic rice beyond levels affordable by many Japanese, patience tended to evaporate. Given the widespread and well-publicized growth in national wealth during World War I, citizens seemed to believe that rice should be readily available. When this belief was betrayed as food costs rose faster than wages, Japanese aimed their resentment both at local officials and at the Terauchi cabinet.

The Terauchi Government's Grain Policy

The central government responded belatedly to what journalists from 1917 began to refer to as the "rice price revolution." The fundamental error of the Ministry of Agriculture and Commerce was to handle rice scarcity as a secondary problem. Rather than correct the basic cause of steep prices, an absolute shortage, Terauchi's ministers set about treating its symptoms. As opposition party politicians pointed out once rioting had begun, the government's aim was to correct distribution problems and curb speculation administratively. Nakakōji himself repeatedly voiced the official view that rice prices were "unnaturally" high owing to the activities of speculators, completely ignoring the existing imbalance in supply and demand.[26] When Nakakōji aired his views during the summer of 1917, Japan's rice reserves had actually fallen 143,000 koku below the level recorded for 1916.[27] Adhering to the Nakakōji line, officials continued their assault on speculators and inadequate distribution during the remainder of 1917 and into 1918.

The initial phase of such efforts, a program organized on an ad hoc basis, consisted of imposing stronger sanctions against brokers. Armed with new imperial ordinances (*chokurei*) and ministerial directives (*kunrei*), the Ministry of Agriculture and Commerce took summary action against those suspected of cornering, hoarding, and manipulating market conditions to force prices upward. In addition to new directives, existing laws for price regulation were extended to cover commodities such as cereals and fertilizers.[28] The Excess Profits Ordinance (Bōri Torishime-rei) of September 1917 was typical of a number of measures intended to prohibit profiteering in goods ranging from rice to coal.[29] The measure's effectiveness, however, was limited to commodity-market transactions and did little to prohibit merchants or landlords from hoarding rice. The ordinance was market-oriented and contained no incentives for farmers to produce more or merchants to increase grain imports. Moreover, it left in place the Diet-imposed duties on foreign rice and failed to alter the official policy to promote grain exports, in effect since 1913.

In spite of stiffer laws, any direct government action against speculators was weakened by dealer resistance and relatively mild penalties for offenders. The case of Oka Hanzaemon, a rice dealer warned in 1918 for market making, illustrates the impotency of the sanction policy. When rice futures hit an all-time high on nationwide grain markets in January 1918, officials in the Ministry of Agriculture and Commerce accused Oka of a hoarding scheme to force prices higher. Oka, the first to be warned under the provisions of the Excess Profits Ordinance, was cautioned against any future infringements of market propriety. He was also ordered to sell out his recently acquired holdings within thirty days and to curtail his market activities temporarily. No further action was taken against this well-known market manipulator. He continued in business and continued to prosper.[30]

The ineffectiveness of government measures was underscored on 1 February when prices for rice futures set yet another record high.[31] In response, the government merely redoubled its efforts in spite of the failure of its piecemeal policies. From May to July 1918 a dozen grain dealers received warnings. Yet, to many brokers and middlemen, the chance for greater profits seemed to outweigh threats of punishment. Public embarrassment and temporary loss of market position were inconveniences, not sufficient deterrents. At the very worst, second-time violators of the Excess Profits Ordinance were liable to a *maximum* of three months in jail and a fine not to exceed 100 yen. First-time offenders were usually only warned.[32] In 1918 not a single major rice dealer appears to have been prosecuted as a second-time offender. As is evident from the continued rise in retail rice prices, from about 25 sen per shō in January 1918 to nearly 50 sen for the same measure in August, the government's hit-or-miss sanctions did nothing to restrain the month-by-month jump in rice prices.[33]

What the policy makers in the Ministry of Agriculture and Commerce could not accomplish with sanctions, they belatedly attempted with stepped-up rice imports. Improving the supply by buying from abroad had a greater chance of success than policing the activities of the many large- and small-scale speculators. Indeed, several private business groups unsuccessfully urged the removal of all duties on rice.[34] In late 1917 the Terauchi government was still reluctant to go as far as complete deregulation. But it was willing to begin bringing in more rice under official guidance and control. Although well intentioned, the shift in policy did too little and was begun too late. By involving major Japanese trading companies in the already overheated rice market, the import program also increased popular suspicions about collusion between the Terauchi cabinet and *narikin*. As was evident in speeches made at urban "citizens' rallies" during the peak of rioting, city dwellers in particular saw trading houses such as Suzuki Shōten as symbols of exploiting nouveau-riche firms responsible for high consumer prices.

Despite increasingly strong demands for a fundamental shift in import policy, it was not until the very eve of rioting that officials in the Ministry of Agriculture and Commerce backed away from government support of grain prices. The Terauchi cabinet had ample precedent for its reluctance. Before 1918 other cabinets, instead of hurriedly flooding the market with cheaper foreign rice, desultorily used increased grain imports as a temporary, stopgap measure. A foreign observer of Taishō politics commented in the 1920s:

> In Japan so large a part of the population has always been interested in the cultivation and sale of rice that, even in days when exports have disappeared and given way to imports for the feeding of the increased population, a low price for rice is regarded with more alarm than a high one.[35]

Rather than use import policy as the chief weapon against shortages, Agriculture and Commerce officials treated the idea almost as an afterthought.[36]

The Foreign Rice Control Ordinance empowered the ministry to carry out the desired fine-tuning of the market. Control regulations promulgated on 25 April 1918, allowed Agriculture and Commerce officials to set the wholesale and retail prices of imported rice and adjust the amount of grain shipped into the country. The actual import, distribution, and marketing of foreign rice was to be left to four major trading companies: Mitsui Bussan, Suzuki Shōten, Iwai Shōten, and Yuasa Shōten. Fueled by widespread resentment against *narikin*, popular rumors during the riots alleged that executives of companies like Suzuki Shōten ordered ship captains to dump rice at sea to push up grain prices at home. There is no hard evidence that profit-hungry trading companies kept rice off the market; indeed, the government took special measures to prevent such abuses.[37] Subsidies provided within the control ordinance assured fair profits to the companies and cushioned against losses that they might incur through higher overseas prices and shipping costs. In exchange for official largess, the Ministry of Agriculture and Commerce demanded that the companies maintain a streamlined operation, one that would hold middlemen costs to a minimum and keep distribution simple.[38]

Although Japan was awash in foreign rice after the riots, the government's early program for imports matched its policy on sanctions in having a negligible effect on preriot grain prices. By July 1918 the average monthly retail price for a koku of polished rice on the Tokyo market had reached 36 yen, a full 10 yen more than the 1917 price. As prices bounded upward, newspaper articles referred to the government's rice policy as a *yabuhebi*, a misguided attempt to do good that yields only new problems.[39]

No longer able to ignore growing criticism from the press and opposition politicians, Ministry of Agriculture and Commerce officials at last decided to carry out a nationwide survey of current rice reserves. On 17 July 1918, notices were sent to all prefectural offices ordering local officials to inventory the actual amount of rice in private and public hands as of the end of July. The measure not only aimed at ascertaining the amount of rice available in Japan but was also intended to locate suspected bottlenecks in the distribution network. Still unwilling to admit that an absolute scarcity existed, ministry officials continued to hunt for secret caches of rice. The press speculated that once the survey was completed, the next step would be some kind of mandatory confiscation and redistribution in order to better balance supply and demand.[40]

Although the survey was intended to check any further inflation in rice prices, its actual effect was exactly the opposite. The government's first mistake was to fan the flames of speculation by failing to release survey results. The air of secrecy surrounding the investigation gave weight to rumors that shortages were far worse than they were previously thought to be. Spokesmen for the ministry made repeated denials of any drastic shortfall, but no one seemed to be listening. Worse yet, unofficial leaks of survey results set off a new frenzy of speculative buying that sent prices even higher.[41]

Overall, the government's rice policy produced only confusion. The more it struggled to contain the "rice price revolution" the less effective its policies appeared. Antispeculation measures, import controls, and attempts to mandate better distribution seemed to increase rather than lighten pressure on the consumer. The worsening situation was soon reflected both in central and in regional markets. During the last week of July 1918, rice shops in some cities were demanding as much as 50 sen for a shō of polished rice—a 60 percent jump in price within only thirty days. As prices went higher day after day newspapers frequently carried dark warnings of public protest if something was not done. In early August the Ministry of Agriculture and Commerce, which now seemed to give credence to such reports, belatedly commenced large-scale distribution of Korean and Taiwanese rice.[42] By this time, however, demonstrations had been going on in Toyama prefecture for over a week. On 9 August nationwide rioting began.

Rioting and Suppression

Chapters that follow will discuss the riots as dissociated regional protests. Here it is useful for understanding both the general dimensions and contemporary official perceptions of unrest to look at the riots as a national uprising. In scale, in distribution, and in the massive mobilization of military and relief efforts necessary to suppress them, the 1918 riots were unprecedented in Japan's modern history. The unrest began on 22 July in a small fishing hamlet in Toyama prefecture, and spread like wildfire in the Kansai region and in each of Japan's rapidly industrializing cities. Between 9 August and 20 August Kyoto, Nagoya, Osaka, Kobe, and finally Tokyo became the scenes of violent rioting involving tens of thousands of protesters. From 20 August to 27 August rioting broke out in Japan's coal-mining areas. In Yamaguchi prefecture and northern Kyushu attacks by miners against company property and personnel led to additional troop mobilization. Force did not automatically produce order: armed miners tenaciously resisted troops and police sent to quell the protests. As a result, mining compounds in Yamaguchi and Kyushu experienced the bloodiest fighting with the heaviest loss of life during the summer protests. Isolated protests continued into October, and in a few locations incidents described as "riots" in the press were reported as late as December 1918.[43] Nevertheless, the state had successfully suppressed the largest protests by late September.

During the period from July to September, 42 of Japan's 47 prefectures reported incidents of varying degrees of severity. Actions included nonviolent sit-ins, peaceful marches to local government offices, grain-shipping boycotts, attacks on grain brokers and merchants, the destruction of rice, and the forcing of rice retailers to sell at a "fair price." Crowds streaming from urban mass rallies, which in cities like Nagoya drew from 40,000 to 50,000 people, also attempted to take their demands to prefectural and central-government officials. In areas where such attempts were stifled, full-scale street battles broke out between crudely armed rioters and heavily armed troops and police. Only the Ryukyus and several Tōhoku prefectures were riot-free between July and September. For eight weeks, disturbances occurred from Hokkaido to Kyushu, in fishing villages, in farm communities, as well as in every major Japanese city. Although Japanese researchers are still uncovering incidents heretofore unreported, reliable estimates indicate that protests occurred in 49 cities, 217 towns, and 231 villages (see table 1).

Statistics vary as to how many Japanese citizens actively participated in the nationwide disturbances. The precise answer is complicated by the unreliability of police records and the lack of any precise definition of what "participation" meant in the context of the 1918 disputes. Estimates of the total number of rioters range from a low figure of 700,000 to a high of 10 million.[44] Matsuo Takayoshi and other leading historians of the riots seem to have abandoned any accurate head count by simply suggesting that more than a million people joined the protests.[45] Whatever the precise figures may be, those who took to the streets represented a sizable proportion of Japans's total population of about 56 million in 1918. The participation figure takes on greater significance when we realize that nonadult members of Japanese families constituted the bulk of Japan's 1918 population.

The rioters' diverse social backgrounds reflected the wide popularity of the protests. With the exception of the independently wealthy, a

TABLE 1.   NATIONWIDE DISTRIBUTION OF RIOTS,
JULY TO SEPTEMBER 1918

Prefecture	Cities	Towns	Villages	Mining Areas	Total
Hokkaido	0	0	0	1	1
Aomori	0	0	0	0	0
Iwate	0	0	0	0	0
Miyagi	1	2	0	0	3
Akita	0	0	0	0	0
Yamagata	0	0	1	0	1
Fukushima	2	19	5	1	27
Ibaragi	0	1	0	0	1
Tochigi	0	0	0	0	0
Gumma	0	1	1	0	2
Saitama	0	1	2	0	3
Chiba	0	2	1	0	3
Tokyo	1	0	0	0	1
Kanagawa	2	3	1	0	6
Niigata	2	1	0	0	3
Toyama	2	10	4	0	16
Ishikawa	1	4	0	0	5
Fukui	1	0	1	0	2
Yamanashi	1	1	1	0	3
Nagano	1	3	0	1	5
Gifu	2	7	6	0	15
Shizuoka	2	20	11	1	34
Aichi	3	14	1	0	18
Mie	1	2	7	0	10
Shiga	1	5	3	0	9
Kyoto	1	4	12	0	17
Osaka	2	12	26	0	40
Hyogo	3	7	14	0	24
Nara	1	3	4	0	8
Wakayama	1	12	13	0	26
Tottori	1	1	0	0	2
Shimane	1	11	37	0	49
Okayama	1	22	28	1	52
Hiroshima	4	19	20	0	43
Yamaguchi	1	6	12	2	21
Tokushima	1	1	2	0	4
Kagawa	2	5	7	0	14
Ehime	1	8	5	0	14
Kochi	1	6	2	0	9
Fukuoka	3	1	0	17	21
Saga	0	0	0	4	4
Nagasaki	1	0	1	0	2
Kumamoto	1	0	2	1	4
Oita	0	2	0	0	2
Miyazaki	0	1	0	0	1
Kagoshima	0	0	1	0	1
Ryukyu	0	0	0	0	0
TOTAL	49	217	231	29	526

SOURCE: *KSNK* 1:90–91.
NOTE: This table does not include multiple incidents of rioting that occurred in a single location or the numerous riots uncovered by local historians working since the early 1960s.

TABLE 2.   AGES OF RICE RIOT DEFENDANTS

Age Group	Number Prosecuted
14 to 17	341
18 to 19	686
20 to 29	3,170
30 to 39	2,229
40 to 49	1,282
50 to 59	384
60 and over	75
TOTAL	8,167

SOURCE: *IKSK*, 215.
NOTE: No age information is available for 18 of the 8,185 prosecuted.

broad cross section of Japanese society was caught up in police round-ups both during and after the riots. Grouping the 8,185 riot suspects formally prosecuted into well-defined economic classes is made difficult by the wide variety of occupation and income groups represented. In Kobe city alone, interrogators placed detainees into more than ninety different occupation categories, a classification scheme that never perfectly matched the particular systems used in other localities. Still, we can see that a large number of the 8,815 individuals prosecuted (a group probably overly representative of city protesters and very likely containing numbers of innocent individuals rounded up by overzealous police) came from poorer, relatively uneducated levels of Japanese society. Traditional craftsmen and unskilled laborers are heavily represented among riot suspects. In Osaka city, for example, 25 percent of those detained gave their occupation as "craftsman."[46] The "premodern" occupational background of riot suspects appears substantiated if we add to the craftsmen category prosecution figures for day laborers, construction workers, rickshaw pullers, street vendors, and other similar groups.

Accurate generalization is difficult, however. White-collar workers, minor officials, farmers, fishermen, journalists, and students also appear with "craftsmen" among those prosecuted for riot-related crimes. As for income levels, relatively few of the "extremely indigent" appeared among those prosecuted for rioting. The 709 suspects considered financially "well-off" far surpassed the 579 arrested from Japan's lowest income level. The mixture of employment and income groups suggests that those who joined in the riots represented a stable cross section of Japanese society (see tables 2, 3, 4).

District Court	Number Prosecuted	Higher School	Middle School	Primary School	Semi-Literate	No Education
Tokyo	299	3	24	211	47	14
Yokohama	40	0	3	34	3	0
Mito	40	0	2	25	5	8
Shizuoka	314	0	5	185	99	25
Kofu	23	0	—	13	8	2
Nagano	31	0	4	26	1	0
Niigata	60	1	1	44	9	5
Kyoto	301	—	—	177	57	56
Osaka	521	—	2	74	185	128
Nara	65	—	—	17	31	16
Kobe	546	1	5	224	143	132
Otsu	35	0	0	7	15	13
Wakayama	565	—	4	222	177	120
Tokushima	18	0	0	4	11	3
Kochi	3	0	0	3	0	0
Takamatsu	70	—	—	16	3	4
Nagoya	556	0	6	306	202	42
Annotsu	459	—	—	128	77	75
Gifu	143	0	0	90	36	17
Fukui	99	0	1	87	4	7
Kanazawa	7	0	0	3	2	2
Toyama	1	0	0	1	0	0
Hiroshima	560	—	4	243	127	112
Yamaguchi	698	1	3	83	40	22
Matsue	332	—	—	106	115	88
Matsuyama	252	0	6	53	139	54
Okayama	517	1	1	200	133	182
Nagasaki	45	0	0	0	45	0
Saga	298	0	1	138	86	73
Fukuoka	717	1	12	363	175	138
Oita	6	0	0	6	0	0
Kumamoto	309	0	9	228	39	33
Kagoshima	3	0	0	1	1	1
Miyazaki	38	0	0	35	3	2
Sendai	132	2	16	93	15	6
Fukushima	48	0	1	38	5	4
Sapporo	34	—	—	—	—	—
TOTAL	8,185	10	110	3,484	2,038	1,384

NOTE: Ministry of Justice officials compiled information included in this table by sur-veying district court prosecutors throughout Japan. Of the 8,185 individuals prosecuted, information on educational and income background is available for only about 7,000 defendants because complete statistics were not provided. For example, Yamaguchi dis-trict prosecutors supplied educational background data for only 149 of the 698 people prosecuted; Sapporo officials provided nothing beyond a total figure of defendants. A dash or a significant difference between the total number of individuals prosecuted in a judicial district and the sum figure of educational or economic background for that dis-trict means that information was not available.

TABLE 4. PEOPLE PROSECUTED FOR RIOTING
(AS OF DECEMBER 1918): GENERAL
INCOME LEVEL

District Court	Number Prosecuted	Safe Income	Prosperous	No Surplus	Financial Difficulty	Extremely Needy
Tokyo	299	1	22	236	39	1
Yokohama	40	0	2	5	8	25
Mito	40	0	1	6	24	9
Shizuoka	314	3	17	63	182	49
Kofu	23	1	0	2	20	0
Nagano	31	1	2	10	12	6
Niigata	60	4	6	13	32	5
Kyoto	301	11	27	84	153	14
Osaka	521	3	12	205	142	27
Nara	65	—	5	13	43	3
Kobe	546	13	33	180	247	32
Otsu	35	1	1	4	27	1
Wakayama	565	19	24	67	345	60
Tokushima	18	2	0	1	1	14
Kochi	3	0	0	0	2	1
Takamatsu	70	—	—	8	8	7
Nagoya	556	24	88	329	112	3
Annotsu	459	2	22	119	126	11
Gifu	143	7	36	62	38	0
Fukui	99	0	3	29	58	9
Kanazawa	7	0	0	2	5	0
Toyama	1	0	0	1	0	0
Hiroshima	560	9	25	176	239	36
Yamaguchi	698	3	5	42	62	37
Matsue	332	19	35	155	86	14
Matsuyama	252	1	4	29	199	19
Okayama	517	4	11	80	324	98
Nagasaki	45	0	0	0	45	0
Saga	298	9	88	107	86	8
Fukuoka	717	10	69	318	276	16
Oita	6	0	0	0	6	0
Kumamoto	309	0	12	94	183	20
Kagoshima	3	0	0	0	3	0
Miyazaki	38	1	2	3	27	5
Sendai	132	2	3	15	64	48
Fukushima	48	0	4	24	19	1
Sapporo	34	0	—	—	—	—
TOTAL	8,185	150	559	2,482	3,243	579

NOTE: The Ministry's survey classified income categories based on a family of three or four members with the following monthly incomes:
(1) "Safe income" (Anzen naru mono): 100 yen or more.
(2) "Prosperous" (Yaya yutaka naru mono): about 100 yen.
(3) "No surplus" (Yoyū naki mono): about 50 yen.
(4) "Financial difficulty" (Kyūhaku naru mono): about 30 yen.
(5) "Extremely needy" (Kyokutan naru mono): at or below 10 yen.

As will be discussed further in chapter 3 on urban riots, several groups that might be expected to appear in the lists of the arrested and indicted are largely missing. Skilled laborers and leftists, who potentially could have provided the protesters with organizational expertise or a more ideological justification for the protests, are absent from prosecution records. This absence of the labor elite can be partially explained by its better wages and working conditions. But more important, workers in major factories, such as those managed by Mitsubishi, Yawata Steel, and other private and public enterprises, also increasingly took their grievances directly to company management instead of resorting to street protests. Although technically illegal, incidents of factory strikes and labor-management negotiation increased significantly during the war years, particularly in large, city-based enterprises. What was true for lathe operators, machinists, and welders, however, did not necessarily apply to relatively unskilled workers. As is evident in the role of coal miners in the riots, semiskilled industrial workers occasionally did take part in protests outside the company compound. This phenomenon was especially common in company towns where the firm's influence on its workers extended beyond factory gates and where joining in the riots could serve to further the laborers' position in disputes with their bosses.

The lack of participation by socialists and anarchists reflects the lack of contacts between these groups and the "masses," as well as the efforts by the police to limit any agitation by those "harboring dangerous thoughts" (*kiken shisō kaihō mono*). In 1918 the Left was still an isolated and largely underground movement, one that had yet to form a uniform ideology or a concrete program for political action. Nevertheless, the government was extremely nervous about the small number of Japanese leftists. Before the summer protests, Metropolitan Police officials had already placed more than a hundred self-styled socialists and anarchists in the category of individuals requiring "special police surveillance." Police routinely questioned anyone connected with suspected political agitators and dogged the steps of individuals designated "dangerous thinkers." In mid-August, as discontent over rice prices threatened to develop into violent protest, the Metropolitan Police ordered that measures against leftists be strengthened. Although the directive did not spell out details, it did permit police to exercise preventive detention. During the riots, Ōsugi Sakae, Arahata Kanson, and others were either formally arrested or administratively detained for as long as several days. Arrests were sometimes arbitrary. In addition to

placing well-known socialists like Yamakawa Hitoshi under house
arrest, police also rounded up and detained over a hundred members of
Japan's moderate labor organization, the Yūaikai.[47]

Overall, the government's precautionary moves against anarchists
and socialists were hasty and unwarranted. Only seven leftists were
formally arrested for having anything to do with the riots. All of them
had already been placed under special police surveillance, and several
were taken in not for rioting but because they had resisted arbitrary
arrest.[48] Of those finally prosecuted for riot-related crimes, none could
be classified as political leaders of any stripe whatsoever. Although
several admitted that they were socialists (shakaishugi sha), their political activities appeared secondary to their main occupations as magazine publishers, reporters, and writers. Of course, others among the
8,185 prosecuted for riot-related offenses may have successfully kept
their political beliefs from police interrogators. Nevertheless, the police
were well informed as to the whereabouts and movements of important
leftist leaders, even those in small regional towns and cities.

Despite the crackdown on leftists during and after the riots, officials
continued to suspect that organized planners following some hidden
and dangerous ideology were behind the unrest. Police therefore questioned thousands of riot suspects in an attempt to ferret out "red" agitators. Yet, aside from a negligible number of radicals who took part in
the riots as individuals, leftists failed to exert any ideological or organizational leadership during the summer rioting. Although leftists later
praised the riots as a first revolutionary step toward mass liberation,
they were as surprised as officials had been by the sudden outbreak of
widespread unrest.

Women and burakumin (members of outcaste communities) also
participated in the riots, albeit not always in a consistent manner. Aside
from the Toyama disturbances, women usually did not take the role of
crowd organizers, nor did gatherings of housewives form the principal
protest groups. In urban disturbances, such as the ones that occurred in
Kobe city, women with children in tow did crowd around rice shops
after male rioters had forced dealers to sell grain at a reduced price.
They were similarly involved in major riots in Osaka, Sakai, Kure, and
Tokyo.[49] Although prosecution records do not provide complete information about the sex of those tried for rioting, very few women's
names appear among those prosecuted, even in urban disputes. The
major exception was seen in the burakumin areas, where women often
took an active role alongside men in carrying out protests against high

prices and in making appeals to officials. In Kyoto city, as in Toyama, buraku women took the initiative in demonstrating for reasonably priced rice.[50]

Burakumin, however, generally did not lead the nationwide protests. Indeed, their participation can best be described as spotty; in buraku where rioting did occur, it was staged on an all-or-nothing basis. Reflecting the *local* solidarity typical of the buraku, the entire settlement either participated or remained completely out of the conflict. Overall, detachment was far more typical, and most buraku remained peaceful as riots raged in surrounding communities. Of 554 designated buraku in 1918, only 32 reported disturbances during July through September. In Osaka, the scene of the largest sustained protests and the Japanese region with the largest concentration of burakumin among the general population, outcastes took little part in the riots.[51]

The minor role played by burakumin was not entirely accidental. Government officials, particularly local leaders, took special precautions to insure that the poorest and most socially deprived members of the population would remain quiet during the riots. In so doing, they supplemented movements already under way to improve the buraku in cities such as Nagoya and Osaka. In many settlements, measures to provide the buraku with extra rice supplies also helped prevent protests.

Despite the relative calm in buraku settlements, the government's need for a convenient scapegoat led to a disproportionate number of burakumin arrests throughout the nation. After the riots the vice-minister of justice, Suzuki Kisaburō, openly attributed random violence and wanton looting to those "acting for burakumin interests." The *Chūō shinbun*, a newspaper with Seiyūkai affiliations, followed Suzuki's line in a series of articles that suggested that as many as 70 percent of the rioters hailed from the buraku.[52] The figure was greatly inflated, but police, who spent an inordinate amount of energy in attempting to pin responsibility for the riots on the buraku minority, acted as if the estimate were valid. Many burakumin suspects had been caught up in arbitrary police sweeps of settlements, during which an abundance of rice in one's grain bin was taken as sufficient evidence of criminal activity. Sentences given burakumin were uniformly severe. Only two individuals, both burakumin, received death sentences for riot-related crimes.[53] Although burakumin made up less than 2 percent of Japan's population in 1918, they accounted for more than 10 percent of those arrested for rioting (see table 5).

Those who joined protests as members of an organized group typically

TABLE 5. PEOPLE PROSECUTED FOR RIOTING (AS OF DECEMBER 1918): SOCIAL BACKGROUND

District Court	Number Prosecuted	Under Special Surveillance	Political Party Connections	Reservist	Youth Assoc. Member	Student	Burakumin
Tokyo	299	—	—	13	—	13	—
Yokohama	40	—	—	5	4	—	—
Mito	40	—	—	9	—	—	—
Shizuoka	314	—	—	52	70	—	—
Kofu	23	—	—	5	5	1	1
Nagano	31	—	—	1	—	1	—
Niigata	60	—	—	9	21	1	—
Kyoto	301	—	—	39	131	—	137
Osaka	521	1	—	5	11	—	19
Nara	65	—	—	11	5	—	16
Kobe	546	1	—	52	29	—	55
Otsu	35	—	—	8	9	—	24
Wakayama	565	—	—	92	75	—	176
Tokushima	18	—	—	3	1	—	—
Kochi	3	—	—	—	—	—	—
Takamatsu	70	—	—	—	—	—	—
Nagoya	556	—	—	80	15	—	—
Annotsu	459	—	—	63	67	1	174
Gifu	143	—	—	24	27	—	9
Fukui	99	—	—	13	5	—	—
Kanazawa	7	—	—	2	1	—	—
Toyama	1	—	—	—	—	—	—
Hiroshima	560	—	—	69	49	1	96
Yamaguchi	698	—	—	26	17	—	—
Matsue	332	—	—	71	83	—	6

District Court	Number Prosecuted	Under Special Surveillance	Political Party Connections	Reservist	Youth Assoc. Member	Student	Burakumin
Matsuyama	252	—	—	50	18	—	8
Okayama	517	—	—	69	102	1	161
Nagasaki	45	—	—	—	—	—	—
Saga	298	—	—	75	—	—	4
Fukuoka	717	—	—	46	37	—	1
Oita	6	—	—	—	—	—	—
Kumamoto	309	—	—	79	61	—	—
Kagoshima	3	—	—	—	—	—	—
Miyazaki	38	—	—	5	22	—	—
Sendai	132	—	1	4	3	—	—
Fukushima	48	—	—	10	—	—	—
Sapporo	34	—	—	—	—	—	—
TOTAL	8,185	2	1	990	868	18	887

SOURCE: *IKSK*, 272–75.

belonged to state-supported institutions. Of 8,185 individuals charged
with riot-related offenses, 990, or more than 10 percent, were members of local military reservist groups (*zaigō gunjin kai*). In some
areas almost 40 percent of those initially detained held membership in
reservist organizations.[54] Among the more than 8,000 riot suspects
officially prosecuted, an additional 868 suspects were members of
Japan's nationwide youth association (*seinen dan*; see table 5). The reservists and the youth groups, joined by local volunteer fire brigades,
had been formally called upon to help maintain order during the protests. Working with police and mobilized troops, officials requested regional reservist groups, fifty-seven youth associations, and fifty-eight
fire brigades to patrol and guard local areas.[55] To the dismay of local
and central-government officials, these auxiliary forces of order at times
dragged their heels or openly disobeyed orders. In Shizuoka prefecture
volunteer firemen responded sluggishly to police calls for assistance in
putting out blazes set by rioters; in Okayama a fire brigade protested
the shipping of rice outside the local area by aiming their fire hoses at
grain baled for shipment. Similar events occurred in Yamaguchi, Shimane, and Hyōgo, where reservists or others in local organizations
assigned to guard rice stores actually joined in attacks against suspected
hoarders and speculators. In Kyoto the head of a local youth association not only joined in but actually led attacks against landlords and
officials unwilling to cooperate in the distribution of rice at reduced
prices.[56]

Officials justifiably viewed with alarm the lack of discipline among
reservists. The events of the Russian Revolution, in which mutinous
troops helped tip the scales against the monarchy, were fresh in the
minds of Japanese leaders. In numerous articles published after the
riots, political commentators speculated that the recent mass uprisings
signaled the beginning of Russian-style class war in Japan. But with the
exception of a few sailors involved in the Kure city uprising, military
men on active duty did not rebel during the riots. In Kobe, however,
unconfirmed reports circulated of clashes between troops and armed
rioters who had been organized in ranks and led by a reservist. As a
result of this incident, the leading regional officer in Kobe assembled a
meeting of *zaigō gunjin kai* members on 20 August 1918, to express his
displeasure at the manner in which reservists had deported themselves.
In dissuading his subordinates from future undisciplined acts he urged
them to maintain their dignity as soldiers:

The reservists are the backbone of this nation. Three years ago the emperor bestowed an imperial rescript calling for reservists throughout the country to be loyal subjects. If we are to serve as the nation's mainstay until the bitter end, we must not act rashly or foolishly. Under the present circumstances, we must be moderate in our behavior. We must be concerned about injuring the reputation of military men.[57]

As would be seen in later reservist association reforms, such concerns were shared by Tanaka Giichi, the group's leading organizer and proponent, as well as other national leaders.[58] The distress over reservists, however, was emblematic of a greater worry, namely, that vast segments of the Japanese population were rapidly becoming disaffected both with their national rulers and with the manner in which they ruled.

The "Candy and Whip" Policy

Harsh sentences for convicted rioters in general represented but one aspect of the central government's suppression-and-relief, or "candy and whip" (*ame to muchi*), policy. The Home Ministry and the Ministry of Justice usually wielded the whip, while the Ministry of Agriculture and Commerce doled out the candy.[59] From 15 August Home Ministry and Metropolitan Police Board officials worked out an eight-point program to deal with the massive protests. The measures included putting police on the alert for any signs of unrest arising from concern over skyrocketing prices. To prevent the spread of rioting, officials were additionally empowered to ban all public meetings convened to discuss the rice problem and to enforce Home Minister Mizuno's ordered censoring of newspaper and magazine reports of the protests. Police were also instructed to take special precautionary measures in buraku areas and to tighten their surveillance of those harboring dangerous thoughts.[60]

In past uprisings the government had called out the military to restore order. In 1884 the government ordered the army to crush the Chichibu uprising. It relied on force again in 1890 during the Sado rice riots, in 1905 during the Hibiya riots, and in 1907 against the Ashio mine workers. Identical measures were used in 1913 during the Taishō "political crisis" and in 1914 against the Nagoya streetcar protesters. Although mobilization had never been carried out across the country, the government did not flinch from taking drastic measures during the 1918 crisis. Altogether the government called on 102,000 troops for service in 26 prefectures at 140 individual locations. Groups mobilized included military police (*kenpeitai*), infantry regulars, and even navy troops.[61] From Sendai in the north to Nagasaki in the south, units of as many as 11,500 soldiers guarded rice exchanges and government offices.

The largest contingents were posted in major cities and the coal-mining districts of northern Kyushu. Troops there usually maintained order simply by being present. But when they were provoked they did not hesitate to use swords, rifles, and machine guns against crowds that sallied forth from behind street barricades to attack the troops with stones, clubs, and sharpened bamboo sticks. Although no soldiers or civilians died at the hands of rioters, more than thirty protesters were killed, and scores more were wounded by police or troops.[62]

Before the outbreak of widespread urban protests, government spokesmen had made conciliatory, even sympathetic, pronouncements on the poorer class's struggle against inflation. But official attitudes quickly hardened when passive protest gave way to street barricades and armed attacks against imperial troops. The punitive treatment of suspected protesters carried over into legal proceedings following riot suppression. Ministry of Justice officials brushed aside press criticism of the use of brutal force and illegal detention on more than twenty thousand suspects.

In the search for riot leaders, especially those believed harboring "dangerous thoughts," legal niceties typically went by the board. Officials reported that several detainees committed suicide during questioning and that others died from unknown causes. Many suspects left police cells injured, with serious deficiency diseases such as beriberi, or psychologically broken.[63] The harsh treatment moved the Japan Lawyers Association to accuse the Justice Ministry of trampling on human rights, ignoring torture by the police, and failing to maintain minimum health standards for riot suspects.[64]

When they had concluded their preliminary investigations, prosecutors formally charged 8,185 suspects, about one-third of the actual number detained or arrested throughout the nation. On the day that mass trials were set to begin in Tokyo, student lawyers before a standing-room-only crowd at the Kanda Seinen Kaikan held their own mock tribunal to adjudge the criminality of the protesters' actions. In this demonstration of public support for those indicted, all of the accused were found innocent. The actual trial, however, progressed along far different lines. On the opening day of the Tokyo proceedings, in which 299 individuals faced charges of rioting and related crimes, the presiding judge, Nagata, disposed of fifty cases in a single afternoon, a pace that he increased to seventy per hearing over the next three days.[65] Sixty defense lawyers, most of whom were volunteers from the Japan Lawyers Association, attempted to slow down the assembly-line dispensation of justice. But the court permitted only a single day for the questioning of witnesses and two days for defense arguments.[66] The Tokyo trials, which began on 25 November, ended less than a month later, on 20 December, with all but thirty-three of the defendants sentenced to prison terms, fined, or both.[67] Two defendants were sentenced to five or more years in prison; eleven, from one to five years; sixty, from six months to a year; and sixty-four, six months or less. Fines ranged from less than thirty to more than a hundred yen.

Throughout the nation most riot trials proceeded with the same alacrity as those held in Tokyo. Hearings en masse enabled most deliberations to be concluded before the end of 1918. Of those initially indicted throughout the country, more than 5,000 were speedily convicted for various offenses. Those convicted, whether for simply receiving rice that a merchant was forced to sell at a discount or for more serious crimes like arson, received stern punishment. Thirty rioters, mostly from the Kansai region, were sentenced to life at hard labor.[68]

The government balanced its show of strength by establishing a national relief fund. With the onset of rioting in Japan's major cities in mid-August, central-government officials announced that the Taishō emperor, deeply aggrieved over the disturbances and concerned for his subjects' welfare, had donated 3 million yen for national relief. The imperial largess was soon surpassed by money from a multitude of donors, both public and private, corporate and individual.

The central government led by providing 10 million yen from the national treasury. On 25 August, Japan's major trading and industrial companies jumped on the relief bandwagon. In the name of Iwasaki Hisaya, the Mitsubishi industrial and financial conglomerate (zaibatsu) contributed 1 million yen, immediately matched by an additional million from Mitsui. Suzuki Shōten, the largest rice importer and a company whose headquarters had been burned to the ground in violent rioting in Kobe, donated 500,000 yen. By the end of August the national relief fund amounted to more than 15 million yen.

Relief funds raised centrally amounted to an impressive total figure. Nevertheless, when the money was apportioned to individual needy communities throughout the nation, imperial generosity provided scant relief. More significant assistance was typically provided on the local level where wealthy individuals, from landlords in farm villages to urban factory owners, opened wide their purses. In Nagano prefecture, for example, less than 5 percent of money raised for rice relief came from the imperial contribution; in Fukui city donations raised between the outbreak of unrest on 13 August and 30 August totaled 66,500 yen, an amount equal to one-half the city's 1917 tax revenue.[69]

Although the disbursement of funds raised centrally did not achieve any lasting improvement in local economic conditions, it did fulfill other symbolic functions. Not only did it express the concern of the nation's highest political and economic leaders and attempt to shame the general public into more tractable behavior; it also, by example, primed the pump of local generosity and encouraged local officials and wealthy individuals to take care of their own.

The central government distributed relief funds among Japan's prefectures, where added donations raised locally provided funds to small rural hamlets as well as major cities. For the "extremely needy" (*goku-hin*), local officials gave free rice or cash subsidies. To those less destitute, rice was provided at a discount determined by the amount of local taxes (*kosūwari*) paid. A lower position on the tax rolls meant a higher possibility of a family's being deemed needy. If sufficiently poor, local residents could receive discount coupons enabling them to purchase foreign rice and fixed quantities of domestic grain at lower than market prices. The coupons often carried a message explaining that the holder was a recipient of imperial beneficence and should be grateful for the emperor's concern. So that there would be no doubt about the source of the aid, sacks of relief grain were boldly printed with the slogan "Imperial Gift Rice" (*onshi mai*). In Kyoto and other cities, local officials also proclaimed "Imperial Favor" days on which rice was sold at ten sen below market price.[70]

During and immediately after the riots, orders for foreign rice poured in to Suzuki Shōten and other rice importers. Thousands of Japanese clutching their coupons lined up at village and town offices, primary schools, and rice stores, where their names had been hastily registered as qualified recipients of aid. Not everyone applauded the aid program. Even before the riots had ended, people complained about the temporary nature of the relief measures. In city riots, speakers at mass rallies condemned token solutions that fell short of establishing a publicly set price for rice and failed to rid the nation of government officials responsible for Japan's distorted economic conditions. Others, finding no fault with the basic concept of rice relief, charged that the program simply did not go far enough. Demanding a broadening of recipient qualifications, they charged that inflation-caused poverty struck the middle class as well as poorer groups.

Many also complained about the use of Korean, Taiwanese, and Southeast Asian rice in the discount-sales program. This again suggests that for many who joined in the riots, the problem in 1918 was not one of absolute privation. Protesters did not want just any rice; they explicitly demanded Japanese rice at a fair price. Reflecting this concern was the fact that foreign rice seldom outsold domestic even when imported grain was offered at a hefty discount. An article that appeared in the 20 August edition of the *Ōsaka asahi shinbun* focused on some of the problems with the discount rationing program:

> Korean polished rice is being handled by rice dealers on the outskirts of town and the grain is often full of sand and dust. What's worse is that because there are few takers of foreign rice many are buying it for animal feed or to process into Japanese sweets. The genuinely hard-pressed poor must spend half the day scurrying about to buy two shō of rice. This greatly reduces the efficiency of husbands and wives who both work. Discount sales? On the contrary, the program has just increased prices [because of the indirect cost of obtaining grain]. The "benefits" of discount sales do not amount to even a tenth of the demand for polished rice. Most city people are, as ever, resigned to paying fifty sen for a measure of rice. Their resentment continues strong.[71]

As the *Asahi* article attests and letters to the editors of Japan's major dailies indicated, people decried government efforts to "fool" them by selling cheap foreign grain. They not only opposed the supposedly oily taste and foul smell of what was popularly known as Nanking rice but also took issue with the government's failure to provide adequate and reasonably priced food supplies. In a few cases, qualified recipients of aid rejected aid in any form.[72]

The government endeavored to overcome popular resistance to foreign rice by working through local officials. During the summer of 1918 the Ministry of Agriculture and Commerce's Provisional Foreign Rice Control Division (Rinji Gaimai Kanri-bu) sent a poster-size directive entitled "Foreign Rice Instructions" to local government offices. It included a complete listing of foreign rice prices, a directory to all branch offices of the four major trading companies handling sales, and suggestions for mobilizing cooperatives, charitable groups, and local government offices in the distribution of "Saigon" and "Rangoon" rice. In its attempt to convince local officials, who were in turn to persuade their constituencies, of the value of foreign grain the directive takes an almost pleading tone. It presented a positive nutritional analysis of foreign rice along with cooking tips (e.g., soak overnight, boil longer, mix with glutinous rice, eat while the grain is warm). But the directive's excessive explanation perhaps clarifies why the public was less than enthusiastic about bargain rice:

> In addition to its use as food, foreign rice is also consumed as an industrial raw material [kōgyo genryō]. Here, however, we will explain its use as a food. Heretofore, the first thing that comes to mind about foreign rice is its petroleum-like smell. This has caused the people to tend to reject it. When foreign rice was [first] imported in 1894 it was shipped in hemp sacks that when woven had been treated in a petroleum oil which resulted in a strong odor. Recently, however, a different oil is being used and the strong odor has completely vanished. First and foremost, it is essential that you understand this. But for the best flavor, it is better to mix foreign rice with domestic rather than cooking it alone.

Such urging, however, did little to instill public confidence. In emergency rice sales in Tokyo, domestic rice outsold foreign rice by a margin of at least three to one, depending on the relief outlet, and in certain wards by as much as ten to one, despite the lower price of imported grain.[73]

The central government's candy-and-whip response to a nationwide breakdown of law and order was uniform and unyielding. The state's response also reveals the perception, shared by contemporary policy-makers and historians who have studied the riots, that the protests were a single convulsive uprising. Yet, as the following chapters will discuss, rioters did not view their actions as part of a single, homogeneous, national event. The disputes invariably involved a variety of differing specific local issues.

A general concern with what might be called a "moral economy" was, however, one widely shared characteristic that linked the 1918 protests. Popular demands for an equitable sharing of local resources, especially during times of stringency, were nothing new in Japan. Riots and other protests broke out irregularly but often during the Tokugawa and Meiji periods. Japanese remembered their past traditions of defiance: in the regional disturbances of 1918, participants often looked back to local traditions to justify their protests and help them decide what actions to take against local leaders. Modern worldwide democratic movements may have contributed to a "mood" that made protests feasible, but the vocabulary of liberal ideology was seldom heard in rural Japanese uprisings in 1918. Traditional elements were particularly evident in the Toyama coastal riots. There the causes and course of unrest strongly resembled incidents that had occurred regularly from at least as early as the Tokugawa period.

TWO

Traditional Protest Along the Toyama Coast

Smoke from a steamship offshore means rice will cost one sen more.

A Toyama saying

The first wave of rioting began almost simultaneously in small towns and villages along Toyama Bay facing the Sea of Japan. The Toyama coast, crowded by mountains on one side and the sea on the other, is part of Japan's "outback" (*ura Nihon*) and appears an unlikely starting place for the unrest that later engulfed the nation. In 1918 the local economy was undergoing gradual industrialization, a process that had accelerated during the late Meiji period. Nevertheless, most of Toyama's workers still labored according to the agricultural calendar and the fishing season rather than the factory time clock. At the end of World War I, traditional occupations—farming, fishing, grain loading, itinerant medicine vending, migratory labor, and workshop craft trades—were still predominant and would continue so until Toyama's industrial "take-off" got fully under way in the mid-1920s. During the Taishō period the prefecture lacked large factories, shipyards, and arsenals, places where strikes and labor disputes were breaking out in Kure, Kobe, Osaka, and Tokyo. At the end of World War I, Toyama remained part of the hinterland, a region outside the mainstream, apparently remote from the rapid social and economic transformation that seemed to overwhelm more central urban areas.[1]

Toyama's coastal towns and villages, however, were not untouched by changes occurring in other parts of Japan in 1918. Toyama fishermen, women stevedores, and factory hands experienced the same hardships resulting from wartime inflation, commodity speculation, and inadequate wages that sometimes prompted industrial workers to strike. In some respects, conditions were worse than elsewhere. In 1918 the general prefectural death rate, at 31 per 1,000 population, was the highest it had been since 1886. Infant mortality stood at 252 per 1,000, up sharply from the 177 per 1,000 recorded in 1912 and a third higher than Japan's national average. And at the peak of the war-boom years more people died from tuberculosis than during any year from 1900 to 1940.[2] Local residents also lacked any immunity to the effects of central-government inflation-control policies that had contributed to the outbreak of unrest elsewhere.

Nevertheless, nationwide inflation alone cannot explain why disturbances occurred when they did in Toyama nor why they were essentially nonviolent. Although 1918 was a hard year, one of greater poverty and sickness, Toyama residents had choices other than that of taking their grievances to the streets. Both before and after the riots, men and women became migrant workers, found new jobs in city factories, and took on additional side-work (*naishoku*) to make ends meet.

Times were difficult, but they were never so bad as to affect the annual schedule of festivals, weddings, and other celebrations. In 1918 Toyama residents took in 5,593 statistical days of plays, sumo matches, *rakugo* performances, and traveling *naniwabushi* recitals. In addition, modern entertainments—magic-lantern shows and movies—were well attended. Local people also had income sufficient to support three daily and two evening papers in addition to twenty-six other periodicals that circulated throughout the prefecture.[3] It might be argued that such diversions were enjoyed solely by wealthier city people. Yet the wide variety of entertainments, traditional and modern, highbrow and lowbrow, suggests that it was not just those who dwelled in Toyama's two cities who supported the arts. Indeed, Toyama officials cited, not poverty but a popular love of luxury, one that "warped the hearts" of common people, as a contributing factor in the riots. After the 1918 protests Nakaniikawa county (*gun*) officials initiated a Scrooge-like "life beautification movement." Directives and posters distributed throughout the coastal towns enjoined the population to stop such wasteful practices as exchanging New Year's greeting cards, holding expensive weddings, practicing flower arranging, and sending funeral wreaths. To return to the austere beauty of the old ways, citizens were told to stop drinking and to keep their clocks tightly wound. Prefectural directives before the rice riots made similar calls for a return to the traditional virtues of thrift and incorrupt simplicity.[4] Perhaps we should not take too seriously local-government campaigns that urged greater individual economizing and deflecting attention from the state's responsibility for poor economic conditions. Nevertheless, in postriot explanations of the origins of the 1918 unrest, neither officials nor rioters suggested that the protests arose from famine or lack of work. In fact, wartime newspapers reported a labor shortage in Toyama's construction industry and workshops.[5]

Although absolute poverty had little to do with the Toyama rice riots, local residents did react angrily to what they considered unjustified economic deprivation. Rioters seldom asked for free grain, but they repeatedly demanded it at a fair price. Throughout the protests they distinguished between relative poverty, which an individual might accept as one's lot in life, and gratuitous exploitation, which was widely condemned. Of course, any precise gauging of a "calculus of pain" aimed at determining the precise point at which acceptance turns to protest is futile. But local residents did appear primarily concerned with maintaining a livelihood well above mere subsistence. As postriot accounts of local living conditions make clear, there continues to be a good deal of controversy about just how poor the rioters actually were.[6] Moreover, if rioting had been a simple reflex action, we might expect to see it in regions where economic conditions were worse than in Toyama. Yet in Tōhoku, for example, where wages were lower and disease rates higher, rioting rarely occurred in 1918.[7]

Rather than hunger, central to the protest was the disproportionately large share that escalating rice prices took from the family budget. Many believed it was wrong to pay so much for something apparently so abundant. True, rice was scarce on a nationwide basis, but this scarcity was hardly evident in Toyama, where rice was the prefecture's most abundant and most profitable product. In 1918 its total cash value was estimated at 46 million yen, a figure that far outdistanced the 8.4 million yen output of Toyama's spinning mills and the 7.6 million yen value of traditional medicines sold by itinerant vendors. Although the harvest was comparatively poor in 1918, rice annually accounted for at least half and as much as 65 percent of the total shipments from Toyama's two principal ports during the war years. At just one major port, Fushiki, stevedores loaded rice valued at 4 million yen in 1918, a year in which farmers suffered poorer yields per acre and the smallest total harvest since 1914.[8]

Men and women daily hauled bales of grain for shipment by steamships waiting offshore (see fig. 4). As far as Toyama's rice supply was concerned, they could see with their own eyes that high rice prices were man-made and not the result of local shortage. When apparently unnatural prices began to nudge food costs beyond what was considered a fair price, Toyama residents took to the streets. Rather than being "rebellions of the belly," however, the coastal riots were expressions of resentment against marketing practices that prevented the local consumption of locally produced rice.[9]

The relationship of wages to consumer costs helps clarify the point at which the acceptance of steep prices shifted to protest. Of primary concern here are the working conditions and incomes of fishermen, factory and migrant workers, stevedores, and those engaged in piecework or side jobs done in the home. The situations of these groups were not unique: "white-collar" workers also found it hard to make ends meet. At a time when Tokyo newspapers estimated that a family of four required about 50 yen per month for simple subsistence, clerks in the Namerikawa town office made only 18.50 yen monthly during the first half of 1918. Toyama primary school teachers took home only 20 yen per month; policemen earned even less.[10] During the riots low-ranking government officials often acted sympathetically toward the protesters. But their roles as representatives of local order—combined with the receipt of special cost-of-living subsidies—restrained them from actually expressing their discontent over the high prices. The focus here is on the working conditions and incomes of the poorer classes whose members actively protested when high rice prices threatened a lower standard of living.

Workers and Wages: Toyama 1918

Fishermen's wives, not fishermen, led the coastal riots. But the insufficient income of the household's male wage earner, which was at the heart of the protest, encouraged women to act on behalf of their husbands and families. Men, who often worked far away from home, were less familiar with specific grievances and were consequently less involved in local disputes. Many men simply were not around when rioting broke out. If present when the disturbances began, they tended to steer clear of the appeals movements and noisy demonstrations, which they considered "unmanly" and "woman's work."[11] Nevertheless, despite the typically belated involvement of men in the coastal riots, it was the declining real wages of fishermen that women often referred to as justifying their protests.

Fishermen either worked the Toyama coast or joined crews that fished northern waters off Hokkaido or Russian territory. Coastal fishing grounds along Toyama Bay had been steadily worked for three hundred years, and productivity declined during the Meiji period, causing fishermen gradually to move their operations northward. As a result of overfishing in local waters and of higher wages, migrant fishermen (*dekasegi*) far outnumbered those who remained home.[12] In 1907 the Russo-Japanese Fishing Treaty gave the Japanese equal rights to fish waters in the Russian Far East.[13] Access to new grounds accelerated an earlier trend for Toyama fishermen to work farther and farther from local ports.

Well before 1918 many families simply departed Toyama for good. In 1883, for example, pioneers from Ikuji moved to Hokkaido to establish a permanent fishing settlement. People from Toyama constituted 15 percent of Hokkaido's population by the turn of the century. From 1902 to 1911 more people left Toyama for resettlement in Hokkaido than from any other Japanese prefecture. Another reason for the growth of Toyama's *dekasegi* fishing industry was the Meiji government's conscious development of Hokkaido. Before 1869 Toyama fishermen had been limited to working only coastal waters; thereafter the central government permitted free access to Hokkaido's fishing grounds.[14]

By 1915 the system whereby fishing bosses (*amimoto*) gained proprietary rights to specific coastal waters also effectively banned most fishermen from working near home. Lacking anything other than muscle and wind-powered boats, which were virtually useless given the *amimoto* monopoly of local fishing grounds, the number of self-employed fishermen declined from 3,929 in 1914 to 603 in 1915. The sharp reduction in the number of independent fishermen was matched by a corresponding increase in *dekasegi* hired workers. The number of *dekasegi* fishermen taking cod, herring, squid, and seaweed (*konbu*) from the waters around Hokkaido, Karafuto, and the Kuriles steadily increased from the 1880s onward.[15]

Employed by *amimoto* in Toyama or recruited by labor bosses representing owners in Hokkaido, hired fishermen worked under an informal contract system. Although they were occasionally accompanied by their wives, who joined the crew as cooks or helpers, men normally left their families behind after signing on a boat. Many remained away from home from March through October, the length of the normal fishing season. After completing a contract with one boat owner, the workers might join another crew without visiting home in the meantime. The opportunity to work as a day laborer in Aomori or Iwate also sidetracked those returning between fishing seasons.[16]

A few boat owners made a good living, but the wage-paid fisherman was far from wealthy. In 1918 the estimated nationwide wages for fishermen ranged between 50 and 95 sen a day.[17] Statistics show that Toyama fishermen, by earning gross daily wages of between one and two yen, did far better than the national average fisherman's wage of 61 sen.[18] But this total wage is not a fair reckoning of the actual income of hired crew members, whose wages came as a share of the season's total catch. A poor fishing harvest caused by seasonal fluctuations or the peculiarities of the fishing ground could substantially reduce the daily catch and thereby lower the fisherman's pay. Such occupational uncertainties brought hardship during the slack season, from July to September. During this slow period many fishermen had to find work mending nets, take jobs in the local hemp-processing factories, or, along with their families, hire themselves out as farm laborers.[19] Bad weather and rough seas, which made fishing hazardous from October to November, forced fishermen to rely on their savings or whatever alternative work they could find. In 1917 the day wage during the winter months was estimated at about 55 sen per man, a pay rate below the national average for fishermen.[20]

Wage deductions made by boat owners also reduced earnings. Migrant fishermen hired by a labor boss and working for an absentee boat owner were especially vulnerable. Absentee owners, living in Hokkaido and beyond the sanctions of the local community, tended to squeeze all they could from the fisherman's wages. The possibility of working for an absentee owner was high in 1918. Of 16,000 Toyama fishermen in 1918, an estimated 7,000, or 44 percent of them, worked away from home.[21] In one town the total number of *dekasegi* fishermen ran as high as 114 out of 200 families.[22]

An official study of working conditions for migrant fishermen in Shimoniikawa county in 1924 reports that fishermen were routinely indebted to boat owners before the fishing season began. In about 1890, boat owners initiated a debt system (*zen shakin*) by which money was advanced to a fisherman by the boat owner or his agent. The advance carried with it a hefty 25 percent interest charge, which was due, paid in full, at the end of the fishing season. Although the money was ostensibly lent for steamship passage to the fishing grounds, workers and owners alike recognized that it was commonly used to pay debts or for family expenses. The advanced wages bound individual fishermen to particular absentee owners much as if the recipient was an indentured servant. The arrangement was hardly accidental. The system, patterned after one used in Meiji spinning mills and other factories, aimed at securing a stable and productive work force for the boat owner by obligating the borrower to work hard to free himself from debt by the end of the fishing season.[23] In the event that the hired fisherman failed to make good his obligation, he might be left broke and stranded in Hokkaido, inasmuch as the boat owner was in no way bound to guarantee the debtor's return passage. Although the licensing and protection of migrant fishermen represented one of the postriot reforms taken in Shimoniikawa, a 1928 study of working conditions indicates that 64 percent of the county's hired fishermen continued to borrow against their wages.[24]

Hired fishermen, regardless of whether they worked local or northern waters, suffered further wage deductions for bait, equipment rental, and damage fees for loss of line and other items.[25] In Shimoniikawa these fees were assessed from the 48 percent of the catch remaining after the boat owner had been paid his obligatory 52 percent of the total seasonal harvest.[26] Even nominally self-employed fishermen were not free from the boat owner's exactions. Those who attempted to work independently on rented boats paid 20 percent of their catch to the boat's registered owner. As they were also required to pay for rights to the *amimoto*'s fishing areas along with charges for equipment, bait, and damaged or lost items, their situation was often only marginally better than that of the hired crew members.

Although the migrant fishermen were ostensibly the main breadwinners for family members left behind, lower fish prices and an uneven fishing season recorded for local and northern waters during 1917 and 1918 prevented them from contributing much to family earnings.[27] Accounts of the Toyama riots repeatedly comment on the inability of those working out of Hokkaido to send anything home; by the close of the 1918 season many fishermen were forced to write dependents for boat and train fare back to Toyama.[28] Even if they did manage to save something from their earnings, an increasingly larger proportion went to pay for rice during the summer months of 1918.

In times of continually rising prices for rice, those working locally in Toyama were hardly in a position to help a stranded family member. Male factory workers in local workshops and factories made approximately seventy to eighty sen for a ten-hour day in 1918, with top wages at about one yen per day on the eve of the riots. Craftsmen were better paid. A skilled carpenter or mason could earn about one yen a day in 1918.[29] But women or teenage girls typically earned only 50 percent or less of what was paid to their male counterparts.[30]

Women also worked outside Toyama. During the 1890s young girls, single women, and even a number of married women, began leaving their families temporarily to work at spinning mills and silk-processing factories in Osaka, Tokyo, Nagano, Gunma, and Fukushima.[31] A prefectural report in 1928 notes that these *dekasegi* workers did not always leave of their own accord but were often ordered to work by husbands and fathers.[32] Statistics kept for the years from 1915 to 1940 indicate that Toyama was by far the largest source of female workers migrating to other Japanese prefectures. During this period an average of 9,043 women left Toyama annually, a migration rate that declined only after 1925 with the opening of additional textile mills within the prefecture. Over one-third of the more than ten thousand women working outside the prefecture in 1918 hailed from Shimoniikawa, the site of the first 1918 protest over high rice prices. With the exception of the year 1931, Shimoniikawa women, in fact, accounted for 25 to 40 percent of those women who left home as migrant workers between 1915 and 1940.[33] The stringent economic conditions indicated by the high *dekasegi* rate may explain why Shimoniikawa women acted earlier than others in protesting the high cost of grain.

The steady stream of female workers leaving Toyama in 1918, however, was not caused by a lack of work within the home prefecture but by the higher wages available outside the region. Women working in Toyama hemp-processing factories earned less than half of the male wage. If they relocated to a Shinshū textile mill, they could make up to eighty sen per day, thereby matching and in some cases surpassing the top salaries paid men in Toyama factories.[34] Although women who left to work in mills away from home bore the expense of travel and the burden of family separation, the incentive of higher pay encouraged more than ten thousand women a year to take jobs outside the prefecture between 1917 and 1927.[35]

In addition to laboring in other prefectures, women also worked as casual stevedores (*nakashi*) and did piecework in their homes (*naishoku*). Those responsible for loading cargo were not really dock workers in the strictest sense of the term. Most of Toyama's shallow ports lacked the long piers and necessary harbor facilities for servicing large steamships. The stevedores spent most of their time putting bales of rice, straw matting, and other goods into lighters, which were pushed off from beaches to steamships waiting in the bay (see fig. 4). Cargo loaders earned their pay by shouldering goods from granaries or warehouses to the lighters. In Uozu, the largest port in eastern Toyama, rice dealers, fish fertilizer merchants, local banks, and the owners of warehouses typically relied on labor bosses or hired women directly to work in loading teams. At the blast of a whistle, the women haulers gathered at warehouses located along the banks of several rivers that ran through towns like Uozu, Namerikawa, and Mizuhashi.

Aside from the women who worked at cargo loading the year around, additional female workers were often hired to carry bales of rice during the peak shipping season. The work was an important source of extra income for Toyama families. The grain that women carried on their backs was destined for markets primarily in Hokkaido; Hokuriku rice represented Toyama's main commodity sold in Hokkaido in exchange for fish fertilizer. Uozu was the single largest depot in this two-way trade, which initially relied on small sailing vessels and increased in volume from 1877 with the introduction of steamships.[36] With the growth of rice exports from the Hokuriku region, women also prepared grain shipments bound for rice exchanges in Osaka and Tokyo. In some instances, the rice was later transshipped to markets in China.[37]

During the peak loading periods the bayside towns were backlogged with rice waiting to go aboard steamships waiting offshore. The cargo ships kept to a tight schedule, stopping along the coast to take on additional goods in the shortest possible span of time. The stevedores worked frantically during the peak periods, often continuing to load the lighters long into the night. Women were paid according to the distance from the storehouse to the boat and according to the number of rice bales they carried. Their pay varied slightly, depending on the employer. Kanagawa Sōzaemon, Namerikawa grain dealer and one of the main targets of attack during the rice riots, paid female loaders one-half sen per rice bale. Pay elsewhere was not appreciably higher; in 1918 a woman's typical return for a day's work ranged between ten and twenty sen. During the peak season wages improved as working hours grew longer. If they had the stamina to work day and night shifts, women could earn as much as forty-five sen per day, a wage rate double that paid to female factory workers.[38] Although many refused to load rice during the riots, local women in normal times valued this backbreaking work. As one female loader recalled in a 1968 interview, "It didn't matter, day or night, whenever a steamship moored in the bay we went out to load rice."[39]

When cargo loading was slow, women worked at home doing piece-work. Their children, many of whom only irregularly attended elementary school, joined them in cutting and pasting paper bags used by medicine vendors, making soles for Japanese sandals (*zori*), and stitching together hemp sacks.[40] Other families involved in the small-scale cottage industry also fashioned straw mats and made handkerchiefs from materials received from wholesalers. Wage levels varied, but estimates indicate that a single adult woman engaged in side-work could make from fifteen to thirty sen per day, depending on the job and the particular wholesaler (*ton'ya*).[41] This was a small yet important contribution to family income, given the rapid rise in prices from mid-1917.

Although economic conditions were not prosperous, both food and work were available. The demand for polished white rice was not determined by nutrition or the unavailability of substitutes. It arose instead from the popular belief that people had a right to buy rice in reasonable amounts and at a just price. In some cases, qualified recipients, out of pride or their dissatisfaction with aid restrictions, simply refused relief rice.[42]

Most studies of the Toyama riots have accepted the popular determination, based on interviews with those who joined the protests, that individual fishermen required about a shō of rice daily. The same amount is suggested as having been necessary for male and female cargo loaders.[43] This rough estimate of a minimum daily rice requirement may very well be inaccurate. It is important, however, not for any scientific validity but as a standard of what was popularly considered necessary to maintain an adequate standard of living. Local people accepted rice priced at a level that allowed a family to maintain itself above subsistence. When nationwide scarcity, inflation, and commodity speculation pushed prices beyond the "reasonable" level, passivity changed to protest.

Rice prices in Toyama began to rise almost a year before the outbreak of rioting, reversing a trend toward relatively low prices that had begun with a bumper harvest in 1914. Local grain prices continued low throughout the first half of 1917 but jumped sharply and continued to increase from late spring onward (see table 6). By July 1918 the depletion of preharvest rice supplies coupled with renewed market speculation pushed up wholesale prices on the Toyama and Takaoka city rice

TABLE 6.   TOYAMA CITY PRICES, 1916–1918

Item	Unit	July 1916 (Yen)	July 1917 (Yen)	July 1918 (Yen)	1917 Increase over 1916 (1916=100)	1918 Increase over 1916 (1916=100)
Polished rice						
Top grade	180 liters	14.00	24.70	33.00	176.4	235.7
Middle grade	180 liters	13.50	24.20	32.00	179.3	240.7
Low grade	180 liters	13.00	23.70	32.00	182.3	246.2
Wheat	180 liters	9.00	13.20	20.00	146.7	222.2
Sake	180 liters	60.00	60.00	65.00	100.0	108.3
Soy Sauce	180 liters	27.00	30.00	33.00	111.1	222.2
Miso	3.75 kg.	3.00	3.20	4.50	106.7	150.0
Kerosene	2 cans	5.57	5.48	7.08	98.4	127.1

SOURCE: Saitō, Kome sōdō, 2.

exchanges. Retail prices climbed even higher in coastal rice depots like Uozu than in the prefecture's major cities. Although rice fields ringed the port town, the rice price at local shops increased by almost one sen per day between mid-July and the first of August.[44]

By early August feeding one full-time working member of a fisherman's, stevedore's, or factory worker's household could take all of a woman's wage and as much as half of a man's. Of course, wage earners had more to consider than simply their own maintenance. In 1918 the average Toyama family included six members, and as rioters later recalled, about two shō of rice were needed to support one's family.[45] This meant that a male wage earner's entire day's wage could be spent just for rice. But Toyama families lived on more than rice; they also had to pay rent, buy kindling and coal, and somehow provide for all the other expenses of maintaining large families. Even if we reject the notion that a shō of rice was needed to keep a worker working, it is nevertheless easy to appreciate that ever-escalating rice prices threatened a deterioration in living standards.

The threat posed by rice prices appeared constant. Instead of suggesting that prices might soon decline, articles in local newspapers predicted that the low level of reserves and new demands on national supplies arising from the planned Siberian Expedition would send rice rocketing to one yen or more for a single shō. Rice prices never in fact reached this level in 1918 or in the years immediately after the riots. But to those living along the Toyama coast the rapid rise in prices during the summer months made predictions of yet another doubling of rice prices appear entirely credible. Officials had instituted cost-of-living allowances to help local-government employees survive the hard times. But nothing comparable had been done for the general population. Later, when rioters explained why they took the initiative to change the situation, they recalled the passivity of local officials.[46]

The "Women's Uprising"

The first step in checking the soaring cost of rice was made on 22 July 1918. After sundown women stevedores and fishermen's wives met at a community well in Uozu to discuss what could be done to hold down prices. They agreed that appeals should be made to influential townspeople; if that proved ineffective, then a stronger protest would be mounted. This course was neither bold nor innovative. Many of the women at the meeting had witnessed or taken part in similar disputes during the Meiji years; just six years earlier several had joined the successful appeals movement for cheaper prices.

The 1918 protests continued from 22 July to 4 October. During this period police recorded thirty individual incidents, some of which continued for several days in Uozu, Namerikawa, Mizuhashi, and Higashi Iwase. Although prefectural police accounts state that exactly 5,142 people rioted, this estimate is probably conservative, given the number of towns and villages that reported unrest.[47] Any precise reckoning of crowd size is, of course, impossible. The riots were fluid, fast-changing events in which disturbances in one place might be joined by protesters from another. Towns along the Toyama coast were not separated by great distances, and in some cases rioters merely had to stroll a few kilometers or cross a bridge to support a dispute in a neighboring town.

Although the composition of the crowd sometimes changed quickly, the participation of women was one consistent characteristic of nearly all the Toyama coastal protests. Of the thirty incidents documented by prefectural police, twenty-three were led and carried out exclusively by women. In directing the sit-ins, marches, and all-night vigils, protest leaders did not rely on refined strategy or explicit ideological justifications for their actions. Indeed, when local socialists spoke at rallies in an attempt to politicize the protest, they were ignored.

Age, sex, and work experience were characteristics shared by riot leaders, not involvement in political parties or activism. Middle-aged and older women presided over tiny strategy meetings as well as the larger rallies held in schoolyards and on the grounds of local shrines and temples. The group in Uozu decided on the targets of the protest and the order in which appeals and protests would be made. Their authority was almost indisputable. Deference to age, personal obligation (*giri*), the position of older women as labor bosses, and their status as household heads contributed to their widely recognized prestige.

Sugimura Hatsu, who had joined the riots in Mizuhashi, stated in a 1968 interview that the "big boss" (*ichiban oyakata*) behind the town protest was Mizukami Iyon, stevedore and wife of a local fisherman. Mizukami was joined by two lieutenants with virtually identical backgrounds. Sugimura described the three leaders, all in their fifties, as being able to outwork men at loading grain. These stern women were respected not only because of their personalities but also because they organized grain-loading teams and directed younger women in mending nets and other tasks. One woman participant in the riots, who was twenty-one years old at the time, later recalled that the respect owed the older women made it difficult for younger women even to hold up their heads in the presence of the female "bosses" (*oyakata*). Even if they were indifferent to the actual decisions made at the well-side gatherings, younger women deferred to the age and experience of these leaders.[48]

During the riots the older women occasionally resorted to pressure tactics to buttress demands for group solidarity. In several incidents leaders demanded that at least one member from each local family join the demonstrations. Failure to comply sometimes resulted in a claque of women gathered at the offending family's door, sarcastically yelling that this household had money and need not worry about high prices.[49] Such coercion, however, was usually unnecessary. Women stevedores led by example and sheer energy. Typically described in accounts of the riots as self-sacrificing, they acted against their own self-interest by boycotting grain loading. They also attempted to persuade male workers to follow their example. When verbal persuasion failed, these tough women prevented men from proceeding with their work.

Women-led crowds were noisy but generally nonviolent. Police temporarily detained a few dozen men and women during the weeks of protest, but all were released after a night or two in jail. No one faced trial or received a punitive sentence for joining the riots.[50] "Riot," in fact, does not best describe the Toyama protests. True, there were angry confrontations between stone-throwing crowds and police. Women also defied authority by convening clamorous rallies at local temples or in front of the homes of wealthier neighbors. Nevertheless, the actions of protesters and officials alike demonstrated a premeditated, almost ritualistic, quality. Local people familiar with the history and course of earlier "riots" drew on their experience in ordering the aims and tactics of the 1918 protest. Their actions hardly seem "riotous" if that means spontaneous, uncontrolled violence. But if what happened in Toyama was not a riot, then what was it and why did it have such a tremendous influence on protests throughout the nation? The answer becomes clearer when we investigate the issues at stake in the Toyama dispute, the background of the "rioters," and their tactics.

The Course of Rioting

Hasegawa Hiroshi and others who have studied the Toyama protests usually present them as occurring in three distinct phases—prelude, peak, and pacification—lasting from 22 July to 4 October, after which calm was restored.[51] This view sees the degree of popular resistance and crowd size as basic to understanding the protests; it loses any sense that the rioters employed calculated methods or that local officials were moved by something other than a desire to expeditiously snuff out unjustified resistance to their authority. According to Hasegawa, in the riot's prelude stage from 22 July to 2 August, protests tended to be small, isolated, and generally peaceful gatherings easily broken up by police. In the peak period, which continued until 8 August, tension mounted. The crowds became larger, angrier, and more persistent: mobs of as many as two thousand confronted rice merchants, police, and officials, and shouting matches escalated into scuffling and property destruction. Local authority was challenged as rioters ignored police appeals to end the protest, gathered when and where they liked, and even laid seige to a local police substation. The pacification stage began on 9 August and lasted until 4 October. Once the crowd's anger had been vented, the urge to riot declined as police used repressive measures and officials made token concessions to restore order. That the riots were fundamentally spontaneous, lacking in leadership, and without conscious political direction is also said to have contributed to the end of the disturbances.

This view of the riots is, for the most part, descriptively accurate if the discussion is limited to crowd size and the transformation from appeals to confrontation. But it poses problems by implying that the riots were akin to acts of nature rather than the result of conscious calculation. A more useful and accurate approach is to look at the riots as incidents of community problem-solving closer to collective bargaining than to spontaneous mob violence; that is, not as "naturalistic" aberrations symptomatic of an emerging "crisis of capitalism" but as historically familiar and proven ways to resolve local conflicts.

The initial period of rioting can be seen as a preparatory stage during which protesters defined the issues and devised strategies for lowering the price of rice. During the petition phase women held meetings, after which they made appeals or carried out some other essentially peaceful protest. During the second stage, corresponding to the peak period of rioting described above, activity shifted from appeals to demands. In demonstrations throughout early August, rioters forced local leaders to pay greater attention to their grievances, end their resistance to the women's appeals, and begin concrete efforts to combat grain scarcity and high prices. The rioters' basic tactic, direct appeal to community leaders believed responsible for rice shortages, did not change during this period. But requests for cooperation did give way to demands backed by threats. All-night vigils, sit-ins, marches on town offices, and the posting of women "guards" at granary doors characterized this phase of the protest. As a result of confrontations during the "demand" period, the protest entered a third stage, in which local officials and influential community members stepped in to change commercial practices and administer a relief program.

Japanese riot studies have termed the third stage a pacification or eradication period. In some localities "eradication" is appropriate to describe the central government's no-nonsense use of troops against rioters. Yet in Toyama, where troops were not called out, the final stage of the protest resembled the settlement phase of a long dispute. "Pacification" does describe the decreasing size and frequency of riots after 9 August, but it fails to explain adequately why protest ended. My own view is that the beginning of significant official relief efforts, those judged an equitable compromise with rioters' demands, had much to do with the ending of the riots. These efforts were not simply cosmetic or short-term, but typically continued to be enforced long after the last protest was supposedly pacified. As will be detailed below, relief measures did not entirely satisfy protesters, merchants, or local officials. The program was a means of coping, one that provided no final solution to the problem of high prices, but by meeting the protesters' minimum demands contributed to a decline in protests from 9 August.

The Appeals Movement

It was not accidental that Uozu women began their appeals movement at a community well. As most families in the fishermen's wards lived in houses without running water, women congregated daily at wells to draw drinking water, prepare meals, and wash clothes. The well was also a spot where women came together to talk. Well-side gatherings (*idobata kaigi*) were regularly held to gossip, discuss local problems, and sometimes to learn about more profound subjects. Itazawa Kanejirō, a longtime Uozu resident, described the "wives' conferences" as lively forums:

> What the women talked about at the well-side meetings touched upon politics, the economy, and the like. The content was very wide-ranging. . . . Labor strikes that broke out here and there, even the government created by those poor laborers who staged the Russian Revolution was brought up.[52]

This account perhaps makes too much of the content of well-side discussions, but the gatherings did serve as a sounding board for local opinion. Literacy was not high among fishermen's wives, and the well-side talks provided information more accessible and pertinent to their lives than could be found in newspapers.[53]

At the 22 July meeting in Uozu women complained of the high cost of rice and what could be done to hold costs down. The method hit upon to deal with the problem was identical to the one adopted in earlier protests: boycott grain shipping. As was suggested by a common saying in use during the Meiji period, "Smoke from a steamship offshore means rice will cost one sen more," it had long been known that shipping Toyama rice to Hokkaido or Osaka created shortages and sent local prices higher. Coastal residents thus perceived a close relationship between shipping and inflated prices.[54]

In the 1918 protests, however, women blamed nearby merchants and not the steamship companies for their problem. They distinguished between local rice dealers, who had it in their power to sell or not to sell rice, and steamship companies, which merely acted upon the merchants' decisions. Throughout the riots women demonstrated that they would change only what they could change. This is not to suggest that the rioters were ignorant of the world beyond Toyama. But they were calculatingly unconcerned with national conditions that made it profitable for local entrepreneurs to ship rice. Indeed, they completely disregarded officials and merchants who attempted to enlighten them on such abstractions as "market structure" and ignored arguments premised on "business is business" attitudes.

At the Uozu meeting the women bosses decided that little would be accomplished by acting individually. The lowering of local prices required concerted group action, which they resolved to begin the very next morning. It was then that grain loading was scheduled to resume aboard the *Ibuki-maru*, a steamship that regularly transported grain from Toyama to Hokkaido. The women would spread the word to other local women, go directly to the beach where rice was being loaded, and request that shipping be stopped.

The following morning forty-six women gathered on the shore. Word of the gathering had earlier reached the Uozu police station, and several patrolmen soon arrived to disperse the crowd. Nevertheless, the women had so sufficiently interfered with grain loading before the police arrived that the ship left without the Uozu rice.[55] The action established the aim of the women's protest, the end of shipments, and the means, direct appeal or, if necessary, active obstruction of grain loading, by which it would be presented.

Following the Uozu demonstration, another appeals movement was staged in Higashi Iwase, a town several kilometers to the west. On the morning of 27 July fifteen women described as members of the "poorer class" (*saimin*) agreed to meet after dark for a march to the homes of well-off townspeople to request a relief program to offset high food costs. After sundown the original group was joined by others, who were out enjoying the cooler evening air, and a large crowd proceeded to Suwa shrine. The police confronted about forty marchers and persuaded them to go home peacefully. The crowd of women returned the next night but were turned away once again by patrolmen.[56] The Higashi Iwase action proved less successful than the Uozu demonstration, but it added another dimension to the protest by demanding that wealthier community members take responsibility for the economic well-being of poorer residents.

The twofold appeal for ending rice shipments and establishing a relief program was restated in a gathering of women held in Tomari a few days later. After an all-day meeting on 1 August, the women decided to hold a "formal" discussion on 2 August at the local elementary school. Those who joined in this meeting decided to present their grievances directly to the town council. They put off the actual submission of their appeal until 5 August so that a five-member representative committee could be selected to meet with local officials.[57] On the same day as the Tomari meeting, a crowd gathered in Takaoka city outside the house of rice dealer Hirano Goheii to demand that he immediately put 1,300 koku of stored rice on the city market.[58] When Hirano refused, the crowd proceeded to the city police station and requested that the police intervene to convince rice merchants to open their storehouses and sell on the local market.[59] The Takaoka appeal, with its request that the police take action to curb rice prices, marked the end of the small, sporadic, largely peaceful appeals that recurred from 22 July to 2 August. The actions served to bring issues of protest before people considered capable of controlling the local cost of living and helped spread the protest from one end of Toyama Bay to the other.

From Appeals to Demands

Strictly peaceful appeals did not end after 2 August. Groups in Tomari, Ikuji, and Miyazaki continued to present their grievances quietly to town council members and grain dealers. Although most historical accounts of the Toyama riots note a clear change after 2 August, hard-and-fast distinctions between the methods used during the first and second phases of the protest are not justified. Nevertheless, the appeals increasingly occurred alongside what the newspapers sensationally described as a "women's insurrection" or "uprising" (onna ikki).[60] The shift from appeals to direct action, although never as dramatic as was depicted in the contemporary press or later historical accounts, developed as those with local influence made promises but appeared to do little.

The first "uprising" broke out in Mizuhashi, a depot town from which large quantities of grain were sent outside the prefecture by steamship and rail. On the evening of 3 August, several hundred Nishi Mizuhashi women, called together by leaders who had planned the rally on the previous day, organized themselves into three smaller groups. One contingent was sent to visit influential people such as stevedore bosses (nakashigashira) and boat owners, while a second set off to make demands of influential town members living in inland wards. A third group went directly to rice dealers and landlords living in Nishi Mizuhashi.

The message carried by all three teams was the same as the one that had been delivered in Uozu and other towns from 22 July to 2 August: stop grain shipping ..nd begin a "public-spirited" (gikyo-teki) sale of reasonably priced rice. How forcefully the rioters pressed their demands is unclear, but the size of the gathering itself was certainly intimidating. Although little survives to show exactly what the women said to those they confronted on 3 August, reports mention that rice dealers were threatened with nasty consequences if they dared move a single grain of rice outside the town.[61]

On 4 August the protest crossed the Shirakawa River and spread to Higashi Mizuhashi. Police reports indicate that this was expected; neither officials nor protesters believed that the previous night's demonstration had resolved anything.[62] Throughout the day women with children in tow met in small groups at the beach. After nightfall they regathered, forming a crowd of nearly seven hundred. Repeating methods used in the Nishi Mizuhashi disturbance, the leaders once again split the group into three smaller divisions, now dubbed "women's armies" (jo gun) in Toyama papers, to march en masse upon the homes of the mayor, town council members, rice merchants, and loading bosses. Local policemen found themselves powerless to control the protest as the women ignored orders to disperse.[63]

In Mizuhashi women enforced the previous night's ban on grain shipping on 5 August when the *Kōmei-maru*, a regularly scheduled steamship running between Toyama and Hokkaido, dropped anchor. A group of two hundred women responded to the ship's arrival by rushing to the beach to block any loading of grain. As the ship was to take on nothing but straw matting, the women did not interfere, and it left port without incident.[64] Later that day, however, carters attempting to move rice through Mizuhashi to Namerikawa were embroiled in a heated exchange when a few women noticed a wagon loaded with rice near the town office. When drivers attempted to move the cart, women clung to its shafts and refused to let it pass. According to their own "rules," the women had scant justification for the action. After all, the rice did not originate in Mizuhashi but was simply en route to Namerikawa. The situation was at an impasse when a local policeman stepped between the carters and the angry women. As the argument grew heated it attracted the attention of a group of men loitering nearby, who proceeded to thrash the policeman. The officer was only slightly injured, but as a result of the incident two men and a woman were arrested.[65]

Among those detained was a woman "general" whom police suspected of directing the Higashi Mizuhashi disturbances and a man believed responsible for orchestrating the riots in the town's west section. Takanobu Rihachirō, director of the Mizuhashi substation, sent the suspects to the Namerikawa station to remove the alleged "ringleaders" from the scene. Police Chief Maeda Jōtarō, Takanobu's superior, took the incident in stride. On the blocking of the grain shipment and Shimaji's beating, he was reported to have said, "It really wasn't much of a crime and sooner or later we'll let them go. The three are rather excited now, so we will let them rest awhile in jail." After the head of the Mizuhashi fire brigade attested to their past good reputations and vouchsafed their future good behavior, the three were released without being charged.[66]

Despite Police Chief Maeda's conciliatory attitude, demonstrations continued in Mizuhashi, Namerikawa, and other towns and villages along the bay. From 5 August the protests tended to increase in number and size and frequently jumped town boundaries. Women protesters, sometimes joined by sympathetic males, seemed to believe that if rioters in a neighboring town or village could not successfully blockade rice shipping on their own, then they should be lent a helping hand.

Joint protests took place in Ikuji-Ishida, and cooperative demonstrations in Mizuhashi and Namerikawa. In the latter incident fifty or sixty women gathered in Namerikawa to press their demands. By 9:30 P.M. this crowd had increased to about three hundred. The protesters' targets included owners of the Rice-Fertilizer Company and the town's three major rice merchants: Kanagawa Sōzaemon, Saitō Nizaemon, and Saitō Asajirō. All were wholesale dealers or brokers and not small-scale retailers. Unlike protesters in other prefectures, Toyama rioters usually left the owners of local rice shops in peace.

The crowd, which eventually snowballed into a gathering of five hundred, first visited Kanagawa, Namerikawa's largest rice dealer. Police orders to cease and desist were ignored, but the demonstration was largely peaceful. Women knelt at Kanagawa's entryway in a traditional gesture of supplication as they entreated the dealer to stop shipping grain and do something constructive to bring down the cost of rice. Receiving no sympathetic response, the crowd finally began to shout, "Are you people deaf?" "Reborn devils! You have no feelings!" The police once again urged the crowd to go home, but protesters only mocked the order by yelling, "Yes, you people who can afford to eat, by all means go home and sleep!"[67] Their jeers and insults continued. It was only when the police promised to bring the issue of shipping and high prices before the town council that the rioters turned homeward.

Before noon on 6 August Namerikawa women marched to the town office to make sure that the police would keep their word. The town journal gives no details regarding the 6 August incident except a terse note, "Town residents, numbering between 150 and 160 people, pushed into [the office]; appealed for reduction in consumer prices."[68] Other accounts flesh out this single-line record of the incident. Saitō Yaichirō's study notes that those who gathered complained that they lived virtually hand to mouth and that even this was becoming difficult as rice prices increased relentlessly. The women also verbally attacked the rice dealers, whom they accused of simply shutting their eyes to the plight of their neighbors. They argued that men like Kanagawa were responsible for the intolerably steep cost of grain and that merchants did nothing to alleviate their plight. Crowd representatives demanded an immediate halt to rice shipping, adding that they wanted nothing for free but that reasonable prices must be restored. This was the message that they asked the clerks to convey directly to the mayor. Clerks rushed about, conferring with superiors and attempting to calm the angry women. At last one came forward to announce that an emergency ward council meeting would be held the next day to take up the issues of relief rice and discount sales. He pleaded with the townspeople to be patient for just for one more day.

The crowd left but did not remain quiet. In the afternoon the *Ibuki-maru*, a steamship returning from Hokkaido, was sighted dropping anchor off Namerikawa. The ship had come to take on rice from the storehouses of the Rice-Fertilizer Company and from Kanagawa's granaries. Aware of the ship's mission, Mizuhashi and Namerikawa women gathered in the fishermen's wards and agreed to ignore the whistle that signaled the beginning of loading. They then set off in two contingents to meet at a nearby shrine and to renew the demonstration at Kanagawa's house.

The first group met at the seaside shrine and then moved to where carts filled with bales of rice had been readied for loading onto beached lighters. They clung to the ropes around the bales while other women, some with babies strapped to their backs, sat in the boats. They screamed and cursed the male stevedores who attempted to prepare the grain for shipment. The men responded coolly, it is said, telling the women not to interfere with the loading. They further explained that they were certainly not responsible for the shipment and advised the women to take their complaints directly to Kanagawa or the others in charge of sending rice outside the area. The men used no force against the women, and although labor bosses encouraged the men to continue their work, the *Ibuki-maru* left port unloaded.[69]

Local women used the same tactic two days later when the *Santoku-maru* dropped anchor near Namerikawa. Once again the male workers finally gave up and the rice was left sitting on the beach. The owners of the Rice-Fertilizer Company, realizing that no one in or near Namerikawa would touch their grain, attempted to break the loading boycott by hiring workers elsewhere. They sent word to labor bosses in Sehama and Hama offering, in addition to the stevedore's wages, five hundred yen for relief efforts in these wards. The offer was rejected by workers who explained that its acceptance would be a slap in the face of Namerikawa people. Later that day the *Santoku-maru* also left port unloaded.[70]

During the 6 August protests in Namerikawa, rumors spread that the night of 7 August would bring a "men's uprising" aimed at punishing Kanagawa.[71] On 7 August the Namerikawa police station informed prefectural officials of the increasing unrest in the town, and in response, six policemen were dispatched to Namerikawa to assist local patrolmen. Later that night a crowd of two thousand men and women gathered at Kanagawa's house, chanting for the end of shipments, lower rice prices, and the appearance of the "master." Kanagawa avoided the protesters but his chief clerk (*bantō*) is reported to have told the crowd:

We aren't doing anything wrong by buying and selling rice. Generally speaking, if you people have so much time to come down here and make trouble, shouldn't you put your energy into side-work? That's what would be good for you.[72]

To a crowd of two thousand angry people this was perhaps courageous but not very clever advice. The demonstrators called the clerk a fool and accused him of heartlessness. They added that Kanagawa was a "filthy old man" (kono kuso oyaji) who had no consideration for the townspeople beyond making piles of money by taking rice from their mouths. The clerk retreated hastily into the house.

The crowd pushed toward Kanagawa's entryway, but a police line prevented any break-in. Patrolmen warned that anyone crossing the threshold would be arrested for unlawful entry. Such threats did not intimidate the rioters, who began throwing rocks against the metal shutters that protected the main gate and windows of the house. The noise brought out Kanagawa's son, who, according to one report, argued that even protests had limits and that this attack had surely overstepped those boundaries. He added that because neither he nor his family determined whether rice would be cheap or dear, they had not caused the townspeople's difficulties. Opponents in the crowd disagreed, noting that rice bought in Namerikawa was two or three sen more expensive than what was available in Toyama city. They excoriated local dealers for busily cornering rice supplies while taking no responsibility for the hardships resulting from their profiteering.

After Kanagawa gave up arguing with the crowd, a Mr. Kagamida tried his luck. Kagamida, a clerk at the town office, was known as a member of Namerikawa's coterie of liberal thinkers. Others like him, especially local socialists, were under police surveillance during the entire course of the Toyama protests. None appears to have had the slightest connection with instigating, influencing, or leading the riots. The gulf separating local progressives from protesters is evident in the crowd's reaction to Kagamida's extemporaneous speech. In urging that there was a better way to deal with high prices than to block local rice shipping, Kagamida explained:

The present situation in our country is one in which wicked merchants spurred by the Siberian Expedition have engaged in market cornering and rice hoarding. That is why rice has shot up in price. . . . Rather [than boycott shipping], we should force merchants to sell as much rice as possible [on the central market]. In this way it will become cheaper. Especially now, we should allow the movement of rice from the storehouses.

Before he could finish, Kagamida was unceremoniously hooted down with cries of "Don't talk like one of Kanagawa's friends!" and "Have you been bought by Kanagawa?" Despite the crowd's reaction, Kagamida's view was generally correct; even local prices were affected by central-market conditions. Demand, as was made clear by the frenetic trading in rice futures on various exchanges, did appear to increase with the expectation of Japanese intervention against the Bolsheviks. Yet, however accurate Kagamida's analysis, it was addressed to the wrong audience. The protesters' interests were not national but decidedly local. They had previously dealt with higher rice prices by boycotting shipping, not by allowing the free movement of grain, and this had effectively drawn attention to their problems.

The head of Nakaniikawa county, along with the county secretary, both of whom had come to Namerikawa to discuss relief measures, also attempted to ease the confrontation at Kanagawa's house. Maeda Jōtarō, Namerikawa's police chief, warned that the presence of the officials would likely do more harm than good, but his advice was ignored. Izeki Toshio, the county head, went on to address the crowd:

> Ladies and gentlemen, from eight tomorrow morning... the Namerikawa town council will take up the question of discount rice sales and other emergency measures.... I am sure that something will be worked out. However, the cost of rice is not to be attributed to any single individual. Neither Kanagawa Sōzaemon nor Saitō Nizaemon can control such things.

He too was cut short by jeers that mocked his polite "ladies and gentlemen" and accused him of defending *narikin*. When he attempted to explain that local rice dealers did not control price fluctuations, he was cursed as a "watchdog of the traitorous merchants" and, in terms reminiscent of the Tokugawa era, accused of being an "evil magistrate." Izeki's companion, the county secretary, fared no better. Protesters threatened to throw him into a nearby river when he told them that if they worked they could eat rice even if it cost one yen per shō.

Despite their apparent anger, the rioters did not attempt to break into Kanagawa's home or storehouses. His property (as well as that of all the others targeted by the protesters) remained intact throughout the disturbance. Furthermore, no injuries were reported by either the police or those who gathered on 7 August. Such restraint is surprising because Kanagawa appeared to embody everything that the protesters opposed: he was a grain broker, a rice shipper, and, owing to his recent business success, a *narikin*. But he was more than this. Despite the angry rhetoric leveled at him, Kanagawa was widely recognized as someone who could do something positive to curtail the high cost of living. He was urged to take responsibility for the local crisis, not simply because of his own individual wealth but because he had repeatedly demonstrated a politically liberal concern for local welfare.

The rise of the Kanagawa family to local prominence was largely the result of Sōzaemon's efforts during the Meiji and Taishō years. From humble beginnings he built his rice brokerage and shipping business into a flourishing enterprise that commissioned large sailing ships, and later steamships, to carry Toyama rice to Hokkaido and Osaka in exchange for fish fertilizer and other goods. Kanagawa's individual success did not distance him from the larger community or diminish his concern for local welfare. He was particularly involved in educational projects. Although he had received only a rudimentary formal education, he recognized the value of learning, not only for the individual's benefit but because educated men were needed to promote local interests. He accordingly supplied money, books, and advice that enabled several bright but indigent students to pursue their studies in Toyama and Tokyo. His establishment of an agricultural experiment station and provision of land for the building of the Namerikawa railroad station are among the projects that had a broader influence on both vocational education and the local economy.[73]

In the Namerikawa rice riots of 1912, it had been Kanagawa who had been selected, along with the town mayor and several others, to formulate and implement relief measures.[74] He was also concerned about the problem of grain scarcity as a national problem. Even before the 1912 unrest, he had begun to speak in favor of the central government's regulation of rice supplies and prices. Between 1910 and 1920 he used his own funds in a private lobbying campaign for greater government involvement in the rice market. Although he himself was a rice broker, he believed that the nation's basic food should not be an object of economic speculation.[75]

He was also active in popular rights politics, and it was no accident that Kagamida, a local socialist, had spoken for pressuring the central government and metropolitan merchants and against harassing the local broker. Kanagawa, the town's largest individual rice dealer, had been Kagamida's ally in the local branch of the Constitutional Protection Association organized several years before the rice riots. He was also friendly with Hirai Kōichirō, the son of a wealthy boat-owning (*amimoto*) family and the coastal region's premier "radical." Although

Kanagawa was put upon by protesters, he neither wavered in his support for democratic politics nor cut his ties with local progressives. On 6 October, within days of the last Toyama riot, he gave a supportive speech at the founding of the Namerikawa Universal Suffrage Alliance in support of the group's work and, along with several activists who had been designated carriers of "dangerous thoughts," put his name to a petition demanding an expansion of the vote.[76]

If they had wanted to, the two thousand rioters gathered in Namerikawa could easily have overpowered the small group of policemen protecting Kanagawa's storehouses. For that matter, they could simply have taken the unguarded rice bales from the beach. Nothing like this happened because the protesters expected that men like Kanagawa would respond sympathetically to their demands.

The crowd's actions and the response of those attacked reveal an almost palpable sense of self-conscious role-playing. In Toyama protests from the Tokugawa through the Taishō period, the same pattern of angry confrontation followed by ameliorative measures recurs regularly.[77] That those involved recognized their parts in the drama is not to argue that fishwives, police, or wealthy merchants were less than serious in their respective actions. But spontaneity, unchecked anger, and destructive violence—characteristics commonly associated with the term "riot"—were largely missing in the Toyama disputes. After his house had been pelted with stones, the younger Kanagawa angrily asked the crowd, "Don't you realize that even an uprising has its limits?" The protesters' actions implicitly answered yes to the question.

On 7 August town and village councils in Namerikawa, Mizuhashi, Uozu, and elsewhere met to discuss implementation of relief programs promised earlier. The deliberations did not restore order immediately. In Namerikawa crowds gathered to add complaints about the proposed aid plan to their demands for halting rice shipping and for lower prices. Rumors had leaked that the town council would supply rice at reduced prices only to poorer families. Some members of the crowd felt that the discount price of 35 sen per shō should be cut to 25 sen and that relief eligibility requirements should be widened.[78]

Despite the grumbling about aid proposals, the Namerikawa-Mizuhashi protests had all but ended by 7 August, when a change in police tactics gave them new life. Prefectural authorities, concerned that "threatening" disturbances modeled after the Namerikawa-Mizuhashi protests might spread to other towns, dispatched high-level police officials to assist in containing the uprising. Once on the scene, they determined what local police already knew: uniformed patrolmen were only minimally effective in stopping the riots. The prefectural police thereupon decided to rely on undercover tactics. On the night of 7 August, plainclothes officers circulated within a throng of twelve hundred protesters gathered at the Rice-Fertilizer Company and Kanagawa storehouses. As the crowd began to thin out police followed suspected leaders to their homes. They did not attempt any on-the-scene arrests but merely recorded addresses which they later handed over to their superiors. The next day, in the safety of broad daylight, Namerikawa police reinforced with a contingent of twenty-seven cadets called up by the Prefectural Police Affairs Section rounded up the people marked the night before. Altogether the sweep netted thirty-eight suspects.[79]

Investigators soon determined that seven of the detainees had nothing to do with leading the previous night's disturbances and released them. But they steadfastly refused to give up the other suspects. Saitō Gyōsan, the head of the prefectural police, and a Mr. Hane, the director of Toyama's Police Affairs Section, were clearly behind this tougher stance. Intent on making certain that the prefecture's largest riot spread no further, their no-nonsense approach called for speedily restoring order by using more policemen and force. To show they meant business, they stationed fifty uniformed patrolmen around the Namerikawa station.

The protesters were undaunted by the display of authority and interference by prefectural outsiders. On 8 August a crowd of a thousand gathered outside the police station and held a noisy rally, demanding the immediate release of those arrested earlier that day. They surrounded the small jail and, indicating their sense of betrayal, shouted insults and asked whose side the local police were really on. Inside the station, Saitō is said to have listened to the views of Namerikawa Chief Maeda Jōtarō and Hane, the prefectural police official. Maeda advised simply talking calmly and sympathetically with the protesters. He argued that the crowd could not be forced to obey orders but might be soothed into compliance. Aware of the local grievances and the issues that spawned them, he stressed that doing anything else might escalate the confrontation. Hane opposed Maeda's characteristically low-key approach as no more than the coddling of law breakers. He argued that the police should go out in force to arrest as many demonstrators as possible. Acting otherwise would only further diminish respect for police authority and weaken local order.

Hane's opinion won out and a group of policemen waded into the crowd, only to be greeted by a shower of stones. Taken aback by the crowd's violent reaction and recognizing the obvious futility of making arrests, the police made no other aggressive attempts to break up the assembly. Both sides waited, and after awhile the din outside the station quieted. Chief Maeda and Saitō Gyōsan then ventured out to speak with the protesters.[80] Whatever these men said was sufficient to disperse the crowd. Hashimoto Ki'ichi, the station's telephone operator on duty during the incident, later recalled that the confrontation ended peacefully:

> I was tense but not overcome by fear. Chief Maeda and Prefectural Police Chief Saitō went out in the midst of the crowd. While they were jostled and pushed about, they never stopped talking. There wasn't anything like a fight between these policemen and the crowd. Perhaps the riots would have been bigger if on-the-scene arrests had been made. Those who had been detained were all released the first thing on the morning of the ninth. I suppose the crowd's action wasn't futile, but I think that's because Chief Maeda handled the situation so well.[81]

With the end of the Namerikawa-Mizuhashi riots, protests along Toyama's coast became less frequent and smaller. At Higashi Iwase, Ikuji, Izurugi, Uozu, and elsewhere women repeated actions taken during earlier phases of the disturbance: they gathered at shrines, blocked rice loading, and presented demands at town offices. Scattered protests continued into autumn in some towns and villages, but these, too, subsided as relief efforts got fully under way.

The Role of Local Police

Response to the rioting came in the form of police-led suppression and community relief efforts. Neither corresponds strictly to the chronology of prelude to peak to pacification because both were actually ongoing from the beginning of the Toyama protests. Based on a tradition of cooperation as well as conflict, protesters and officials acted moderately in resolving the incident. During the twenty-five days on which multiple incidents of rioting occurred, even prefectural officials, who viewed the protests as a more serious breach of civil order than did local police, never found it necessary to mobilize troops against the protesters. Town and village officials, perhaps under duress from prefectural superiors, sometimes supplemented the police with men from the outside, but they usually treated riot control as a local matter.

In part, tactical considerations account for the moderate control measures. Small contingents of local patrolmen, even when augmented by additional prefectural police cadets, had their hands full. Large gatherings provided opportunities to make arrests, but they also carried the risk, as was evident in the Namerikawa police station incident, of escalating the conflict. By arresting women "generals" or other suspected ringleaders, police accomplished little and made problems posed by the shipping boycotts and demonstrations more difficult to resolve.[82] This left police in a quandary. Rioters no longer followed verbal orders, but stronger actions brought the risk of escalating the confrontation. In those few incidents in which police waded into crowds to make arrests, they had been pelted with rocks. This not only was unpleasant for the individual patrolman but also revealed a lack of police authority in the inability to control the situation. The relative mildness of attempts at suppression and the light penalties imposed on riot suspects did not mean that local authorities were lax in trying to contain protests before they grew into larger, more destructive disturbances. According to Toyama prefectural police records, Uozu constables had picked up rumors of the first demonstration even before it began. Such efficiency was typical. Prefectural statistics show that few crimes went unsolved in the region. Arrest and prosecution rates in 1918 were well over 90 percent in cases of murder, arson, assaults, and extortion. Even 80 percent of common theft cases were solved.[83]

The riot policy of the police, one that favored conciliation over the cracking of heads, arose as much from necessity as from choice. In the Toyama protests (as well as in virtually all incidents of rioting throughout Japan during the summer of 1918), rioters overwhelmingly outnumbered policemen. In Namerikawa, for example, approximately two thousand people, or 20 percent of the town's total population, joined the protests. During the early stage of rioting, police managed to scatter crowds simply by ordering people to go home. If they were disobeyed, they sometimes rushed into the crowd and threatened arrests. Such methods worked when the gatherings were smaller, isolated, and joined by fewer male participants. But as the protests grew larger and more threatening and as people from several towns or wards joined in, rioters began to ignore police orders.

Police attempted to compensate for their small numbers by using the local terrain to their advantage. The towns and villages along Toyama Bay were linked by bridges and narrow roads in 1918. The police used these for crowd control by stationing men at bridgeheads and at key intersections along the rioters' circuitous routes. Using these bottlenecks, patrolmen attempted to limit gatherings before they became un-controllable. But such techniques of containment were only minimally successful. In the Ikuji-Ishida incident, for example, women protesters confronted by police on a country road simply took paths through the rice fields to reach their destination. In the Namerikawa protest, Mizuhashi residents who found bridges blocked by police barricades came by boat to join the demonstrations. Within the densely packed fishermen's wards there was little that police could do to prevent smaller crowds from growing, in one policeman's words, by "threes and fives" to form crowds numbering eventually in the hundreds. Despite police efforts to channel the rioters' movements, small groups always managed to converge from several directions on the target of their protest. In Namerikawa demonstrators assembling in this manner were able to meet in crowds numbering from one to two thousand for three or four days without being particularly hindered by local authorities.

Once crowds had gathered, the handful of local police could only appeal to the protesters' own sense of self-control. Accordingly, the police stressed cooperation over conflict, often presenting themselves as honest brokers desiring to deal positively with the rioters' demands. Local patrolmen typically followed Chief Maeda's line in handling the protesters. While they sympathetically listened to the appeals of smaller crowds, they reasoned with, cajoled, and made promises to larger groups. In some instances they used this paternalistic "reasonable" approach while plainclothes police were removing the crowd's leaders. But it should be noted that resorting to undercover agents represented prefectural, not local, policy. In Namerikawa police trailed suspects only after prefectural police officials interfered in the dispute. As a result, the outsiders, oblivious to local sensitivities, created greater unrest in their haste to stifle the protests.

Police could not completely control the crowds, but they did manage to go about their business as best they could, largely unmolested by the rioters. That protesters took no aggressive actions aimed specifically at local police might be interpreted as reflecting fear and respect for the authorities. Police, after all, held an officially sanctioned monopoly on the use of legal force, although using such force against women would probably have brought widespread condemnation or, worse yet, more violent protests. The police likely considered such an eventuality in moderating their behavior. The townspeople on their part did not demonstrate any deep-seated or absolute deference to the local authorities. Protesters, by haggling with patrolmen and seldom accepting their word as final, treated the police as middlemen between people without formal political power and high officials. Indeed, rioters often made their first appeals at the local police station. When police fulfilled their official duty as guardians of local order by rounding up suspected riot ringleaders, the protesters reacted as if they had been betrayed. One of the insults repeatedly hurled at police was "Whose side are you on anyway?"[84] The protesters probably knew that the police had divided loyalties and were not totally sincere in acting on their complaints against rice merchants and officials. But this did not stop them from relying on the police to attain specific goals. During the coastal riots, police boxes and local stations were never the primary targets of attack, in contrast to riots in Kobe, Osaka, Nagoya, and Tokyo where policemen were attacked and police buildings were routinely set upon, trashed, and sometimes burned to the ground. In some instances the urban rioters attacked police simply because they were police. But in Toyama it was only when police appeared to betray local interests or wavered in fulfilling promises that they became targets. The Toyama rioters attempted to enlist the police in their cause whenever possible and seldom treated the local constable as a class enemy.[85]

The police seemed to view their own role somewhat ambiguously. On one hand, they were charged with maintaining local order, which, during the riots at least, required the use of various tricks and tactics; on the other, they also lived in the community, suffered from low wages, and appeared genuinely concerned with local welfare. They could not single-mindedly act on the rioters' behalf, even if they had wanted to. But they did not resort to the use of arbitrary force when their orders were ignored, nor did they call for prefectural troop mobilization to act for them. When arguing with rioters, they reiterated what had become the unofficial official line: high prices were created by central markets, and no amount of local protest could change this. Yet, while asserting that making a fuss served no purpose, police endeavored to find a local solution to the crisis. In effect their actions, which demonstrated that protest could in fact lead to correction, belied their words. A clear example of this occurred in Isurugi, where police called in protest leaders to warn against any expansion of unrest *and* to inquire about their demands. Similarly, the local police chief of Tomari asked the neighborhood rice dealers to commence selling polished rice at thirty-five sen per shō, a price several sen below the prevailing market rate, before protests began in his town. The chief's request was taken as an order, and discount sales were begun immediately.[86] Such unilateral action was uncommon, however. More often the police, acting as intermediaries between the public and officials, responded by meeting with town council members and influential private individuals to work out the amount and kind of relief possible given local resources. Once an aid program was decided on, the police played an instrumental role in carrying it out.

Official Response to Tokugawa and Meiji Protests

The riots were settled in government offices as well as in the streets. But before we consider the remedial measures taken in 1918, it is useful to consider the antecedents to aid programs in the Taishō period and the significant continuity in the way local officials, whether Tokugawa samurai magistrates or Taishō town mayors, responded to the protests. Harada Tomohiko, extending research begun by Aoki Kōji, has documented 865 cases of city and town rioting (as distinct from rural *ikki*) between 1600 and 1867. Many of the Tokugawa disturbances occurred in the Hokuriku regions of Echizen, Etchū, Echigo, and Kaga. In Etchū, which included modern-day Toyama prefecture, 40 major riots broke out in castle and country towns during the Tokugawa years.[87] In some aspects these town riots resembled village uprisings (*murakata ikki*).[88] But unlike the more prevalent countryside protests, the town disputes centered on consumer issues and urban politics. Townspeople (*chōnin*) rioted over rice prices, extraordinary tax levies, devaluations of paper money, and official malfeasance. Rice riots, unlike agrarian uprisings, were not always the direct result of famine or absolute scarcity, but resulted more often from high prices. In some cases there was not a one-to-one correspondence between prices and protest. During three peak periods of urban unrest (1781–1788, Tenmei; 1830–1843, Tenpō; and 1865–1867, Keiō), riots were not triggered by every jump in local prices. Protest more frequently occurred when people with political influence did nothing to check the spiraling cost of living. Rioting broke out when rice wholesalers (*ton'ya*) appeared to join hands with retail merchants in market-cornering schemes, and when officials responded indifferently to such manipulation.[89]

The rioters resorted to various tactics to call official attention to their grievances. In Toyama the blocking of grain shipping (*tsudome*) was by far the most common. In the Tokugawa period, as in 1918, towns along the Toyama coast served as marshaling points for grain transshipment, and it is not surprising that records of blockades and loading boycotts date back to 1690.[90] More boycotts occurred, or were perhaps simply better documented, toward the end of the Tokugawa period.

Little can be said with certainty about the social and economic background of seventeenth- and eighteenth-century rioters. Existing records suggest that only males were punished in most incidents. But as we move toward the end of the late Edo period, official documents begin to speak of the active role of fishermen's wives in several protests. The 1858 riots in the coastal towns of Himi and Hōshōzu (now Shinminato city) provide verifiable examples of a long tradition of women's involvement in Etchū protests.[91]

During July 1858 fishermen's wives in Himi appealed to officials and wealthier townspeople to take steps to curtail the high cost of rice. On 16 July, when ships from Kaga arrived to take on tax rice, an angry crowd gathered around the bales that loaders were preparing to transport to sailing ships moored offshore. The rioters, reported to have accused the workers of indirectly pushing prices up by making homegrown grain scarce, attempted to seize the bales. The port headman (*kumiaigashira*) and his subordinates managed to scatter the crowd. But fishermen in forty or fifty small boats later rowed out to the cargo ships, boarded them, and cut their sail rigging, forcing the rice that had been loaded to be returned to shore. That night women and children gathered in front of the town office (*kaishō*) to complain that high rice prices would drive them to starvation if something was not done. Later, a crowd of about three hundred men and women, marching to the trill of bamboo pipes, made their way through the town to carry out attacks on the homes of rice merchants.

The Hōshōzu riot took place a few days after the Himi disturbance. It followed the same pattern: women appealed for aid; they accused rice dealers of hoarding and cornering rice; the protesters seized or destroyed the property of merchants and wealthier neighbors. During the summer months of 1858, similar riots occurred in Uozu, Mizuhashi, Higashi Iwase, and other coastal towns.

Police and officials responded to these incidents much as they would in 1918. The day after the Himi protest domain policemen (*yoriki*) brought together town leaders (*machi kimoiri*) and other influential community members to talk over remedial measures. After some haggling, they decided to cut rice prices from the market price of 104 mon to 85 mon per shō. Discount sales offices were soon established, and rice was sold at reduced prices from 18 July. To pay for the program, wealthier families were ordered to "donate" to the poor. Once aid was dispensed, the protest quieted. In Hōshōzu officials instituted similar measures, but samurai representatives from the magistrate's (*daikan*) office also placed fourteen rice dealers under house arrest for market manipulation.

Although official responses to these riots were similar to those of the Taishō period, Tokugawa law was far more severe in its punishment of dissenters. Death, usually by decapitation or crucifixion, was the standard penalty imposed on protest leaders, even when the magistrate dealt positively with the protesters' demands and, in so doing, implied that there was some justice in their complaint. In Himi, for example, officials mandated lower rice prices and punished merchants. But they also combed the wards of fishermen and dock workers for three men suspected of leading the riot. The suspects were sent to Kanazawa for interrogation, where two of the three were sentenced to death—one by decapitation, the other by crucifixion. As a warning to others who might contemplate disturbing the local order, both men were returned to Himi for execution, where their heads were to be exposed in a public place. After 1868 simple rioting was no longer a capital crime.

Because the Meiji Restoration inaugurated many political and economic reforms, one might expect that the *tsudome*, or shipping boycott, would have faded away. In fact, the basic causes and course of protests changed little. True, tax rice was no longer shipped from the Toyama coast to the domain seat in Kanazawa. But the new Tokyo government, hungry for revenue, had its own plans for centralizing taxes and encouraging the export of grain to central metropolitan markets. Thus Toyama consumers still periodically found themselves hired to load locally produced rice that they could not afford to buy in neighborhood shops.

The "feudal" Tokugawa government may have given way to a new, increasingly unified state, but the growth of an increasingly centralized rice market, a development facilitated by improved steamship transport and faster communication between grain exchanges, exacerbated rather than eased old frictions. Shortly after the Restoration, Toyama's high yield of rice made Etchū rice the third cheapest in the nation.[92] Provincial grain merchants and agents from central markets soon took advantage of the local surplus and low prices to ship rice to Hokkaido and rapidly growing Japanese cities where both prices and profits were higher. Exporting took on an international dimension in 1878 when

Ministry of Finance officials, acting on reports of famine in China, urged Toyama rice dealers to take advantage of this new demand. Wholesalers in Takaoka and Fushiki responded enthusiastically; one individual broker exported 60,000 koku from Toyama before the famine had passed. While dealers profited, domestic consumers felt the effects of the reduced supply. The 1878 harvest had already been reduced by flooding and insect infestation. With the China exports, supplies declined even further. By the second half of 1878 prices had jumped steeply, and not long after the increase, officials reported "women's uprisings" (*onna ikki*) in coastal towns and villages. The cycle of grain exports followed by higher prices resulted in forty-four coastal protests between 1869 and 1912.[93]

The rioters' basic tactic, blocking shipments, continued unchanged from the Tokugawa period, but several new developments are evident after 1868. Women, especially fishermen's wives, more often joined in the Meiji protests. Their larger role in the riots reflected their more prominent position in coastal communities. The expansion of migrant fishing—a product of the new freedom of movement allowed commoners—and the end of restrictions on the size of coastal vessels took Toyama men farther from home for extended periods. In the absence of husbands, wives became the acting heads of households.

The opening of coastal ports to steamship trade and the rapid annual expansion of rice shipments after the Meiji Restoration also brought about changes in women's work.[94] In addition to part-time work as field hands, menders of nets, or fishmongers, common jobs available to women during the Tokugawa period, women now began to hire themselves out as cargo loaders. As workers who prepared rice shipments and as housewives who purchased grain at the local store, women developed a keen sensitivity to the relationship between grain supply and price fluctuations. The independence of Toyama women as household heads and free workers also provided the confidence they needed to defy male authority. In many ways their behavior in the home and at work contravened the central government's newly developing ideology that declared women to be politically passive "good wives and wise mothers." Indeed, this model of proper feminine deportment does not appear to have penetrated very deeply into Toyama during the Meiji or even the Taishō years. What Ella Lury Wiswell wrote of Suye village women in the 1930s certainly applied to an earlier generation of Toyama women:

Officially, as all over Japan, they occupied a subordinate position, but they did not act as if they did. It is true that women had no role in village administrative affairs and at home they followed the standard pattern of subservience to the husband, but in day-to-day contact with men, in their social role at gatherings, and their outspokenness, they certainly acted with greater freedom than any Japanese female city dweller.[95]

If anything, the Toyama women were more assertive than those described by Wiswell. It is hardly surprising that twenty-three of the forty-four major Meiji protests were women-only uprisings.

The transition from Tokugawa to Meiji also meant a change in how local officials responded to women-led protests. In general, the frequency of unrest and legal reforms caused them to treat minor protests in a routine and restrained manner. After demonstrations at city or town offices and following the occasional riot-caused cessation of trading on the Takaoka or Toyama exchanges, officials appointed a committee to work out relief measures. In addition to drawing on town or city treasuries, they also ordered wealthier individuals and rice merchants to make "donations." Following the riots in 1875, a single well-off (*fugō*) Namerikawa resident supplied 1,250 of his poorer neighbors with rice for forty days.[96] More often, relief was a collective effort. Once sufficient money was raised, community leaders set up rice kitchens to provide boiled rice or rice gruel (*okayu*). Sometimes Meiji rioters also received grain discount coupons or subsidies in hard cash.[97]

Relief Efforts, 1918 and 1919: Namerikawa-machi

Like their counterparts in other towns and villages along the Toyama coast, Namerikawa councilmen were well aware of how previous town councils had responded to riots.[98] After the first reports of unrest reached the Nakaniikawa county office, a communiqué was sent to Katō Jinzaemon, Namerikawa's mayor, requesting information about the situation. The message noted that "the recent movement by the poor cannot be considered an unprecedented event. Similar actions have likely occurred in the past." It inquired about the particulars of the recent disturbance and requested background information on previous uprisings. The communiqué included a questionnaire that required Katō to provide the reasons for the protests, a description of them, an account of contemplated relief measures, and whether bands of women and children had been involved.[99]

Katō's reply detailed measures taken by the town council in the July 1890 and July 1912 protests. Writing of the 1890 riots, he suggested that the actions of local officials could either contribute to or prevent unrest:

> The high cost of rice caused the poor to become alarmed about rice shipping [from Toyama] ports. Their concern led to attempts to prevent stevedores from moving grain. The town office carried out discount sales of rice in order to *prevent* a disturbance [emphasis added].

He noted that rioting was avoided entirely in July 1912, thanks to the town council's swift action:

> [The poor selected] a general representative who came to the town office and presented and appeal. At this time, rice discount sales were begun. There was not a single incident of the poor forming ranks and marching.

Katō served as Namerikawa's mayor in 1912 as well as in 1918. He was familiar with the earlier riots and personally directed relief efforts that led to nearly identical aid programs in both incidents. But his reports to the county office never mentioned that women protesters had forced the town council to implement relief. He pointedly avoided using terms like "unrest" or "uprising"; instead, he disingenuously noted that candidates for public assistance had been "discovered." To help those discovered to overcome difficulties resulting from high rice prices in 1912, the town set up six sales branches in different wards where rice could be purchased at a subsidized discount rate from 5 July through 30 September. During this period officials raised 1,500 yen in donations from "public-spirited" individuals, which they used to buy rice from a Kobe grain dealer for distribution to 230 poorer households. In May 1918, months before the outbreak of protests, the local chamber of commerce again bought and distributed foreign rice at a discount to Namerikawa's poorer households. This action, however, did not avert the later unrest perhaps because an additional order was not delivered as scheduled or, more likely, because the narrow scope of this unofficial relief effort did not meet the demands for expanded assistance.[100]

On 7 August 1918, eighteen members of Namerikawa's town council and five major rice merchants officially met to decide how best to deal with the latest protests. Their proceedings might be taken for a carbon copy of the record of earlier disputes. Under the heading "Issues

Decided" the minutes of the meeting detailed the measures to be adopted:

1. From 8 August until 17 September, for a period of forty days, rice will be sold at reduced prices.
2. Domestic polished rice will be sold for 35 sen per shō.
3. Restrictions on the sale of rice to the poor are as follows:
   (a) [Sale will be limited to] households at level three or below [on the local tax rolls] (1,016 households).
   (b) Those at tax levels three to five [will be eligible for aid depending upon] special circumstances.
   (c) Each person in each eligible household will receive an average purchase allotment of .35 shō per day.
   (d) The proportion of domestic to foreign rice will be two-thirds Japanese rice and one-third foreign rice.[101]

The council further decided that rice dealers would be assessed 20 sen for each koku of rice held as of 31 July 1918. Although called a "contribution" (*kifu o nasu koto*), the assessment was a precisely calculated estimate of the amount of rice held locally and was expected to bring nearly two thousand yen into the newly established relief fund. Additional "contributions" of two yen per household were also levied on several hundred Namerikawa families. Using this fund the council approved an initial purchase of foreign rice from the Kobe office of Suzuki Shōten. To speed up relief efforts it also agreed to buy five hundred koku of rice from local holders at forty yen per koku. The purchase price was a bit below current market rates but above the proposed discount price (thirty-five yen per koku) at which it would be sold to the needy.[102]

The arrangement penalized rice dealers by forcing them to "contribute" twenty-five sen for each koku of stored grain.[103] Officials took the edge off these sanctions by using town money as well as donations from other sources to buy rice from these merchants at a reasonably high price (forty yen per koku). The rice dealers could not complain too loudly, because they were at least able to sell the rice that the loading boycott had prevented from being shipped to central markets. But they were actually making contributions to buy their own rice. The difference between the price of forty yen per koku at which the town purchased rice from grain dealers and the thirty-five yen per koku at which it was sold to poorer residents was covered by donations from the town's major rice brokers. In return, three hundred koku of the five

hundred koku to be purchased locally was bought from Kanagawa
Sōzaemon and from the Rice-Fertilizer Company.[104]

The Namerikawa council's 7 August decision neatly answered the
rioters' demands and to a lesser extent the merchants' requirements by
(1) taxing grain holders and freeing up local supplies, (2) subsidizing
local relief with mandatory "contributions," and (3) providing a market for the grain that local merchants could not sell outside Toyama
because of the shipping boycott. The plan effectively found a middle
ground where the rioters' grievances were redressed and the targets of
the riots also had their interests considered. The protesters "won," but
the rice merchants did not really lose.

In Namerikawa the town council initially acted on its own to remedy
the causes of the unrest. As riots broke out throughout the nation the
central, prefectural, and county governments became involved in
varying degrees in local relief efforts. The national government provided
limited funds to fuel programs in Toyama and other prefectures. Meanwhile, prefectural and county officials channeled money to towns and
villages; they coordinated orders for foreign rice, supervised shipping,
and kept the books on the cost of aid programs. Prefectural and county
officials also asked town and village councils for information about the
success of the remedial measures and new signs of unrest.

The Home Ministry and the Ministry of Agriculture and Commerce
nominally controlled the entire program. The program was finally implemented in the towns and villages, however. The central government
apportioned relief funds among the prefectures, which in turn pooled
those funds with money drawn from prefectural treasuries and donations solicited locally. Prefectural officials funneled this money to county
governments, which parceled it out to towns and villages within their
jurisdiction. In directives sent to prefectural governors, Home Ministry
officials specified that relief funds be used to buy foreign rice and make
compulsory purchases of local grain according to the provisions of the
recently promulgated Emergency Grain Expropriation Ordinance.
Toyama prefecture received 19,000 yen as its share of the imperial contribution; 1,027 yen of this was forwarded to Namerikawa.[105] Of the
38,000 yen given to Toyama by the zaibatsu and other donors, 5,100
yen was transferred to Nakaniikawa county and a proportionally
smaller sum was sent to the town. The imperial and other donations
were delivered in cash to Namerikawa on 29 August.[106]

The prefectural government, in compliance with central-government guidelines, attached specific instructions for the use of this money. A total of 34,263 coupons allowing for a three-sen discount on rice were to be distributed to 1,016 households in Namerikawa, thus making aid available to 5,588 individuals. The prefectural authorities required that the coupons carry a message that the gift came from the emperor. Officials and policemen were to visit the homes of the poor to distribute aid personally. In face-to-face meetings with relief recipients, they were to explain that the emperor was deeply troubled by the recent unrest and to encourage the poor to respond with appropriate gratitude. The indigent were to be "kindly counseled and advised that [such imperial beneficence] would not become a customary practice. The recipients should be directed to make greater efforts." Prefectural authorities also instructed the program's local implementers to consult grain dealers in carrying out relief efforts. They were to inform wholesale and retail rice merchants that the discount coupons would be coverted at face value from the portion of the imperial gift and other donations held at town and village offices. Local program coordinators were instructed to keep strict accounts concerning use of the imperial gift.[107]

The national relief policy dovetailed neatly with the measures that the Namerikawa town council had already taken on 8 August. The town now had more money than it had expected and smoothly pushed ahead with its relief efforts. On 25 September Mayor Katō reported to Izeki Toshio, the head of Nakaniikawa county, that town officials had canvassed the poorer wards to register eligible aid recipients and placed the registration ledgers at established discount sales outlets. The poor, reported to be "deeply moved by imperial graciousness," accepted 27,586 discount coupons (representing 276 koku of rice) in the emperor's name during the first two weeks of distribution.[108]

Influential Namerikawa townspeople also worked to instill a sense of gratitude among aid recipients and to reconcile local conflict. Mayor Katō, town officials, and the police visited the poorer fishermen's wards personally to investigate living conditions, and they directly oversaw rice sales at the seven outlets opened in each of the town's wards.[109] Namerikawa's major rice dealers were also enlisted in relief efforts. Aside from a donation assessed on rice holders, about a hundred people made additional contributions, resulting in the pooling of 4,951 yen in the town's own relief fund. The three largest contributors were none other than the three major targets of the riots: the Namerikawa Rice-Fertilizer Company (955 yen), Kanagawa Sōzaemon (811 yen), and

Saitō Nizaemon (330 yen).[110] These rice dealers also volunteered the use of their businesses as sales outlets. As a result, the poor now received rice from the hands of those they had attacked earlier.

The selection of Kanagawa and others to distribute relief rice made logistic sense. The town, after all, bought rice from these major merchants, and drawing it from their storehouses for on-the-spot sale eliminated the trouble and expense of hauling the rice to another location. But relying on merchants to dispense relief grain served other purposes than just simple convenience. Having the targets of the protest provide aid demonstrated that the community had not been irrevocably split by the riots. A few days after the noisy demonstrations, rioters and the objects of their attack were both involved in an extensive relief plan that threw them together and indicated that social relations within Namerikawa had not changed significantly with the recent unrest.

Historians of town rice riots in the Tokugawa period have noted that calm returned almost immediately after a protest. People went about their daily routines the day after rioting had culminated in demolished homes and attacks on rice dealers. Although the Taishō riots were less destructive than the earlier protests, much the same thing happened in 1918. The smooth return to routine probably had less to do with notions of cathartic violence than with riots being almost a standard part of town life in the Meiji and Taishō periods. Riots, hardly revolutionary events, put social groups in contention but also confirmed community cooperation. The rice dealers were made to pay more than merely a symbolic penitence. In addition to levying additional fees for stored grain, officials warned them against future attempts to manipulate rice prices. The grain held by major dealers like Kanagawa and the Rice-Fertilizer Company was already subject to confiscation and mandated sale according to the central government's Grain Expropriation Ordinance. Local rice dealers undoubtedly found it in their best interest to cooperate.

By allowing the officially chastised targets of the protest to assume leading roles in the aid program, town officials intended to make poorer residents feel grateful and reflect upon their acts. Yet punishing the merchants also appeared to legitimate the rioters' conduct. The Toyama protesters, who but a few weeks earlier had blocked rice shipments, now found rice pouring into the area by ship and rail. Protest worked.

The relief program that was instituted after the riots went far beyond the original forty-day period originally planned by Mayor Katō and the town council. The mayor kept in constant touch with county and prefectural officials, repeatedly requesting their cooperation in buying and shipping foreign rice to the town. Sales to the needy were extended five times, and the relief program was expanded when signs of unrest reappeared in July 1919. Town records do not indicate precisely when postriot relief efforts ended. As late as October 1919, however, the director of the Toyama Internal Affairs Division reported to county officials that the delivery of 150 sacks of foreign rice would be delayed because of railroad construction.[111] This indicates that direct aid continued for at least fourteen months after the riots were supposedly pacified.

Local officials, aside from responding to the protesters' immediate demands to stop shipping and make rice affordable, took steps to assure that rice riots would not recur. County officials recognized that the poor in their jurisdiction required a more permanent welfare policy. In December 1918 they sent a directive to Katō, encouraging town officials to implement a long-term relief plan. The measure called for coordinating relief efforts with the local chamber of commerce and organizations such as youth and veteran's associations. Town leaders were specifically advised to encourage the consumption of foreign rice and other inexpensive foods and to ensure an adequate supply of these items. Other recommendations included the establishment of job-finding services, a program of aid for the unemployed, and the encouragement of frugality, savings, and by-employment.[112]

In Namerikawa, Police Chief Maeda took charge of surveying the town's economic conditions and investigating the local standards of living. He reported his findings to the town council on 27 June 1919, at a meeting attended by county officials. Because Maeda's investigation indicated that Namerikawa's poorer families still needed relief, the town council authorized funds for ongoing financial aid and rice relief to 1,048 Namerikawa households.[113]

The program of continuing aid was supported at the prefectural level. Rice prices continued high in 1919, thus creating conditions for renewed unrest. Realizing that exhorting the poor to be frugal and to take additional side-jobs would not prevent rioting, the director of Toyama's Internal Affairs Division advised city and town mayors to put in place the administrative machinery to make relief efforts possible *before* unrest occurred. He specifically urged that "methods should be planned before those [already poor] drop into the ranks of the extremely impoverished." Local police were called on to institute contingency plans for dealing with any new problem with rice prices.[114] Religious, educational, and volunteer organizations were also enlisted to use their stabilizing influence to help maintain local order. Of more concrete significance, the prefecture subsidized public markets to provide goods directly from the producer to the consumer. The first three markets opened in 1919 in Toyama city, Takaoka, and Tomari. A Takaoka official explained the thinking behind the public markets:

> We intend to sell at inexpensive prices. Items will be priced at least 10 to 20 percent below market. Prices will not only be cheaper, they will also be uniform. There will be no lusting after profits due to inevitable pressures from the open market. Up to now, one little event would send prices spiraling, creating difficulties [for everyone].[115]

By the end of 1919 prefectural and local efforts had restored order to the Toyama coast. A mid-year report in 1919 noted that economic conditions had already improved in Namerikawa. Wages had risen sharply, enabling the poor to cope better with consumer prices. Residents were also said to have become accustomed to inflation and to have begun economizing in anticipation of temporary jumps in the cost of certain goods. The livelihood of fishermen and their families, the poorest segment of the Namerikawa community, had also improved. The 1919 fishing season was a good one, and fishermen and women stevedores made more money at grain and fish-fertilizer hauling. Opportunities for side-work had also increased. During the second half of 1919 women and children could make two or three yen a day working at home.[116] Despite a generally optimistic economic outlook, the town mayor reported that there were still deeply impoverished families. The town had provided these families with aid and would continue to. Aid would not be provided, however, in response to rioting. Although "unrest" was observed in June 1919, the riots did not recur.

In later years Toyama residents joined in other disputes. From the autumn of 1927 through 1928 a protest over high electricity rates strongly resembled the Taishō movement for lower rice prices. Residents in Namerikawa and other coastal towns demanded a 35 percent reduction in power rates. Local residents held rallies, shut off the power to their homes, organized nightly patrols when the company turned off street lights, and returned light bulbs. According to Hamada Tsu, a participant in both the rice riots and the "electric power dispute" (_denki sōgi_), protests over high rates also aimed at shaming officials of Toyama Denki Kabushiki Kaisha by such tactics as processions to company offices. In one incident, bulbs that had been collected throughout Namerikawa were placed in a coffin and returned ceremoniously to the power company.[117] Local elites, including town officials, wealthy merchants, and "socialist thinkers," were instrumental in resolving the dispute. Following orderly protests that culminated in negotiations involving local residents, the prefectural governor, and company officials, Toyama Denki reduced rates by an average of 12.9 percent in August 1928. Although the *denki sōgi* of the late 1920s in Toyama and elsewhere await further study, they seem to demonstrate the same dynamic of traditional community cooperation, as opposed to class conflict, evident in the 1918 coastal rice riots.

Local cooperation perhaps explains the weak popular response to organizational appeals made by the region's small group of socialist activists. Toyama's local progressives, cognizant of the opportunities for broadening their own political aims, sought to lead various protest movements. They gained a modicum of local support during the 1920s and early 1930s, but they were successful because they backed popular opinion rather than because popular opinion backed their ideology. In Namerikawa, Hirai Kōichirō, Matsui Shijirō, and other local activists played a central role in organizing the widely supported electric power dispute. Nevertheless, their "Social Masses Party" (*Shakai taishūtō*) took only three of twenty-four town council seats in the 1929 elections. Hirai's own platform called for the public management of electric utilities, public housing, free clinics, public crèches, and expanded welfare. But he was not one of the socialists who won office. Although residents were quite willing to cooperate with local elites who professed socialist programs in resolving conflicts that affected popular interests, ideology alone did not garner significant support.

What might be called "pragmatism," or perhaps more cynically from the leftists' position "popular opportunism," can also be seen in the region's tenant movement. In Namerikawa the merchants and landlords central to settling the rice riots and electric power dispute were also involved in negotiating settlements over agricultural rents, eminent domain, and other quarrels concerned with agricultural land. Despite an economic position in the town that suggested the local elites were a class apart, others had no aversion to dealing with them in resolving a number of conflicts.

This pragmatic attitude may also help explain the weakness of the trade union movement throughout Toyama. Statistics for Toyama indicate that between 1923 and 1935 the maximum number of unions organized in any given year never surpassed eight, with a total membership of 414 individuals (1935). The highest number of strikes for any year between 1921 and 1935 was only six. Moreover, the growth of the union movement was inconsistent. For example, from 1930 to 1931 the number of unions declined from five to one, and total membership fell from 427 to 187 individuals. This pattern differs significantly from national trends. Until the mid-1930s Japan's unions expanded progressively both in number (from 432 unions in 1923 to 965 in 1935) and in membership (from 228,278 in 1923 to 387,964 in 1935). In contrast, the labor movement in Toyama tended to wane instead of wax in the years after the riots.[118]

Conclusion

Although coastal residents participated in protests and strikes after 1918, rice riots, so frequent in the Meiji and early Taishō periods, did not recur. Much of this "domestic tranquillity" can be attributed to the official response to the riots, which was generally well suited to the popular demand for rice at a fair price. Excepting charity extended to a small number of the poorest households, town officials offered nothing for free. Instead, they worked energetically to place rice within affordable limits. There was obviously an element of "submissive repression" in their actions. Officials made full use of imperial sanctions and played upon aid recipients' gratitude and sense of moral obligation (*giri*) in personally enacting relief programs. Cash assistance, which in some towns amounted to a daily allotment of a few sen per individual, also suggests that authorities conceded but little in order to avoid changing much more.

    Yet to view official actions simply as repressive tactics does not account for the speed at which aid was provided. Nor does it fully explain why local officials willingly took on the burden that riot relief placed on local financial resources. In Namerikawa alone a partial accounting of the relief program indicates that relief rice worth more than 47,000 yen was sold within the town.[119] Aside from the financial burden (which was disproportionally carried by wealthier residents), town officers dealt with rioters' complaints against local rice dealers and corrected abuses stemming from alleged market manipulation. Such actions appeared to coordinate the interests of all involved in the conflict and to restore local order. The contending groups in the riots—

the poor, officials, and grain dealers—reached a settlement, but none achieved an unqualified victory. Although concessions were made on all sides, each group was dealt with as if its interests were legitimate. Other factors, of course, contributed to the absence of protest along Toyama Bay after 1918. Local economic conditions and national-level politics had changed, and Korean and Taiwanese rice was pouring into the home islands at a stepped-up rate. The expansion of industry in Toyama and the extension of voting rights also provided alternatives both for making a living and for political expression. But in addition, the manner in which the 1918 disputes were settled locally played an important part in preventing future riots.

High prices for rice were a nationwide problem in 1918. Yet people dealt with it in a variety of ways, depending on the local understanding of the causes and possible cures for the condition. In Toyama residents responded to threats to their standard of living with a series of largely nonviolent protests. The methods employed in these demonstrations can be characterized as "traditional" in that they had been used repeatedly in the past in similar times of high prices. But these traditional protests were not apolitical. Popular disturbances represented a collective awareness of the efficacy and the limitations of protest in solving specific problems. The problem during the summer months of 1918 and for months thereafter was the fundamental political question of who gets what, when, and how.

Contrary to views of the riots that stress the spontaneous and unconscious nature of popular protest, the Toyama rioters set about resolving the crisis caused by rice prices in a rational and effective manner. They identified what they believed to be the causes of steep prices and short supplies (transshipping and hoarding) and applied pressure on political leaders and merchants to limit these practices. Until the limitations resulted in lower prices, protesters also demanded relief rice and subsidization to prevent their standard of living from declining still further. The politically influential and the wealthy provided the requested temporary aid in a remarkably short time.

The Toyama demonstrators' full use of their political options is a point not usually emphasized. By staging noisy protests, the unenfranchised poor could influence officials to take up their grievances and actually alter the policies of local government. The purposeful side of the rioters' actions has been neglected by a misplaced emphasis on the spontaneous character of the riots and the absence of any concrete plan for a social restructuring. Evident in the rioters' aims and motives and in the response of community leaders is a presumption that the local political system was still considered workable. What occurred was neither a mindless Jacquerie nor an incoherent attempt to create something new. Rather, the riots and the official response to them represented a popular demand that economic problems be addressed and that cooperative relations between groups, temporarily out of kilter, once again be balanced. Protest was intended to eliminate the problem of high prices for rice, not to be the first step in class revolution.

Although the immediate issue was rice prices, at stake in the Toyama riots were larger, nonlegal, essentially moral questions of community right and wrong. By taking to the streets, protesters expressed their concern over the rights of the poor, the duties of political leaders (elected or otherwise), and the responsibility of the rich. In understanding the significance of the protesters' acts and the response of the larger community, the elements of both class cooperation and class conflict must considered. Although the economic interests of contending groups in Toyama were clearly different, people lived with still-meaningful traditional concepts of how the community should function in a world shaped by market forces. This is not to suggest that towns like Namerikawa in any way resembled political Shangri-las where genuine conflict never occurred and harmony prevailed unbroken. Conflict of interest was real in Toyama. Town officials and rice dealers gave nothing that was not demanded. But local conflicts were muted by a recognition of the rights and responsibilities of community members. Although it might have appeared that one group's socioeconomic interests were irrevocably opposed to another's, the popular conception of how the community should run moderated class conflict.

In Toyama this indirectly expressed concept of a moral economy worked remarkably well. In making demands on the community and in responding to such demands, each group seemed to recognize that it had rights, duties, and responsibilities that went beyond what was required by law or abstract market forces. By responding with relief efforts soon after the disorders broke out, the politically influential and the rich acted on the demands of the poor in a traditional and effective manner. As a result of the rioters' vigils, appeals, and threats, protest declined rapidly.

Although a traditional moral economy seemed to work in Toyama, elsewhere the "women's uprising" was viewed very differently. Press reports consistently exaggerated the level of violence and distorted the issues involved in the coastal area protests. Typical headlines in Osaka and Tokyo newspapers reported that rampaging women had destroyed merchants' houses, beaten or threatened officials with death, and even attacked rice-carrying steamships.[120] In describing the riots in terms of class conflict, reporters also suggested that they should be seen as threatening object lessons aimed at Japan's political leaders. The manner in which Toyama events were conveyed in the press contributed to the outbreak of disturbances throughout Japan and may have added to their violent nature. The precedent of the "women who stood up in Toyama" was referred to by protesters throughout the nation. The fundamental misunderstanding of what actually took place in Toyama had a significant influence on the methods and aims of rioters in the rest of Japan.

THREE

The City Riots
Mass Protest and Taishō Democracy

I am constantly and greatly apprehensive that in the midst of
the present difficulties in society caused by price rises, we also
see the confusion of old and new thought; and it is possible
that these conditions will ferment chaos from dangerous
thoughts.

> *Yamagata Aritomo to Tokutomi Sohō,*
> *7 February 1920*

The rise in prices and the importation of anarchism fan each
other and will give rise to a major social revolution. The
primary school teachers, the police, and petty bureaucrats are
budding socialists. . . . You cannot imagine how much the
thinking and the ideals of the young today are confused. I am
convinced of this. . . . Please destroy this letter.

> *Tokutomi Sohō to Yamagata Aritomo,*
> *9 February 1920*

Within days of the Toyama shipping boycott, massive rioting broke out
in every major Japanese city. The sudden burst of unrest shocked government officials and, as is indicated by the Yamagata-Tokutomi correspondence, continued to worry them long after the last 1918 protest
had been quieted.[1] Before mid-August Home Minister Mizuno Rentarō, who initially referred to the coastal riots as a "trifling regional
matter, a commotion raised by Toyama fishwives," had taken no
special steps to prevent or speedily suppress urban rioting.[2] Police,
kenpeitai, and reservist associations went about their normal daily
routines. Regular army units had not been put on special alert and
continued to drill in preparation for intervention against Russian Bolsheviks in Siberia. Only after rioters had rallied in crowds tens of
thousands strong, erected street barricades from which they battled
police, and set buildings ablaze were troops finally mobilized.

The failure to recognize the Toyama protest as a dangerous precedent reflected official attitudes similar to Home Minister Mizuno's. De-

spite alarmist articles in major city newspapers about hunger, popular hatred of the *narikin*, and the threat of class war, government leaders did not foresee an expansion of unrest.[3] After all, Japan was not Russia. Although tensions between labor and capital certainly existed, the state, at least before the riots, appeared unified. Respect for the imperial institution was strong, and "socialism" was generally considered a dirty word by rulers and ruled alike.

Mizuno appeared correct in playing down the importance of the Toyama incident in his suggestion that such disturbances would occur only where local traditions and peculiar economic conditions justified popular protest. Japan's major cities had seen rice prices double between 1868 and 1870 and double again between 1874 and 1875 without the citizens of Tokyo or Osaka taking to the streets.[4] By contrast, Toyama, with its long history of actions mounted by rancorous but otherwise nonviolent "women's armies," was the scene of repeated appeals during the Meiji period to halt the movement of grain outside the region. Moreover, the second incident of rioting after Toyama occurred in a fishing village in Okayama, a place where the causes (rice shipping) and methods of protest (shipping boycotts) strongly resembled those in the "fishwives' uprising." Difficulties in the rice-producing periphery appeared only tangentially related to those in rice-consuming cities. Central-government bureaucrats probably assumed that the Toyama and Okayama authorities, who had successfully dealt with such local problems in the past, would do so again in 1918. The need for precipitous action was not clearly evident, for the conditions in Japan's major cities seemed far different from those in the hinterland.

There were also other, more directly political, reasons for the central government's blasé attitude toward early signs of unrest. Although ministerial officials were privately fearful of a red contagion behind the riots, they publicly dismissed popular protests as isolated outbursts of ignorant rabble-rousers. During the course of the riots Mizuno at times urged local officials to demonstrate "sympathy" and "concern" for citizens experiencing "livelihood" problems. Nevertheless, his directives were aimed at putting down unrest created by those who knew not why they acted.[5] Political restraints, of course, prevented the home minister from acting otherwise. An acknowledgment by Mizuno of the seriousness of the Toyama incident or the validity of rioters' complaints would have been taken as an admission of some fundamental flaw in the Terauchi cabinet's rice policy. Because officials were initially reluctant to draw out the threatening implications of protests in remote coastal districts, they discounted it as a precedent for urban unrest. In their certainty that riots *like* the shipping boycott would probably not recur, they failed to consider the possibility of riots very *unlike* the Toyama incident.

The city uprisings were more than a simple replaying of the Toyama dispute in an urban setting. True, city riots did share features of protests elsewhere. High prices for rice contributed to unrest wherever it occurred in 1918. Poorer residents typically filled out the ranks of rioters whether the dispute took place in a fishing hamlet, a farm village, or an industrial city. Moreover, city rioters also saw the rice prices that imperiled their right to existence (*seizon-ken*) as a violation of traditional morality.

Yet the urban riots went beyond the traditional protests in their sweeping indictment of national politics as practiced in 1918. Government leaders such as Yamagata and Mizuno were shocked by the city protests, not only because the unrest was unexpected, widespread, and difficult to quell but also because the rioting represented a massive rejection of the new Japan by great numbers of its citizens. Five decades of sweeping economic and social change appeared endangered. Genro, central-government bureaucrats, and military men could more easily grasp the causes of traditional uprisings, or *ikki*, mounted by a handful of fishwives and farmers in prefectures far from the political center; as Mizuno suggested, such peripheral protests harked back to "premodern" values. But what of rioting in the capital and in virtually every industrial city, where diverse groups abandoned appeals to traditional paternalism and presented explicitly political demands? The people at the conservative political center feared that these city riots portended a class war that would lead to the end of government dominated by genro, military men, and compliant party politicians. Such fears appeared well founded in 1918. The rhetoric and actions of urban rioters made it clear that city dwellers were aware of national political issues, identified themselves as citizens of Japan and not just of a town or a village, and were willing to use mass protest in changing government policy.

Although the sudden blossoming of "Taishō democracy" manifested by the riots was upsetting to bureaucrats and party politicians, particularly to those who believed in a strict division between rulers and ruled, the actual threat presented by the riots was less ominous than the letters of Yamagata and Tokutomi suggested. The actions of city rioters rejected aspects of the existing political system, but not the system itself.

In particular, protesters sought to reform structures that distributed wealth and political prerogatives unevenly. Speakers at "citizens' rallies" (*shimin taikai*) often posed two related questions: Who was responsible for the shrinkage of the average worker's real wage while the overall economy was flourishing? Why did most Japanese have no political rights to change this obvious inequality? These were worrisome questions to genro, bureaucrats, and party leaders. But they did not represent the disintegration of society or the spread of anarchistic contagion. Rather, I will argue, the city rioters' words and actions demanded the integration of popular interests within the Meiji constitutional order. This demand is particularly evident in rioting that occurred in Nagoya from 9 to 17 August.

The Nagoya Riots

The Nagoya citizens' rally on 9 August was the first incident in a series of major urban protests (see fig. 5). Police reports note that the unrest began when small groups gathered after nightfall in Tsurumai Park, the site of repeated mass meetings during the next nine days. Throughout the day rumors circulated by word of mouth or in handbills that all concerned citizens should gather at the park for a discussion of the crisis in rice prices. No individual or organization scheduled this spontaneous meeting, and no one came forth to accept responsibility for it. During the hot, sticky summer months, crowds customarily congregated in the park after sundown to stroll around its central fountain, listen to free band concerts, and enjoy the relatively cooler evenings outdoors. But the 9 August gathering was different. Newspapers had carried word of the Toyama "women's uprising" throughout Japan. In Nagoya, where rice prices were increasing daily during July and August, mere rumors of a meeting to discuss "livelihood problems" (*seikatsu mondai*) were sufficient to attract a crowd.

By 10 P.M. more than five hundred people had gathered around the Tsurumai fountain. Although the rally was supposedly a "speech meeting" (*enzetsu kai*), no one stood to address the crowd formally. Nevertheless, there was no doubt about why everyone had gathered: shouted slogans condemned the ineffectiveness of the government's rice policy and stressed the need to "smash" (*uchikowase*) middlemen rice brokers.[6] Despite the heated language, this rally was peaceful compared with the street violence that came later. The only disturbance occurred when the crowd stoned an automobile carrying finely dressed geisha and their customers, which had attempted to drive through the park. Such expressions of anti-*narikin* resentment ran like a common thread through each of the urban riots.

The crowd's aggressiveness worried police, who remembered the burning of streetcars, attacks on the homes of trolley line executives, and the trashing of police boxes that had occurred in a 1914 protest against increased trolley fares. That three-day uprising, which had required the mobilization of four companies of regular army troops to restore order, had also begun with a citizens' rally.[7] Following reports of unrest at Tsurumai, officials at the Monzen police station called up all off-duty officers. Although the police anticipated further unrest on 9 August, they made no attempt to disperse those gathered, and the crowd left the park voluntarily.

The next evening a crowd gathered once again at Tsurumai. According to the Monzen police station report, many who came believed that a local newspaper company was to sponsor a "speech meeting" to discuss the rice problem; others had read press reports that an unsponsored rally would be held. In fact, the only event scheduled for 10 August was an outdoor evening concert of military music. But even it had been canceled by police authorities wary of any event that might draw a large crowd.[8] Throughout the evening, crowded streetcars and trains brought city residents to stations near the park entrances. By 8 P.M., thirty-five hundred men, women, and children milled around the park bandstand; at 9 the crowd exceeded thirty thousand.[9] As the gathering increased in size people here and there called for the sponsors of the meeting to show themselves and to begin the speeches. Finally, several employees from the Okamoto Automotive Company climbed atop the bandstand and declared that the rally was open.[10]

A tinker, a day laborer, and a medical student were the first to address the crowd. They attributed high rice prices to hoarding farmers and to market-cornering grain brokers whose individual greed caused the impoverishment of great numbers of common citizens. The speakers castigated the central government for countenancing these outrages. They singled out major companies like Mitsui and Mitsubishi for their irresponsible concern for profits above all else. None of the speakers advocated direct action to deal with widespread "livelihood problems." Nevertheless, several hinted that good citizens might be required to act on their own if petitions to Nagoya's mayor and the prefectural governor failed to improve conditions.[11]

Uniformed and plainclothes police, alarmed at the direction the rally seemed to be taking, soon moved in to disperse the crowd. At about eleven o'clock patrolmen from the Monzen station, reinforced by policemen called up from other city stations, cleared the bandstand. After declaring the meeting closed, they successfully drove lingering groups from the park. But on 10 August and on successive days thereafter, those who had been unceremoniously pushed into the streets refused to go home. Instead, they regrouped into crowds several thousand strong and charged through the city's central shopping district, throwing rocks at shop windows and smashing street lights as they attempted to make their way to Komeya-chō, the city's central grain-dealing district. A guard line of more than a hundred uniformed police officers blocked the streets and bridges leading into Komeya-chō and prevented the rioters from confronting the rice dealers. Although crowds continued to loiter nearby into the early morning hours, police had the situation under control.[12]

The pattern of protest established during the first two days of unrest continued for another week. Unlike the Toyama disputes that occurred both during the day and into the night, the urban riots were usually after-hours events. From sunrise until late afternoon, city residents went about their normal day-to-day business. But after dark, people began streaming into Tsurumai Park or other central meeting places to listen to impromptu speeches by day laborers, postal workers, journalists, and a great many who declined to identify themselves. Following the orations or even in the middle of the rally, authorities attempted to break up the meeting forcibly. Once pushed into the streets or conducted there by crowd leaders, smaller groups attempted to make their way to the Nagoya Rice Exchange, major grain dealerships, and government offices.

On 11 August city officials stepped up their efforts to deal with the growing crisis. A little after midnight, Nagoya's mayor, Satō Kōsaburō, called the city council into emergency session. The council members speedily agreed to allot 31,400 yen for the purchase of foreign rice and to set in place the administrative machinery to carry out city-wide discount sales. Their plans called for local officials to dispense foreign rice at ward offices for four hours daily from 12 August. To defuse criticism, they stipulated that the grain would be sold at its cost price of 19 sen per shō, the only restrictions being those regulating the hours of sale.[13] The scheduling of public sales from 4 to 8 P.M. served a dual purpose. These hours not only proved convenient for people returning home from work to purchase grain but also corresponded to the time that crowds began to gather in different parts of the city. The Nagoya Rice Retailers Association followed the city council's lead. Within hours of the mayor's emergency meeting, the association's directors met and decided that discount sales of foreign rice at cost price would be carried out at rice shops throughout the city.[14] To assure that grain supplies for relief efforts would remain steady, Mayor Satō requested central-government officials to make large amounts of foreign rice available to the city. Aichi's governor, Matsui Shigeru, repeated the mayor's request to Minister of Agriculture and Commerce Nakakōji, emphasizing that help from the central government was essential for overcoming a shortfall in local grain supplies.[15]

These official and nonofficial efforts were well publicized. On 11 August all Nagoya newspapers reported the city government's actions. Meanwhile, rice dealers posted signs near the entrances to their shops announcing the decision of the retailers association to sell foreign grain at cost price. Yet, despite government and private relief efforts, the crisis in and around the city worsened. Police reported finding handbills in villages on the outskirts of Nagoya that called for concerned citizens to join the Tsurumai mass meetings. Rumors also circulated that the buildings of specific grain merchants, suspected of market cornering and hoarding, would be burned to the ground.[16]

Anticipating trouble, Nagoya police officials strengthened their crowd-control measures. They posted additional uniformed and plainclothes police around Tsurumai Park and Komeya-chō. The Monzen and Egawa stations, which held jurisdiction over the park and the rice-exchange district, served as command centers from which police authorities directed the activities of additional patrolmen called up on 11 August. They also ordered stations in peaceful areas, both inside Nagoya and in nearby counties, to send all nonessential personnel to the Monzen and Egawa command centers. To avoid overextending the police lines, patrolmen were held in reserve at the two stations. If rioting broke out in a new location or if crowds threatened to overwhelm police contingents, these additional units were to rush to the trouble spot.

Approximately eight hundred policemen were mobilized to keep order on 11 August, a number several times over the normal deployment.[17] The written instructions given by the police chief of the Egawa station provide a clue to the attitude of the authorities:

1. It is strictly forbidden to draw swords.
2. To prevent losing swords, a strong cord must be attached to your weapon.
3. Do not take any excessive action. Rely upon persuasion and calm actions.
4. Crowd control must be carried out in organized units.
5. A commanding officer will be assigned to each position. His orders are to be obeyed.
6. Orders [from the command post] will be sent in cases where the crowd is to be routed.
7. In the event that you are wounded, you are not permitted to draw your sword. The sword should be kept sheathed in its scabbard and used as a club if self-defense becomes necessary. At all times you must keep in mind [that you are not to bare your sword].[18]

One of the patrolmen assigned to temporary riot duty at the Egawa station recalled later that the station chief reacted angrily when pressed about the possible need to use sabers against the protesters. The commanding officer is reported to have told the assembled patrolmen, "Those of you who can't handle this without drawing your sword, write out your resignations." None of the policemen resigned. To make doubly sure that sabers would not be used, policemen wound strips of white linen around both blades and scabbards.

At the Tsurumai citizens' meeting on 11 August authorities' worst fears of an expanded protest were realized. Police observers noted that, in contrast to the crowd of the previous night, few women or children joined the throng of people who streamed into the park after sundown. They were also alarmed by many in the crowd who carried clubs and wore straw sandals, footgear more practical than clumsy wooden geta for escaping a policeman. To all appearances the crowd had come ready for confrontation.[19] By 9 P.M. fifty thousand people had gathered once again in the park. They marched through the city, renewing their attacks on police boxes and smashing shop windows as they made their way to Komeya-chō. Unlike riots in other cities, however, there were relatively few reports of looting or forced sales of rice during the Nagoya riots. When the crowds finally reached the outskirts of the rice-trading district, their advance was halted by police lines. Rioters tried repeatedly to push past the police cordon into the avenues leading to the grain exchange. Fistfights and scuffling broke out, and the patrolmen soon resorted to their swords to defend against the rioters' clubs and sticks. Despite intense street fighting in which twenty-nine patrolmen and an unknown number of rioters were injured, the police managed to repulse the crowd's surges into their lines and arrest thirty-three rioters.[20]

The previous night's melee did not dissuade city officials from putting their relief plan into effect during the daylight hours of 12 August. On that day 6,457 residents purchased 290 koku of rice at Nagoya ward offices. Prefectural authorities also assembled government-designated grain importers to ascertain the level of available rice supplies within the city. The meeting, which revealed a shortage that was worse than expected, led Aichi officials immediately to renew their request that the Ministry of Agriculture and Commerce make an emergency shipment of between 70,000 and 80,000 bales of foreign rice to the Nagoya area. Prefectural officials also arranged to buy 7,000 bales from the Nagoya branch of Suzuki Shōten as a stopgap measure intended to continue discount sales until additional supplies arrived.[21]

Such efforts, however, did nothing to stem the enthusiasm for crowd protest. Police responded to rumors of unrest by posting additional patrolmen and mobilizing *kenpeitai* mounted police to keep order around Tsurumai Park. They also sent 325 uniformed officers to guard Komeya-chō. Nevertheless, by ten o'clock that night a crowd of thirty-five thousand, described by police as "laborers and young people," had gathered around the park bandstand. Smaller groups were also reported in other parts of the city.[22]

Speakers at the Tsurumai rally on 12 August continued their verbal attacks on government officials and grain dealers. But the content of the speeches had undergone two significant changes. First, several of the speakers sought to legitimate rioters' actions by invoking an imperial sanction for the protest. They asserted that the Terauchi cabinet's alleged misdeeds were an outrage perpetrated against the emperor as well as an offense to Japanese citizens. Speakers suggested that the rioters' actions, taken in defense of both the emperor and the people, were entirely justified. Claiming that the current government had lost the confidence of the people, they demanded that Terauchi and his ministers submit their resignations. One speaker contrasted the shameful, self-serving acts of particular ministers with the selfless behavior of General Nogi Maresuke. Another suggested that, in the good old days, disgraced officials would have expiated their misdeeds by committing seppuku. Now, he lamented, the nation's leaders felt that they need only print excuses (*kōjitsu*) in the newspapers and all would be forgiven.[23]

The second change came in the speakers' harsh criticism of Nagoya's police force. Despite explicit instructions that swords were not to be drawn against rioters, word had spread that police had indeed used such weapons indiscriminately the previous night.[24] On the morning of 12 August the head of the prefectural police division met with reporters to state officially that sensational allegations of police brutality were completely unfounded. His statement was publicly supported by Aichi's governor, Matsui.[25] The lengthy and well-publicized denials notwithstanding, many speakers at the Tsurumai rally on 12 August treated the rumors as established fact. They condemned the wanton use of swords against civilians as indefensible and eulogized the victims as individuals brutally prevented from exercising their "twentieth-century" right to gather freely and express opinions. One speaker ended his remarks by asking rhetorically, "Can there be any worse crime than the wounding of so many law-abiding citizens?"[26]

Not everyone was critical of local officials. Unlike the Toyama rioters who unanimously confronted their representatives, several speakers at the citizens' rallies commended Aichi officials (but not the central government) for doing their best to deal with the grain problem. A few even condemned the crowd's actions as unduly excessive, while others defended police tactics as an excusable exercise of official duty. Such opinions clearly did not reflect the feelings of most of the people attending the rallies. Yet, in contrast to the one-sidedness demonstrated by the Toyama protesters, the city crowds allowed those holding contrary opinions to express their ideas freely. With the exception of the police, all who chose to speak were allowed to do so, and the speakers often made fiery speeches. But curiously, their remarks invariably concluded by urging the protesters to use only peaceful means. The sincerity of such appeals is questionable. Although the speakers stressed that they were simply concerned citizens, not "ringleaders," and that they in no way wished to instigate violence, their call for moderation was perhaps little more than a transparent attempt to evade subsequent prosecution. After all, uniformed and plainclothes police observers as well as the military secret police (*kenpeitai*) were always present to arrest later those speakers that they could identify.

Nevertheless, the frequently repeated appeals for peaceful methods should not be entirely discounted. One speaker, for example, quite prudently observed that riot-caused property destruction would only mean heavier taxes for Nagoya citizens. For others, the need for restraint went beyond economic considerations to issues of "civilized" behavior and civic pride. Two unidentified speakers expressed themselves on these concerns at the park rally on 12 August:

[First speaker.] My friends, last night Komeya-chō was attacked. The cause of the explosion in rice prices is Terauchi's unconstitutional regime [*biriken*; the term, after a popular pointed-headed doll, was a commonly used pun referring to both high-handed politics and to Terauchi's close-cropped, bullet-shaped head]. But attacking Komeya-chō, smashing gaslights along the street, and the like is uncivilized (*hibunmei-teki*). I resent that kind of behavior. But I am not one who wishes to bend you from freely expressing yourselves and thereby completely achieving the goal of reducing rice prices. Still, in carrying out your resolve, I can only hope that you will use peaceful methods.

[Second speaker.] Why have we filled this park to overflowing for the last three nights? What is the point? The answer goes without saying—to attempt to reduce the price of rice. But I have also heard of last night's attack on Komeya-chō and the boldly hostile action against the police. Don't you think that such behavior greatly disgraces us in the eyes of foreign nations? Aren't hostile acts against the police a betrayal of our civic duty?[27]

The Nagoya riots peaked on 12 and 13 August. On 12 August three thousand rioters at Hijiebashi, near Komeya-chō, stormed police lines in an attempt to take the rice-trading district. Crowds armed with boards torn from fences and with tiles stripped from roofs attacked police and mounted *kenpeitai* units in a see-sawing battle through narrow lanes and around the bridges that spanned the ward's many canals. After an hour of attacks and counterattacks, regular troops, requested by Governor Matsui, finally arrived to reinforce police lines. But the rioters were not intimidated. For hours, hand-to-hand fighting continued in darkness broken only by fires set by the rioters. Similar clashes occurred near the prefectural governor's residence and city offices. Once again police and troops halted the rioters' advance in both Komeya-chō and at Nagoya's civic center. But regaining control came at a cost. At Komeya-chō alone, rioters wounded forty-two policemen. Before order was restored, crowds had also destroyed six police boxes, damaged the property of ten rice dealers, and set several small fires. Arson, which carried the death penalty in 1918, was no small crime in cities built largely of wood. That protesters would resort to such methods indicated to city officials how far control had slipped from their hands. Police now gave no quarter and, during this single day of unrest, arrested more than a hundred people for rioting.[28]

Despite, or more likely because of, the previous day's violence, on 13 August prefectural and city officials renewed their efforts to make inexpensive rice available to a wider segment of Nagoya's population. But this had become more difficult. Justifiably alarmed by the events of the past four days, most of the city's retail rice dealers had closed their shops. In retrospect, the grain retailers may have acted prematurely. Thanks to police protection and the rioters' restraint in usually targeting major wholesalers and not retailers, only a few rice merchants suffered serious losses during the nine days of rioting. Nagoya rioters, of course, had many opportunities to enforce a "just" price or simply to take what they wanted, as rioters in other cities often did. There were scores of small, neighborhood rice shops scattered throughout the city. Yet despite the availability of targets, rioters tended to attack the rice-exchange and grain brokers concentrated in Komeya-chō. Still, one can easily imagine the widespread sense of panic among rice retailers during the long hot nights when smashed street lights and cut power lines left entire city blocks in darkness. No one could tell when rioters might redirect their ire from the large dealers to the neighborhood rice store. But had the retail rice shops been attacked, the crowd would likely have been disappointed. Owing to riot-caused disruption in Nagoya's wholesale market, many rice retailers found it difficult to restock rice inventories; some shops had nothing left to sell.[29]

The prefectural and city governments stepped in to mend the disrupted channels of distribution between rice wholesalers and consumers. Ward offices sold an additional three hundred koku of foreign rice at cost price on 13 August. On the same day Kondō Yūzaemon, a wealthy Nagoya businessman, gave the relief effort an unexpected boost by donating 100,000 yen to Aichi prefecture. Supplementing Kondō's contribution with other private donations, prefectural officials contracted for the purchase of an additional ten thousand koku of rice.[30]

Contrary to the alarming reports of shortages that Governor Matsui sent to the Ministry of Agriculture and Commerce, his public announcements assured city residents that rice was in ample supply. In his 13 August statement, however, he did acknowledge that distribution problems existed. To overcome them, he warned, expropriation would be used against hoarders and market cornerers.[31] A separate, abbreviated notice issued under the auspices of Aichi prefecture and posted in public places throughout Nagoya described current grain-reserve levels and steps that should be taken by those requiring assistance:

1. At present Japan's nationwide domestic rice reserves total 17 million koku. Our prefecture possesses 500,000 koku of the national reserves.

2. Within the next few days, an additional 72,000 bales of foreign rice will be delivered.

3. Distribution of foreign-rice discount coupons will be greatly increased.

4. People experiencing difficulties should obtain coupons from the police [station in their local neighborhood].[32]

Not long after the notice appeared on the morning of 13 August, crowds began to queue up outside police stations throughout the city. Within a few days police had issued fifty thousand rice-discount coupons. On 14 August the city council further amended the plan by reducing the purchase price for foreign rice to fifteen sen per shō, a level well below cost price. It ordered domestic rice to be reduced to thirty sen, a level fifteen to eighteen sen lower than the current retail prices.[33]

While officials dangled the carrot of lower rice prices with one hand, with the other they groped for a heavier stick with which to put down the rioting. On 13 August authorities stationed 209 policemen around Komeya-chō and reinforced them with two companies (400 men) of regular troops placed near the Hijie bridge. An additional platoon was sent to guard the Nagoya branch of the Bank of Japan. To quell any unrest emanating from Tsurumai Park, regular mounted troops replaced *kenpeitai* guards. Together with an antiriot squad of 60 uniformed police sent from the Monzen station, they prepared to disband any gathering that might take place in the park.

To prevent riots in individual neighborhoods, the Nagoya branch of the Imperial Reservists Association mobilized reservists throughout the city to maintain a "self-defense watch" (*jiei-teki keikai*). Although the city was not formally placed under martial law, bands of reservists were to discourage residents from leaving their homes after sunset. They were to act peaceably; none of the reservists carried arms nor were they authorized to use force. The head of the city's reservist association simply requested its members to use their personal authority to keep peace in the city's wards. Nevertheless, the reservists were ordered to coordinate their efforts with those of the police. They were to be especially watchful for arson attempts and suspicious activity within their local neighborhoods.

By tightening security within city wards, officials attempted to choke off protest at its source. They seemed to believe that if residents remained off the streets, large gatherings could be prevented. Again, these efforts proved unsuccessful. If anything, the bottling up of residents in the city's wards only served to aggravate already widespread resentment against the alleged heavy-handed techniques used by police. According to the *Nagoya shinbun*, popular resentment against the actions of police and troops, especially on the sword issue, continued to run high on 13 August. Rumors also circulated on 13 August that the rioters intended to burn down the Egawa police station. The police took these threats seriously, and patrolmen began moving records out of Egawa station to other stations for safekeeping.[34] Grain brokers in Komeya-chō had taken similar precautions on 11 August when they moved valuables, records, and in some cases families outside the area.[35]

On 13 August police attempted to limit access to Tsurumai Park. But by eight o'clock a crowd of five thousand had once again gathered around the bandstand. An even larger group remained just outside the park. Before the speeches could begin, the chief of the Monzen station addressed the crowd:

> The recent riots breaking out throughout the land have come to the attention of the emperor. We have received word that His Majesty, deeply troubled [by this situation] has graciously bestowed a significant grant [for relief measures]. Let us acknowledge his benevolence. Tonight go no further. Return to your homes. If you do not disperse I will use my official authority to disband this gathering.[36]

The crowd, which had listened attentively to the first part of the policeman's short address, shouted and booed when the chief used the words "official authority." Seeing that his speech roiled rather than calmed troubled waters, the police chief immediately ordered his men into action. Within minutes uniformed police and mounted soldiers rushed in, forcing the crowd to flee the park. Throughout the night individual crowds of as many as fifteen thousand rioted at different locations within the city. A group of three thousand surrounded the Monzen police station and showered it with rocks. Other groups renewed attempts to march on the prefectural governor's official residence and to break into Komeya-chō. But once again the center held, and by 1 A.M. the city was quiet.

After 13 August a more permanent order was gradually restored. Police barricaded Tsurumai Park, preventing the reconvening of citizens' meetings. Although groups continued to gather outside the park for several days, these smaller crowds made no serious attempt to defy police lines. Those that persisted in protesting found a new rallying ground at the Ōsu Kannon temple, where ten thousand gathered on 14 August. People met at the temple during the next three nights, while sporadic rioting went on in other parts of the city. On 14 and 15 August police resorted to force to scatter the crowds congregated on the park-like temple grounds. But on 17 August, when several hundred had gathered to hear a socialist denounce the government, the police easily arrested the speaker, and the crowd quietly obeyed orders to disband.[37] Officials stepped up their relief efforts, and disturbances became smaller and less intense after 14 August. On 15 August city officials opened additional outlets for discount sales and reduced the price of domestic rice to twenty-five sen per shō. These sales, which cost the city nearly 2 million yen, continued until 31 October.[38]

Rioting in Other Cities

The Nagoya riots were followed by protests in every major Japanese city. The day after the first Nagoya mass meeting, representatives from Kyoto's burakumin wards visited police stations and noisily demanded action against high rice prices. Riots began in Osaka, Kobe, Hiroshima, and Kure on 11 August, and were followed by mass gatherings in Tokyo and other cities from 12 August. Urban unrest, first reported on 9 August, eventually spread to thirty-eight cities and continued until the quelling of the Sasebo uprising on 20 August. Only several Tōhoku cities and virtually all of Okinawa remained riot free during the summer months.

Although widespread, city protests were unequally distributed. The largest, most violent, and lengthiest riots occurred in the industrializing Kansai and Kantō regions. Most lasted only two days or, more accurately, two nights. The Nagoya riots (9 to 19 August) went on longer than disturbances elsewhere. But Tokyo, Osaka, Kyoto, Kobe, Kure, and other cities also experienced unrest for as long as a week. The end of the protests can be attributed to the speedy and positive response of city officials to the rioters' demands. In addition, the rioters' needed to return to a regular work schedule. After a workday of ten to twelve hours, it took extra energy to remain on the streets, rioting—and some-times reveling—into the early morning hours. And revel the rioters did. Observers among the protesters and the police noted that rather than being somber, funereal gatherings of the grim-faced poor, the gather-ings were festive, and as in the traditional *matsuri* (festival), rioting included processions, chanting, dancing, and drinking. The coincidence of the riots with the Bon holiday and the Tanabata celebration of the seventh day of the seventh month (according to the old lunar calendar) partially accounts for the often-cheerful mood and easy gathering of crowds in some cities.[39]

In addition to official concessions and the physical exhaustion of rioters, police and troop intervention helped end the city protests. Prefectural governors, who held direct jurisdiction over major cities in the Kansai and Kantō, quickly recognized that relying on local police forces was not sufficient to maintain order. After a day or two of citizens' rallies regularly followed by attacks on urban business districts, all major cities were placed under virtual martial law. Governors ordered troops mobilized, imposed dusk-to-dawn curfews, and in several cities enjoined police to treat any gathering as a potential mob.[40] In Osaka emergency ordinances required that residents stay indoors after sundown and banned any gathering of five or more people during the daylight hours. Violators were subject to a month in jail. Police officials also suspended night runs of the Osaka City Electrified Railway and, anticipating an action that the Home Ministry later ordered nationally, censored local press reports of the riots.

But even the early enforcement of such measures did not immediately restore order or prevent massive rallies. Estimates of the number of participants in the urban riots bear out this point. Police figures indicate that a total of 130,000 people (out of a city population of 437,000 in 1918) took part in the Nagoya protests. This figure was reached by totaling estimated crowd sizes over several successive nights and obviously includes protesters counted more than once. Nevertheless, there is no doubt that a sizable proportion of the city's residents joined in the citizens' rallies and rioting. Indeed, the actual number of participants was probably higher than police reports indicate. For example, where the police counted 15,000 people in a single rally in Tsurumai Park, a postriot report issued by the Aichi prefectural office estimated that 30,000 actually attended the meeting.[41] Although there is no absolutely reliable source for crowd size, it is clear that the most massive uprising occurred in Osaka, where approximately 232,000 city residents joined the protest. Estimates of the total number of rioters in other major cities indicate that 10,000 took to the streets in Kyoto and at least 50,000 in Tokyo.[42] When we consider that individual rallies drew crowds estimated at 20,000 to 50,000, figures for total participation appear conservative.

Crowds made up of tens of thousands of people did not, of course, act as a single unified group. Citizens' rallies often served as a central gathering from which rioters formed bands of a few hundred to several thousand to march in the streets or attack specific targets. In Kyoto, Kobe, Osaka, and other cities the roving crowds initially demonstrated self-control. Their leaders visited retail rice dealers and forced the masters of small shops to sign agreements to sell rice at a rate that the crowd considered fair, usually about twenty-five sen per shō—that is, at the level of about a year before prices skyrocketed. The merchants who agreed to the rioters' terms were forced to paste signs outside their shops announcing their intention to sell grain at between 40 and 50 percent below the going market rate. In some cases, rioters (or women gleaners who followed them) purchased rice immediately after riot leaders had forced merchants to accept the crowd's price.

Rioters responded variously to shop owners who refused to deal with them. In some cases they simply left an amount of money that they deemed sufficient to cover the cost of the rice, sacked the grain, and left. In others they threw the merchant's rice in the street and broke up the shop. Dealers who claimed depleted stocks but were later found to have hidden grain or left it with others for safekeeping usually received rough treatment.

The longer the unrest continued, the greater the tendency for the self-control demonstrated by rioters during the first days of protest to weaken. Genuine "fair prices" were no longer fixed, and rioters increasingly left only insignificant payments that fell far short of the actual value of items carried away. The goods taken also began to include items other than rice. In Osaka, for example, rioters tossed ten-sen coins in the direction of the shop owner as they made off with bags of coal valued at two yen each. In the final days of rioting in Osaka and Tokyo, police reported incidents of plain-and-simple looting. To mask their identities, looters occasionally smashed street lights or cut electric lines, throwing entire neighborhoods into darkness.[43]

A possible explanation for the escalation of property destruction and incidents of looting in the urban protests is the absence of face-to-face relationships between rioters and the targets of their attacks. In disputes in small towns and villages, which often occurred during both the day and the night and in which rioters seldom bothered to mask their identities, recognized social ties between protesters and their targets worked to moderate the rioters' actions. The almost mannerly conduct of rural rioters was notably absent in the cities. Except in those relatively few protests where burakumin played a leading role, the urban crowd was typically made up of mutually anonymous members. But personal ties softened conflict even in the city riots. In Osaka and Nagoya bands of rioters often traveled across town to protest against rice dealers or other targets outside their own neigborhoods.

Urban protests that began peaceably shifted rapidly from marches on grain brokers to armed conflict with police. In some cities rioters also used arson against grain-importing trading companies, a few retail rice stores, many police boxes, and, in Kobe, a progovernment newspaper company. These attacks, intended to destroy property, were seldom genuinely random. In Nagoya the primary target was the grain-trading district, home to major rice brokers; in Kobe it was Suzuki Shōten, the company rumored to have clandestinely influenced Terauchi's ministers to promote the company's business illegally. Rioters also attacked stores that charged excessive prices or sold inferior goods (or both). Businesses and offices of specific government agencies directly connected with rice-price regulation, especially in Tokyo, were sometimes set upon, but private homes rarely suffered attack. Ward offices, schools, and temple buildings where rice was stored for relief distribution came through the protests unscathed. Officialdom, from cabinet members to city mayors, appeared horrified by what appeared to be an unprecedented national uprising of the have-not class and the implications that such unrest held for the future peace of industrializing cities. But considering the tens of thousands involved in the city riots, the protests were far less destructive than they might have been.

The editors of Nagoya's official city history note that property destruction during the riots was largely limited to structural damage, in particular to buildings of rice dealers and to police boxes. Their summary assessment is that although the protests were massive, actual losses were light. In postriot testimony, Yamazaki Tsunekichi, a Nagoya protest leader, explained how crowd control was exerted:

> We did not encounter much resistance as we moved along, but there were incidents in which shops on both sides [of the street] had their windows smashed. [When that happened] leaders stepped in front of the crowd and gave the order "Halt!" which immediately stopped our movement forward. The goal from start to finish was to negotiate with rice dealers for lower prices. Those fellows who used force as a lesson [to merchants in general] were themselves thrashed. After that, random violence declined.[44]

Throughout the protests private individuals rarely suffered physical attack, but rioters did not spare police and troops that attempted to disband gatherings or limit the crowd's free movement. In rioting in Osaka, Kobe, and Tokyo, the assaults upon peace-keeping authorities were often unprovoked. When they simply performed their official functions, police were accused of siding with the rich against the poor and thereby became the crowd's enemy. Policemen's use of swords and guns against their fellow citizens fed the sense of outrage that manifested itself in retributory attacks on specific police stations. It made little difference to the protesters that the police and imperial troops were acting on behalf of the Taishō monarch.

Unlike rioters in the rural tumults who ignored, evaded, or attempted to enlist local policeman in their cause, city rioters actively challenged the forces of order. Their persistence is depicted in eye-witness accounts such as the following description of street fighting in Kobe on 13 August, when four civilians died of bayonet wounds:

> Finally at around eleven that night, bugles blared the arrival of a support group of two platoons. The basic strategy of these fresh troops was to drive pockets of stone-throwing rioters from side streets [along the main avenue]. To do this, the soldiers fixed bayonets to their rifles, divided into four groups, and set in place a machine gun. They then began the attack. I was lying in a ditch from where I could see the assault repeated several times. After the crowd fled, wooden sandals [geta] and hats lay scattered like leaves blown in the wind. . . . But when the crowd realized that the machine gun fired only blanks, they rallied and returned, throwing sandals and rocks. The machine gun may have fired blanks, but the bayonets were real enough. A man slashed in the thigh fell into my ditch. My white suit, already covered with mud, was now wet with blood.[45]

Despite the intensity of clashes between crowds and troops, neither a single soldier nor a policeman died at the hands of rioters. Throughout the nation, however, more than thirty civilians were reported killed. Half of them died in the city protests; the remainder were killed in coalfield labor disputes.

Issues Fueling Protest: Traitorous Merchants, Government Malfeasance, and Citizens' Rights

The specific issues that brought people into the streets for consecutive days of fighting with police and troops varied somewhat from city to city. Rioters in Nagoya, Osaka, and Tokyo, for example, seemed as concerned with central-government mismanagement and the "right" of free expression as they were with food costs. But protesters in Kyoto and Kobe, where crowds forced retail merchants to sell grain at a popularly set fair price, appeared more interested in purely economic issues. Yet such differences were more of degree than of substance because the rioters' concern over economic and noneconomic issues were usually intertwined.[46] Furthermore, the riots themselves spawned a number of subsidiary issues. In Nagoya and Tokyo the question of the limits of legitimate police force provided protesters with an additional *casus* belli. In Kyoto, Osaka, Kobe, and other cities with large burakumin settlements, the breakdown of local order also allowed indirect protests against this group's second-class citizenship.

One of the common concerns voiced by rioters everywhere was the cost of rice, the staple item in the Japanese diet. Four days before the outbreak of rioting in Tokyo a newspaper article declared that only the city's labor elite any longer made an adequate living and asserted that 90 percent of the capital city's population "faced starvation."[47] The statement greatly exaggerated conditions within Tokyo. Yet it was true that urban workers, both blue- and white-collar, found it increasingly difficult to make ends meet during the summer months of 1918. Again the economic problems faced by poor and even middle-class workers were not due to widespread unemployment. The war boom, which profited Japanese light and heavy industries, created new opportunities for city employment. But no matter how hard one worked, inflation and the rapid increase in the cost of rice outstripped any increase in daily or monthly wages. Widespread individual poverty appeared in the midst of corporate prosperity. Soeda Azenbō's song "Carefree" (*Nonki bushi*), which became popular during the summer of 1918, bitterly expressed the prevailing resentment over contemporary conditions:

> Showing magic lantern images of plundering *narikin*,
> A teacher at a broken-down school tells his pupils
> With honest work this could be you.
> He's teaching them success.
> Ah, aren't we carefree!
>
> It's because we are poor, we Japanese are great!
> Atop that, our patience is first-rate.
> Prices know no ceiling as they rise.
> But supping boiled water and rice gruel,
> We somehow survive.
> Ah, aren't we carefree!
>
> Eating Nanking rice, being eaten by Nanking bedbugs.
> Living in the likes of pig sties.
> Japanese citizens don't have voting rights,
> But we are proudly arrogant nonetheless.
> Ah, aren't we carefree.
>
> Swell, swell, our nation's might swells.
> The tyranny of the capitalists swells.
> My wife's belly swells.
> The ranks of the poor swell.
> Ah, aren't we carefree![48]

TABLE 7.   RETAIL RICE PRICES IN MAJOR
JAPANESE CITIES AS OF 9 AUGUST 1918

City	Price (sen per *shö*)
Nagoya	45.00
Kyoto	47.00
Hiroshima	48.00
Osaka	55.00
Tokyo	57.50
Kobe	60.80
Moji	67.00

SOURCE: *KSNK* 3:3.

The song's sentiments were echoed in the daily press. Newspapers in
Tokyo, Osaka, and other cities documented the widening gap between
family income and expenses by printing representative family budgets.
These reports pointed out that junior-grade civil servants, school-
teachers, low-ranking company employees, not to mention day laborers,
rickshaw pullers, cooks, and carpenters, could no longer afford to pay
their monthly rice bill.

The degree of increase in rice prices was not as severe in Nagoya as in
Kobe, Osaka, or Tokyo (see table 7). Even when urban retail prices
reached record high rates in mid-August, rice could still be obtained for
several sen less in Nagoya than elsewhere. Nevertheless, the local press
predicted that the time was fast approaching when one yen, sufficient
for purchasing four measures of grain in 1917, would no longer buy
even a single shō of rice.[49] The market tended to bear out such pessimis-
tic estimates. On 1 August the average retail cost of domestic polished
rice in Nagoya stood at thirty-five sen for one shō. By 10 August, the
day of the first massive Tsurumai rally, the price had jumped to forty-
six sen for the same amount of grain, a whopping 30 percent increase in
less than two weeks. In most cities the price of rice had doubled within a
single year. The increase was even more rapid in Kobe, Moji, and other
cities, where the cost had risen by more than 50 percent within five
weeks.[50]

Rice dealers agreed with the central government in attributing
shortages to distribution problems rather than to any absolute scarcity.
But rather than accept responsibility for shortages, they often blamed
farmers for man-made insufficiency. A Nagoya grain dealer who
made regular buying trips to rural areas presented the problem in the
following terms:

Most [dealers] make advance purchases of two or three *to* and try their hardest to fill the orders of their best customers. Before setting out to buy rice, the dealers are resigned to paying a somewhat higher price [than usual]. But there actually appears to be no rice out there. This is not only a local problem. You can go as far as Mino or Ise [and it's just the same]. Yet we know from the recently announced Ministry of Agriculture and Commerce survey of rice holdings that, even today, in every corner of the agricultural villages there are two or three farmers holding ten or more koku of rice. These farmers have already sold off 70 to 80 percent of last year's harvest, but they stubbornly refuse to sell the remainder until the new rice [crop] is in. On account of this, I go out every day, scurrying here and there to buy rice. But lately I usually return empty-handed.[51]

From early July, Aichi prefectural officials with the cooperation of the Railroad Board (Tetsudō In) moved to increase grain supplies in Nagoya by allowing the free rail shipment of rice. But ironically, this measure worsened scarcity within the city. Farmers and rice brokers used the free shipping privilege to send rice outside the prefecture to markets where they could demand a higher selling price. A report by county officials on 16 August noted that 2,000 bales of rice had been sent out of Aichi county since the elimination of grain-shipping charges. The draining of rice from the area sparked an increase in local prices in the countryside surrounding Nagoya. Seeing prices climb day by day, farmers became increasingly reluctant to release grain reserves for sale in the city.[52]

Increased shipping of rice outside the prefecture, combined with the holding of stocks in the countryside, caused a sharp fall in Nagoya's rice reserves during July. On 15 July the Tōkai and Nagoya warehouses reportedly held 77,673 bales of domestic and 21,012 of Taiwan rice. On 31 July their combined holdings of domestic had fallen by 57 percent to 44,209 bales, while the supply of Taiwan rice had increased only marginally to 23,568 bales.[53]

In Nagoya many rice dealers bought as much rice during July and August as their capital would allow. The rush to buy limited supplies resulted in a division between large and small dealers in Japan's major cities. On the one hand, major wholesalers (like one merchant who bought 600 bales of rice from Fukui prefecture) stored grain within the city in anticipation of higher prices. On the other, smaller wholesalers and retailers, whose capital proved insufficient to compete in the over-heated market, were sometimes forced out of business.[54] Smaller retailers that somehow managed to survive the harsh market conditions attempted to protect their limited stock as long as possible. Some refused to sell to anyone but their best customers. Others mixed foreign grain with domestic, adulterated the grain with chaff, or limited the amount they would sell to their customers. In several city riots customers attacked retailers who had resorted to such supply-stretching methods.

In Nagoya rioters blamed both farmers and merchants for the high rice prices. Speakers at the 10 August Tsurumai rally presented the following analysis of the problem:

> The soaring cost of rice seems to be something that can't be helped. We raise a commotion and say that the government is rotten. But [high prices] are caused by certain market cornerers and rich farmers who hoard rice. First of all, Japan is not a country lacking in rice. What we must first do is punish those seeking to corner the market and hoard grain.[55]

> In short, the wrong-doers are the government merchants [seishō] and the hoarding landlords. [They] have forgotten any sense of obligation [on] in their pursuit of "profitism" [mokeshugi]. If we wait any longer to chastise these groups we will surely starve. Everyone, rise up! If we dilly-dally we'll be run over by a cart loaded with rice bales.[56]

Despite the crowd's apparent awareness of the shared responsibility for expensive rice, it was the large urban rice dealers who took the brunt of the rioters' attacks because there was little that city dwellers could do to check rural rice hoarding effectively. They had neither the time nor the resources to seek out "greedy landlords." Even at the peak of city rioting, rioters diligently pursued their daytime jobs and only joined street protests during their free evening hours. In any case, the urban rioters had no specific idea as to the identity of their rural enemies. Speakers at the mass rallies talked much about dishonest rich farmers and landlords. But the words had an abstract, symbolic sound to them. When the speechmakers and petitioners proposed specific and concrete plans to deal with high prices, these city people usually failed to present any clear program for dealing with rural hoarders.

Urban rice merchants, particularly major brokers like those concentrated in Nagoya's Komeya-chō, provided convenient and identifiable targets. But more than convenience led rioters to focus on the rice dealers. Speakers at citizens' rallies castigated grain dealers for their self-serving interference with the supply-and-demand relationship between rural producers and city consumers. In Nagoya brokers were described as "parasites" and "evil germs" that produced nothing but discord throughout society. To chastise this enemy crowds repeatedly attempted to break into grain-trading firms in Nagoya, Kobe, Moji, and Osaka.

An "exploitation-immiseration" explanation, one that social scientists often use in accounting for mass uprisings in rapidly industrializing cities, is somewhat helpful in understanding the rioters' targeting of grain wholesalers and brokers. According to this theory, urban popular protest occurs

> as a reaction to the spread of exploitative capitalist property relations which implied an actual reduction in opportunities and well-being for masses of people. Falling real wages and the decline of independent producers are two possible indices of exploitation and immiseration at work.[57]

On several points, the Japanese city riots bear out this interpretation. City populations generally suffered from a sharp decline in real wages during the period from 1914 through 1918. In the Nagoya riots craftsmen and traders ("independent producers") constituted the main force behind the street protests. But economic desperation, perhaps a necessary "cause," was not, of itself, a sufficient reason for the riots. As we shall see in the discussion of the background of city rioters, paupers did not fill the ranks of protesting crowds. Moreover, even though economic distress was clearly present, the causes for it were linked to an understanding that popular pressure could alleviate the situation. Protest was not solely the result of high prices for rice, as can be seen in action taken by urban rioters against realtors and *narikin.*

In city riots crowds expanded their attacks beyond rice merchants to include other "economic" enemies, such as residential landlords, pawnbrokers, loan sharks, and real estate agencies. Many of the incidents during the 1918 unrest were grounded in long-standing grievances. In 1912 Kure residents had formed a tenants protection association to force lower housing rents. After three years of protest and negotiation, the association won a significant rollback in rents. In June 1918, when city landlords attempted to increase rents by as much as 65 percent, members of the association once again mounted a movement for rent reductions. Although the precise role of the association as an organized group in the rice riots is unknown, it is clear that rents as well as rice provided a source of conflict in the city protests.[58]

Demand in excess of supply accounted for both housing and grain shortages. Japan's urban population had doubled from 5 to 10 million between the turn of the century and 1918, a rate at which new construction could not keep pace with the flow of newcomers into the city. Kobe was hit particularly hard by the housing shortage. From 1914 to 1917 an influx of workers into Kobe's shipbuilding, steel, and light industries caused the city's population to balloon by 22.1 percent, a growth rate higher than any other Japanese city during this period. As a result, housing for Kobe's 600,000 residents was woefully inadequate. In 1918, although more than 33,000 new residents crowded into the city, only 4,664 new housing units were built. Based on an estimated occupancy of five people for each unit, the new construction covered only about one-third of the demand. In 1919 the vacancy rate for city housing was virtually zero; of Kobe's 120,000 apartments and houses, only 84 were reported vacant. The strong demand for housing made it easy for landlords and real estate agencies to demand high rents. In some areas of the city, tenants complained that their rents had doubled in 1918.[59]

Shortages in Osaka and Tokyo were as bad as those in Kobe. By 1919 the demand for housing in Osaka was estimated to have exceeded supply by 50,000 units; between 1912 and 1921, rents had doubled. An annual report on housing in Osaka observed that the situation was tantamount to a virtual "denial of residency rights" (ijūken kyohi). In Tokyo the record demand for housing was considered a crisis, not only because of the shortage but also because middlemen unscrupulously exploited renters. The late Meiji period and the opening years of Taishō saw residential tenants and small businesses subject to what was popularly, and aptly, called "earthquake trading" (jishin baibai). During these years land speculation caused urban real estate prices to double and ownership to change hands quickly. When deeds were transferred, the residential or business tenant—those atop the land—had few rights to challenge demands from new landlords for increased rents or eviction. When ownership shifted, the basis for business and community life shook, bringing disastrous consequences. These were particularly dire to small-scale businesses and longtime residents whose economic existence depended on a loyal clientele with whom, over the decades, they had developed business ties based on familiarity and trust. The Japan Lawyers Association was frequently involved in suits and political lobbying to protect both residential and business tenants threatened by land speculation. But their attempts to prompt legislation that would protect residency rights did little to stem abuses.[60] One study notes that by 1919 "illegal activity became so rampant among real estate agents that the Bureau of Social Affairs of the new municipal government set up a special office for directing home-seekers to houses and rooms for rent, a function assumed by each ward office later."[61]

During the Kobe uprising crowds of rioters attacked and destroyed the offices of the Heishinkan agency (see fig. 6). Seventy percent of all Kobe housing was rented, and the Heishinkan managed more than 50 percent of the city's rental housing. The company was notorious for abusing its monopolistic control of the real estate market. Renters complained that the Heishinkan charged high service fees from building owners and at the same time demanded rents from tenants in excess of what the landlords stipulated. The company was also widely resented for its involvement in the high-interest-loan trade and for using policemen as dunners and bill collectors.[62] One rioter, who was sentenced to prison for joining in the attack on the agency, testified at his trial:

> The apartment I rented was managed by the Heishinkan. At first the rent was 3.80 yen. But . . . was [soon] raised to 5 yen. I was selected as a tenants' representative to negotiate with the agency. I asked for a reduction to 4.70 yen [but nothing came of it]. People in general thought that the Heishinkan was simply merciless.[63]

Rioters criticized the Heishinkan's willingness to gouge tenants in the same terms they used against grain dealers. They viewed the company as but another middleman group unfairly taking advantage of scarcity. As crowds surrounded the agency's main office on 12 August Harufuji Otokichi, a dockworker later sentenced to eighteen months for rioting, addressed the gathering, saying, "Rice is expensive because the evil rice dealers boost the price. Rents are high because of the likes of the Heishinkan. We should wipe them out." The crowd immediately followed his advice.[64]

Popular resentment aimed at rental agents was a specific manifestation of general ill will against *narikin*. As commonly used, the term referred to a wide variety of entrepreneurs who had prospered during the war years in everything from one-man concerns to major enterprises such as Suzuki Shōten. People labeled *narikin* were popularly viewed as having become wealthy not by dint of their own efforts but as a fortuitous consequence of the European war. Many rioters also believed, with some justification, that the phenomenal success of their companies had been achieved by keeping wages low, taking advantage of scarcity, and ignoring the resulting inflation-caused deterioration in living standards. In short, rioters attacked the unfair sharing of the fruits of Japan's industrial success. While the rioters' actions represented a general attack on the *narikin*, speakers at mass rallies made more specific accusations. Sunaga Inosuke, a day laborer who spoke at a Tsurumai Park rally, argued:

> Citizens of Imperial Japan include the rich like the Mitsuis and the Iwasakis and those like us, the poor living off their day wages. Ours is a country of equals. We observe the same laws. The rich and the poor have the same rights. Since the outbreak of the European war many industries have rapidly developed, bringing their owners tremendous profits. But in contrast [to these rich people], our income is extremely low. We must therefore press those men of wealth [*shihonshi*] to increase wages by 30 to 40 percent. [This is how to deal with] the rice problems.[65]

Speakers at other rallies demanded that the directors of "monopolistic companies" (*dokusen kaisha*) accept a degree of responsibility for the riots by making generous donations to relief efforts.[66]

As we saw in the destruction of the Heishinkan, rioters also sought to punish the *narikin* directly by destroying their property. The most spectacular of these attacks occurred in Kobe, where thousands of rioters surrounded the offices of Suzuki Shōten, the largest of the government-designated grain importers. Within minutes the building was set ablaze as onlooking crowds cheered "banzai" and struggled against fire fighters sent to put out the rising flames (see fig. 7). In other cities as well, rioters attempted to destroy Suzuki Shōten buildings and even attacked subsidiary enterprises owned by this symbol of the *narikin*.[67]

Not all of the urban rioters' assaults were directed against major companies. In some cities people who indirectly benefited from the *narikin* "life style," which was typified by ostentatious free spending and fast living, also became targets of attack. In Kobe, Osaka, and other cities crowds rampaged through entertainment districts. Rioters harassed geisha and broke the windows of expensive restaurants, bars, movie theaters, brothels, and mansions of the rich. The crowds's urge at times appeared to be toward a kind of crude leveling, in which the definition of *narikin* was stretched to include anyone who made a comfortable living or was connected with *narikin*. Such popular resentment even led to attacks on streetcars. Since many rioters could afford trolley fare no more than they could the more lavish entertainment enjoyed by richer city residents, not even mechanical manifestations of the nouveaux riches escaped attack.[68]

Action against *narikin* again points to the applicability of the exploitation-immiseration argument as well as explanations based on "rising expectations." But the rioters' acts against *narikin* also suggest a demand for full-fledged citizenship. Grounds for both economic and political resentment were widespread and obvious. Japan had at long last become a creditor nation in 1918, yet many of its individual citizens were in debt and struggling to earn their daily rice. Only the *narikin* seemed to benefit from government policy; only "hoarding landlords" and the nouveaux riches possessed the wealth requisite to obtain voting rights. At the citizens' rallies, speaker after speaker asked rhetorically who had provided the wealth of the newly rich that gave them rights over common people. From the crowd's standpoint, the answer was, of course, the great mass of laboring people who continued to be both economically and politically second-class citizens.

The city rioters' actions and rhetoric suggests that they held the central government ultimately responsible for the predations of grain dealers and *narikin*. In mass rallies in Nagoya, Tokyo, and Osaka speakers attacked the Terauchi government as culpable not only for its muddle-headed grain policy but for actively conspiring with rice importers to force up domestic grain prices. Kubota Hisao, one of the Tsurumai speakers, presented his indictment of the Terauchi cabinet in the following terms:

> Hasn't the Terauchi cabinet bought up 8,000 koku of rice and and commisioned certain traitorous merchants [*kansho*] to export grain overseas? That is why rice is expensive. Didn't Gotō Shinpei conspire with one of those merchants [i.e., Suzuki Shōten's Kaneko Naokichi] to export 45,000 koku of wheat flour? Isn't this why rice dealers everywhere are involved in market cornering? . . . We must use public opinion [*yoron*] to smash the Terauchi cabinet.[69]

One of the rioters' chief aims was to bring down the Terauchi cabinet and replace it with a government that would protect the commonweal. As Kubota noted in his address, rioters viewed public opinion as a potent weapon for changing political policy. It was, moreover, one of the only weapons available to the great majority of Japanese citizens still without the franchise in 1918. With no voice in electing the national government, protesters sought to change Japan's national leadership by exerting pressure from below. City residents saw little alternative to taking actions that the organized political parties, which appeared more intent on sharing power with "transcendent" bureaucrats and military men than with commoners, refused to take.

In Osaka the city's branch of the Kokumintō sponsored the first citizens' rally to attack the Terauchi government's economic policies.

But after a vociferous crowd had gathered, intent more on discussing livelihood problems than on partisan wrangling, party leaders completely disassociated their organization from the protests. The withdrawal of party sponsorship, however, did not lessen popular enthusiasm for forcing political action on the problem of rice prices. In several incidents individuals from the crowd stepped in where party men feared to tread. At the height of the Osaka riots, for example, a citizens' rally appointed a three-man committee to meet with the governor of Osaka prefecture (*fu*) and the city's mayor. The conference between the popularly selected crowd and municipal officials reveals how the riots were viewed both by protesters and by local officials.

The committee, which consisted of a university student and two others selected at an indoor mass meeting, was at first refused an audience with Governor Hayashi and Mayor Ikegami. But their persistence at the entrance to the governor's official residence paid off, and after being thoroughly searched, they were allowed to state their case before the two highest local officials and the city police chief. Governor Hayashi was especially solicitous, pouring cold beer for his guests and commenting sympathetically on their exhausted appearance. After the required courtesies had been exchanged, Hirano Itarō, the student, was allowed to make his appeal. He explained that the situation was critical and that only the public fixing of rice prices could ease the desperation of Osaka's million citizens. Hayashi responded that Osaka officials, too, were vexed by the issue of rice prices. "Nevertheless," he added, "the fundamental problem falls within the jurisdiction of Terauchi-kun and Nakakōji-kun [that is, the prime minister and the minister of agriculture and commerce]. It is beyond the realm of my authority. [Fixing a public price] is absolutely impossible." The committee members accepted this explanation but continued to press the governor and the mayor to at least convey the idea of mandated prices to the central authorities. The officials promised to do all they could. After the discussion had ended, policemen waiting outside attempted to arrest the petitioners on the spot. But the Osaka police chief intervened and they were allowed to leave the governor's mansion, only to be arrested later as they made their way back to the rally.[70]

Despite the obvious close cooperation among local officials, city police, and mobilized troops, speakers at mass rallies seldom attributed ultimate responsibility for high prices to city or prefectural representatives. If anything, urban crowds expressed a peculiar kind of nationalism, in which they identified with local officials and the emperor but regarded the Terauchi cabinet as inimical to the interests of city dwellers. Kawamura Enji, another Tsurumai speaker, captured the mixture of nationalism and antigovernment sentiment in his 11 August speech:

> Has not the national prestige of Imperial Japan been promoted abroad in wars against China and Russia? Has not that been achieved by battling to plant the flag of the rising sun [*nisshoku*]? Everyone here represents Nagoya's flag of the rising sun. We are citizens in whose veins runs the blood of the Meiji emperor. But today, because of the soaring price of rice, we find it hard to live. This situation is due to the worthlessness of the present cabinet's rice regulation policy. That policy has allowed dishonest merchants to corner rice. The present government must be brought down. For the time being, however, we must reduce rice prices. There is no way to achieve this other than appealing to the mayor and governor. In the event our appeal is unsuccessful, then we must bear down on the traitorous merchants. But you must not use violence. To do so would be a stain on the honor of the cautious people gathered here.[71]

The theme of appealing to the local government to achieve the rioters' aims was one repeated daily during the Nagoya riots. Some of the speakers at mass rallies, however, were less than optimistic about the effectiveness of petitioning city and prefectural officials. Several Tsurumai orators described the mayor and councilmen as nothing more than the people's "chief clerks" (*bantō*). They further argued that the rice-price problem created by the Terauchi cabinet and grain dealers was just too big for the clerks to handle.

Yet even those critical of the ability of local officials to deal with the problem did not suggest that local representatives were responsible for shortages. Nor did rioters blame the emperor for the errors of his ministers. Protesters at the Hibiya rally in Tokyo shouted slogans calling for the resignation of the Terauchi cabinet, the sacking of the minister of agriculture, and the smashing of the *narikin*. But not a word was spoken against the emperor. In fact, speakers tended to justify their attacks on rice dealers by suggesting that they were carried out on behalf of the monarch. In the words of a Nagoya rioter:

> At bottom, the soaring cost of rice is a crime perpetrated by the Terauchi cabinet. It is a matter of the utmost urgency that we act as soon as possible to bring down this government that has violated the will of the people. . . . Our emperor is greatly saddened because his subjects have [suffered] because of high rice prices. Like all of us, he is troubled by the traitorous merchants. . . . Many such merchants are right here in Nagoya. We must punish [them].[72]

Speakers at rallies recommended attacks against merchants and *nari-kin* only if appeals to local leaders proved ineffective. But crowds often moved against both the central government and grain merchants regardless of relief efforts undertaken by city officials. Following citizens' rallies, rioters in Nagoya and Tokyo repeatedly organized large groups to protest at government offices and rice-trading districts. Police lines in both cities usually prevented crowds from reaching the main targets of their respective protests. In Tokyo, however, rioters were able to stone the windows of the Ministry of Agriculture and Commerce building as well as attack the home of the minister of agriculture and commerce.[73]

Rioters criticized attempts by police and troops to prevent demonstrations and gatherings as interference in their legitimate right of popular protest. This was most evident in Nagoya, where rioting took on a strong antipolice coloring after the first few nights of unrest (see fig. 8). Speakers at Tsurumai rallies condemned alleged police excesses as acts carried out by the "agents" not of the emperor and his subjects but of the Terauchi cabinet and *narikin*.[74] As police stepped up measures to prevent gatherings and as the crowd's rhetoric and actions became more extreme, speakers at mass meetings held the police rather than protesters responsible for escalating the incident. A postal worker at one rally accused the police of failing to realize that the age of feudalism had ended and that Japanese citizens now possessed "freedom of speech" (*genron no jiyū*). He attempted to prove his point by claiming that police had ignored the civil rights of "peaceful" protesters, who sought only to "negotiate" with rice dealers.[75] Other speakers encouraged protesters to resist police attempts to suppress their movement:

> Last night we went to Hijiebashi in order to negotiate peacefully with the dishonest merchants in Komeya-chō. But the police, misunderstanding [our actions], not only used force against us but bared their swords, wounding old people, women, and children. Nagoya people have no self-respect [*ikiji nashi yatsu*]. If they had they would reach their goal.[76]

Crowds who listened to the antipolice speech responded that they indeed possessed self-respect and would follow crowd leaders in fighting to achieve their "goal." Although rioters voiced respect for the emperor, they had none for police or imperial troops. As they had done when speakers targeted the government and rice merchants for attack, rioters now moved against the police (see fig. 9).

The expansion of relief efforts did little immediately to defuse the widespread resentment against the police. One speaker at the Ōsu Kan-

non temple rally criticized discount rice sales based on private donations as inferior to the public setting of grain prices. But it was not only
the tokenism inherent in the aid measures that angered him. From his
perspective, the worst feature of the relief measure was the entrusting
of the police with dispensing the discount coupons. To the Tsurumai
speaker, receiving aid from the hands of the police represented nothing
more than a repressive measure intended to shame unruly citizens.[77]

In general, the political concerns expressed by the 1918 rioters
strongly resembled those evident in the 1905 Hibiya riots and the 1913
Constitutional Protection Movement. In the earlier protests rioters called
for the resignation of the cabinet, criticized individual ministers for mis-
handling national administration or ignoring the popular will, and accused government officials of condoning police brutality.[78] Although
the 1918 riots were more concerned with domestic than with international issues, urban rice rioters made essentially the same demands, criticisms, and accusations. In 1918 as well as in 1905, rioters also claimed
the emperor as their ally. It was to him that speakers at mass "citizens'
rallies" appealed for the removal of allegedly incompetent ministers,
and it was in his name that they justified their sometimes violent acts. In
a series of urban disturbances in the years after the Hibiya riots of 1905
in Tokyo, city dwellers sometimes attempted to petition the city or prefectural government for redress just as rioters did in 1918.

The practice of overtly political urban protest did not have the long
tradition of the almost mannerly give-and-take evident in the Toyama
riots; Nagoya, in fact, was not a hotbed of popular protest during the
Tokugawa or the Meiji period.[79] Instead of looking to a more distant
past, urban protesters took the Hibiya riots, the 1912 and 1913 "political crisis," and the 1914 Nagoya streetcar riots as precedents. The
rioters' actions in 1918 as well as in 1905 clearly indicated whom urban
crowds considered inimical to their interests. When police or troops
blocked their protest, crowds turned on the forces of order, inflicting
physical injury and destroying police property.[80] As an expression of
democratic nationalism that demanded respect for the person and the
rights of the individual and pledged loyalty to the emperor but not to
unpopular policies or policy makers, the 1918 city riots represented an
emerging convention of avowedly political protest.[81]

This convention, however, did not see revolution as a solution to the
urban rioters' problems. Official fears notwithstanding, rioters made
absolutely no attempt to establish some kind of alternative to Japan's
imperial system. Speakers at Nagoya rallies lambasted farmers, mer-

chants, and entrepreneurs as being un-Japanese (*hikokumin*), castigated elected politicians and appointed officials as being no more than replaceable clerks (*bantō*), and called for an expanded movement to "unify the spirit of the nation's people" (*kokumin no seishin o itchi suru*).[82] Yet no one questioned the right of the Mitsui family to own property or the emperor to rule through his cabinet. Quite the contrary, as speakers at mass rallies made abundantly clear, rioters justified their actions in the name of emperor and country. But a proviso was implied: economic wealth should be more equally distributed and His Majesty's ministers must be "loyal," something that they could prove only by following the will of the ruled.

Although speakers at citizens' rallies sometimes used traditionally moralistic rhetoric, the massive gatherings themselves were a new and modern phenomenon rarely seen before the Taishō period. In attacking the Terauchi government and recommending a government-set price for rice that would be adjusted to inflationary conditions and real income levels, rioters used a modern political vocabulary alongside their appeals to traditional morality. Freedom of expression, government mismanagement, citizens' rights, the rejection of transcendent cabinets—these were the concerns repeatedly expressed in the citizens' rallies.

Aside from following the rather schizophrenic official view of the riots, which declared that the protests were apolitical while hinting that they represented the handiwork of a worldwide revolutionary socialist conspiracy, few central-government officials were willing to attribute conscious political motives to the rioters. Yet the urban protests were a very clear attack on the incumbent political regime. Their criticism of policy and policy makers was, in the words of one rioter, a legitimate expression of "twentieth century" freedoms.

Rioters and Citizens:
City Protest and Political Integration

Police and trial records provide the most reliable indication of who took part in the city riots. Admittedly, using such sources poses problems. Massive crowds made it difficult for police to distinguish active rioters from casual onlookers. Consequently, arrests were made on a catch-as-catch-can basis as police rounded up those who offered the least resistance. Arrests were often made after the riots had ended, a tactic that led detainees to complain that they had been unjustly taken into custody simply because they had been caught up in the crowds or had happened to be in the wrong place at the wrong time.

A second problem with arrest records as an indicator of participation in protests arises from the government's strict attitude toward rioters, whether real or suspected. The urban riots represented an unprecedented breakdown in civil order that officials naturally did not wish to see repeated. To deter any future use of violent mass protest that might test and, more important, reveal the weakness of state authority, central-government and local officials used stern measures against riot suspects. The fear that "apolitical" violence might escalate into political terror—as it seemed to have done in so many nations in 1918—was widespread among central-government officials. Even Yoshino Sakuzō and similarly liberal intellectuals, who supported an expansion of democratic freedoms, saw rioting as raising the specter of class war.

During the city uprisings such fears led police and prosecutors to rely heavily on circumstantial evidence to justify the detention and indictments of riot suspects. An excess of rice in the family bin or receipts signed by merchants who had agreed to sell rice at a discounted price became damning evidence of complicity in the protests that justified at least temporary detention. If goods had been received, the recipient could be charged with theft or extortion, even if "fair price" money had been left.[83]

Preliminary investigation by court prosecutors reduced the number of riot suspects indiscriminately rounded up during and after the riots. In Nagoya, where more than a thousand people were initially detained for rioting, only a little over two hundred were finally prosecuted for joining the protests. The proportion remained fairly constant in most other major cities; only one out of every four or five rioters detained was eventually tried.[84] Nevertheless, even after prosecutors had reduced the pool of those indicted, many suspects were found guilty not because they actually took part in riotous acts but because the central government's deterrence policy required that all accused be harshly punished. The government's attitude was made clear by Suzuki Kisaburō, vice-minister of justice:

> Stern punishment is the only way to deal with the recent incidents of rioting. Some rioters set out to burn and pillage. Others, brazenly and in broad daylight, committed crimes little different from robbery. In view of these acts, there is no basis for sympathizing with such people. Other rioters perhaps did not intend to act violently. They thought that they would merely watch the action and in so doing became mixed into the crowd. Still others, overwhelmed by the riotous mood, lost their heads in the heat of the moment and joined in stone throwing. Nonetheless, we should not sympathize with these people either. If we overlook the ones who committed crimes because they were controlled by the psychology of the crowd, we will foster the

TABLE 8.   OCCUPATIONAL BREAKDOWN OF PEOPLE
INDICTED FOR RIOTING IN FOUR MAJOR CITIES
(percentages)

City	Laborer	Crafts	Factory	Sales	Other[a]	None
Nagoya	20	22	26	11	17	3
Osaka	33	22	12	20	22	0
Tokyo	21	40	9	9	16	4
Kobe	23	25	22	14	13	2
Kyoto	47	18	19	12	5	0

SOURCES: NSNK 1:252–63 and 3:320–35; Yoshimura, "Kansai ni okeru kome sōdō," 23; Abe, "Hyogo-ken ka no kome sōdō," 7; and Matsuo, "Kyoto chihō no kome sōdō," 134.

NOTE: Percentage totals equal less than 100 because of rounding.

[a] "Other" includes intellectuals (interi such as journalists and teachers), farmers, fishermen, entertainers, and others whose occupation was unclear.

notion that violence can be used to achieve the goals of such people. In the end national order will be destroyed.[85]

Despite the obvious flaws in arrest and trial records, a degree of homogeneity is evident among groups detained and prosecuted for rioting in Japan's major cities. Along with the testimony of those who admitted their involvement in the riots, later interviews, press reports, and the official record provide a general, if imperfect, profile of urban protesters.

According to lists of people tried for rioting, most city rioters were twenty- to thirty-year-old males who worked in traditional trades. A sprinkling of newspaper reporters, students, and government employees were included among those tried in Tokyo, and a number of skilled factory workers among those prosecuted in Nagoya and Kobe. Very few of the unemployed (or those who reported that they had no occupation) took part in the riots (see table 8).

Although the occupational background of riot suspects is well documented, less is known about their individual income levels and educational attainments. In general, Japanese studies refer to the urban rioters as "people of slender means" (saimin) or, less poetically, as indigent and poorly educated members of the lower class. The definition is lacking in precision, but Matsuo Takayoshi suggests what the term implies in his analysis of 289 rioters prosecuted in Kyoto (203 from Kyoto City). According to Matsuo's research, 52.9 percent of the rioters earned thirty yen or less per month, an income level that allowed for little more than subsistence. They also tended to be poorly educated. Although 61 percent of Kyoto rioters had attended at least a year or two of elementary school, 19 percent had received no formal education and none had attended middle or high school.

Although representative of Kyoto city, the group studied by Matsuo is atypical of city rioters throughout the nation because of the high proportion of burakumin (48 percent) among those arrested in Kyoto.[86] It is also unusual in that it included more than twice as many (47 percent) unskilled laborers among those arrested than in Nagoya, Tokyo, Osaka, or Kobe. In Kyoto the riot suspects' burakumin status may have made them *saimin*; but generally, *saimin* status did not automatically transform the poor into rioters.

An analysis of arrest and prosecution records from other cities provides a different profile, which indicates that rioters represented not the riffraff but a stable cross section of the cities' populations. They were not a disintegrating fringe group, but just the opposite: urban residents with family roots, old or freshly put down, integrating themselves into new or changing circumstances of the industrializing city.

Figures for nationwide prosecution show that 81 percent of the people who faced trial for riot-related crimes were males aged twenty to forty-nine; a full two-thirds of the 8,185 individuals for whom prosecution records exist were aged twenty to thirty-nine. These national proportions parallel statistics for those arrested in city riots. In other words, the participants in riots were not misguided youths but mature male wage earners and heads of households.

The arrested rioters' *honseki*, or registration of permanent or original domicile, also indicates that they were not part of a floating, disoriented population. Many were, of course, new to the city. But this should take nothing from the new resident's identity as a city person or, more simply, a citizen in the term's fullest implications. Deciding to change one's *honseki* was a momentous step. As Irene Taeuber has observed, a transfer of permanent domicile "involved the relations of individual to family or of branch to main family [thus] decisions to transfer *honseki* from areas of ancestral origin to areas of permanent residence were not made casually or quickly."[87] People who changed their domicile registration were putting down new roots.

It was not, as modernization studies sometimes suggest, the alienated sojourner who joined in the 1918 riots.[88] In Nagoya we in fact see a positive correlation between permanent domicile registration and length and intensity of protest. In that city, where riots lasted longer and citizens' rallies were larger—and rice prices cheaper—than in any other urban area, nearly 70 percent of 210 riot suspects had either Nagoya city or Aichi prefecture domicile registration. In Kobe, Japan's fastest growing city in 1918 and the scene of violent street fighting and the fire attack on Suzuki Shōten company headquarters, 56 percent of those indicted for riot-related crimes had domicile registration within the city or Hyogo prefecture.[89]

Historical documents do not indicate whether the suspect's *honseki* was old or new, but they more than suggest that the city residents were keenly interested in issues that touched on their identity as urban citizens. It was ironic when speakers at city rallies excoriated "hoarding farmers," because they themselves may well have immigrated only recently from the countryside. But the irony was more apparent than real. It did not take long for the newcomer to the city to shed all but a sentimental attachment to the countryside as he or she adjusted to the new realities of urban life.[90]

The city riots in fact opened up new political possibilities for those who joined in them. Several protesters found that the riots made them aware of what could be achieved by mass-based movements, and it is easy to understand how pressure from below energized movements for expanded suffrage, women's rights, and free labor organization after 1918. An example of how protest could move an individual into the political process, rather than signal alienation from it, is seen in the career of Yamazaki Tsunekichi. An itinerant tinker at the time of the riots, Yamazaki had been one of the first to speak at the Tsurumai Park rallies. His involvement, however, came about indirectly:

> At the time I was an artisan, shouldering my tools as I made my rounds repairing metal buckets and the like. I worked at public hydrants where groups of housewives gathered. There the talk was of nothing but the high cost of rice. I especially recall hearing rumors that Mitsui, Suzuki, and other grain importers charged with bringing Taiwan rice to the main islands had dumped rice into the sea to bring prices higher at home. That made me angry. I read in the August 10 newspaper that there would be a citizens' meeting at Tsurumai Park concerned with the rice price problem.[91]

The newspaper, the *Nagoya shinbun*, was financially controlled by opposition party Kenseikai members and took a critical stand against the Terauchi government before and after the riots.[92] Despite the paper's appeals for mass protest, Yamazaki did not rush to the park. After working a long day in oppressive heat, he decided to rest at home. But his stifling room did not permit sleep, and later in the evening he found himself wandering toward the park. Once at the rally he discovered that although a large crowd had gathered, no one came forward to speak. Screwing up his courage, he stood up. In his first speech he explained by way of self-introduction that his original home district was Kōchi, the birthplace of Japan's first political party, the Jiyūtō. He had only recently come to the city, but as a citizen of Nagoya he felt justified in speaking out against hoarding farmers.

Yamazaki not only spoke. He also joined the leaders of the crowd after it was pushed from the park. He recalled that although the self-appointed leaders were young, they were not gamblers or yakuza-type gangsters. He also noted that this was the first time that he had ever experienced the thrill of standing at the forefront of a mass movement (*Sono toki jibun wa hajimete taishū undō no riidaa to naru omoshirosa o shitta*). After his initiation, Yamazaki joined in the riots every night. He spoke at the Ōsu Kannon temple as well as at Tsurumai rallies and took part in clashes at police barricades in Komeya-chō. In his words, he had "all of a sudden" (*itsu no manika*) become a riot leader.

About a week after the riots had ended, he was arrested. Police interrogators repeatedly accused him of being a socialist agitator, to which he replied that, on the contrary, he was a loyal imperial subject. Despite his insistence that he was loyal to the emperor and Japan, his participation in the protests resulted in police detention pending possible indictment. As he later recalled, this was a valuable experience. The riots had given him a taste of the power and possibilities of mass political action; being thrown into jail impressed him with the inequality inherent in Japanese society. Although he was indicted and tried, Yamazaki was, to his surprise, found not guilty and released. But instead of causing him to be content with his individual good fortune and to shy away from further political involvement, the experience served as the beginning of what became a lifelong political career.

In 1920, when *Nagoya shinbun* reporters led in forming the Nagoya Laborers Association (Nagoya Rōdō Kyōkai), Yamazaki joined as one of the group's first members. Later he himself organized the Nagoya Free Laborers Union (Nagoya Jiyū Rōdōsha Kumiai). His efforts at worker organization soon brought him once again into conflict with the police. For encouraging a sandal-makers strike he was arrested for violating Article 17 of the Peace Preservation Law. He was again found innocent. On his release he continued to organize craft workers. In the antileftist terror following the 1923 Kantō earthquake and as a result of pressure exerted by Nagoya authorities, the Nagoya Free Laborers

Union was forced to disband. Yamazaki temporarily toned down his
labor activities, although he continued to make his home available to
the city's near-destitute labor organizers. It was at this juncture that the
once self-avowed "imperialist" moved from strict labor organization
into proletarian politics.

From the mid-1920s to 1927 he worked behind the scenes in the
Labor-Farmers Party. In 1927 he moved from the shadows to run successfully on the party's ticket for a seat in the Aichi Prefectural Assembly, a position he attempted to use as a springboard for election to the
national Diet. Although his bid for national office was frustrated during
the prewar years, he continued to be politically active as a member of
his party's central executive committee. During the 1930s leftist parties
were disbanded, and Yamazaki was sent to the Manchurian front for
the duration of the war. In 1946 he was finally elected to national office
and reelected twice after that, as a Japan Socialist Party candidate.[93]
Yamazaki's rise was, of course, exceptional. But other riot leaders, such
as Hirano Itarō and Yamamoto Kenzō, met with government officials
during the protests and engaged in organized politics thereafter.[94] They
were part of the urban crowd, representative of its interests and backed
by its members, who increasingly supported labor organization and
mass politics in the years after the riots.

The people who stood behind Yamazaki and similar activists were
neither destitute nor socially marginal. A survey of the backgrounds of
thirty-three riot suspects arrested in Osaka indicates that the protesters
were family-supporting men long employed in traditional trades.[95]
Although all were far from wealthy, most testified that they had enough
to get by. Several went so far as to describe their income level as "middling," an assertion not simply made out of face-saving pride because
one-third of the suspects had savings accounts, a few owned their own
homes, and one even possessed rental property.

In the police and prosecutor's survey of "character and conduct"
(*seishitsu gyōjō*) and "local popular opinion," (that is, *sehyō*, or "reputation"), the most common comments were that the individual suspect
was "diligent" (*kinben*) at his work and possessed a generally upright character. This estimation was supported by an investigation of previous
criminal offenses. For two-thirds of the those arrested, their involvement in the riots was their first brush with the law. Of the eleven who
did have records, eight had been arrested for minor gambling offenses.

The blanket *saimin* designation, which connotes pauperism, slums,
and marginality, is also contradicted by the occupational background

of Nagoya suspects. Forty-eight percent of those indicted were workers in skilled crafts and trades (see table 9). Included were laborers in the region's famous pottery and industrial ceramics factories, blacksmiths, foundry workers, and carpenters. They were not employed in the occupations associated with skilled heavy industry, but neither were they unskilled laborers. More important, crafts- and tradespeople represented the great majority of the work force, far outnumbering skilled workers in new industries. Although the wartime boom had brought more workers to Japanese cities than at any period before 1914, the labor force in cities such as Osaka and Nagoya was concentrated not in large-scale, mechanized factories but in smaller workshops that relied on skill. In Kobe, for example, 96 percent of city factories in 1914 employed between five and ninety-five workers. A survey of Osaka in 1924 further indicates that of 18,900 factories, 83 percent were enterprises with five or fewer workers.[96]

Such workers, employed individually or in small shops, did not have even the modicum of protection afforded workers in large enterprises under the 1911 Factory Law. The law, which went into effect in 1916, limited working hours for women and children, mandated at least two days off per month, and curtailed work after midnight. The measure was ridden with exceptions that allowed easy evasion. Moreover, by the time this cautious measure was finally implemented, it was already irrelevant for many major industries. Large firms, especially zaibatsu enterprises employing five hundred or more workers, had already gone beyond the law's minimum provisions so as to retain a loyal work force. Yet those employed outside heavy industry, a group encompassing a majority of workers in every city, neither received significant legal protection nor benefited from the better conditions provided by large enterprises. The factory law itself applied only to factories with power-driven machinery, to shops that employed at least ten workers, or to workplaces deemed hazardous. According to Yazaki Takeo, "the total number of factories, including workshops employing less than five workers, is reported to have reached 1,551,000 in 1919, in which case the factory law would have applied to only 1.6 percent of all factories."[97]

People in the traditional crafts and trades, with neither workplace bargaining leverage nor reliable employment security and with the feeling that they were the ones who suffered when prices spiraled, sought redress in street protests. Japanese government officials and party leaders lamented this breakdown in worker discipline. Yet given the

TABLE 9.   OCCUPATIONS OF PEOPLE INDICTED FOR RIOTING IN NAGOYA

Laborers (20%)

Occupation	Count
Hired laborer	24
Day laborer	11
Construction worker	2
Other	4
TOTAL	41

Craftsmen / Tradespeople (22%)

Occupation	Count
Blacksmith	10
Tinsmith	4
Cabinet maker	3
Lacquerer	4
Carpenter	4
Fitter	3
Jeweler	2
Craftsmen Unspecified	1
Shoemaker	2
Stone carver	2
Tansu cabinet maker	1
Seal carver	1
Box maker	1
Cooper	1
Plasterer	1
Measuring box maker	1
Paper lantern maker	1
Clock box maker	1
Buddhist altarpiece maker	1
Tatami maker	2
Tortoise shell carver	1
TOTAL	47

Workshop / Factory Employees (26%)

Occupation	Count
Ceramics worker	15
Brick maker	5
Foundry worker	4
Arsenal worker	5
Dyer	3
Casting worker	2
Bicycle factory worker	2
Lead plant worker	2
Clock factory worker	1
Saw mill worker	1
Spinning mill worker	2
Machine weaving worker	1
Glass plant worker	1
Knitted goods factory worker	1
Tile factory worker	1
Print shop worker	2
Metal detailing worker	1
Weaver	1
Other	4
TOTAL	54

Sales and Vending (11%)

Occupation	Count
Sweets vendor	3
Footwear sales	2
Hat sales	2
Fishmonger	2
Sundries sales	1
Lumber sales	1
Fruits and vegetables sales	1
Ink products	1
Snack vendor	1
Tinsmith supplies sales	1
Beef retailer	1
Cotton goods sales	1
Pickle sales	1
Bean curd sales	1
Knitted goods sales	1
Kindling, coal sales	1
Other	2
TOTAL	24

Other (17%)

Occupation	Count
Farmer	10
Carter	6
Rickshaw puller	4
Delivery man	2
Tailor	4
Barber	2
Publishing company employee	2
Gardener	1
Office worker	1
Sumo announcer	1
Exchange employee	1
Newspaper employee	1
Mining engineer	1
TOTAL	36

SOURCE: *KSNK* 1:252–63.
NOTE: Seven of those indicted (3 percent of the total) indicated that they had no occupation.

limited alternatives for improving economic conditions, the rioters' actions appear reasonable. If they did not take their grievances to the street, where were they to take them?

Workers in the steel, shipbuilding, electrical machinery, machine weaving, and other modern industries had different options and, not surprisingly, few from these occupational groups appear in prosecution records. Workers in major industries, who generally enjoyed a better standard of living than those in semiskilled trades, agitated for higher wages at their workplace rather than in the city streets. In Kobe, for example, Mitsubishi Shipyards employed 27,000 workers in 1918, but apparently few of the company's employees were involved in mass rallies, raids on rice dealers, or the burning of Suzuki Shōten. The ship-yard workers did, however, stage a strong protest within the company compound.[98]

Incidents similar to the Kobe shipyard protests became more fre-quent from the middle of World War I. In 1916 some 8,413 Japanese workers participated in 108 factory strikes and work slowdowns. By 1917 the number of labor protests had tripled to 398 incidents involv-ing 57,309 workers. This trend continued in 1918, when 66,457 laborers took part in factory strikes or work slowdowns. But the 1917 and 1918 labor actions differed from earlier strikes in that protests' targets involved more factories employing larger numbers of workers.[99] The upsurge in labor protest reached an unprecedented level on the eve of the rice riots. In August 1918 a total of 26,000 workers joined factory-based struggles for higher wages and better working conditions, a monthly figure matched on only one other occasion during the prewar period.[100]

Labor unrest on company property sometimes paralleled the rioters' street actions. During the protest on August 9 at the Mitsubishi Ship-yards in Kobe, workers moved from a work slowdown to a "riot" when the management responded to their demands for a 50 percent wage increase by offering to raise wages by only 30 percent.[101] As was the case in the Mitsubishi incident, the labor struggles frequently did not yield all that the workers desired. Nevertheless, as rioting spread across the nation many large enterprises compromised with workers by increasing wages or instituting cost-of-living allowances. In Nagoya factories, management and workers organized "factory hygiene com-mittees" (*kōjō eisei kai*) to settle labor disputes. In other cities plant management set up "relief associations" (*kyūsai kai*) to assure the basic welfare of all employees by providing rice subsidies and bonuses.[102]

According to the letter of the law, strikes were illegal. But in practice both private enterprise and the state countenanced a degree of collective bargaining. Unions may have been banned, but workers in important enterprises—particularly steel, shipbuilding, and arsenal work—found that collective actions could wrest concessions on wages and working conditions. The example of factory strikes in heavy industry may have contributed to the willingness of people in traditional occupations to defy authority.

Burakumin, Socialists, and Yakuza

Unlike the urban industrial workers who joined organized labor movements at large factories in increasing numbers, workers in semi-skilled or traditional trades had no comparable avenue for protest. This was especially true for the burakumin members of these occupational groups. Although nominally liberated from their pariah-like status by the Meiji reforms, burakumin continued to suffer from social and economic discrimination. The rapid increase in rice prices worsened the already difficult circumstances of many living in burakumin ghettos. If we accept exploitation-immiseration as the primary cause of the urban riots, then burakumin, as the poorest of the *saimin*, had the strongest economic reason for joining the protests.

Burakumin, however, did not generally lead the nationwide protests. Indeed, their participation can best be described as spotty; in buraku where rioting did occur, it was staged on an all-or-nothing basis. Reflecting the local solidarity typical of the buraku, either the entire settlement participated or it remained completely out of the conflict. Overall, detachment was far more typical, and most buraku remained peaceful while riots raged in surrounding communities. Of 554 designated buraku in 1918, only 32 reported disturbances from July through September. In Osaka, the scene of the largest sustained protests and the Japanese region with the largest concentration of burakumin among the general population, outcastes took little part in the riots.[103] Other large buraku settlements (located in Wakayama, Nara, Hyogo, and Fukuoka prefectures) were also largely quiet as nationwide rioting broke out. Even in Hiroshima prefecture, which had a burakumin population of nearly twenty-four thousand in 1918, officials reported only minor unrest in burakumin areas.

The minor role played by burakumin was not entirely accidental. Government officials, particularly local leaders, took special precautions to ensure that the poorest and most socially deprived members of the population would remain quiet during the riots. In so doing, they supplemented buraku improvement movements already under way in cities such as Nagoya and Osaka. In Aichi, the location of 2,285 buraku households, the prefectural government's efforts successfully discouraged the large burakumin population from taking any significant role in the riots.

The preriot improvement movement in Nagoya buraku required nonburakumin policemen to live within the local community. Together with the head of the local reservist association, the primary school principal, and buraku headmen, the policemen were charged with managing the community's self-help efforts. When rioting began in Nagoya and outlying areas, resident policemen assembled burakumin to warn them against joining the protests. Policemen also required local leaders to turn away organizers coming into the settlement in the hope of enlisting burakumin in attacks against grain dealers.[104] In many areas these steps, along with measures to provide certain buraku settlements with extra rice supplies, nipped protest in the bud. Although disorders occurred throughout Aichi prefecture, burakumin were not among those prosecuted later at the Nagoya district court for riot-related crimes.

Despite evidence that burakumin did not take a leading role in the riots, they figure prominently among those who faced prosecution. Burakumin made up less than 2 percent of Japan's population in 1918, but they accounted for more than 10 percent of those arrested for rioting. According to statistics for both urban and rural areas, 30 to 40 percent of the people arrested for rioting in Kyoto, Mie, Wakayama, and Okayama were burakumin.[105]

The high rate of burakumin arrests can be partially attributed to the predisposition of national and local officials to shift responsibility for the city riots to burakumin, a policy that emanated from the highest levels of the government. In a directive sent to police authorities throughout the nation on 19 August, Home Minister Mizuno Rentarō stated: "Incidents of rioting have spread to all regions. [Unrest] has a particularly strong connection with the buraku. At present we must restore calm . . . but I feel it is also necessary to teach [the burakumin] a lesson for future reference."[106] Following the riots, the vice-minister of justice, Suzuki Kisaburō, seconded this view; in his estimate many of those arrested were "acting on behalf of burakumin." The *Chūō shinbun*, a newspaper with Seiyūkai affiliations, followed Suzuki's line in a series of articles asserting that as many as 70 percent of the rioters hailed from the buraku.[107] The figure was highly inflated, but police, who spent an inordinate amount of energy attempting to pin responsibility for the riots on the buraku minority, acted as if the estimate were valid. While national leaders and the progovernment press stated the unofficial policy of blaming burakumin, prefectural authorities carried it out by ordering police to make sweeps of even those urban buraku that had not reported unrest.[108]

A second reason for the high proportion of burakumin among those arrested for rioting was the way in which they joined the riots. Unlike other city residents, who participated as individuals, burakumin often acted in identifiable groups. Crowds of burakumin from the Imamiya district of Osaka, from Yanagihara in Kyoto, and from Ujigawa in Kobe poured into police stations to demand relief or visited grain merchants to force discount sales of rice.[109] Members from different buraku, linked by intermarriage or other ties, sometimes acted as a single group. Although women participants were rare in most city riots, crowds of women as well as men took part in burakumin street actions. The unity demonstrated by burakumin rioters was seldom seen among other occupational or neighborhood groups. Solidarity within buraku districts strengthened demands for lower rice prices. But the tendency for burakumin to act in fairly homogeneous groups also provided a convenient target for authorities, who already suspected that burakumin were behind the riots.

Burakumin unity was a localized phenomenon. Whereas the residents of several buraku might act in concert, those in other prefectures (or even within the same city) took absolutely no part in the rioting. In contrast to the heavy participation of burakumin in the Kyoto city riots, burakumin leaders in Nagoya and Osaka acted to keep local residents out of the conflict, a feat they accomplished by working with police to provide relief rice and by keeping careful tabs on the movements of buraku residents. In Osaka buraku "bosses" directed the peace-keeping efforts. Their attempts to supply the buraku with rice and to keep rioters outside the settlement help account for the relatively low proportion of burakumin among the protesters in Osaka, the site of the most massive of the urban riots. This spirit of cooperation with authorities was by no means universal. In Okayama prefecture burakumin joined with nonburakumin in rioting but were arrested in a number disproportionate to their actual involvement. As an expression of resentment at being singled out for responsibility, buraku leaders in several settlements mounted a boycott (*fumai undō*) of relief rice.[110]

Central-government and local police authorities also gave special attention to leftists suspected of playing a role in the riots. Both during and after the riots, they expressed their belief that socialist agitators had incited the urban poor to join the protests. Following the first demonstrations in Nagoya, police reported that "socialists and juvenile delinquents" (*shakai shugisha furyō seinen*) had encouraged crowds to carry out nighttime raids against rice dealers.[111] Writers for the *Kōbe shinbun* also saw leftists behind the violence. According to the newspaper, the rioters' rampage through the city resulted from the combined efforts of three types of groups: "agitators" (*sendōsha*), "driving forces" (*gendōsha*), and "blind followers" (*fuwaraidō*). The agitators, socialists, and anarchists, were said to play upon the resentments of the poor against the rich in order to intensify class conflict. Their lead was followed by *saimin* in general and burakumin in particular, who acted as the driving force that carried out the fire attack against Suzuki Shōten and the *Kobe shinbun* company headquarters. Blind followers, carried along by the excitement of the movement, helped the core group achieve their aims by making the riots larger and more uncontrollable than they might otherwise have been.[112] The Kobe paper was not alone in expressing views about the rioters' coordinated actions in the urban protests. The *Kokumin shinbun* and other dailies suggested that the rioters' carefully thought-out actions were intended to protect group interests. The writers for these papers also occasionally expressed doubts about the ability of crowds to take such actions without some kind of leftist leadership.[113]

Publicly, government leaders played down the role of socialists in leading the city riots. They initially gave no credence to press reports suggesting that agitators had somehow orchestrated the riots as a means of striking the government at its weakest point, domestic economic policy. They also discounted press reports, like those in the Kobe newspapers, that the riots represented leftist attempts to unite *saimin*, burakumin, and other disadvantaged groups against the state. But official action belied public pronouncements. As the riots continued and became more violent, officials within the Home and Justice Ministries appeared increasingly alarmed over the possible ideological force behind the unrest. As in Nagoya, riots in urban areas quickly escalated from simple protests against high rice prices to more complex struggles that typically included political sloganeering and speechmaking.

In Tokyo the Metropolitan Police Board officials (Keishi-chō) began to round up socialists for administrative detention on 13 August. From 13 to 30 August, Ōsugi Sakae and Arahata Kanson, along with 25 other socialists, anarchists, and people under special surveillance, were held in police custody.[114] After the forcible suppression of the riots, it was clear that official concern over leftist agitation had been unfounded. Of 8,185 people arrested for crimes related directly to the riots, only two were designated as agitators requiring special police surveillance (*tokubetsu shisatsumono*).

In the nationwide arrest statistics "progressive thinkers" (or even people associated with legal political parties) were overshadowed by members of groups officially considered supportive of national goals. In contrast to the negligible role of leftists, 990 reservists (or 12 percent of those detained nationally) and 868 youth association members were arrested for riot-related crimes.[115] Despite the apparent lack of participation by political activists, police interrogators nevertheless pressed suspected rioters to admit socialist leanings. Yamazaki Tsunekichi later recalled that his interrogators refused to believe that common people could express political opinions. In his words: "The policeman said that I was regarded as socialist agent. But on the contrary, I was an imperialist [*teikoku shugisha datta*]."[116] He might have added that he was also a reservist.

Yamazaki's sense of social justice mixed with nationalism seemed shared by many who took part in the riots and might be seen, as Charles Tilly suggests, as the "rubbing together of urban and pre-urban value systems."[117] Police reported that protesters sometimes carried Japanese flags as they marched through city streets and cheered "banzai" after successfully attacking *narikin* establishments. In Kobe yakuza took an especially active role in negotiating with local grain dealers for reduced rice prices. Police records do not indicate how many of those arrested for rioting had ties with yakuza groups. Testimony by participants in the Kobe riots, however, suggests that the self-appointed leaders of attacks upon Suzuki Shōten and other *narikin* targets had strong yakuza connections.[118] Takeda Hōichi, who interviewed several of the yakuza crowd leaders, noted that these individuals were not even marginally involved in organized local politics. But they did possess a strong sense of social justice. The yakuza who later discussed their actions during the riots described themselves as carrying on the tradition of Sakura Sōgorō, the leader of a famous Edo-period peasant uprising (*ikki*) who gave up his own life in organizing popular resistance against unjust rulers. Yakuza interviewed by Takeda stated that they acted in the heroic *gimin* tradition, one of public-spirited self-sacrifice, and attacked only those they considered harmful to community interests. They asserted that they took no rice for themselves during the riots but called out neighborhood housewives to take grain that they had extorted from grain merchants.[119]

Despite the heroic self-description of yakuza deeds furnished decades after the riots, this socially marginal group cannot be credited with instigating the 1918 city riots. Nor, contrary to the assertions of central government officials and conservative newspapers, did burakumin or leftists provide the "agitation" (*sendō*) or the "driving force" (*gendō*) behind the protests. Yoshikawa Mitsusada, in his 1937 official report on the riots, observed that "political ruffians" (*sōshi*) often stood at the forefront of the protesting crowds.[120] Yet, there is little evidence to suggest that their roles represented the playing out of a conspiracy carefully planned by people on the edges of mainstream society. Instead of the "alienated," the primary support for the city protests came from mainstream groups largely composed of craftworkers and tradespeople.

Postriot Changes in Urban Social Policy

Following the troop-led suppression of rioting in Nagoya, city officials continued relief measures begun in the midst of the uprising (see figs. 10 and 11). Relying on the city's share of the imperial contribution of 3 million yen, private donations, and city treasury funds, Nagoya's city council authorized both discount rice sales and the distribution of free grain. Over the ten-week relief period, rules governing aid changed so as to conserve domestic rice supplies and gradually wean city residents away from dependence on relief. To overcome consumer resistance to foreign rice, the needy were eventually prevented from buying Japanese rice unless they purchased an equal measure of foreign grain. On 31 August Nagoya officials announced that discount sales of both domestic and foreign rice would be replaced immediately by sales of a more palatable variety of Taiwanese rice. On the same day the city council assembled a total of 4,090 representatives of poorer Nagoya families (*saimin*) at ward offices throughout the city to present each family ceremoniously with two shō of rice purchased with funds from the imperial contribution. The move appeared intended to take some of the sting out of replacing sales of discounted domestic rice with Taiwanese grain. But the use of Taiwanese rice, even when combined with token gifts presented in the emperor's name, fell short of total success. On 21 September Nagoya's city council once again authorized discount purchases of foreign and domestic rice and simultaneously announced new rules limiting aid to people paying three yen or less in national taxes. The sales of foreign, domestic, and Taiwanese rice continued until 31 October.[121]

Funding for the massive relief effort came predominantly from local contributions. Compared with the huge sums contributed by major corporations to national relief, individual donations to Nagoya's campaign ranged from thirty to about three thousand yen.[122] Using the private donations, central-government funds, city revenues, and proceeds from the grain sales, the city raised 2.2 million yen. This amount was more than sufficient to cover the 1.9 million used in the distribution of 67,000 koku (6.7 million shō) of rice during the relief period.[123]

Nagoya's public took full advantage of the city's relief efforts, but the measures did not meet with universal approval. City newspapers reported scattered complaints about the narrowness of the program and its failure to meet the needs of middle-class city residents who suffered because of inflation and high food costs. Those qualified to receive aid complained about long lines and insufficient supplies of rice at ward-office distribution centers. Even after waiting in line for several hours, they were often turned away because the day's grain allotment had already been sold out. The distribution of coupons was also criticized. While white-collar workers criticized the program as too limited in scope, poorer recipients of aid charged that "wealthy" individuals were fraudulently obtaining coupons, causing poor people to go without.[124]

These minor complaints reflected a larger concern. During the Nagoya riots, speakers at Tsurumai and other rallies repeatedly criticized discount sales, short-term subsidies, and gifts of imperial grain as unsatisfactory substitutes for an effective policy for the regulation of rice prices. The state already monopolized or heavily regulated such products as tobacco, salt, and alcohol—all for the benefit of the national treasury.[125] Speakers at the citizens' meetings demanded that the central government take responsibility for regulating grain prices, not as an additional means of bolstering tax revenue but to better protect the citizens' livelihood. They also suggested several methods, including pegging grain prices to wages or simply mandating a maximum retail price, to achieve fair retail prices and market stability.[126] In the wake of the riots, writers for local Nagoya papers took up the question of public regulation of grain prices and supply. An article in the *Nagoya shinbun* of 21 August repeated criticisms of the city's relief efforts as little better than stopgap measures. Journalists noted that cities like Nagoya were especially vulnerable in times of short supplies and recommended that the central government protect urban consumers by fixing maximum limits on grain prices.[127]

Prefectural and city officials had no authority to set limits on the price of rice. Nagoya officials did, however, respond to calls for setting maximum grain prices by supporting a public-market program. The idea of public markets, or stores that would provide consumers with food and other goods at regulated prices, was supported both by private individuals and by the press. Shortly after the riots, Nagoya's mayor and city council commissioned a study to investigate the replacing of temporary discount sales with a more permanent system of subsidized markets. On 16 September the city council decided that widespread demand justified going ahead with the public-market plan.

On 15 November the city opened the first two markets. The shops offered rice, coal and kindling, vegetables, spices, meat, and other items at lower than retail prices. The success of the first two markets led to the opening of an additional two outlets on 1 December 1918. The strongly favorable public response to discount markets created problems in maintaining public order. In the early morning hours, long before the stores opened, it became common to see crowds of customers waiting in lines stretching for six or seven blocks. In some cases rice was sold out before all the customers had an opportunity to make their purchases. At one location the rush to buy grain resulted in customers stampeding through the store, injuring seventeen women and children.[128] Despite such problems, urban residents and the press welcomed the markets. Nagoya officials, who also saw the program as a success, cooperated in expanding outlets to fourteen locations in 1918 and 1919. In Osaka monthly sales passed a million yen during the early 1920s; in Tokyo two years after the riots the number of public markets totaled sixty-six.[129]

In addition to the public-market program, private philanthropic groups in Nagoya sponsored lunch rooms (*kan'i shokudō*) as a means of providing inexpensive meals to laborers and low-income workers. With support from city officials, the program's four main organizers began soliciting contributions on 18 August. Donations flowed in, and by 4 September the fund had reached 19,000 yen. On New Year's Day 1919 the first of three planned lunchrooms was opened. Popularly called "democracy" lunchrooms or "commoner dining halls" (*heimin shokudō*), these inexpensive restaurants later became the "salons" of Nagoya labor organizers.[130] In them individuals like Yamazaki attempted to gain popular support for movements toward unfettered labor organization, expanded suffrage, and women's rights, all of which grew to new strength in the decade after the 1918 riots.

As part of this increased attention to urban social welfare, existing agencies were expanded and, in some cities, special departments were established to extend assistance to the city poor. Osaka prefecture and Osaka city, which had sponsored public markets before the riots, took the lead in upgrading small government sections or subsections into full-fledged welfare divisions. Within a few years of the organization of Osaka city's Social Division, all of Japan's major cities had similar agencies.[131] In the drive to improve social services, urban political leaders often led in the establishment of subsidized public markets, housing-assistance offices, workers' lunchrooms, and even day-care facilities for working mothers. The new emphasis on city government as an agency for social welfare represented a departure from the traditional view of welfare based on individual charity from the purses of well-off private citizens or the emperor.

Conclusion

Whereas the Toyama riots were essentially a single-issue dispute carried out in a traditional manner, the city riots represented a more modern awareness of the political use of mass protest. Although city rioters referred to the *gimin* tradition and included groups like the ya-kuza, they had more recent precedents for their protest. If anywhere, the antecedents of the 1918 city riots are to be found in the 1905 Hibiya riots, the 1913 urban uprisings resulting from the Taishō political crisis, and the 1914 Nagoya streetcar riots. These earlier mass protests aimed at achieving political and economic objectives by popular action directed against the makers of government policy. Like the 1918 rice riots, they included elements of widespread antigovernment and anticapitalist sentiment expressed by city crowds whose only effective political weapon was street protest. In the earlier Taishō protests, mass meetings, political speeches, demonstrations at government offices, and attacks upon police—whom many perceived as the teeth and claws of government policy makers—represented the unen-franchised citizen's powerful vote of no confidence in his government. City rioters resorted to the same methods with telling results in 1918. Speakers at mass rallies demanding that the entire Terauchi cabinet resign had their demands met within weeks of the last city riot. In the end, even central-government officials, who could dismiss the Toyama protest as a simple commotion raised by uneducated women, could not resist the popular indictment of their policies raised by city rioters.

The massive 1918 city riots marked a change in popular attitudes toward the state. Articles in liberal newspapers, magazines, and intellectual journals drew out the full implications of the protests in interpreting them as a collective demand for expanded democratic rights. An editorial in the 15 December 1918 *Tōyō keizai shinpō* was representative of periodicals ranging from *Chūō kōron* to *Hōji koku*. Responding to a government statement of the "need" for discipline to quiet the people's hearts, it offered counterproposals:

> How about universal suffrage? This, too, is something the people's hearts desire. . . . How about legally recognizing the right of labor organization? Something else desired by public sentiment. To put the matter simply, the recent unrest springs from "the unequal distribution of power and wealth." A "fair distribution" is what the public really longs for.[132]

The analysis was, of course, an intellectual and partisan interpretation. Yet it differed little from the views expressed at citizens' rallies. Writers and rioters appeared to agree that rather than an oligarchic constitutional monarchy, a popular constitutional monarchy was needed. The urban crowds' words and deeds pressed for an order similar to Yoshino Sakuzō's "people as the base-ism," or *minpon shugi*, which asserted that popular welfare was the state's basic concern and that all government policies should be based on public opinion. Transcendent cabinets that excluded popular political participation had no place in this order. As if to emphasize this point, the announcement of the replacement of Terauchi's government with a party cabinet was celebrated in a rally in Yokohama that drew crowds from throughout the Tokyo-Kanagawa region. Of the public's euphoric mood following the riots the journalist Maeda Renzan noted:

> The nation's citizens have welcomed Hara Takashi with a shout of joy. Yet this does not mean that they have expectations of Hara's statesmanship. For most their welcome stops at celebrating a commoner prime minister and the emergence of a genuine party cabinet (*jun seitō naikaku*).[133]

In embracing Hara the symbol if not Hara the man, the public rejected what social commentators called "aristocratic politicians." The change in popular attitudes frightened the genro and advocates of "transcendent" or "national unity" government.[134] The public increasingly regarded such fine-sounding phrases as meaning little more than that a small self-selected group should lead and citizens should docilely follow.

At the very moment that the nation's military and bureaucratic leaders demanded unity and support for armed intervention against the Bolsheviks in Siberia, the public appeared to turn its back. In 1918 individuals and labor groups no longer asked "What can we do for the greater glory of the Japanese empire?" The question shifted to what the state could—and should—do to improve the material and, by implication, the political quality of people's lives. In the words of a Nagoya rioter, the time had come to raise a flag representing the interests of common citizens.[135] If this required challenging central government authority in order to find their own place in the emerging political order, the urban rioters appeared entirely willing to do so.[136]

Fig. 1. The Western-dressed *narikin*, with characteristic paunch and cigar, depicted as creating a false scarcity that lifts rice beyond the reach of the traditionally dressed Japanese housewife.
Source: Sakai and Shimizu, eds., *Kindai manga, 5: Taishō zenki no manga*, 67.

Fig. 2. *Narikin* at play. At the end of an evening of entertainment, the *narikin* patron lights a hundred-yen note to
allow a geisha to find his shoes in the darkened entryway.
Source: Nihon Kindai Shi Kenkyū Kai, *Gakuhō Nihon kindai no rekishi: Minpon shugi no chōryū*, 50.

Fig. 3. Western-dressed paupers (*yōfuku saimin*; *saimin* is literally "people of slender means"). The emerging middle class was hit hard by inflation and higher rice prices. This satirical cartoon depicts the new Western-style generation (the teacher, "salaryman," artist, jailer, etc.) as faring far worse during the war boom than industrial laborers, who could benefit from overtime, bonuses, and family labor. The caricature of the paupers in Western clothes notes that they had become the best customers of urban pawnshops. The cartoon originally appeared in the Tokyo *Asahi shinbun* two months before the onset of major urban riots.

Source: Sakai and Shimizu, eds., *Kindai manga, 5: Taishō zenki no manga*, 94–95.

Fig. 4. Grain loading on the Toyama Coast, 1918. Courtesy of the Nameri-kawa City Historical Museum.

Fig. 5. The 13 August "Citizens' Rally" in Hibiya Park.
Source: Nihon Kindai Shi Kenkyū Kai, *Gakuhō Nihon kindai no rekishi: Minpon shugi no chōryū*, 86.

Fig. 6. The Heishinkan in the aftermath of Kobe city rioting. Courtesy of the Kobe Shinbun Company.

Fig. 7. The burning of Suzuki Shōten. Courtesy of the Kobe Shinbun Company.

Fig. 8. Upper: Mounted *kenpeitai* troops confronting rioters during the Nagoya riots. Lower: Infantry troops mobilized for riot suppression in Kyoto on 12 August.
Source: Nihon Kindai Shi Kenkyū Kai, *Gakuhō Nihon kindai no rekishi: Minpon shugi no chōryū*, 87.

Fig. 9. Ridiculing the forces of order. The urban riots revealed strongly negative popular attitudes toward the police. This cartoon mocks the curfew put into effect to control rioting. Caption: "Look here, don't you people know about the prefectural order banning a group of five or more from strolling about? With that baby on your back, that makes six and calls for punitive measures!" Courtesy of the Ōmiya Shiritsu Manga Kaikan.

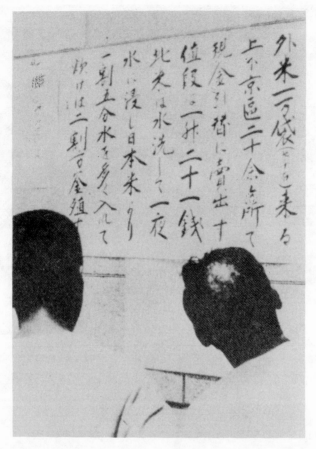

Fig. 10. Announcement of public sales of discount grain in Kyoto. Foreign rice was sold within the city at twenty-one sen per shō from 12 August.
Source: Nihon Kindai Shi Kenkyū Kai, *Gakuhō Nihon kindai no rekishi: Minpon shugi no chōryū*, 85.

Fig. 11. Discount grain sales in Kobe. Courtesy of the Kobe Shinbun Company.

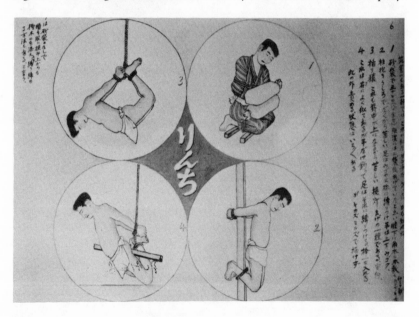

Fig. 12. Punishments as examples to others (*miseshime*) in a Meiji period mine.
Source: Yamamoto, *Chikuhō tankō emaki*.

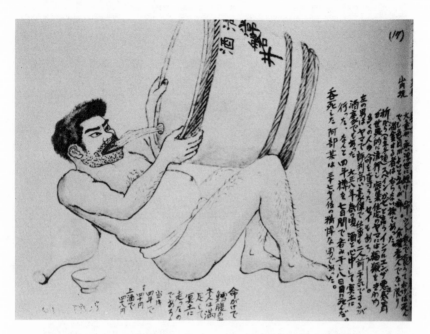

Fig. 13. The miners were known as great drinkers, supposedly content with a short, carefree existence. According to the caption, they disdained to save money and enjoyed spending freely on food and sake. Pictured is one miner famous for his physical strength ("able to easily perform the work of two men") and liquor capacity ("akin to a codfish"). He reportedly drank himself to death. Source: Yamamoto, *Chikuhō tankō emaki*.

Fig. 14. Attacking the company store at a Chikuhō region mine. Caption: "Although the miners smashed or threw out everything else in the store, they carefully and gently carried the sake barrels outside. Everyone was allowed to drink their fill." The circular inset shows one of the riot leaders dispensing cash found in a strongbox inside the company store. The money was given as "membership allowances" to people who joined the attack.

Source: Yamamoto, *Chikuhō tankō emaki*.

Fig. 15. Miners destroying goods at a company store. Caption: "Despite widespread newspaper reports about attacks upon noncompany merchants, we miners did not do this. We only raided the company store."
Source: Yamamoto, *Chikuhō tankō emaki.*

Fig. 16. A Mineji rioter hurling dynamite at troops. According to the caption, he refused to come down and the soldiers finally shot him.
Source: Yamamoto, *Chikuhō tankō emaki.*

Fig. 17. Dancing at Bon. Mineji miners gathered the day after rioting was suppressed to continue their dances.
Source: Yamamoto, *Chikuhō tankō emaki.*

Fig. 18. Rioting rewarded. As a result of rioting at one of the Yamauchi pits, the company unilaterally announced concessions at another of its mines where no rioting had yet occurred. As a precautionary measure, however, troops were dispatched and put on alert at the peaceful mine. The sign in the circular inset states that henceforth miners will receive one yen for each box of coal produced and a fifty-sen allowance for each day they enter the pits. Day laborers will be given a 20 percent raise in wages. Polished rice will be sold to all at twenty-eight sen per shō. Referring to the dynamite used by miners in rioting at the sister mine, the caption states: "Hey! The explosion at Kamio really worked. Another blast might bring wages even higher!"
Source: Yamamoto, *Chikuhō tankō emaki.*

FOUR

The Rural Riots

Consumer Protests
and Tenant-Landlord Riots

If there is good government there will be no rioting, no
matter how poverty-stricken the peasants may be.

Motoori Norinaga, 1730–1801

Farming is the basis of the nation; farmers are the nation's
treasure. Japan is yet an agricultural nation in which seven-
tenths of the citizenry live in rural districts, and seven-tenths of
these are tenants. Nevertheless, long-standing evils have come
to overflow into the fields . . . as capitalism has encroached
upon the countryside.

Declaration of the Japan Farmer's Association, 1924

Japan in 1918 as in 1924 was still a predominantly agrarian state,
but the economic boundaries dividing urban from rural were blurring at
a pace never before experienced.[1] As the Meiji transformation expanded commercial networks and created new transportation and communication systems, the process of integration accelerated, particularly
in towns and villages within the orbit of burgeoning cities along the
Pacific coast and in western Japan. The Russo-Japanese War and World
War I, which stimulated industrial growth and a concomitant mass
migration of excess sons and daughters from farm fields to urban workshops, further quickened the economic linking of city and countryside.
For those who worked the land the expansion of commercial networks
and the possibility of factory employment brought both new depen-
dencies and new opportunities. Farmers relied increasingly on a
national commodities market to sell the rice they grew and to buy the
rice they ate. They also availed themselves of a labor market that, while
releasing them from ties to the land and to landlords, exposed them

to the insecurities inherent in swings between economic growth and recession.

Tenants, landlords, and others living in the countryside both welcomed and resisted the expanded involvement in the commodities and labor markets. Greater participation in the national economy provided outlets for locally produced goods and opportunities for work, thereby promising a better material life for all, if not for all equally. Increased ties between urban and rural economies also undermined the cooperation needed for rice production and, consequently, for the livelihood of many landlords and most tenants. During the Taishō period farming still required the heavy use of human labor. At least amicable relations were essential for the effective financing of fertilizer, the sharing of water rights, and the carrying out of scores of other tasks essential for growing and marketing rice.

The 1918 riots made manifest the strains in the countryside that were the result of the rapid merging of agrarian and industrial economies. Popular discontent was widespread; for each incident of city rioting there were more than ten rural protests. Despite more than four hundred reported incidents of town and village unrest, not all farmers everywhere rioted. Nevertheless, the huge number that did join in demonstrations, rice confiscation, and attacks on landlord property shocked the central government.

National leaders were disturbed not only by the scale of rioting but also by the shattering of nearly four decades of relatively peaceful conditions in the countryside. Peasants had rebelled against many of the reforms introduced during the opening years of the Meiji Restoration— the use of the Western calendar, the abolition of domains, conscription, and the reorganization of land ownership. During the new government's second decade, centrally enforced tax reforms, deflation policies, and other economic programs continued to fuel farmer opposition to changes that touched upon almost every aspect of their lives. Nevertheless, since the unrest associated with the Freedom and Popular Rights movement of the 1880s, significant rural disturbances were few. Although there was an increase in the number of tenancy disputes in 1917, an average of less than ten such disputes were recorded for each year from 1901 through 1911.[2] The mid-August outbreak of widespread rural rioting in 1918, soon after the city uprisings, called into question the effectiveness of Meiji-Taishō state-building policies.

This chapter focuses on two types of riots in the industrializing countryside, the consumer and the tenant-landlord protest. In contrast to the Toyama shipping boycott, the aims and tactics inherent in these Japanese rural disputes strongly resemble those associated with market riots, or *taxation populaire*, in eighteenth- and nineteenth-century Europe. As will be discussed further, both the Japanese and the European rural protests had common roots in community disputes between landlords, political groups, and other wealthy interests, on the one hand, and poorer residents, both farmers and factory workers, on the other.

In the first, and by far the most common, type of riot, rural consumers responded to high prices for rice by forcing retail grain dealers to reduce market prices and by bringing pressure on local leaders to institute relief efforts. They also carried out retributive attacks against village officials, landlords, and rice dealers to demonstrate their concern over local "welfare" and "justice." As in protests elsewhere, the issues involved went beyond the cost of rice to raise questions of local political responsibility.

The second type of village or town protest, which occurred in at least fifteen incidents of rural rioting, arose from clear-cut disputes between landlords and tenants over land rents. Although the first stirring of the tenants movement, characterized by the forming of tenant associations and other coalitions of farmers, began well before the 1918 rice riots, the movement did not attain national scale until the early 1920s. Nevertheless, in 1918 a number of tenant groups took advantage of the widespread breakdown of law and order to harass and make demands upon landlords.

In contrast to the consumer riots, in which local residents protested the inability of officials to keep high food costs down, the second type of riot involved the questions of how much "compensation" a tenant should receive for his labor and what rights he had to cultivate a particular parcel of land. These disputes were related to the consumer protests in that the tenancy system prevented tenants and even independent farmers from being entirely self-sufficient. Full-time farmers as well as part-time cultivators and day laborers depended on the retail market for rice and other consumer goods. Conflicts over land rents might, while appearing unconnected to protests over consumer rice prices, in fact demonstrate the producers' awareness that with lower rents more money could be used for food. With the rapid increase in prices during the summer months of 1918, this of course became an important consideration in deciding whether to press the landlord for rent reductions.

Rent disputes also reflected the desire of tenant farmers, particularly people who owned fields as well as worked them for landlords, greater access to the rice market. Their involvement in the market was to sell rather than to buy grain. As Nishida Yoshiaki and others have demonstrated, by the late Meiji period "tenants" had become an increasingly diverse group, differentiated by land wealth, degree of control of postharvest grain surpluses, and direct involvement in commodity marketing.[3] A number of the 1918 riots clearly indicate the frustration of middling landowning tenant cultivators unable to take full advantage of soaring rice prices because of landlord demands for rent payments in kind.

The consumer and producer forms of rural rioting were linked by their occurrence in towns and villages near urban centers. The majority of the rural disputes were concentrated in the Kansai, Chūgoku, and Kanto prefectures of Osaka, Kyoto, Hyogo, Okayama, Hiroshima, and Saitama. But they also broke out around industrializing cities in Aichi and Shizuoka (Chūbu), Kagawa (Shikoku), and Kumamoto (Kyushu). With the exception of rioting in Fukushima prefecture, neither the consumer nor the tenancy types of riots, however, occurred in Japan's more purely agricultural northeastern region. In Iwate, Aomori, Akita, and Yamagata prefectures only one incident of "unrest" was reported.[4] Despite the high price of rice and a generally more impoverished standard of living in the northeast, protests for lower retail prices for rice or reduced land rents were virtually unheard of.

Why did rioting occur in some rural regions while quiet prevailed in others where economic conditions appeared to provide conditions ripe for popular protest? In seeking to answer this general question, the following analysis explores the characteristics of rural unrest as distinct from protests elsewhere. The Kansai riots have been selected to demonstrate the salient characteristics of rural riots by consumers and producers. The incidents discussed by no means provide an exhaustive examination of the hundreds of rural protests reported during 1918. They are, however, generally representative of disputes not only in the Kansai but throughout Japan where industrialization and an ongoing tenants movement heightened conflicts within the village or rural town.

The Furuichi Riots:
Farmers, Button Makers, and New Money

The consumer riot, whereby protesters expressed concern over village justice, rice prices, and political authority, occurred throughout western

TABLE 10.   OCCUPATIONS OF FURUICHI RESIDENTS, 1920

	Main Occupation		Subsidiary Occupation or Work Engaged In by Family Member	
Type	Male	Female	Male	Female
Farming	408	13	350	732
Mining	1	0	0	0
Manufacturing	342	40	180	375
Commerce	114	39	101	206
Transportation	24	2	16	32
Public- / Self-employed	60	21	37	96
Other	3	3	2	4
Domestic work	0	1	0	0
None	23	33	37	71
TOTAL	975	152	723	1,503

SOURCE: *KSNK* 2:92.

Japan. In these disputes farmers and workers attacked local officials, landlords, and rice dealers held responsible for driving up grain prices. They also called meetings to persuade officials to take positive relief measures such as selling rice at a discount or disbursing communal funds. There were, of course, variations in individual protests. Nevertheless, in the riot of 12 and 13 August in Furuichi, once a predominantly agricultural town on the outskirts of Osaka city, we can see the broader characteristics of the rural consumer riot as it occurred throughout Japan.[5]

In 1918 Furuichi, now known as Hibikino city, was a small community divided into four major divisions (*ōaza*) that had been separate "natural" villages until their amalgamation into a single administrative township in the 1880s. Outside the town's central district, with its concentration of public offices, police station, and homes of wealthy residents, lay three farming areas. Although the town was but thirteen kilometers from Osaka, well within commuting distance to the city's factories, most of Furuichi's 3,733 residents (611 households) listed farming as their main occupation in the 1920 national census. Many town residents, however, supported themselves by nonagricultural employment (see table 10).

Although no records on tenancy are available for the town itself, statistics for Minami Kawachi county indicate that almost half of the county's farming population worked as full-time tenants. If we add the number of people who both owned land and tilled it for others, the percentage of tenant farmers rises to more than 75 percent of the farming population in the district. Apart from 136 families with relatively large holdings in excess of two chō, 90 percent of Minami Kawachi's farmers cultivated extremely small plots of one chō or less. Households with fields of between two chō or more than five chō accounted for only 1 percent of the landowners in the county.

Furuichi tenants paid land rents in kind, typically at a rate of 60 percent of the harvest. In addition to rent, landlords also required that each five-to (three-bushel) bale of rent rice contain an extra shō (half-gallon) to cover spillage. The high rents contributed to a critical grain shortage faced annually by tenants and smallholders throughout July and August. During this preharvest period, many farmers depleted their own rice reserves and were forced to borrow from landlord families. The difficult economic position of tenants and smallholders seems to suggest constant conflict within the town. Yet this was not the case. Before the 1918 riots tenants expressed little hostility toward the holders of larger tracts of paddy land. In Furuichi tenants commonly referred to the landlord households respectfully as "parent" families (oyake) and acted humbly in their presence.

Customary deference was not the only reason for the lack of open conflict between landowners and tenants. A three-member committee formed to mediate disputes between farmers and landlords provided a channel for resolving differences over rent and terms of tenancy. Superficially, the committee functioned as a neutral arbitration group. Because its members served only after being approved by the landlord-dominated town council, however, the committeemen proved more sympathetic to the interests of landlords than to those of tenants. In 1918 only one of the three negotiators was a farmer who actually worked the land, and in the years following the riots, the negotiating committee was displaced by associations organized by tenants to represent their own interests.

In addition to mediating rent disputes, the committee concerned itself with a variety of activities ranging from funding local festivals to confirming town council members. Its formal role in Furuichi politics, however, was largely symbolic. Membership in the town's twelve-man council was not determined by popular ballot but by wealthier community members who resolved among themselves the question of who was most qualified to serve as mayor and council members. In the selection process the committee solicited the opinions of townspeople and provided an apparently popular seconding of the council members nominated by landlord families. This closed arrangement, in which influential families approved the three-man mediation group which in turn confirmed the landlord-dominated Furuichi council, enabled one homogeneous group to strongly influence town politics. Only after the 1925 suffrage expansion did anyone other than a member of Furuichi's landlord families hold a council seat.

Historically, the same group that dominated local politics had monopolized the town's economic life. From well before the Meiji Restoration, landlord families ran local stores, owned pawnshops, and loaned money at high interest rates. The basic funds for these commercial endeavors derived, of course, from the rice surplus that landowners marketed with the help of a local broker. After 1868 the landlord families continued to rely on the annual harvest to provide money for local commercial investment, including the pooling of resources to raise capital for a local bank. As is indicated in table 11, local landlords were not only involved in nonagricultural businesses but were also expanding their commercial activities beyond such traditional pursuits as pawnbroking.

Despite the long-standing and continuing economic vitality of the old landed families, a new group had emerged in the 1890s to challenge the landlords' domination of the local economy. The rivalry sprang from the opening of shell button factories in and around Furuichi. Established without landlord financing, these enterprises produced the single most profitable manufactured product in the county.

By 1918 the button business was thriving. Since the start-up of manufacturing shortly before the Russo-Japanese War, the scale of production and operation had expanded steadily. The first factory, Matsuo Button, began with only a handful of workers, but by 1918 it employed about a hundred craftsmen, a work force that expanded to three hundred in 1920. Aside from a main factory, in which shells were cleaned, cut, shaped, and drilled, the company maintained several smaller workshops, each of which employed from ten to fifteen button finishers. Four other button factories, with twenty to thirty workers each, also provided work for Furuichi residents.

The factories paid their employees on a piecework basis. Wages for men and women averaged between 70 sen and 1.20 yen per day or between 20 and 30 yen per month in 1918. The workers occasionally

TABLE 11. FURUICHI'S LANDLORDS

Name	Size of Holding (chō)	Secondary Occupation, If Any	Town Council / Other Office	Attacked During Rice Riots?
Shimizu Michitsugu	30	—	No	Yes
Morita Hiromitsu	20	Postmaster	Yes	Yes
Hatayama Tsunesaburō	8	School principal	Yes	Yes
Nishitani Tokusaburō	5	Bank director	Yes	Yes
Nishitani Iwazō	3	—	Yes	Yes
Hosoda Kazuichirō	3	Pawnshop, clothier	Yes	Yes
Hatayama Shūhei	2	—	No	Yes
Takauchi Iku	2	General store, coal, kindling	No	Yes
Shatani Seijirō	2	—	Yes	Yes
Morita Honji	Unknown	Moneylender	Yes	Yes

SOURCE: Watanabe, "Ōsaka-fu Furuichi-machi no kome sōdō," 90–93.

complained about the low pay, but their grumbling did not develop into strikes. The plants' small-scale operation and the deferential ties between bosses and workers helped prevent wage disputes. For many Furuichi residents the subsidiary or main income earned in the button factories provided a desirable and relatively secure alternative to the precarious economic life of a tenant farmer. Workshop wages were not particularly high, but the worker was free from paying for seedlings, fertilizer, tools, and all manner of other expenses borne by the tenant farmer. Moreover, because button factories were the only local industry of any significance, workers had little choice but to take conditions as they found them. The alternatives were to look for work outside Furuichi or return to farming, but neither guaranteed significantly better wages or greater economic security.

The landlord families in Furuichi did not appreciate the button factories' influence on the community. The workshop owners represented "new money" without ties to the older landlord group. They did not rely on the landlord-capitalized bank but maintained financial and business relationships with material-supplying wholesalers (*ton'ya*) in Osaka and Kobe. Landlord resentment led to strained relations almost from the outset of button production. In one dispute landlords complained to local police that the "unsanitary" (*fuketsu*) shells used in button making necessitated nothing less than closing down the new workshops. Factory owners were forced to curtail operations temporarily, but by banding together they successfully resisted demands that production be halted permanently. Although the conflict over dirty shells was finally resolved, competition between old landlords and new entrepreneurs worked against any permanent improvement in relations between these groups. According to a Furuichi policeman, the landlords' complaints had little to do with fear of pollution but stemmed from a concern over the loss of tenant labor.

The button-factory owners diminished the landlords' collective role as the town's leading patronage group by providing an economic alternative to reliance on the old money elite. The erosion of authority, however, was neither sudden nor complete. Before and after the riots and sometimes in the midst of an angry gathering at a landlord's doorway, tenants and others dependent on peaceful, if not cordial, relations with the people who controlled the town council and surrounding rice fields continued to act deferentially toward the *oyake*. Nevertheless, the possibility of alliance with the new factory managers and of additional employment opportunities allowed superficial courtesy to give way more easily to direct conflict. The Furuichi riots were thus symptomatic of a gradual but fundamental change in the governance of the town. The shift became permanent in 1925. Seven years after the riots and following the broadening of the local electorate, a new group, which included factory managers and former tenants, gained seats on the town council. The once-indisputable *oyake* dominance had given way to local rule by a group more broadly representative of the population.

Two versions exist as to how the riots started in Furuichi. The first, based on a police investigation of 1918, asserts that unrest began after a regularly scheduled meeting of the local youth association (*seinen dan*). Toward the close of the association's meeting on 12 August, someone reported that a local rice dealer was consistently cheating town residents by selling short measures and mixing large amounts of bran into his rice. These complaints led to a more general discussion of rice shortages, high prices, and how the town government should deal with these issues. It was finally decided that Furuichi's landlord-dominated council should take the lead in initiating discount sales of rice. To motivate the old elite, a four-man negotiating committee was formed to meet with town representatives.

According to the police report, none of the four men selected at the meeting represented landowning families. The group included Kikui Yūzō, a button-factory owner, head of the county button manufacturers association, and representative to that group's national organization. Kikui led the negotiating committee. He was assisted by his brother-in-law, Ueda Yasutarō, a technical-school graduate who later ran his own construction company and became one of the town's wealthiest residents. His postriot activities on the town council enabled Ueda to rise to the position of Furuichi's mayor in 1945. The committee was filled out by Nishida Eisaburō and Kitada Isaburō. Nishida, a relative newcomer to the town, was known as a poetry-loving local intellectual and was regarded by town residents as a champion of the underdog, or "gentleman ruffian" (*shinshi goro*). His profession and source of income remains unclear, and the police analysis of the Furuichi riot suggests that he had a "past." Kitada Isaburō served as town stationmaster and owned a watch shop conveniently near the rail line. Aside from Nishida, whose mysterious background and reputation as more ruffian than gentleman caused many local people to regard him warily, the committeemen were respected citizens known for their concern for local welfare.

Although the police report presents a clear, detailed account of the meeting at the youth association hall, a second postwar study compiled by a research team led by Watanabe Tōru found no substantiation for this version. According to Watanabe, town residents remembered that before rioting broke out people took part in numerous small gatherings to discuss rice shortages and high prices. Yet none could recall a single formal meeting. In fact, one witness later testified that "the [negotiating committee] was not specially selected, they just decided on their own to call themselves a committee."[6] Watanabe's interviews with Kikui Yūzō and Ueda Yasutarō, the button-plant owner and his brother-in-law, tend to support this version. The new-money entrepreneurs nevertheless maintained that, formal meeting or not, their social position, combined with requests from townspeople, required that they investigate local grain reserves and the relief plans of the town council.

Whether self-appointed or selected by general consensus, the negotiating committee began its work on 13 August. Nishida and Kitada took the first step by going to the town office to inquire into the amount of rice on hand locally. Officials at the town office told them that an inventory carried out in compliance with a 1 August order from the Ministry of Agriculture and Commerce had revealed that rice stored in Furuichi amounted to a paltry 16.8 koku. The negotiators reported their findings to representatives of the town's neighborhoods gathered at the youth association hall. Kitada added his personal view that the actual amount of rice on hand was more than a thousand bales, a far larger figure than the one officially reported. Before the meeting adjourned all agreed that the matter required further discussion and decided to meet later at the town shrine to enable more town residents to join in their proceedings.

While these deliberations continued, word spread throughout Furuichi that the town council had independently decided on a relief plan. Learning of this, the four-man negotiating committee once again visited the town office. Interviewing the mayor's representative, they discovered that several landlords had contributed 20 koku of rice to be sold at a discount from 15 August. The unpolished grain (*genmai*) would be sold at 26 sen per shō in fixed amounts of .5 shō for each adult and .3 shō for each child in a family. Kikui and his fellow committeemen carried the news back to the neighborhood representatives, who in turn provided details to residents throughout Furuichi.

In reporting the relief plan the negotiators misrepresented one crucial point. Contrary to the council's intentions, the committee stated that the relief measures would be virtually unrestricted: all Furuichi residents would be allowed to take advantage of the cheaper prices. The council members' actual program was, in fact, much more modest. They had indeed purchased rice at the market price of about 40 yen per koku for resale at 26 yen per koku (the 14-yen difference to be made up by local contributions). But they intended to limit sales to the town's poorer residents.

The initial report of the four-man negotiating committee raised high expectations only to shatter them later. Why Kikui and his group incorrectly reported the council's plans is unclear. They simply may have misunderstood the proposed relief program or may have reported its details before the plan was completely worked out. The negotiating committee, after all, did not cooperate closely with the Furuichi council. Indeed, the meddling of self-appointed ombudsmen probably irritated officials already resentful of the interference of Kikui and his upstart friends in their affairs. From the old guard's perspective, relief efforts were the responsibility of Furuichi council members, the town's formal representatives and the owners of the local grain surplus. As guardians of local welfare, council members had taken it upon themselves to unilaterally plan aid measures and saw no need to confer with Kikui or anyone else.

Kikui's erroneous reporting of relief plans may, however, have resulted from more than a simple lack of communication between landlords and button makers. Watanabe's postwar study suggests that town officials intentionally misinformed the self-appointed negotiating committee so as to embarrass them in the eyes of the townspeople. Another possible interpretation is that, rather than the landlords, it was Kikui and company who acted deviously. By promising generous relief measures, which the town's treasury could ill support, the negotiating committee may have sought to reveal the landlords' incompetent handling of local affairs. The exact motives of old and emerging elites is murky. What is clear is that both sides were attempting to manipulate the crisis in rice prices to their own advantage.

On the evening of 13 August a town council spokesman announced that the rumors about relief had been grossly misrepresented. According to his explanation, the town had received only a hundred yen in donations. If discount sales were to be open to all for a fifty-day period, then about eight thousand yen would be needed. He insisted that the town did not have the money for such wide-scale relief and that such an ambitious program had never been contemplated. The actual plans aimed at providing relief to only one section of the community, which was limited to the sick and indigent at level five and below on local tax rolls (*kosūwari*).

In Furuichi the *kosūwari* (a city, town, and village tax levied from 1872 on the household income and property of residents in these administrative units) was levied according to income levels ranging from one to two hundred. The extreme bottom of the scale, level one, referred to people with virtually no property, whereas level two hundred included only the town's wealthiest residents. The council's plan to limit discounted grain sales to residents at level five automatically disqualified most townspeople from receiving assistance. People expecting town-wide relief reacted angrily to the revised plan, with even destitute families complaining about the narrow scope of the council's relief measures. After the riots one poorer resident recalled that he and others felt embarrassed about being singled out as charity cases:

> We might have wanted rice sold [cheaply], but to be given relief rice would mean our registry records would be marked ["welfare recipients"]. It would be a blot lasting until our grandchildren's [generation]. Even though we wanted it, we would not go and buy [the rice].[7]

Before rioting began on the night of 13 August, a crowd of towns-people went to the button factory to seek out Kikui Yūzō and the other members of the negotiating committee. The crowd grew larger as several of its representatives angrily questioned the negotiating committee members to ascertain whether they had intentionally deceived them with misleading reports. Outside the factory office a few individuals began making extemporaneous speeches. Hosoda Yoshikichi, an umbrella craftsman, is reported to have said: "The [negotiating] committee and the buraku representatives have tried their best. But as for us, what have we done? Isn't it each and everyone's problem? Hurry up, ring the temple bell [the signal for emergency or natural disaster] and smash the landlords [*oyake*]." His appeal to the crowd was seconded by Matsumoto Motoyoshi, a farmer. Perhaps disgusted with the contentious wrangling of the old patrons and the new-money leaders, he urged the crowd to become their own "go-betweens." He himself was ready to take responsibility for whatever punishment might follow (*Orera ga kon'ya wa kimoiri shite yaru. Washi ga ato no koto wa hikiukete yaru*).

At about midnight someone did ring the temple bell. Electric power, normally shut down during fires or other calamities, was cut through-out the town, sending people scurrying into the streets to see what had happened. Most returned to their homes immediately, but a gathering of about forty continued to mill about the town's temple. Several policemen and the negotiating committee soon rushed over to calm the situation. They urged the group to go home, promising that rice would be sold at a discount from the next day. After a brief scuffle, the would-be peacemakers, outnumbered and ignored, could do nothing but leave the crowd to its own devices.

Following the temple meeting, a roving band of townspeople began attacking the homes of landlord families (see table 11). They first called on Morita Honji, a rich farmer and moneylender. After pelting his home with rocks, the crowd wound its way through Furuichi's central section, affording identical treatment to the director of the local bank and owners of the town's pawnshop, grocery store, and other businesses. Gradually, the crowd grew to about three hundred, 30 percent of whom were women. With rocks and clubs they damaged fences, smashed ornamental gateways, and broke up the latticework on the outside of the landlords' homes. In two or three places, they also broke into houses, damaging sliding screens and furnishings.

Although there were three rice dealerships in Furuichi, only Nakano Kosaburō's was set upon during the hour and a half of rioting. The town's largest rice dealer, Nakano was resented for his close ties with the *oyake* families. More than the other two rice dealerships, his store bought, milled, and sold the landlords' surplus grain. Nakano was also rumored to have plotted with the town's influential families to drive up local rice prices. According to the police version of the riots, town residents suspected him of having regularly deceived customers by selling less than full measure and by mixing chaff into rice. To punish Nakano rioters broke into his store and carried bales of rice and barley into the street, ripping them open and scattering the grain onto the roadway. Inside the store they overturned bins of rice and spilled their contents over the floor. No one attempted to carry off rice or other property, nor were incidents of theft reported during the course of the rioting.

The crowd remained in the streets during the early hours of 14 August. After the first wave of attacks, someone suggested that the pro-testers attack the landlords a second time. While they were debating the suggestion, Matsunaga Torakichi, a rice miller, arrived to announce that from the next day he would sell rice at twenty-five sen per shō. His words quieted the rioters, and the gathering began to break up.

The question of precisely who participated in the disturbance is not easy to answer. The courts prosecuted twelve individuals for leading or joining riots. But this was hardly representative of the number that actually joined the roving bands. Moreover, some of the alleged ringleaders maintained that they were not involved in the riots, even though they resigned themselves to accepting responsibility. The testimony of Furuichi residents indicates that three hundred or so actually joined in the attacks, a cross section of town residents including tenant farmers and button-factory workers.

There is little ambiguity about the focus of the crowd's attack. None of the targets appear to have been randomly selected. Striking only the homes of town council members or wealthier town residents and Nakano's rice dealership, the attacks were limited to the property of individuals who had become the focus of resentment over the limited relief plan. During the riots tenants continued to act deferentially to their own landlords. They scrupulously avoided attacking landlords with whom they had a direct personal relationship. This is not to say that the town's landlords escaped the riots unscathed. Popular resentment against the landlord group was sufficiently strong and landlords sufficiently numerous to assure that most of them were attacked, in some cases more than once. In only one incident did the crowd intervene to prevent damage to the home of a "good" landlord, Shatani Seijirō, who later provided funds for the rioters' legal defense.

Relief and Prosecution

As in rioting elsewhere, the Furuichi incident resulted in the immediate implementation of the kind of relief plan desired by local residents. The day after the disturbance, the town council moved to sell rice for twenty-six sen per shō. During the first four or five days the discount sales were open to all without regard for the purchaser's status on the local tax rolls. But the rice supply soon ran out, forcing the council to amend its fifty-day plan to make grain available only to those below tax level twenty. Although this disappointed some residents, it nevertheless represented a more liberal program than the original plan, which denied aid to anyone above *kosūwari* level five. After the riots residents continued to complain about the tax-based limitations that denied relief to many townspeople, but the beginning of the police investigation stifled further protest.

Local patrolmen began by interrogating Kikui Yūzō. Kikui maintained his innocence, arguing that he and the other negotiators had done all that they possibly could to prevent violence. When asked to identify crowd members, he disingenuously replied that darkness made it impossible to recognize anyone. Kikui was later released without charges, and the police did not interrogate any other committee member. The investigation eventually focused on residents of the northern section of town. Although the police found it difficult to find witnesses willing to testify against suspected rioters, a patrolman claimed that he had recognized certain voices and had actually seen several people from this part of town among the crowd. It was largely as a result of his testimony that the twelve people were charged with rioting (see table 12).

With the exception of a bicycle shop owner, the indicted represented Furuichi's poorer residents. Three were employed in button factories, and the rest held low-status and low-paying jobs as fruit vendors, barbers, and umbrella craftsmen. Only one was a full-time tenant farmer, which again suggests that alternative employment with "new-money" enterprises helped embolden people to move against the old landlord families. The rioters' income levels (based on their position on the local tax rolls) indicates that ten of the twelve would have been eligible for relief rice even on the basis of the town council's original plan to limit discount sales. Although several of those arrested had criminal records for petty crimes such as gambling, theft, and brawling, most had not been previously involved with the law. Found guilty on 9 October 1918, all of the rioters were sentenced to prison terms, although one defendant later had charges against him dismissed. According to postwar interviews, they were considered by their jailers to be "men of meritorious service" (kōrōsha) for helping reduce rice prices, and were afforded relatively kind treatment. On the basis of their previous clear records and good behavior, most were released after serving two-thirds of their original prison sentences.

Several of those who were tried insisted initially that they had nothing to do with the riots and protested their indictments. Unidentified town residents, however, urged them to accept punishment for the town's sake. They warned that continued protestations of innocence would only prolong the police investigation, which might result in more arrests. Suspects were also promised that their families would be looked after during the trial. In the event that they were sentenced to jail, certain townspeople also pledged help in starting their lives again.

The defendants finally capitulated, but little came of the promised support from town residents. Although the prison guards may have respected convicted rioters more than common criminals, most Furuichi townspeople were less generous. Kikui Yūzō, the button factory owner, and Shatani Seijirō, the "good" landlord whose property was spared during the riot, did help defray several defendants' trial expenses. But in general the families of those indicted bore their own defense costs and received no economic assistance after eleven of the twelve defendants were sent to jail. Ueda Yasutarō, another negotiating-committee member, later attempted to raise funds for a homecoming party for those released after serving their sentences, but the project met with little enthusiasm. To show his gratitude and the town's, Ueda finally used his own money to host a *naniwabushi* recital of traditional songs and stories for those released from confinement.

A major issue in the Furuichi riot was the failure of established town officials to assure local welfare. This is not to suggest that rice prices per se mattered little to the rioters. But the rural protesters viewed measures taken (or not taken) by local leaders as of equal, if not of greater, importance than grain dealers' attempts to maximize profits. The merchant's social role was, after all, to make money. In general, the rice dealer's fellow townsmen judged him by a different standard, regarding the merchant's scruples more leniently than those of officials responsible for local welfare. In many disputes rioters first pressed their demands upon wielders of local political influence and then, almost as an afterthought, attacked grain dealers.

Yet the distinction between political and economic targets in the rural riots should not be overdrawn. In Furuichi as in numerous other small towns, the groups that controlled local government and exerted economic clout often overlapped. In many incidents, attacking the landlords who served as village councilmen was tantamount to attacking grain holders and profiteers. The popular redress of local grievances therefore accomplished the twofold purpose of punishing official malfeasance and making cheaper rice available to local residents. By rioting, those without formal political power forced authorities to deny their own immediate economic interests to act on behalf of the general welfare of the town or village. The pattern resembled the one seen in Toyama. But there was an important difference. The Toyama protests attempted not to overturn local political relations but to return them to their preriot state. Fishwives and grain loaders returned to their calling, Kanagawa and the other grain merchants to theirs. But in the Furuichi dispute, the rioters and their more prosperous backers used unrest to further loosen the reins of political control once firmly held by the town's landlord elite.

TABLE 12. PEOPLE TRIED FOR RIOTING IN FURUICHI

Name	Age	Education	Occupation	Income Rank	Character	Prior Offenses	Family Remarks	Sentence Sought	Given
Matsumoto Motoyoshi	51	—	Farmer	Below 5 on tax rolls	Reportedly bad character, gambler.	2 months for gambling, fined 10 yen	7; daughter working as prostitute	4 years	3 years
Maruoka Chōhei	20	—	Liquor shop employee	Below 5	Good character, but likes violence.	—	—	$3\frac{1}{2}$ years	$2\frac{1}{2}$ years
Shiono Shōsaburō	21	Primary, fifth	Button maker	Below 5		—	—	3 years	$2\frac{1}{2}$ years
Takahashi Sanji	23	Upper-primary graduate	Button maker	—		—	—	3 years	$2\frac{1}{2}$ years
Ueda Komatarō	35	—	Toothbrush maker	—	Violent when drunk, now abstaining from drink. Bad character, gambler.	—	—	4 years	3 years
Hosoda Yoshijirō	42	—	Umbrella craftsman	—		Cockfighting, fined 2 yen	—	4 years	3 years
Kikui Ei'ichi	24	—	Bicycle sales	50–60 yen, economically well-off		—	—	3 years	$2\frac{1}{2}$ years

Name	Age	Educa-tion	Occupation	Income Rank	Character	Prior Offenses	Family Remarks	Sentence Sought	Given
Koike Noriyoshi	37		Button maker	Below level 5	Rumored to be a gambler.	Theft, served 2 months	5	4 years	3 years
Kodera Tsuneyoshi	37		Barber	—	—	—	7	2½ years	2 years
Nakano Torakichi	35		Fruit vendor, fire brigade leader	—	Fined 50 yen for fighting; 30 yen for gambling.	—	—	3½ years	Charges later dismissed
Kishimoto Sadakichi	22		Button maker	Level 2	—	—	—	1½ years	8 months
Kondō Kisaburō	26	Primary, second year	Matchstick maker	1 yen daily, below middling, level 6	Hardworking, known as leader capable of inciting others. Strong personality, bad behavior, good family relations.	—	—	1 year	8 months

SOURCES: *KSNK* 2 (1959): 106–8; Watanabe, "Ōsaka-fu Furuichi-machi no kome sōdō," 89–104.
NOTE: Only partial information is available for the defendants. Remarks on the character of the accused reflect police and prosecutor opinion.

Other Kansai Protests

Other incidents of rioting in the Kansai generally followed the pattern seen in Furuichi. While small committees negotiated with the locally influential, larger crowds attacked the property of landlords or town councilmen until aid measures were implemented. In multiple incidents, protests continued until the relief program was tailored to meet popular demands. Where local leaders unilaterally worked out aid plans, protesters acted to ensure "fairness." In practice this typically meant forcing officials to broaden eligibility requirements or reduce already discounted rice prices to an even lower level.

In some cases rioters additionally sought an equitable division of what they considered a commonly held resource. An example of rioting over communal funds occurred in the Nakano hamlet of Fujiidera in Osaka prefecture. In Fujiidera, a predominantly agricultural village, residents demanded that, instead of rice relief, local officials allocate money for relief from the village's common fund (*kyōyūkin*). Their request was not unprecedented, for farmers had previously been allowed to borrow from the fund during the July-to-August preharvest grain shortage (*hazakaiki*). On 13 August, however, several villagers demanded that the fund be disbursed to all needy residents. When village officials failed to respond to the demand, the crowd took to the streets. Much of the attack was directed against the property of Tsujita Sentarō, the manager of the common fund, and against the homes of his relatives because of his reluctance to divide village resources and his suspicious management of the common fund.[8]

In incidents of rural rioting in the Kansai, residents similarly threatened and attacked specific local representatives. In Minami Kudara village, also in Osaka prefecture, crowds moved against the village headman, Hashimoto Heitarō. Postriot accounts of the incident report that Hashimoto took no particular stand on whether relief should be given. Nevertheless, his indifference to difficulties faced by other villagers and his reputation for stinginess (*ketchi*) were used to justify the attack on his home.

A similar incident in which villagers judged the attitude of local leaders rather than any specific act occurred in Mozu village. In Mozu as in Furuichi, the village council took the initiative in planning discount sales. At first its actions seemed to have prevented the kind of protest occurring in nearby towns and villages. But at a meeting convened to settle relief measures, Tanaka Shingo, one of the town's wealthier landlords, obstructed the aid program by refusing to provide his grain for local sale. Tanaka argued that he could still get as much as fifty-five yen per koku for his rice and that he was not going to sell it at the price of thirty-five yen per koku offered by the Mozu council. Villagers reacted speedily to Tanaka's indifference to community welfare by forcing their way into his house and methodically breaking up its furnishings. Because Tanaka was away, crowd leaders explained their actions to his mother. They promised that the vandalism would stop the moment she agreed to sell rice at twenty-five yen per koku, ten yen below the selling price set earlier by the village council. Tanaka's mother, claiming that the price was too low, at first refused to negotiate. But as the vandalism continued, she gave in. The rioters took all the rice held in Tanaka's storehouse except what they deemed necessary for the family's use.

Although some crowd members advocated taking charge of the grain on the spot, a majority agreed to wait until the next day to pick up the rice. As in Toyama, Furuichi, and elsewhere, no one attempted to break into Tanaka's granaries directly, and nothing was taken until the rice holder "consented" to sell grain at the crowd's price. The following morning, 17 August, Tanaka duly turned over thirty-seven bales of rice to the village council, which were immediately put up for public sale.

In Mozu rioters and targets alike seemed to conform to the unwritten rules in effect in Furuichi and many other sites of rural rioting. These rules permitted the destruction of property but ruled out thievery; allowed for threatening demonstrations, but did not permit physical force against individuals. The unwritten code also required people who could provide aid to be denied the option of not participating once relief plans were set. On their part, those who were attacked seemed to accept the popular judgment by turning over rice, increasing donations for discount sales, and honoring pledges to broaden relief efforts. These rules were seldom violated. Despite the immense scale of town and village rioting, theft and assault—features of urban rioting—rarely occurred.

The moderation of the rioters' actions might have stemmed from the limited and isolated nature of the conflicts. Although rioting was widespread in the countryside, almost all incidents occurred independently in a single village or town. Word of unrest in one particular location undoubtedly stimulated a similar riot in a nearby town or village, but a joint protest of three or more villages was unheard of. Except for incidents involving burakumin and the Toyama protests, rioters usually did not join in protests even in towns or villages neighboring their own. The closed nature of social relations in rural communities made local protests very much like private family disputes. Residents might disagree over particular issues, but personal relations kept the dispute within the "family" and moderated the rioters' methods.

A second reason for the relative mildness of the rioters' methods and for the ready compliance of their targets, was that protesters seldom asked for more than officials were able to give. In the Mozu incident, for example, the rioters' actions did little more than carry out relief measures already approved by the village council. Violence occurred when grain holders such as Tanaka were able but unwilling to extend aid. At Tanaka's house rioters took only his surplus grain, leaving the stores of rice that were required for his family's use. The crowd did not intend to ruin Tanaka financially, although their mandated fair price for his grain was set punitively below what was originally offered by the council. But they were willing to force his compliance and censure his reluctance to join an aid program that would generally benefit the local community.

In other incidents, such as the Hiraoka village disturbance in Osaka prefecture, violent confrontations between officials or attacks on recalcitrant individuals proved unnecessary. A single noisy gathering in front of the town or village office prompted officials to institute relief efforts. Threatening but largely nonviolent measures taken throughout the Kansai region and central Japan included the posting of handbills and the sending of anonymous letters. The posters typically called for meetings to discuss "livelihood" problems, demanded cheaper grain prices, and threatened wide-scale retribution for profiteers, hoarders, and officials who had become lax in their duties. Anonymous letters to prefecture, county, and town offices or to grain-dealer associations carried similar messages. In Ashida village in Hyogo, for example, the head of a local ward (*kuchō*) received a letter warning that his house would be "drenched in oil and burned to the ground" if he did not personally take steps to assure the sharing of village wealth.[9] Attempts to follow through on such threats were rare. Nevertheless, posters and letters made officials aware of popular unrest and increased their willingness to institute aid programs.

Numerically, rice dealerships were more often the targets of protest than town or village offices were. In part, this is simply because grain dealerships far outnumbered local government offices. Yet it is important to note that, as in the cases of Furuichi and Mozu, rioters criticized town or village councils for condoning profiteering by rice dealers. In resorting to direct action against grain merchants, rioters merely took steps that local officials appeared reluctant to take.

An incident where rioters clearly achieved the twin goals of prompting political action and redressing grievances against grain dealers took place in Kamioka village in Kyoto. There a crowd estimated at about a hundred gathered at four local rice dealers and demanded that rice be sold at thirty-five sen per shō instead of at the market price of forty-seven sen per shō. Residents were said to be motivated to usurp the role of the village council because of official action taken in the neighboring town of Kizu to lower rice prices. When Kamioka officials failed to follow Kizu's lead, villagers bypassed their legal representatives and approached the rice dealers directly.[10] Again, the incident was by no means unique. In twelve of the twenty-five rural riots in Hyogo prefecture, protesters demonstrated against and attacked rice retailers and dealers, particularly those charging high prices or obstructing relief plans.[11]

Rural rioters usually directed demands for popular redress against officials, grain dealers, and wealthier town residents. But there were also incidents with little overt connection to rice prices. Yoshimura Tsutomu notes in his study of rioting in the Kansai region that villagers, in harassing the locally influential, occasionally appeared bent on simple chastisement for past unspecified grievances. In some cases they did not even bother to demand reduced prices for rice or relief donations.[12] In the Furuichi riots, the cost of grain was important, but the protests also represented a clash between old and new money for greater control of local politics and the town's economic life. The hungry did not initiate the action. It was the work of an apparently self-appointed negotiating committee, a group composed not of poor farmers but of plant managers and relatively well-off members of the local intelligentsia.

The arena for narrow political rivalry provided by the rice riots can likewise be seen in disturbances at Ōharano village in Kyoto. After demonstrations resulted in lower rice prices, villagers joined together again to carry out an "antiboss" struggle against the village headman, Sakaguchi Toyojirō. In trial testimony following the riots, Sakaguchi is described as

> a stubborn and opportunistic man who has no compunctions about troubling others if it serves his own self-interest. He possesses an extremely bad reputation within the village. . . . In mid-1916 he was involved in a shady deal involving public land and in February 1918 was known to have swindled another person out of a land parcel bordering his. He is a notorious womanizer whose previous acts have damaged public morals.[13]

Although the headman's popularity had never been very great, the specific incident that led to the attack on him had little to do with his bad reputation and even less with the cost of rice. In 1918 Ōharano residents had unanimously agreed to the placing of utility poles on privately owned land to facilitate electrification. But when it came down to actually installing the poles, Sakaguchi blocked the project by hiring workmen to remove them from his property. His action not only interfered with plans to bring electricity to the community, it also obstructed traffic along the roadway, inconveniencing fellow villagers.

After rioting had proved effective in lowering rice prices, Ōharano residents turned their attention to their notorious village headman. In late August villagers held a rally and unanimously demanded Sakaguchi's resignation. He refused, saying that as he had done nothing illegal, there was no point in discussing the matter. His obstinacy only increased the anger of his opponents. Villagers held a raucous mass meeting in front of the headman's house until Sakaguchi appeared to apologize publicly for his past actions. His bowing before the crowd apparently ended the "antiboss" struggle. The record of the Ōharano riot makes no mention of whether Sakaguchi continued as headman or relocated the offending utility poles.

Rioters, Local Organizations, and the Consequences of Protest

Arrest and trial records, basic sources for determining who rioted, provide only a small sampling of those who actually joined in protests. In Furuichi, police and postriot studies agree that at least three hundred people, or approximately 10 percent of the town's total population, took part in the August unrest. Yet only twelve people were tried for riot-related crimes. Police, outnumbered and virtually powerless in every disturbance, rarely apprehended anyone during the rioting. But even waiting until protests had quieted before rounding up suspects did not guarantee that the real culprits would be found. Local people often proved unwilling to testify against one another or, if the victim of an attack, to press charges. Further complicating the problem was the tendency for local residents to band together so as to minimize punishment from outside the local community. In Furuichi this practice extended to providing investigating officials with a small token sacrificial group, one that included a number of the community's poorest and most vulnerable members, to take the community's collective punishment.[14]

Arrest and prosecution records do generally indicate the economic and social background of rural rioters. One of the first things apparent from these sources is that, in contrast to the varied occupations of participants in massive urban disturbances, fairly homogeneous groups carried out the smaller protests in small towns and villages. In fourteen incidents of rural rioting in the Kansai area, farmers, craftsmen, unskilled laborers, and vendors constituted the main occupational categories of those charged with rioting. Of 203 people arrested, 91 (45 percent) gave farming as their occupation, 17 (8 percent) were part-time farmers with other jobs, while the remaining 95 (47 percent) represented workers in small factories, day laborers, carters, fruit vendors, shop employees, and workers in similar low-paying jobs.[15] In short, about half of those prosecuted for rioting in the Kansai were farmers, and half were a mixed group of farmers, petty tradesmen, and laborers—a proportion fairly representative of the population of urbanizing small towns and villages throughout the region. According to prefectural arrest records, farmers made up approximately 50 percent of those arrested in Hyogo and 75 percent of those in Kyoto disturbances.[16] The prefectural statistics do not, however, reflect the degree of involvement in farming. It is likely that many who listed their occupation as farmers also took part in some kind of side-work.

Prosecution records and case studies also suggest that rural riots more often involved local organizations than urban protests did. In contrast to city protests, in which mutually anonymous individuals participated in mass citizens' rallies, the smaller-scale rural disputes were composed of people who knew each other from local youth associations, reservist groups, or volunteer fire brigades; in some instances rioters belonged to all three groups. It was hardly accidental that police records traced the beginning of the Furuichi disturbance to a meeting at the local youth association hall. In incidents of rioting elsewhere, the organization's officers and membership also took an active role in the disturbances.

In rioting in Mozu village in Osaka, where a single landlord's refusal to provide grain effectively sabotaged relief plans, the director of the youth association, Kudō Ichino, designed and executed a detailed plan to force relief measures. Kudō, who also served as Mozu's Shinto priest, met with five other youth association officers on 15 August. They decided that the association, as a group, would break into the homes of the recalcitrant landlord to force him and other wealthy residents to turn over their surplus rice. Taking charge of the rice, the group agreed to sell it directly to needy villagers. To ensure that the action would be smoothly coordinated, association members were ordered to dress in black. Kudō, as group leader, would wear white, for easy recognition by his followers. The plan was successfully carried out, and the proceeds from the sale of the rice were handed over to the original owners of the rice.[17]

Youth association, reservists, or fire brigade members also played leading roles in the "antiboss" struggle in Ōharano village in Kyoto and in other disturbances in Hyogo and Osaka.[18] Members of these groups formed action committees, met with village or town officials, and negotiated with rice dealers. As is evident in the careful planning that went into the Mozu riot, few disturbances in which the local organizations participated were entirely spontaneous. Leaders scheduled times and places for assembly, relayed word about attack plans and targets, established "fair" prices, and carried out relief measures. In some cases they scheduled demonstrations and attacks for times when local police were least likely to become involved.

The members of these local organizations seemed clearly aware of local power relationships. Moreover, as we have seen in Furuichi and elsewhere, they understood that such relations were in flux. In protests that punished recalcitrant old leaders to the benefit of emerging new elites, the actions of youth association and other groups were multifaceted. They reflected a local consensus, helped organize effective actions, and served as a vehicle for achieving the rioters' aim. But as in Toyama, their political horizon was clearly limited. Unlike the urban rioters, who saw rice prices and shortages as problems resulting from central-government policies, the rural protesters dealt with these issues within the confines of their own town or village.

The rioters' actions were not, however, entirely economically determined. Members of local voluntary organizations active during the protests included relatively well-off rural community members. In more purely agricultural villages, middle farmers joined associations and participated as group members in the riots, and in industrializing towns such as Furuichi, middle-class residents took a leading role in the protest. In cases where the riots formed part of an antiboss or other more overtly political struggle, the participation of wealthier residents appeared to be an extension of an ongoing local power struggle.

Aside from ulterior political motives, however, solidarity with poorer residents seemed to result from group obligation (*giri ishiki*), peer pressure, and an individual sense of moral outrage. Organized to maintain ethical as well as nationalistic values, youth associations and reservist groups helped foster the emotional outlook and values that facilitated criticism of and actions against indifferent officials and self-serving grain dealers. Although Meiji-period volunteer associations were formally organized at the behest of the central government, they had succeeded and been influenced by earlier autonomous organizations (for example, youth groups [*wakamonogumi*], fire brigades, and field protection groups). Given their functions on the local level, the new groups might be compared to old wine in new bottles—except that most of the earlier autonomous village organizations continued to exist in the Taishō period. The membership of the reservists or youth associations typically overlapped with that of the festival committee, fire brigade, or crop protection group. Moreover simply joining a national organization did not magically transform the individual villager, who might be worried about how to pay the rice bill or incensed by the unequal sharing of local resources, into a model citizen of imperial Japan. Despite the intentions of central government planners to use the reservists associations and other bodies as a means of strengthening loyalty to the state, these organizations also advocated the values and interests of the local community. Indeed, during the 1918 rural riots, the concern of these groups for local welfare seemed to override their respect for national law.

In stressing the spontaneous nature of the 1918 riots, historians have emphasized the negligible role of reservists or youth associations as identifiable groups.[19] Nevertheless, the most common feature of the more than eight thousand riot suspects throughout the nation was membership in a reservist or youth association. This fact and its implication of loyalties divided between respect for national law and concern for local welfare was not missed by national leaders either during or after the protests. At the peak of rioting, the central government did not hesitate to mobilize regular troops, but the official attitude toward using reservists to restore order was decidedly more cautious. Although scores of reservists and members of youth associations were asked to stand guard duty, they were not sent to clash with rioting crowds or make arrests on the scene.[20] Official reluctance to order local volunteers into a more active role might be explained by the sheer novelty of the nationwide mass rioting. Never in the half-century of the Meiji government's existence had local order broken down so thoroughly, and never before had local groups been called upon to remedy the situation. Yet before 1918 reservists, youth associations, fire brigades, and similar local groups had been called upon to keep the peace and assist in rounding up felons, including murderers and robbers. A more likely reason for the central government's hesitation in using auxiliary forces in 1918 was that officials were not at all sure how these groups would respond. They had cause for concern. In rural rioting in Osaka, Okayama, Kyoto, Hyogo, Shizuoka, and Yamaguchi prefectures, reservists and youth association leaders were identified not simply as having joined in the rioting but as leading local people in confiscating grain, putting it up for public sale, and "inspecting" the storehouses of grain holders. In several prefectures, local fire brigades responded slowly to fires intended to destroy the property of landlords or grain dealers and occasionally turned their fire hoses on rice stored for shipment. The failure of reservists or youth association leaders to proclaim that such actions were carried out in the name of the local organizations does not mean that these associations, as organized groups, were uninvolved in the protests. To have identified local groups as responsible for riotous acts would not only have been tactically stupid but would also have exposed a large section of the local population to punishment. As we have seen in repeated incidents of rural rioting, it was common for suspects to assert that they acted as individuals or, in the midst of a protest, to offer to take personal responsibility for what was clearly a group action.

Central-government officials concerned with local reservist and youth association branches seemed to see through the fiction of "individual action": after the riots they expressed concern about the reliability of these groups in maintaining local order. Their fears went beyond the issue of domestic peace. After all, if reservists and youth associations could not be relied upon within Japan, what might members of these groups do when recruited into the military for service abroad? The question was of particular concern to Terauchi Masatake. Before being driven from office by the rice riots, Terauchi had committed Japanese troops to intervene against the Bolsheviks in Siberia. As the head of the Imperial Reservist Association he expressed his shock at the recent acts of reservists, in a directive sent to each regimental district headquarters in October 1918:

> For military men to forget their basic duty, to throw themselves into the vortex of riots, and to undergo arrest—these are ugly sights. Yet many have been arrested, have refused to follow regulations on the proper wearing of uniforms, and have obstructed [reservist] mobilization. We must restrain such reckless behavior. Make it your constant aim never to sully the honor of military men![21]

Such statements of concern notwithstanding, popular support for reservists associations temporarily declined after the riots. Membership in

Osaka reservists associations fell precipitously, and association officers complained that, despite the institution of dinner meetings aimed at encouraging participation, attendance at some branches had fallen by 50 percent. It was said to be difficult to hold meetings because only officers would turn out. Other observers noted that reservists were reluctant to wear uniforms or donned them on inappropriate occasions, as one reservist had done to make an ironic statement during a labor dispute against the Mitsubishi company.[22]

The willingness of associations to act contrary to national policy and laws during the riots arose from links between them and previous organizations that had existed for the benefit of local residents rather than the state. As Fukutake Tadashi observed in his study of rural society, even after the central government's reorganization of local associations in 1910,

> there was no feeling that these organizations had been foisted upon them from without. Villagers felt it their natural duty to pay for the *seinen dan*, the women's association, and the volunteer fire brigade from the meager fund in the village treasury. Since the organizations were thought of as intertwined with, rather than independent of, the hamlet, their growth had the feed-back effect of fostering hamlet unity.[23]

During the summer period of rice shortages members of village organizations saw cause for protest all around them. Farmers could not afford to eat what they produced, landlords often acted like rural *narikin*, and officials seemed unwilling to institute relief. The view of many of the rural rioters was summed up by a Kyoto protester who described grain shortages as created by those having "no moral sense" (*dōtoku shin no nai*).[24] When the government in Tokyo seemed far away and indifferent, residents did not feel compelled to march in lockstep with the state. On the contrary, members of voluntary organizations often reverted to the more traditional function of their forerunners—that is, maintaining local values according to their own lights. It seemed of little consequence that their actions violated the larger national order and the letter of the law.

Nevertheless, officials—and surprisingly, rioters as well—expected a price to be paid for breaking laws and overriding the authority of politically and economically influential community members. In all of the cases discussed above, riot leaders faced stiff prison terms for their actions. Yet the prospect did not dissuade them from taking direct action. In Furuichi one of the leaders of the rioting reflected the mood of many of the participants in his willingness to take individual responsibility for their collective actions. His resigned attitude was typical. In many incidents of rural rioting, crowd leaders confronted protest targets face to face, wore white, and made no serious attempt to conceal their identity. Disguising themselves was probably pointless in any case because strangers were few in the small communities where rioting occurred. Nevertheless, the rioters' open actions seemed to arise not because it was futile to mask identities but out of an understanding that coercive acts meant punishment.

In Furuichi this understanding extended even to those who initially protested their innocence but finally yielded to group pressure to prevent an expansion of arrests. Fellow townsmen who counseled arrestees to accept indictment appeared not the least concerned about the guilt or innocence of riot suspects or whether actual perpetrators ever faced trial. Of greater importance was the presentation of a token group to authorities to accept the punishment all expected. Trial and imprisonment represented the price for achieving the rioters' goals. In a manner strikingly similar to that of rioters punished during Tokugawa peasant uprisings (*murakata ikki*), those indicted put up little protest when called upon to bear the burden of not only their own rebellious actions but those of others as well.

Rioting carried a heavy price, but it also achieved the immediate goal of rice relief. In purely agricultural villages, one-third to one-half of all residents received aid.[25] In Furuichi and elsewhere expanded aid measures coordinated with a national relief program remained in effect for fifty days or longer. Even after that period, officials continued to buy foreign rice and urged local dealers to cooperate in keeping prices low.

Tenants and poorer local residents also gained permanent advantages as a consequence of the riots. The rioters' actions demonstrated that decisions by officials, landlords, and grain dealers were subject to popular redress. Having challenged local authorities by taking government into their own hands on one occasion, rioters established a precedent for future disturbances and a greater sharing of local political control. This precedent was especially evident in the tenants movement, which gained momentum after the 1918 riots had demonstrated the effectiveness of protest. Kansai and Chūbu, the regions of the most widespread rioting in 1918, were also the most active during the organized movement for tenants' rights in the 1920s.

There was not, however, a perfect correspondence between the towns and villages that experienced rioting in 1918 and those that later became involved in conflicts with entrenched wielders of local authority.

Postriot changes in local political relations were shaped by the particular manner in which officials and landlords dealt with protesters, as well as by the rioters' sense of "guilt." In some places the uprising seemed to provide a kind of catharsis. After the riots local elites were more considerate in their handling of town or village affairs; people who had rioted and thereby been exposed to the strong and immediate deterrent of stiff prison sentences became more quiescent. Even though popular sentiment tended to support the rioters' actions, arrest and imprisonment were nonetheless considered shameful. At times, community attitudes toward convicted rioters seemed based on a double standard. In Furuichi, for example, local residents encouraged those arrested to accept responsibility for the uprising and promised financial aid to their families. But after those convicted had been released from jail, neighbors did not help them start their lives over. Economic loss compounded social sanctions. The long imprisonment of a main wage earner or contributor to family income left many families in a worse situation than they were in before the protests began.

Some of those targeted for attack during the riots found that turning the other cheek eased tensions within the community. In trials against suspected rioters, landlords and other locally influential residents sometimes refused to press charges, and several even helped to defray defense costs. By playing on feelings of indebtedness and using their paternalistic position as "parent families," landlords and community officials helped stave off sudden shifts in political or economic relationships as a direct result of the rural riots. But once local authority had been challenged, in some cases with impunity for all but a few, the willingness of local elites to forgive and forget could also be viewed as weakness. As was evident in Furuichi, where within a decade of the 1918 protests a new group had displaced the landlords on the town council, attempts to return to a more stable, paternalistic order were not always successful.

Tenant-Landlord Riots:
Hōryūji, Nara

Hōryūji, now known as Ikaruga-chō, in many ways resembled Furuichi. A mixed farming and manufacturing village, nearly 46 percent of its 398 households farmed extremely small holdings of two or three tan or worked as agricultural tenants.[26] As late as 1933, 62.1 percent of village farmland was tenant-cultivated. While half of the working members of Hōryūji's population of 2,070 tilled the land, the other half found jobs in vegetable-oil processing, silk production, weaving, transportation, and shipping. During the Shōwa years, agricultural work rapidly gave way in importance to commercial and industrial employment. According to prefectural statistics, the proportion of cultivators to other types of workers in Hōryūji was lower than the rate for Nara prefecture (49.9 percent farmers in 1933) as a whole, or for Ikoma (45.9 percent), the village's home county. While some farmers had become full-time workers in manufacturing and commerce, during the agricultural off-season others supplemented their incomes by working in Osaka city, which was linked to Hōryūji by rail and telephone lines. During the Taishō period, however, farming still provided the villagers' primary source of income. Despite increasing occupational diversity, an estimated 90 percent of the yen value of the village's production came from farming in 1918, and most of this from Hōryūji's twice-yearly rice crop.

Disputes between tenants and landlords over the profitable rice harvest had occurred well before the 1918 riots. One recurring source of conflict was the proximity of the Osaka grain market. Large landlords annually shipped off grain for marketing in the nearby commodities exchange. This practice usually corresponded with the period of shortage before the new rice was harvested (*hazakaiki*), a time when local tenants, because of high in-kind rents, found their own reserves of food rice already exhausted. From at least as early as 1897, tenants regularly appealed to landlords to defer rents or lower rates in times of shortages and poor harvests. A 1912 study of village agricultural conditions notes that such requests were no longer being made on an individual basis. According to the report, tenants had closed ranks and were now "making excuses" for nonpayment and clamoring for negotiated rent rates.

Following a drought in 1913, tenants again asked for lower rents, a request that landlords simply ignored until 1914 when tenants began a boycott of Hōryūji's local primary school. Tenant representatives explained this unconventional tactic by stating that "because of poor harvests, tenants are impoverished. If children are not sent to work, we cannot make a living. We cannot [afford] to educate them." The landlords might have told the boycotters to suit themselves. The education of peasant children was, after all, not their concern. But the widely supported action proved extremely embarrassing to the village council. This group, composed entirely of landlords, took pride in the hamlet's association with Hōryūji temple. Village leaders had dedicated the primary school to the spirit of Shōtoku Taishi, the Japanese paragon of learning and a symbol of cultural values. For local people to boycott the school because Hōryūji's prominent families were unwilling even to discuss rent reductions suggested that village leaders were both stingy and hypocritical. The action mocked town elders who urged pupils to emulate Prince Shōtoku in taking every opportunity to fill their minds and at the same time failed to provide parents the means to fill their youngsters' stomachs. Not long after the boycott began, Hōryūji's headman negotiated a compromise in which landlords reduced rents temporarily, and the tenants' children returned to school.

Emboldened by the boycott's success, tenants demanded a 20 percent rent reduction after the 1915 harvest. When landlords again ignored the request, tenants simply withheld 20 percent of the rent rice. Landlords responded by threatening to take stern measures against everyone who joined the action. In 1916 the Tatsumi family, Hōryūji's wealthiest landholding group and the village's first family, followed up these threats by summarily evicting from Tatsumi land all rent-withholding tenants.

Tatsumi's high-handed action at first united rather than weakened the farmers' resolve to continue the protest. Tenant leaders argued that if everyone returned Tatsumi land, the resulting economic loss to the village's single-most important family would yield a significant victory in the struggle with landlords generally. But concerted landlord pressure and the bribing of a key protest leader eroded popular support for action against Tatsumi. Nevertheless, the tenants in the Go-chō section of Hōryūji, where most Tatsumi land was concentrated, continued the protest by returning their holdings. Individual tenants in Hōryūji and sympathetic farmers in neighboring Tomisato village, also unhappy with Tatsumi's high rents, later joined the dispute. The protesters returned ten chō of land in all, but only after cutting all remaining grain standing on it.

Tatsumi Hei'ichirō, the family's patriarch, responded to the tenant boycott by hiring several dozen unskilled burakumin workers (*hisabetsu burakumin*) from a nearby village to work his land. He housed the workers in tents within the family's compound and attempted to direct their work. Despite his best efforts, the countermeasure at first appeared on its way to dismal failure. The newly recruited farmers were willing workers, but they lacked seedlings, oxen, necessary tools, and perhaps most important, experienced farmers to oversee their work.

Tatsumi withstood the boycott, but he was not able to do it on his own. Aware of the test of wills involved, other landlords united behind his family. They supplied needed tools, livestock, and fertilizer and also ordered their own tenants to provide seedlings. The dispute ended when the village head once again intervened to bring both sides to terms. The tenants, however, gained little. In the end, landlords still refused to lower the 1915 rents. Their only concessions were to re-extend cultivation rights to the evicted tenants and to "consider" (*kōryo*) assisting needy tenants in purchasing fertilizer.

Insect infestation and a dry spell in 1917 once again reduced the Hōryūji harvest, rekindling requests for lower rents. This time, cultivators pressed their demands in a more orderly fashion by forming a committee to coordinate negotiations. With organization came an escalation in demands: rather than 20 percent, tenants now demanded a 30 percent rent reduction. In turn, the local landlords unified their own ranks by drawing up a new "landlords association contract" (*jinushi kai keiyakusho*). The agreement, which each association member was required to sign, stipulated that all landlords must aid any single landlord in incidents in which tenants returned holdings. It added that landlords would jointly file legal suit against any and all tenants withholding rents.

The tenants committee and the landlord "contract" represented a new phase in the conflict. Never before had farmers formally organized against landlords, and never before had landlords found it necessary to explicitly unite against the village's small-scale cultivators. Moreover, until the 1917 dispute, neither party in the rent struggle had called on outside legal authorities to settle their differences. Yet when tenants withheld 30 percent of the rent due on the 1917 harvest, a group of twenty-two landlords, acting according to the letter of their association contract, filed suit in the Nara District Court demanding rent payments in full.

The still-unresolved legal proceedings contributed to the two days of rioting that began in Hōryūji on 14 August 1918. But the protests involved other villagers than those named in the landlords' suit. Two groups with overlapping memberships led the dispute. The first, the ten-member tenants committee, acted in a quasi-legal manner. On 14 August several committeemen went to the village office to call upon Saeki Umetarō, Hōryūji's headman, to discuss rent reduction and the lawsuit against local tenants. They told Saeki that if the rent controversy was not amicably settled, then a violent uprising like the one in Osaka city might break out in Hōryūji. The meeting with Saeki represented little more than an opportunity for tenants to make thinly veiled threats. Once the committee had attempted to pressure Saeki, its members took no further part in the disturbance. Although they occupied the village office throughout the rioting, they neither encouraged nor hindered the rioters, who stopped by the village office now and then over the next two nights.

A second, larger group of about a hundred tenant farmers, laborers, and tradesmen took part in face-to-face confrontations with landlords. This crowd gathered at the village office, throwing rocks and noisily demanding that local leaders reduce rice prices, provide relief, and settle the tenant-landlord lawsuit. After this demonstration they began a circuit of landlord homes.

It would be difficult to describe as "attacks" what happened on the nights of 14 and 15 August. The crowd was certainly intimidating, but not aggressive. At the Tatsumi residence, for example, rioters beat on the compound gate and called for Hei'ichirō to appear. But when no one answered the door, they made no attempt to break in or damage property. Instead, members of the crowd simply squatted around the entryway while Morita Ainosuke, a tenant later sentenced to seven years in prison for leading the riots, allegedly yelled to those inside the house: "If you don't open up, we'll just wait here until morning." Aside from verbal threats, the most aggressive action taken by rioters was to throw stones and bang on gates and doorways. None of the landlords sustained significant property damage.

The rioters visited the homes of fourteen landlords during the protest, demanding only that the landlords "lend" them rice. The crowd is said to have acted politely in making its request. For example, as twenty or thirty people gathered outside one landlord's door, one of the leaders reportedly opened the exchange with the customary greeting "Excuse us for troubling you" (*Ojama o shite sumenu*). Nevertheless, it is not surprising that landlords felt threatened by the noisy gatherings. No one had warned them that crowds would appear in the dead of night, banging on their doors and demanding "loans." Moreover, rioters and landlords alike realized that words like "loan" or "borrow" were merely a verbal nicety for "forced contribution." One of the crowd's leaders made this clear in testimony at his trial:

> Although we said we had come to borrow rice, we came in a large group late at night or in the early morning hours. . . . No matter what method we used, there was no thought about returning [the grain]. We went on pell-mell to the next place and the next after that, saying we've come to borrow rice. . . . No one intended to return anything.

In one confrontation the target of the attack, a landlord and former village headman, faced the crowd at his doorway and demanded to know precisely who was borrowing his grain. Voices answered that the loan would be to everyone, that everyone wanted to borrow his grain. No one, however, stepped forward to take responsibility for the loan, nor did anyone mention repayment.

The landlords responded in several ways. Some, like Tatsumi, refused to open their doors and thereby avoided face-to-face confrontation. Others told crowd representatives to proceed through proper channels, to place their requests before the village council. Despite the variety of responses, most landlords eventually turned over several bales of rice to the rioters, the Tatsumi family excepted. Several landlords did not wait to be asked but simply left bales of rice outside their doorways. Others enlisted their own workers to deliver the grain to the open area in front of the village office designated by protest leaders as the central collection point.

After the first night of rice borrowing on 15 August, town leaders called a meeting of the local reservist association and requested that its members intervene to put down the protest. But only 20 of the group's 173 members, landlords almost to a man, appeared at the meeting. Rank-and-file reservists refused to get involved, explaining that rent reductions and other issues leading to the riots were a problem for landlords and tenants to solve and had nothing to do with them. This was, at best, a half-truth. Many of the reservists were tenants who had little to gain by taking the landlord's side in the dispute and likely benefited from the borrowing expeditions. According to Teruoka Shuzō's detailed study, reservist leaders, in fact, took a leading role in demanding that rice be lent and later joined negotiations for local relief. They were active in attempting to resolve the dispute, but they proved unwilling to act exclusively on the landlords' behalf. Although landlords were predominant among the local association's officers, they could not convince the group's general membership to stop the rice borrowing. In the years following the riots, prosperous landlords came to regard the association as unreliable in protecting their interests as they were displaced as officers of the group by independent farmers, tenants, and merchants.

During the night of 15 August landlords, expecting a renewed round of rice borrowing, turned to the tenant committee to control the crowds. Saeki, the village headman, told the committeemen gathered at the village office that the bands of roving borrowers were extorting rice.

He warned that the committeemen shared responsibility for the disturbance; once things settled down, they would be legally as culpable as
those who directly forced landlords to loan rice. One committeeman
disingenuously responded to Saeki, saying: "From the start we simply
appealed for a solution to the tenants' problems. We have nothing to do
with the rice borrowing that's going on everywhere. We don't know a
thing about it." Strictly speaking, this correctly described the committee's actions during the riots. None of its members, calmly sitting at the
village office, made any overt attempt to direct the crowds marching
through Hōryūji. Yet even though they did not lead the rioters, they
also did not deter rice borrowers from their midnight visits to landlord
homes. Moreover, the committeemen who had symbolically taken over
the village office appeared to approve passively the actions of rioters
who delivered expropriated grain to their doorway.

As in Furuichi, the riots ended without forcible suppression by police
or troops. After collecting relief rice and chastising the landlords, the
protesters returned home to await official reaction. The response took
the form of relief measures and arrests, the carrot-and-stick approach
seen in nearly every incident of rioting. After several meetings at Tatsumi Hei'ichirō's residence and the village office, Hōryūji's landlords and
councilmen decided that aid should be extended to all local residents
below a minimum level on local tax rolls. Funds for the program came
from "compulsory donations" (*kyōsei kifukin*) contributed primarily
by Hōryūji landlords. The council used the contributions to buy rice
and subsidize the difference between the market and discount sale
prices. Although local officials ordered the "borrowed" rice to be returned to the landlords, the council's relief measures meant in effect
that landlords were, as we have seen elsewhere, simply buying rice from
themselves. In this manner, they made available 160 bales of grain for
relief distribution.

Landlords also agreed to end their dispute with tenants over the
1917 harvest. Relying on local police as negotiators, the compromise
agreement reduced rents by 7.5 percent. The settlement was far below
the 30 percent demanded by tenants, but it was nonetheless the first
time that landlords had given in. Some tenants grumbled about the
small size of the rent reduction, but complaints were muted when the
landlords agreed to drop their lawsuit against people who had previously withheld rent.

Arrests followed the institution of relief measures. In early September
police took into custody seven members of the tenant committee as well

as fifteen others suspected of inciting a riot, extortion, and illegal entry. In a preliminary decision handed down in May 1919, they were all found guilty as charged. In a second hearing, however, the initial judgment against the seven committeemen was reversed and the remaining defendants received somewhat lighter sentences. Nevertheless, the noncommitteemen all served prison terms for their role in the riots.

The committee members' guilty verdicts were probably overturned because they had carefully avoided taking any active role in the riots. Although authorities charged them with leading the disturbance, none had left the village office or joined in the visits to the landlords' houses. Yet this was not the only reason for their release. The efforts of capable attorneys retained by landlords on the committeemen's behalf probably played an important role in reversing the verdicts. In retrospect, the landlords' leniency appears more shrewd than compassionate. In supporting the tenants committee, a group that had acted moderately during the riots, the landlords' apparent attitude of forgive and forget separated the tenant leaders from the other defendants. The tactic weakened the solidarity of landlord opposition and obligated the tenants' leaders to the very landlords whom they had challenged in past rent-reduction struggles. By helping gain the freedom of the committeemen, the landlords temporarily bolstered their influence in the village.

As for the fifteen noncommittee defendants, the charges against them were not dismissed nor were their sentences reduced to fines even though property damage and physical assaults did not occur during the Hōryūji disturbance. Aside from one defendant who died in jail before sentencing, the rest received sentences ranging from eighteen months to seven years at hard labor. Those people who paid most dearly for the protests were members of the village's "lower-class." Ten of them were part-time tenant farmers, most of whom also worked as rickshaw pullers, vendors of used goods, or day laborers. Only one could be described as financially well-off.

The differential treatment afforded the two groups of Hōryūji defendants reflects the complicated fracturing of village unity. While the tenants committee contained a larger number of landowning tenant farmers, the rice borrowers represented landless tenants, tradesmen, petty merchants, and laborers. These groups acted in concert to pressure prosperous landlords, but their specific aims were not identical. The tenants committee, from first to last, demanded lower rents; rice borrowers demanded grain and relief donations. The former group was more concerned with production, whereas those who made midnight visits to landlords requested rice for their own and for other needy villagers' immediate consumption.

In tenancy disputes that predated the 1918 riots, better-off farmers had complained about the system of rice inspection that required them to give a large share of their first-quality grain to landlords as rent payments in kind. They protested rent rates not because they lacked food sufficient for their own subsistence but because high rents reduced their marketable grain surplus.[27] During the Taishō years, Hōryūji cultivators actually paid less rent than they had paid during Meiji and enjoyed a large increase in surplus grain retained after rents had been paid.[28] When the wartime inflation caused a jump in fertilizer and tool prices and other production costs, however, market profits diminished. Small-scale rice sellers could only accept market conditions as they found them. The only "variable" that might be changed was the amount of rent rice turned over to landlords, and it was this that the tenants committee hoped to adjust to their advantage during the 1918 riots.

Large landlords recognized that the two groups' demands were qualitatively different. Because, in the long run, prosperous landowners had more to lose by acceding to demands for rent reductions, they tried to win over the tenants committee with lenient treatment and negotiation. The large landlords demonstrated a healthy respect for the tenants committee, whose members had, superficially at least, acted "legally" during the riots and themselves aspired to become landlords. The mixed group that had taken the law into their own hands in midnight raids to extort rice merited less concern. From the standpoint of families such as the Tatsumi, the rice-borrowing riffraff could rot in jail.

The distinction between the two groups may have been clear-cut to large landowners, but the tenants' committee and the rice growers were not opposed to each other. Not only did they share the aim of pressuring the village's most prosperous residents, they also had at least one member in common. Morita Ainosuke, the leader of the borrowers, was himself a landowning tenant and small-scale rice miller marginally involved in grain trading. During the rioting he ran back and forth between the homes of large landlords, where he pressured Tatsumi and others to donate grain, and the village office, where he reported to the tenants committee. Although Morita received a stiff sentence of seven years, he was not ostracized by his fellow villagers on his return from prison. Despite his reputation as an enemy of the big landlords, he rose to a position on the village council in the years after the riots.[29]

Morita's important role in village affairs after the riots suggests the degree of economic and political reorganization in Hōryūji after 1918. The change in the fortunes of large landowners is evident in the transformation of landholding patterns between 1917 and 1927: over the decade Tatsumi holdings fell from 175 chō to 151 chō; the holdings of Yasuda Saburō, the village's second largest landowner, decreased from 86 chō to 50 chō. The decline continued even more sharply during the 1930s. In contrast, the holdings of landowning tenants either increased or held steady during the 1920s. Not only did larger landlords divest themselves of their fields and the rancorous relations with tenants that came with them, but they also reduced rents. Between 1912 and 1927 rent paid by cultivators declined by an average of approximately 15 percent. Ten percent of that reduction came after the riots.[30]

Tatsumi and other prosperous landowners lost political influence and prestige as well. Despite landlord attempts to win over the tenants committee, the old order was not restored. Villagers held Tatsumi and others partially responsible for the 1918 protests and condemned their uncompromising conduct in the earlier tenancy disputes for having brought Hōryūji's problems before outsiders. Following the riots, unity among landlords steadily deteriorated. In 1928, when several landlords called for renewed litigation against nonpaying tenants, few landlords joined in the dispute despite the continued existence of the landlord contract. During the 1920s the role of larger landlords in Hōryūji governance also declined as independent landowning tenants, tenants, and merchants replaced them on the village council.[31]

Although the Hōryūji incident represents the best-documented case of tenant-landlord conflict during the 1918 riots, similar incidents also occurred in Fukushima, Saitama, Aichi, Osaka, Okayama, Shimane, and other prefectures.[32] These protests shared characteristics evident in the Hōryūji dispute: the primacy of demands for lower rents, the participation of tenants organized into formal committees or associations, and a rather lengthy history of worsening relations between landlords and tenants.

A study in 1922 by the Ministry of Agriculture of a tenancy dispute in Kasadera village (Aichi prefecture) reflects several of the causes and consequences of the tenant-landlord riots. After the nationwide outbreak of rioting, Kasadera tenants demanded rent reductions in September 1918. Investigators noted that no drought or extraordinary hardship had sparked such a request and that the dispute, in fact, had been smoldering for at least a year before the riots. In seeking the underlying causes for the protest, the Ministry of Agriculture report noted several major factors applicable to tenant-landlord conflicts generally:

1. Landlords lack any paternal feeling for their tenants [*onjō zenzen nakarishi koto*].
2. Tenants have lost respect for police since the 1918 riots.
3. Outside speakers exhort tenants that it is natural [*tōzen*] to press their demands.
4. Tenants are aware that alternative work is available in Nagoya if landlords are reluctant to pay adequately for their labor.
5. Absentee landlords do absolutely nothing for the village.
6. Success in litigation against landlords has made tenants confident and rigid in their views.[33]

In Kasadera as in Hōryūji, tenants' protests differed significantly from the simple consumer riot. The tenant's struggle represented an ongoing dispute over land rents and tenure rights and not an immediate need for lower rice prices or relief measures. In these disputes, ad hoc tenant committees and, in some towns and villages, formal tenant associations played a leading role. With varying degrees of success, they used the opportunity provided by widespread uprisings to further their own movement, reasserting demands on landlords that had been made long before the 1918 riots and continued for years after their suppression. The tenant-landlord riots, therefore, can be seen as the escalation of long-standing conflicts intended to assert greater tenant control over the land and its produce.

The Absence of Protest in the Tōhoku Region

While rioting swept the rest of Japan, the agricultural northeastern prefectures remained quiet. The absence of protest is curious because the retail price of rice was generally higher throughout the region than in Tokyo. Wholesale prices were also steep. In fact, the price of rice futures in Tsuruoka city, in the heart of the Shōnai rice-producing region, was among the highest in the nation.[34]

One reason that rioting rarely broke out in Aomori, Akita, Iwate, and Yamagata prefectures can be found in the preventive measures taken at all levels of local government. As early as April 1918, for example, Yamagata's prefectural governor, Yorita Keijirō, sent directives to officials urging that they take steps to assure food supplies, distribute foreign rice, and crack down on suspected grain speculators. In late August the governor continued to monitor relief efforts. In his instructions to county officials and police departments, he described their efforts as being responsible for Yamagata's escape from the turmoil that had engulfed the rest of the nation. While congratulating them for a job well done, he also cautioned against complacency. Local officials and police should continue to make sure that aid was distributed equitably and uniformly. Anything less, he warned, would fuel feelings of injustice, which might result in rioting.[35]

Such vigilance seemed to work: only a single case of "unrest" was reported in four of the six Tōhoku prefectures. Although these prefectures did not experience rioting, the central government nevertheless provided them with a share of the imperial contribution and the national relief fund. In Yamagata alone, these monies, combined with donations raised locally, resulted in the disbursement of relief rice worth more than 47,000 yen.[36] As in Toyama, prefectural police and community leaders used the emperor's generosity to quiet signs of unrest. Aid measures were not taken in reaction to specific uprisings but as a precautionary response to disturbances occurring predominantly in central Japan.

Rice relief undoubtedly helped assure calm, particularly in the larger towns and cities where officials first looked for signs of unrest. But the aid program does not entirely account for the remarkable lack of regional protest. Indeed, the preemptive measures did not always work. In Fukushima, for example, a month before rioting broke out prefectural and local officials had attempted to prevent unrest. In Fukushima city the Rice Dealers Association met with the Chamber of Commerce to arrange discount sales on 15 July. In addition, prefectural police cracked down on rice retailers suspected of price gouging. In July police inspected 4,318 grain dealerships for irregularities that might give rise to protest. They found that nearly 1,600 of the merchants had violated the law by using unacceptable measures, adulterating rice with sand or other foreign objects, and weighing grain improperly. Although most of the offenders got off with a warning, 450 rice dealers were fined for their actions. Fukushima grain dealers themselves also took steps to head off unrest. Before the onset of rioting in Kitakata township, for example, merchants posted signs offering rice at twenty-five sen per shō and turned on their electric lights to let it be known that they had opened their shops and were willing to do business. Similar steps were taken in Wakamatsu city, Kōriyama, and other urbanizing towns throughout Fukushima. Despite the thoroughness of such efforts, destructive rioting nevertheless occurred in Tōhoku's single most industrialized prefecture.[37]

Stable ties between landlords and tenants were more important than aid programs in preventing unrest in the countryside. With the exception of Fukushima, Tōhoku was relatively peaceful during the early years of Japan's tenants and farmers movements. Of all tenancy disputes recorded for Japan between 1917 and 1931, Tōhoku accounted for only 8 percent, while the Kansai and Chūbu regions made up 60 percent of the total.[38] During the period from 1917 to 1921 Okinawa, Aomori, Iwate, Akita, and Yamagata—the prefectures free of riots during the 1918 disturbances—were the only prefectures where not a single tenancy dispute was reported.[39] Although the number of Tōhoku disputes increased dramatically from 1932, the region was practically inert during the 1920s when an active tenants movement was growing in industrializing central Japan. Despite higher grain prices and tenancy rates in the more purely agricultural Tōhoku regions, where relations between landlords and tenants remained stable, farmers did not attempt to use the opportunity afforded by widespread rioting to protest consumer prices or land rents. A still-viable patronage system based on economic dependency and bolstered by traditional values was central to staving off unrest in the northeast.

Paternalism, or patronage, or its more recent sociological permutation, "clientelism," has been criticized as a concept containing a built-in conservative bias that obscures sociological or historical analysis by replacing a "real" understanding with a fixed normative functional-consensus view of social relations.[40] Those who seek to use paternalism are said either to demonstrate their own "false consciousness" or to impose an unreal image of societal harmony upon their subject. There may be some basis to such criticisms, although it seems difficult to judge whether another's consciousness is "false" or otherwise. In any case, paternalism seems particularly appropriate for an understanding of the absence of rioting in Tōhoku in 1918. As used here, I have relied on the definition developed by anthropologist Alex Weingrod, who explained the study of patronage relations as "the analysis of how persons of unequal authority, yet linked through ties of interest and friendship, manipulate their relationship to attain their ends."[41]

In the case of Japan, this definition might be usefully amended by striking the word "friendship" and underscoring the word "ends." Genuine cordiality may help but is not necessary to the successful working of paternalism. In Japan the system appears to have been, and perhaps still is, grounded in pragmatism. As John W. Bennett and Iwao Ishino have observed of patron-client relationships in a variety of Japanese social contexts, paternalism "is sanctioned or not sanctioned not at the level of values but at the level of practice."[42] Since function is more important than form in such relations, it is not surprising that ties between patrons and clients change over time or are simply discontinued when either side is faced with new economic or political circumstances. In Hōryūji and Furuichi, paternalistic ties tended to go unnoticed until they began to break down. But once farmers marched against the landlords, cutting ties with old *oyake* families and rejecting the values that supported them, inequities in the old paternal order were soon called into question. In incidents of rural rioting in the Kansai region, landlords responded to the new challenge to their local dominance by resorting to legal coercion to enforce authority that had previously been grounded in custom. As in other rural riots near Japan's industrializing cities, alternative economic options and the appearance of new interest groups, whether button-factory managers or tenant-union organizers, quickly transformed old relationships. The change, in turn, helped engender rearranged political ties within the local communities.

The stability of tenant-landlord ties in Tōhoku during the Taishō period was based on the conscious paternalistic efforts of landlords to care for their tenants' needs. The Yamagata-based Honma family, Japan's largest landholders, charged some tenants as much as 75 percent of the rice harvest in rents. Cultivators nevertheless accepted these rental terms without opposition until the 1930s. In fact, tenants preferred to work for the Honma than for landlords who charged lower rents, as a popular Tōhoku saying suggested: "If one must be a tenant, it is best to be a tenant of the Honma."[43]

Four major reasons accounted for the popularity of families like the Honma. First, the conservative large landlords tended to concentrate their energies on farming rather than on other business or political activities. Second, the major Tōhoku landlords (such as the Honma, Ōtaki, and Sakai) entered into formal written contracts with their tenants. Under normal circumstances these agreements, in effect, assured the cultivator's right to work the holding for as long as he desired. Third, the Tōhoku landlords were generally more willing than their counterparts in central and southern Japan to lower rents voluntarily during periods of reduced harvests or during periods of steep consumer prices for rice. And finally, large Tōhoku landlords, unlike their counterparts in western and central Japan, were not as involved in direct competition with landowning tenants for access to rice markets.

The Tōhoku landlords' emphasis on farming is indicated in the Honma family code. Written during the Tokugawa period and in effect until the postwar land reform, the document is primarily concerned with the landlords' social duties. As the code notes, these duties included looking after the welfare of tenants:

> The prosperity of the landlord depends on his tenants. Only when all are blessed with a sufficiency can all live in peace and harmony. Reserve one-quarter of your wealth for assistance to the tenants.[44]

During the Meiji and Taishō periods landlords such as the Honma directed a variety of agricultural improvements intended to benefit their tenants. In Yamagata some of the improvements carried out by landlords, many of whom had received special training at agricultural colleges, included expanding irrigation systems, standardizing field sizes, introducing new strains of rice, training tenants in the efficient use of fertilizers, and promoting horse plowing.[45] Such changes increased productivity and probably benefited the landlord at least as much as the tenant. A better harvest meant that the cultivator's after-rent share increased, but the landlord, who was not responsible for such expensive items as fertilizer, oxen, and implements, typically retained at least half the harvest. Nevertheless, prosperous Tōhoku landlords, who often provided the initiative and sometimes the capital for field improvements, did not press tenants to pay proportionally higher rents simply because harvest yields had increased. For example, one study of the Honma's successful attempts to raise rice productivity notes that Meiji-period changes in fertilizer types and usage increased yields in one sample village from 2 to 2.5 koku per tan. The Honma did not raise rents but allowed the surplus to accrue to the tenants. By the Taishō period a number of Shōnai landlords had abandoned the collection of rents as a fixed percentage of harvest and accepted instead a fixed number of bales of rent rice annually. In effect, the tenants could keep any additional productivity that they might wrest from the fields.[46]

Compared with the modest means of most cultivators, the large Tōhoku landlords appeared fabulously wealthy. Yet tenants did not seem to view their relationship with landlords in a zero-sum manner; that is, as one in which the landlords' prosperity meant the tenants' impoverishment. This attitude may have stemmed from the realization that the tenants' incomes could improve thanks to the landlord's efforts to raise rice productivity. According to a farmer's saying from Iwate, "The master's footprint is the best fertilizer of all."[47] The adage does not indicate that tenant-landlord relations were strife-free, but it does suggest that cultivators perceived an advantage in the landlord's active engagement in farm management. Even incremental improvements in harvests probably meant more to poorer farmers than they did to already prosperous landowners.

The larger landlord's success in raising productivity paid off perhaps as much in self-satisfaction and social prestige as in more bushels per acre. What R. P. Dore wrote of "energetic and keen agriculturalists" during the Meiji period applied to many prosperous Tōhoku landlords during the Taishō:

> They were, many of them, men of intelligence and energy who believed sincerely in technical efficiency and high productivity as ends in themselves. And they interpreted their duties as landlords to give them the right, or rather the duty, to lead their tenant, "for their own good." That it was also for the landlord's own good was doubtless ever present in their mind, but there was never the less, an element of sincere idealism—within the framework of traditional values which accepted the social and economic gap between landlord and tenant as part of the order of nature.[48]

The involvement of families like the Honma and the Ōtaki in raising agricultural productivity and their concern for tenants are exceptional when compared with landlord practices outside Tōhoku. During the Meiji and Taishō periods, the number of absentee landlords and the number of landowners engaging in nonagricultural business increased, particularly in industrializing central Japan. Even landlords who remained in the local town or village tended to be more occupied with commercial enterprises than with tenant welfare. Many landlord families such as those in Furuichi and Hōryūji, who had diversified into sake brewing, banking, and retailing, appeared interested only in the capital that rice harvests produced.

In contrast to the landlords in central Japan, many Tōhoku landlords willingly formalized ties with their tenants in a written contract. One might expect contracts to have been unnecessary given the long traditions of paternalistic relations between major Tōhoku landlords and their tenants. The use of such legal instruments even implies that oyabun-kobun ties (fictive "parent-child" or "master-follower" relationships) were weakening rather than continuing strong. In the Hōryūji tenancy dispute, the landlords' resort to contracts did indicate a breakdown of the old order. But contracts in Tōhoku, whether written or verbal, fulfilled a different social function. Rather than being agreements that might bring to bear the pressure of outside legal authorities on tenants if terms were violated, the contracts served as guarantees that social superiors would provide a basis of livelihood for their charges. Rather than snaring the tenant, they bound the landlord. It was not until the 1930s, when the collapse of rice and silk prices brought widespread agricultural depression, that smaller Tōhoku landlords forced tenants from the land. During this period contractual violation became a basis for legal action by tenants against their putative social betters.

Outside Tōhoku, formal written agreements were rare during the Taishō period; only 30 percent of all tenancy agreements in the nation in 1921 were written.[49] The contracts between Tōhoku landlords and tenants typically stipulated tenancy rates and conditions (such as inefficient farming) that might result in the return of land to the landlord.[50] The Honma family provided contracts that allowed tenants to work a designated plot of land for up to five years. Yet because the contracts were usually extended automatically, they in effect guaranteed the tenant permanent cultivation rights. It would have been inconceivable for the Honma family to break a contract and turn the land over to a tenant willing to pay higher rents. In some cases successive generations of the one tenant family continued to farm the same plot of Honma land from the Meiji period into the postwar years.[51]

From the tenant's standpoint, one of the most attractive features of the written contract was the clause stating the landlord's willingness to reduce rents during periods of poor harvest. In contracts like those extended by the Ōtaki family, the landlord agreed to reduce rents unless the poor harvest resulted from tenant negligence. The practice of rent reduction varied in different regions of Japan; in some places landlords reduced rents even if no written contract compelled them to. In general, however, the willingness of large Tōhoku landlords to offer rent reductions set them apart from landlords in central Japan. According to Dore's study of the tenancy system:

> The degree of bad harvest necessary to provoke a rent reduction varied, but surveys noted that in the more paternalistic north even a small reduction in harvests of only 10–15 per cent would be recognized as requiring reduction in rent, while in the more impersonal contractual districts around Tokyo the landlord would be reluctant to recognize even a fall of 50 per cent.[52]

In some cases tenants were excused from paying any rent at all. According to a recent study of the Honma family:

If the crop was smaller than twice the rent, or when the yield was 1.5 koku per tan, the rent was reduced to 0.7 koku. If the crop was less than 30 percent of the normal yield, the tenant did not have to pay rent. At times, reliable tenants were permitted to pay back rents gradually, over a period of years. These were, in effect, the same means by which the *han* guaranteed Shōnai residents a modicum of security during the Tokugawa period.[53]

In contrast to the Hōryūji landlords, who granted a rent reduction of no more than 7.5 percent in the years preceding the rice riots, the Honma's formula for rent reduction was remarkably magnanimous. It appears even more so when we consider that the Honma not only forgave rents during hard years but also allowed tenants to retain more of the harvest during good years or when improvements increased the productivity of the family's lands.

Although many of the terms offered tenants by prosperous north-eastern landlords appeared generous relative to conditions elsewhere, it would be naive to think that Tōhoku paternalism was grounded only in the landowner's high-mindedness. A long-term village study conducted by Japanese researchers during the 1920s and 1930s provides a glimpse of the specific factors, environmental, political, and economic, that made for durable landlord-tenant bonds in the region. It also points out the extent of control that patrons exerted over their clients.[54]

Tōgō-mura, an administrative village created in 1890 by the amalgamation of seven preexisting "natural" villages, had a population of 3,217 in 1920. In size it was comparable to both Furuichi (3,733) and Hōryūji (2,070). But it differed from them in two important ways. First, it was a one-product village in which virtually all residents depended on rice farming for their livelihood. A full 90 percent of Tōgō's working population were either full- or part-time farmers who, if they did own a patch of land, also sharecropped for local landlords. In this village, the yearly rice harvest accounted for 97 percent of agricultural produce, with the remaining 3 percent represented by soy beans, barley, and red beans (*azuki*), all of which were grown for local consumption, not for the market. In the 1920s the Sakai family encouraged its tenant farmers to diversify into sericulture by promoting mulberry cultivation and silk-worm rearing, but the effort faltered, as is indicated by the negligible contribution of silk to village income in the early 1930s.[55]

Another indication of Tōgō's reliance on rice and landlords is evident in the village's lack of involvement in government programs to diversify, and thereby strengthen, the local economy. Since the promulgation of the Industrial Cooperative Law in 1901 rural communities throughout

Japan had established "industrial associations" (*sangyō kumiai*) to promote nonagricultural pursuits. These organizations interpreted "industrial" rather loosely in their attempts to create by-employment, such as weaving straw goods or making hemp rope. In the northeastern countryside they actually functioned as rural cooperatives, extending loans for fertilizers and organizing buying associations.[56]

Even these state-supported organizations elicited little enthusiasm in Tōhoku. At the fourth national meeting of the Industrial Cooperative Association in 1909, a report on recent developments in Tōhoku noted that, despite the desperate need for cooperatives, the northeast continued "half paralyzed" as a result of inadequate financial institutions. The concern of the national association notwithstanding, the pace of *sangyō kumiai* organization in the region continued to be slow during the Taishō period.[57] As late as 1933 Tōhoku generally and Yamagata prefecture specifically lagged behind other farming areas in the establishment of industrial associations. At a time when only 10 percent of towns and villages outside Tōhoku lacked *sangyō kumiai*, in Yamagata the figure was 25 percent. During the 1920s not only were northeastern branches fewer but their activities were also more limited than elsewhere, a situation that led the Imperial Agricultural Association to criticize existing Tōhoku groups for their passivity.[58]

Tōgō villagers did not establish an industrial association until 1936. But villagers did not seem to miss the organization. Tōgō, located in the heart of the Shōnai Plain's rich rice-growing region, managed without the forestry, mining, and small-scale manufacturing recommended by the associations. In fact, such recommendations seemed irrelevant to local conditions, both environmental and economic. As the authors of the Tōgō study noted in the early 1930s, it was rice that was important:

> It goes without saying that it is the use of cultivated rice fields that constitutes the basis of the various aspects of the farmers' lives. There is no other pursuit that even approaches it in importance. Their lives are based on rice, they live through rice, and it is no overstatement to say that their existence is entirely dependent upon it.[59]

The second feature that distinguished Tōgō from Furuichi and Hōryūji, as well as Tōhoku from other regions, is the powerful role of landlords in controlling the rice market and thereby the local economy. In Tōgō a majority of all farmers owned a scrap of land here and there, but the ownership of large, diverse paddy and upland fields was concentrated in a few hands. There were no button factories or nearby workshops to provide alternative employment and, along with it, competition for control of a loyal work force. Villagers did leave Tōgō, but when they did, they left permanently. They were usually not *dekasegi* workers commuting to work elsewhere but the second or third sons of farming families, or tenants unable to maintain themselves locally.[60]

The structure of the Shōnai rice trade reinforced patron-client dependency. The region's primary cultivators could and did bring their rice to market. Yet compared with tenants, particularly landholding tenants in central and western Japan, Tōhoku cultivators more often sold grain through landlord intermediaries. A Ministry of Agriculture survey of the ownership of rice stored in agricultural warehouses between 1920 and 1933 reveals that the amount of grain commissioned by landowners (*tochi ni tsuki kenri o yū suru mono itaku*) versus that of cultivators (*nōgyō o itomu mono itaku*) was far higher in Tōhoku than in the Kinki region. In 1920 cultivators in western Japan commissioned a little more than half the rice in the granaries surveyed; the corresponding amount for Tōhoku was only 33 percent. During the same year the amount of cultivator-owned rice in storehouses in Yamagata prefecture amounted to only 10.1 percent of all rice commissioned.[61] These figures demonstrate two significant differences between landlord-tenant economic ties in Tōhoku and those outside the region: first, landlords controlled a greater percentage of the after-harvest grain surplus in the northeast; and second, primary cultivators in the region correspondingly had less direct market access than in western Japan.

In Shōnai, the Sakai family, which had been the domain's ruling house during the Tokugawa period, played a key role in marketing grain through their agents and warehouses. The system mandated that most of Tōgō's first-quality rice production be exported to Tokyo and that tenants either sell or subsist on second- and third-grade rice. The best grain reached the central market by one of three routes: through the Yamai warehouse, the Tsuruoka Exchange, or the government's rice-inspection warehouse. The Yamai warehouse, a joint-stock company founded in 1894, which Count Sakai controlled as principal shareholder, was the largest middleman marketing agency. The enterprise was no single granary but a network of main and subsidiary warehouses spread across the Shōnai Plain. In the early 1930s the Yamai company accounted for two-thirds of all rice shipped by the three largest brokering agencies and did approximately ten times the volume of business handled by the government's rice-inspection warehouse.[62]

Although a money economy had certainly penetrated all of Japan by the twentieth century, the rice-ticket system begun by the Yamai warehouse in 1894 and still in use into the 1930s provided an alternative to the coin of the realm. When farmers exchanged their grain in the company's central or branch warehouses, they received rice tickets that were locally recognized as entirely negotiable instruments, honored by buyers and sellers of rice, and used for rent payments. Among the contemporary explanations given for the system's persistence was that its use assured rice quality because the warehouses also served as inspection stations. In essence, farmers who traded grain for tickets received certification that their rice met national market standards. The tickets also facilitated rent payments, helped settle accounts accurately between landlord creditors and tenant debtors, and supplemented currency circulation throughout the region.[63] But perhaps the most fundamental reason for the continuance of the system was that, in the closed tenant-landlord exchange relationship, it was largely unrivaled.

Landlords' economic activities extended beyond the issuance of proxy currency to involvement in local finance. Tenants regularly borrowed additional money for springtime planting. Their biggest outlay was for fertilizers, which accounted for 70 percent of the loans made to Tōgō farmers during the 1920s and 1930s. Many landlords expected and accommodated this need. In addition to extraordinary loans that might be made at any time, the Honma family in Sakata annually offered tenants an advance of ten yen for each 1.2 tan of rented land. Cultivators might seek planting loans from banks, but here again they were often still dealing, albeit indirectly, with their landlords. Tōgō villagers could make fertilizer loans from the Hypothec Bank of Japan, the Sixty-seventh Bank, the Tsuruoka Business Council Bank, the Honma family, or directly from fertilizer dealers. With the exceptions of the Hypothec Bank and the fertilizer dealers, however, all of these institutions were either totally controlled or dominated by landlord groups.

The predominance of landlord families in financial institutions was not all that made farmers turn to them for assistance. The landlords also extended better terms than their competitors. In contrast to the Honma family, which extended fertilizer loans at 7 percent interest, the Hypothec Bank charged at least 7.4 percent, while fertilizer dealers charged a heavy 10 to 12 percent.[64]

During the period of widespread rioting in Japan's southwestern prefectures, large landlord families like the Sakai and Honma in Yamagata continued their control of local economic life and fostered their image as regional patrons. They made well-publicized efforts to appear as their tenants' caretakers. An article in the *Shōnai shinpō* on 15 August, for example, notes that Count Sakai, the former Sakai daimyo, had purchased a hundred bales of rice for distribution to former retainers and made lesser donations for town and city relief efforts.[65] The Honma family, more liberal than Sakai in its contributions, donated five thousand yen to the Sakata township, an additional five thousand to Akumi county, and smaller amounts to other towns and villages. Yet when prefectural officials pressed the Honma family to put more grain on the local market, they were refused. A spokesman for the family explained that, because nearly seven hundred koku was being withheld for tenant relief, more grain could not be released to local markets.[66] In rejecting the government's request the Honma family made it clear that tenant well-being was its first priority. This kind of concern was rare in areas where tenant-landlord riots took place.

Conclusion

Comparing what occurred in the Toyama dispute with European food riots in the eighteenth and nineteenth centuries reveals certain parallels in ostensibly different forms of protest. If they had occurred in France, the Toyama coastal riots might be described as an *entrave*, that is, a

> rural form of grain riot, in which wagons or barges loaded with grain were forcibly prevented from leaving a locality. . . . The entrave tried to restrict the local grain supply to local consumption, and at reasonable prices.[67]

The widespread rural riots that followed the Toyama protest bear an equally striking resemblance to the "market riots" and "price fixing" disputes (*taxation populaire*) characteristic of eighteenth-century English and French uprisings. Rioters moved beyond a simple boycott, demanding that rice prices be fixed and forcing local officials to institute adequate relief measures. In her study of the market riot, Louise Tilly notes:

> Food riots had several forms which show a definite change and development over time. The market riot, an urban version, was usually aimed at bakers whose prices were too high or whose loaves were too few, at city residents who were suspected of hoarding supplies of grain in their houses, and at government officials who failed to act swiftly to ease a food shortage. . . . The market riot and the entrave were polar opposites. The market riot was a sign that not enough grain was available in a local urban marketplace.[68]

Although Japanese rioters were obviously not concerned with loaves or bakers, the targets and tactics evident in both the French and the Japanese protests are remarkably similar. R. B. Rose, in his study of price riots and English public policy, elaborates upon categories of protest that seem to apply to the Toyama protests as well as to later Japanese rural riots:

> Grain riots . . . may be divided into four classes, varying from a simple outbreak of looting, through riots directed against the transportation and export of corn, to direct action by rioters to impose fixed prices on the market, and attempts to force local magistrates to decree maximum prices by mob pressure.[69]

At first glance, Tilly's and Rose's categorizations seem to capture several of the essential differences distinguishing the Toyama protest (*entrave*) from the expanded protests in other rural areas (market riots, or *taxation populaire*). But the fit is not perfect. The market riots, described by Tilly as a form of urban protest, occurred in the Japanese countryside as well as in cities. Moreover, both Tilly and Rose suggest that the various forms of European grain riots changed significantly over time, one form developing from another. In the Japanese protests, however, the riots most comparable to the *entrave* and the market riot occurred simultaneously.

The level of Japanese rural industrialization and the character of tenant-landlord relations help account for differences in the otherwise remarkably similar forms of European and Japanese rural riots. In Japan the distinctive characteristics that once separated primarily agricultural rice-producing regions from urban areas diminished rapidly during the nineteenth and twentieth centuries. During this period the Meiji government's support for extensive industrialization accelerated the integration of rural regions near major cities ever more tightly into the national market. The integration, however, was not uniform. Whereas the Japan Sea side of Japan, including the Hokuriku and Tōhoku regions, remained relatively underdeveloped, the Pacific side, from Fukushima prefecture southward, underwent rapid industrialization. By 1918 the populations of formerly remote villages and towns, particularly in the Kansai and Kantō regions, were increasingly engaged in commercial or manufacturing work in addition to agricultural occupations. The accelerated pace of industrialization, stimulated by a heightened wartime demand for finished products, prompted an unprecedented number of farmers to take side-work in city factories or become part-time day laborers. Others, especially tenants or the second or third sons of smallholders, quit farming altogether, relocated in urban areas, and became full-time wage laborers.

A shift in the pattern of agricultural occupations and landholding also took place in the rural hinterlands of larger cities in central and western Japan. In Hyogo prefecture, for example, the number of farming households decreased between 1914 and 1918, as did the number of families involved exclusively in agriculture. Case studies of villages and towns in Kyoto and Osaka prefectures indicate that even where farming was ostensibly the family's main occupation, part-time farm laborers, both self-employed and wage-paid, far outnumbered full-time farmers.[70] The tendency for small-scale independent farmers and tenants to work in small factories as day laborers, as carters, peddlers, rickshaw pullers, and in similar nonagricultural jobs, is best documented for the Kansai but also occurred around other growing cities. It was in the semiagricultural belts surrounding major Pacific coast cities that the greatest number of rural riots occurred in 1918.[71]

The impact of increasing industrialization and the occupational transformation in the countryside can be seen in the changing economic and social role of landlords. During the Meiji and Taishō periods, many landlords had expanded their economic interests beyond farm management into grain trading, sake brewing, pawnbroking, high-interest moneylending, and banking. In rural or semiurban towns and villages adjacent to industrializing cities, landlords often became absentee proprietors with only the slimmest economic ties to their home districts.[72] Ann Waswo has observed that, although there were important regional variations, after 1900 landlords in general stepped up their investments in nonagricultural enterprises as they became less directly involved in the actual cultivation of their landholdings. Exacerbated clashes (including the 1918 riots) between landlords and tenants were symptomatic of the changing social ties between these groups. In part, these conflicts occurred because traditional economic ties persisted in the midst of changing social relationships. Landlords who had diversified their interests and taken on new roles as modern businessmen, often living outside the village, were less engaged in day-to-day interaction with tenants and less solicitous of their concerns.[73]

Even though landlord paternalism tended to give way to a hard-headed, strictly interest-based concern for tenants, economic ties between landlords and cultivators changed more slowly. The persistence of traditional economic relationships was most conspicuous in the tenancy system. Although the 1873 tax reform loosened the state's control over landowners, it did nothing to alter the relationship between landlord and tenant. According to the new tax law, landowners no longer paid taxes in rice (*nengu*) to the domain government but were instead assessed a cash tax of 3 percent on the value of their holdings. The law was silent on the position of the tenant who, until the end of World War II, continued to pay rents in kind at rates of 50 percent or more of his harvest.[74]

By instituting a money tax while leaving the tenancy system unchanged, the reform left tenants at a distinct disadvantage. Although taxes were reduced for landowners, tenants received no corresponding reduction in rents. Even if he owned his own land, the smallholder found it difficult to take advantage of the reduced tax rate. Ronald Dore notes:

> The change to a money tax . . . placed on the peasant the costs and risks of marketing his rice. Living at or near the subsistence level, he was often forced to sell his rice as soon as it was harvested when the market was most unfavorable. Richer peasants could afford to hold off until the price rose, and many landlords reaped a double advantage by acting as rice brokers.[75]

The collection of rent in kind as a fixed share of the harvest could potentially benefit the tenant, of course. In times of poor harvests paternalistic landlords might consent to reduce the amount of rent due. In fact, landlords in the more traditional, less-industrialized Tōhoku prefectures regularly carried out such reductions. But the attenuated social relationships between tenants and landlords, particularly in industrializing rural regions, tended to nullify the possible advantages of the system of payment in kind.

The unprecedented high price of rice in 1918 revealed another facet of the inequality inherent in the traditional tenancy system. Although record price levels would appear to have profited all producers, benefits more often went to larger landlords, especially ones who doubled as rice dealers. It was the landlords who received rent in kind and could afford to keep rice off the market in anticipation of a higher selling price. The small-scale independent farmer, tenant, or part-time cultivator not only had less to market after rents were paid but also suffered because inflation offset the benefits of higher market prices.

In his study of tenants and smallholders in Fukushima prefecture, Shōji Kichinosuke has demonstrated that during the Taishō period the cost of small-scale rice farming in some cases equaled or exceeded the income that the cultivator could expect to receive by marketing the rice harvest.[76] In 1918 the small-scale farmer's inability to wait for the best market price, the meager size of his grain holdings after paying rent to the landlord, and the increasing cost of fertilizer, tools, and labor tended to lower his standard of living. Many farmers simply could not afford to eat the rice they grew. Forced to turn over a large proportion of their best-quality grain to landlords as rents, tenants and land-renting smallholders often sustained themselves and their families on cheaper foreign rice or with porridges made from barley and mixed grains. A commentary in the *Hinode shinbun* of 3 September 1918 notes:

> Small farmers and tenants [*shonō ika kosakunin*] are increasingly unable to maintain themselves [and their families] with their share of the agricultural harvest. To make ends meet, many have taken side jobs. Middle farmers [*chūnō*] are similarly troubled. Even if they have produced enough rice to meet day-to-day needs, they have completely exhausted any surplus by the end of the year. Only rich farmers have the luxury of money and financing. . . . Consequently they face no necessity of hurriedly selling grain. On the contrary, some use it for speculation.[77]

A petition submitted by the Toyama Nōsei Kurabu, a farmers' organization, to the Terauchi cabinet in the summer of 1918 also voiced the decidedly mixed feelings of farmers toward local changes wrought by greater involvement in the national economy during World War I. As it details key aspects of the predicament facing the rural population during the wartime years, it merits quoting at length:

> The gradual decline in rice prices since 1914 has disrupted the economy of farm households. All aspects of farm management have tended toward "passivism" [*shōkyoku shugi*] as income and outlay have failed to offset one another. Pushed to the extreme of exhaustion and worry, many have abandoned agriculture and now are concentrated in cities or live elsewhere. Despite the gradual but sharp rise in rice prices since the spring of 1917, the wounds caused by the [1914] fall [of rice prices] have yet to heal. Moreover, the sharp increase in rice is but a side effect of the inflation born of the European war, which caused a tremendous increase in various prices. As a result [of inflation], farm households have seen expenses rise. The farming population, long inured to passivism, has responded by struggling to reduce outlay. Farmers have tended to look toward skyrocketing rice prices as a means to lighten the anxieties that arose from the previous period of impoverishment. . . . [Nevertheless], profits derived from the [recent] jump in prices have gone to only one section of farm households and merchants. Farmers generally have been unable to share equally in [the improvement].[78]

The Toyama riots suggested a course of action to remedy the immediate economic problems faced by rural consumers and tenant farmers. Other rioters, whether in cities, farm communities, or mining camps, referred to this incident in carrying out their own protests. Outside Toyama, protesters probably had only hazy impressions of what actually occurred in the coastal uprising. The Toyama rioters' limited aims and their generally nonviolent methods were distorted by press reports that often depicted the first protest as a wholesale uprising fueled by elemental class conflict.[79] Regardless of the popular understanding, or misunderstanding, of the Toyama riots, it would be less than correct to describe the rural riots as simply imitations of the women's uprising. Neither inflammatory press reporting nor high prices for rice alone determined where riots would occur. These were merely contributing causes that facilitated protests where industrialization and deteriorating tenant-landlord relationships had already increased the possibility of unrest. In many rural towns and villages, these protests were an opening wedge, behind which came a more permanent realignment of political and economic ties within the local communities.

The basic stability of landlord-tenant ties in Tōhoku helped avert the turmoil that came with the 1918 riots and much of the conflict inherent in the tenancy movement of the 1920s. Even into the 1930s, when the focus of the movement had shifted to the northeast during the harrowing years of the Great Depression, large landlords fared far better than smaller landowners. Paternalism, an asymmetrical relationship rather than a balanced exchange, is one in which a landlord often benefits more than the tenant. Patron-client relationships therefore entail much that is simply unfair and, if economic or social conditions change, may give rise to dissent. Nevertheless, in Tōhoku in 1918 normative justifications—and the fact that landlords often offered better terms than the few economic institutions competing for the cultivator's business—made a degree of inequality acceptable. Indeed, during those periods of crisis when high rice prices threatened the livelihood of Tōhoku tenants, the landlord could reaffirm his role as a good provider by defying local authorities or acting against his own short-term interest. This is precisely what the Honma and other major landlords did in 1918.

FIVE

The Coalfield Riots
Riot as Labor Dispute

But though the interest of the laborer is strictly connected with
that of society, he is incapable either of comprehending that
interest, or of understanding its connection with his own. His
condition leaves him no time to receive the necessary
information, and his education and habits are commonly such
as to render him unfit to judge even though he was fully
informed. In the public deliberations, therefore, his voice is
little heeded and less regarded, except on some particular
occasions, when his clamour is animated.

Adam Smith, *The Wealth of Nations*

Fraternal spirit is very strong among mine-workers in
consequence of the peculiarly hazardous condition of their
work. Formerly the patriarchal system of boss and follower
ruled the mine-worker's world, but this is being displaced by
the modern materialistic habit.

Japan Year Book, 1921–22

The coal mine riots in 1918 were essentially labor disputes with few
similarities to more traditional rural protests or overtly political city
riots. Miners used the opportunity provided by nationwide unrest to
further their struggle against the owners and managers of Japan's sizable coalfields. Their protests demonstrated scant concern for preserv-
ing the paternalistic relations between company and worker that had
existed before the riots. Nor did the miners' actions have much to do
with liberal political ideas. What did concern them was wages and
working conditions and the right to negotiate both with company management. In forcing concessions on these issues, miners sometimes
rioted. In addition to undisciplined protests, they also resorted to
strikes, labor slowdowns, and petitioning. Company management and
police officials were familiar with these tactics. Although the law un-

equivocally prohibited strikes, coalfield labor disputes had steadily escalated in the decades before 1918.

Coal's profitability as well as its vital contribution to Japan's rapid emergence as the first Asian industrial power forced both private enterprise and the state to tolerate increasing worker dissent. Exported first to China in 1898 and to other countries thereafter, coal fueled Japan's domestic industrialization and provided a profitable source of foreign revenue. By 1913 the mostly bituminous, or soft, coal dug from Japan's extensive fields accounted for one-half the total value of the nation's mineral production. The development of this single resource was no accident. The Meiji government promoted the export of coal, one of Japan's few surplus natural resources, as a way to reduce trade deficits. With state support for overseas sales, the export value of coal exceeded 32 million yen by 1918. Mitsui Bussan, Mitsubishi, and other large trading companies were the immediate beneficiaries of the coal boom. The central government entrusted them with the international marketing of coal, and they parleyed success with this single commodity into the creation of far-flung trading networks that grew to encompass markets for other goods. Mitsui, for example, began selling bunker fuel in Shanghai during the 1880s; by 1914 its trade network had grown to include forty sales offices throughout Asia. Two years later the company's coal, along with other manufactures, was being marketed in Europe as well as in China and India.[1]

Several Tokugawa domains had exploited local coal deposits, particularly after renewed Western contacts in the middle of the nineteenth century. But rapid increases in production did not really begin until fifteen years after the Meiji Restoration. Output, which in 1874 stood annually at 208,000 tons, expanded to a million tons by 1883 and doubled to 2 million tons in 1888. Production grew thereafter by 1 to 2 million tons each year, reaching 31 million tons by 1919.[2] Until the postwar recession and glutted markets of the early 1920s, coal prices moved in only one direction: upward. Despite the ability of companies to achieve ever higher annual production records, demand still outstripped supply. Booming economic conditions during World War I exacerbated this imbalance, causing coal prices to treble between 1915 and 1919.

Although the central government nominally owned all rights to the nation's mineral wealth, the introduction of a concessionaire system in 1873 transferred actual mine management to private hands. According to the 1873 Mining Law, large industrial concerns as well as private individuals could obtain a fifteen-year concession in exchange for royalties paid to the central government. In 1890 the law was amended to allow private concessionaires permanent exploitation rights.[5] Mitsui originally limited its activities to marketing the government's coal, but the profits that accrued from de facto ownership soon involved the company in direct mine management. While Mitsui gained control of the Miike fields, Mitsubishi monopolized the rich Chikuhō mines. Both companies continued aggressively to buy up additional concession rights during the 1890s. The venture proved so profitable and grew so rapidly that Mitsui officials established Mitsui Mining as an independent division in 1890. Coal was just as important to Mitsubishi: between 1894 and 1899 it accounted for 45 percent of Mitsubishi's total assets and 60 percent of company profits; between 1905 and 1908 coal's contribution to total profits grew to 75 percent. By 1900 the government's policy of favoring the emerging zaibatsu as leaders of Japan's industrial growth enabled Mitsubishi, Mitsui, and a few other large firms to gain control of Japan's ten largest coal mines. "One-man" concessions, the smallest a mere forty acres, continued to exist. But they were ill equipped to compete with zaibatsu concessions, some extending over thousands of acres, which benefited from economy-of-scale production.[3]

The zaibatsu-dominated holdings lay atop coalfields in four regions: Hokkaido, the Jōban area of Honshu (mainly in Fukushima and Ibaraki prefectures), southwestern Honshu (Yamaguchi prefecture), and northern Kyushu (Fukuoka, Kumamoto, Saga, and Nagasaki prefectures). These fields varied in size and richness. The Chikuhō deposits in northern Kyushu were by far the largest. Extending three hundred square miles beneath the Onga Valley, this single field provided approximately 80 percent of domestic coal production in 1905.[4]

The exploitation of these resources posed formidable problems. Much of the coal in both Kyushu and southwestern Honshu lay in undersea beds and therefore required sinking deep shafts from onshore entrances or drilling from natural and man-made islands offshore. Some of the tunnels that were extended during the Meiji period ran for more than a thousand feet below sea level. The heat at this depth was intense, typically reaching between 120 and 130 degrees fahrenheit.[5] Ventilation, transportation, and especially seawater leakage created constant problems for mining engineers.

These engineering problems were life-and-death matters to underground workers. Pumps and seals made of supposedly impermeable mud helped keep the pits dry. Nevertheless, shaft flooding occurred often and with devastating results. In 1914, in two separate but almost identical accidents, seawater broke through the pit walls, trapping and killing eighty miners at the Maeda Colliery and more than a hundred miners at the Higashi Misome mine in Ube. Mainland mines also took a heavy toll in miners' lives. Accident and death rates at dry pits in the Chikuhō fields, the site of Japan's largest coal deposits, were extremely high. Whether the mine was wet or dry, explosions caused by pockets of methane gas posed a constant danger to all mine workers. In 1914 a single blast at a Kyushu colliery took 669 lives, the highest death toll in Japanese mining history.[6]

Overall, the death and accident rates in the coal mines not only topped those in other industries but also surpassed rates in metal mines.[7] Accidents happened on the surface as well as underground. Mining statistics for 1920 show deaths and injuries caused by falling rocks, collapsed shafts, gas explosions, runaway carts, load derailments, dismemberment by ropes and cables, asphyxiation, dynamite explosions, boiler ruptures, locomotive accidents, steam burns, and electrical shocks.[8] After 1914 the rate of accidental deaths declined somewhat from its peak of 1,572, recorded for that year. Still, compared with other industries, coal-mining accidents were unusually frequent during the Taishō period. In 1918, 682 miners died and nearly 139,000 were injured in more than 127,000 underground and surface accidents. Despite the dangers, many sought work in the coalfields. In 1918, of 464,727 miners of all types, 287,159 were coal miners. By mid-Taishō compounds like the sprawling Mineji complex of five collieries with a total resident population of 30,000 had become fairly common.[9]

Coal mining was not simply a male calling. Collieries employed more than 80,000 women in 1918, 25 percent of whom worked underground. The mine companies, especially smaller operations, also hired boys and girls under fourteen as pit workers. Those working underground often did so in male-and-female mining-hauling combinations or in ten-person teams. Companies offered larger wage advances to married men, whom management preferred because they were more likely to remain on the job, and it was not unusual for husbands, wives, and sometimes children to labor in the same crew or carry out separate jobs within the mining compound.[10] If men and women worked together, the women often hauled the coal dug by the men. In some mines men and women were given identical tasks. On the equality of working conditions, one woman miner recalled:

Women and men did the same kind of work. . . . It's not true that women were weaker physically. . . . There was a woman who used to lift up huge chunks of coal that men could not carry. . . . My happiest time as a miner was when we went to the Nishitan Mines. There if a man was paid one yen, a woman was paid one yen, too.[11]

Such equality was rare. Female workers typically earned only 80 percent of the male worker's wage regardless of the job done. But this rate was at least "more equal" than what women working in spinning mills and textile factories received.[12]

During the Meiji and Taishō years, mining teams worked virtually around the clock. Day-and-night shifts at Kyushu coal mines lasted for eleven hours in 1917, and it was only in 1918 that management at many mines consented to a nine-hour shift. Although the work was dirty, dangerous, and exhausting, it was not complicated. During the 1920s major companies introduced electric drills and other power-driven equipment. But in 1918 a pickax, a lantern, a shovel, and a box were still the miner's basic tools. Getting to the coal, sorting it, and processing it involved various subsidiary occupations. The mine company thus employed timber men, porters, mine helpers, dressing hands, smelters, and guards in addition to face workers. Nevertheless, surface workers were a minority, outnumbered by underground workers four to one in 1918.[13]

Whatever the workers' specific tasks, they all suffered from difficult living conditions within the mine compound. The need of the government and the coal mine companies for increased production contributed to the neglect of the miners' health and welfare. In 1888 Matsuoka Yoshikazu, a journalist for *Nipponjin*, focused public attention on the horrific conditions at the Takashima mine. The Takashima pits, located on a small island off Nagasaki, had originally been worked by convicts. According to Matsuoka's report, conditions had not improved after Mitsubishi, which took over the mine in 1881, began using free labor. Takashima workers, ill-fed and inadequately housed, suffered from a variety of contagious diseases. Although nominally free to come and go as they pleased, miners were virtual prisoners bound by debt, unfair contracts, personal ties to labor bosses, and at times real ropes and manacles.

The overseer's right to beat miners who were deemed slackers suggests the prevailing slave-labor conditions. At Takashima and elsewhere public punishment was decided not by legal authorities but by crew bosses. As a lesson to others, a "lazy" worker, one who had attempted to run away or had broken mine rules, might be trussed up and whipped in front of fellow workers.[14] (See fig. 12.) Matsuoka's revelations created a widespread public outcry for mine reform, to which some companies responded in the 1890s by improving living conditions. But the degree of improvement did not immediately or substantially correct the many health and welfare problems that continued into the Taishō period and thereafter.

Kagawa Toyohiko, the Christian social reformer, visited several of the Kyushu mines shortly after the 1918 rice riots. He reported that the term for company-supplied housing, "barns" or "sheds" (*naya*), proved to be an unintentionally apt description. Kagawa thought that the sheds, jammed closely together, poorly ventilated, and receiving inadequate sunlight, were more suitable for inanimate tools than human beings. He estimated that family members using company housing had less than a single tatami-sized sleeping space (about three by six feet) for every two people. These crowded conditions went beyond the problem of individual living quarters. In many of the mines, residents suffered health problems because of inadequate facilities. At the mine visited by Kagawa, for example, twenty households shared a single toilet. As a result of overcrowding and poor sanitation, diseases spread rapidly. Common illnesses in the mines in 1920 included typhoid, dysentery, tuberculosis, beriberi, syphilis, gonorrhea, anemia, and intestinal parasites, to list but a few. Kagawa also noted that Japanese miners suffered from the chronic and disabling black lung disease.[15]

Despite wretched conditions within the mines, miners were not entirely without legal protection. During the Meiji period the central government established the Mine Inspection Office as a watchdog agency to guarantee that mine owners would maintain minimum working standards within the mines. By law, each concessionaire was required to submit company rules governing their workers and could not operate unless these received approval from the inspection office. Yet the central government did not provide legislation aimed directly at improving working conditions in the mines until the promulgation of the 1890 Mining Order (Kōgyō Jōrei). The passage of this ordinance, which was helped enormously by Matsuoka's *Nipponjin* articles, was hardly a piece of bold legislation. Beyond stipulating that workers be paid at regular intervals and receive care in case of accidental injury, the ordinance provided little other protection. The Mining Order was followed in 1905 by the Mining Law (Kōgyō Hō), which did little more than stipulate minimum ages for working and minimal relief measures.[16]

Although provisions for the health and welfare of mine workers existed in the law books, the degree of enforcement was, at best, hit or miss. Coal was too valuable, its production too economically and strategically important, and the industry too large to be effectively policed. If the statutes were intended to end riots by workers, they were also singularly unsuccessful. Despite ordinances and laws, miners repeatedly protested working conditions between 1870 and 1900. The Takashima miners, not surprisingly, staged five violent uprisings between 1870 and 1883, all of which were brutally suppressed.[17]

Many of the early protests resembled spontaneous slave revolts in reaction to inhuman conditions. But as coalfield unrest became more frequent after the turn of the century, protests also became better organized. In settling grievances, miners relied on strikes, petitions, and negotiations with management rather than blindly destructive attacks. In the 1904 Miike strike in northern Kyushu, miners presented the following demands to company management:

1. Wages should be raised to match those of workers in other Miike mines.

2. Additional pay should be given for work in difficult places.

3. Coal-box weighing regulations should be changed to provide larger allowances for boxes considered underweight.

4. The company should subsidize oil for miners' lamps.

5. Horses instead of men should be used for underground transport.[18]

They made similar demands without resorting to riot in disputes in 1889, 1895, 1904, and 1908.[19]

Nonviolent strike tactics were not limited to Kyushu. The 1907 Poronai mine "riot" in Hokkaido actually began as a peaceful protest in which miners petitioned management, listing grievances not unlike those cited by the Miike workers. Rioting did not occur at Poronai until management, which had originally approved worker demands following a peaceful work stoppage, reneged on its earlier promises.[20] Both the miners' methods (rioting after peaceful strikes) and the issues in dispute (pay, working conditions, and subsidization), which were typical of these early protests, were identical to those of the 1918 coalfield riots. The character of the disputes did not change in 1917 and 1918, when miners struck more often than workers in any other industrial sector.[21]

By the time stronger protective legislation covering both mine and factory workers was introduced with the 1911 Factory Law, the larger mining companies, goaded by various protests, had also taken steps to improve working conditions. Many companies established clinics within the mine compound or partially paid the medical bills of workers injured on the job. Although the coverage was limited and often paid less if the accident was considered the miner's fault, medical protection at larger mines was more comprehensive. At zaibatsu operations, for example, management provided the injured worker's family with a living allowance based on a percentage of the miner's daily earnings, in addition to covering medical costs. Yet even these benefits were limited in duration and provided only meager disability compensation. As late as the Taishō period, compensation for specific disabling injuries (the loss of a limb, blindness, or crippling) seldom amounted to more than one year's pay given to the miner or his family in a lump sum. Most companies did pay at least a portion of the miner's funeral expenses in case of accidental death.[22] Aside from this dubious benefit, the quality of aid extended to miners was at best uneven. In general, smaller companies did less for their workers than the better-managed zaibatsu concerns.

Understandably, one would not readily become a miner if other opportunities were available. Indeed, before the Meiji Restoration, the mine work force had been composed largely of social outcastes. Domain governments sometimes ordered *eta* to work the pits. In addition to this "unclean" pariah class, landless and impoverished peasants, déclassé ex-samurai, and ex-convicts could also be found working the mines. The "criminal element" was always present, not only because the mines provided exile to fugitives but also because the pits used convict labor.

Despite the Meiji leaders' attempts at social leveling by fiat, the image of the Tokugawa miner as low-class, marginal, and vaguely menacing continued strong during the Meiji period. One study notes that "the miner came to be regarded as an outcast whatever his origin, and this inferior status remained well into the twentieth century, affecting the attitude of mine owners to their employees, and thus the shape which 'familial' management practices took in the industry."[23] This statement is certainly valid. But during World War I the stigma attached to being a miner, if still strong, was at least more ambivalent. The nation's apparently insatiable demand for coal created a labor shortage, which required higher wages and brought more "mainstream" workers into the pits. Mine work was even promoted as a needed service to the state. Nevertheless, a popular saying suggested that to fall to the status of a coal miner was to inflict a punishment on one's parents.[24] The protagonist in Natsume Sōseki's *The Miner* (1908), a novel set in a copper mine, presents the common attitude of "respectable" society toward people who became miners:

> There are many kinds of laborers in this world, but it seemed to me that the lowliest and most cruelly used was the miner. Far from finding it "pretty good" that I could become a miner so easily, I viewed the prospect with a great deal of alarm. If someone had told me that there are species still lower than the miner, I would have found the concept unimaginable, as if I had been told that there are many days left to the year after December 31.[25]

Although many became miners simply for the better pay available during the years of high demand, the mines also continued to attract people outside respectable society. Former *eta* (now burakumin or *shin heimin*), dispossessed farmers, Korean immigrants, ex-convicts, and convicts on "loan" to the coal companies were still recognizable groups in mines of the Taishō period. But even pit workers with no links to an outcaste or disdained ethnic group did not escape the wider public's suspicion. Miners were often literally "outsiders" who hailed from distant prefectures, drifted from job to job, and seemed to deserve their image as low-class vagabonds.

Although many became miners simply for the better pay available during the years of high demand, the mines also continued to attract people outside respectable society. Former *eta* (now burakumin or acceptance. Some studies have suggested that a special kind of esprit de corps traditionally existed among miners. Because of their status as an outcaste group and because of the danger involved in working in the pits, mine workers were said to look after one another on and off the job. Ties of duty, loyalty, obligation, and superior-inferior relationships (*oyabun-kobun*), also characteristic of the samurai tradition, peasant communities, and yakuza, were said to be stronger among miners than among other social groups. The miner was reported to live in a network of social relationships that provided the individual with security and help in time of need in exchange for loyalty and service to other miners. A 1909 English-language Japanese government report on the industry provides a glowing, idealized description of the abstract code governing relationships between miners:

There exist peculiar usages among miners. . . . The oaths of allegiance to chiefs by protégés and to their brethren are observed with religious strictness. It is expected that the instructions of the boss are to be obeyed whether they are right or wrong. These chiefs are in intimate communications with one another, so that in case a miner goes from one mine to another, seeking employment, etc., he may rely upon receiving kind treatment if he gives the name of his chief. His new friends will go to no little trouble to find employment for him and will often give him money to cover his traveling expenses. This peculiar spirit of fraternity is utilized for the *control* of miners; and it is difficult to realize how implicitly the commands of these chiefs are obeyed and how well order is preserved. . . . The absence of strikes may generally be accounted to the kind treatment accorded to miners. (Emphasis added.)[26]

The description overlooks the many labor disputes in the coalfields during the late Meiji years. Indeed, the report barely mentions the system's primary aim of controlling the labor force. Even more misleading is its suggestion that the "peculiar usages" inherent in the crew boss or *naya* system derived from espirit de corps among fellow miners instead of a contractual relationship between mine owners and labor recruiters. Such domination was considered necessary because, even though some workers found security and refuge in the mines, many did not stay long. Hazardous working conditions, the inadequacy of care for injured or disabled workers, and the social stigma associated with the work caused some miners to quit the fields as soon as they could. Pit workers also periodically returned to their home prefectures or jumped from colliery to colliery in pursuit of higher wages. As late as 1910 it was not unusual for mines to have an annual employee turnover rate of 120 percent, which created obvious difficulties for keeping production at consistently high levels.[27] Although never very successful, the *naya* system was intended to staunch the constant flow of workers between mines.

During the Taishō period larger firms moved increasingly toward direct management control, but the crew-boss system persisted in a modified form until 1945. Even zaibatsu mines relied on bosses to recruit, oversee workers, and assure a steady labor force at the pits. Prior to 1900 mine owners typically entrusted the crew boss or barracks head (*nayagashira*) with total responsibility for recruiting and hiring mine workers. As a middleman between management and labor, he acted as guarantor for the coal miners he hired. He also furnished the miners with tools, food, and furniture and helped situate new workers in a bunkhouse (*hanba*) or family living quarters.[28] All of this he did for a fee, which the miner was expected to repay in hard cash and loyalty.

Debts owed the crew boss might not be called due immediately. In 1918 the demand for additional miners to work the Jōban fields led crew bosses to offer generous advances for tools, traveling costs, and even bedding. Repayment would be made later by deductions from the miner's wages. But there was a catch: the miner was also expected to buy household goods from the boss at rates usually higher than retail. The acceptance of an advance left the worker obligated beyond the initial amount of money received. If the boss was sharp and the miner less than careful, debts grew, causing the pit worker to become a fixture in the *nayagashira*'s "stable."

Maintaining his stable was the crew boss's primary function, and in the Jōban mining region the successful *nayagashira* was sarcastically referred to as a "nonworking miner." One researcher who spent 1918 investigating conditions in Fukushima suggested that the crew boss was more procurer than simple labor broker. The resemblance extended not only to the *nayagashira*'s work but to his personal appearance. Mikami Tokusaburō noted that a typical Fukushima boss, who might be found hanging about train stations regaling prospects with promises of good wages, free rent, and subsidized food, typically wore flashy clothes and at least one large finger-ring. He reportedly sought out the young, the inexperienced, and the seekers of something better. On accepting his invitation, new miners were expected to follow directions, accept job assignments, and be grateful. In the Jōban mines the smaller "nonworking miners" had seven or eight men in their *hanba*, while the largest controlled approximately four hundred workers.

In fairness to the crew bosses, their work was not without risk. Miners might abscond from one stable and go to another, especially when enticed by higher wages. Such fickleness often brought recruiters into competition for the pit workers' services. When a rival recruiter was caught in a stronger boss's territory, the poacher might be beaten. Nevertheless, *nayagashira* could not always prevent workers from fleeing in the night or, as the pit worker's slang coarsely described the rampant absconding, placing a sail between the buttocks and blowing away. When this happened, any advances or loans were lost.[29]

The boss was not, however, entirely dependent on direct payments from working miners. He also pocketed a finder's fee provided by the company. For directing pit work, figuring and distributing wages, settling disputes between miners, and punishing those who violated mine rules, he received a percentage of the miner's pay or a commission based on the amount of coal produced.[30] With worker management entrusted entirely to his hands, the *nayagashira* had ample opportunities to abuse his wide-ranging power. That he took advantage of these is indicated by a number of riots and strikes in the Meiji period, protesting the bosses' power to determine wages and punish miners.

The *naya* system in its "pure" form ended with the beginning of zaibatsu control of Japan's major mines. With the trend toward direct management of workers, the *nayagashira* was often incorporated into the mine company organization as a foreman or a regular worker, although in smaller mines the crew boss continued to hold a position of authority. In the modified system the mining company limited the *nayagashira*'s control of miners by prohibiting him from taking a direct cut from worker wages or depending on their production for his income. Although management weakened the role of the individual boss, mine companies nevertheless continued the *naya* system. In fact, a 1922 government study of Kyushu mines with over a hundred employees found that 60 percent of them still used the crew-boss system in one form or another.[31] The paternalistic form of management persisted, even in larger mining companies, because of the companies' need to attract and hold a stable, reliable labor force. While doing away with some of the worst abuses inherent in the *nayagashira*'s traditional role, mine management nevertheless attempted to preserve authoritarian and paternalistic ties between bosses and pit workers in new bonds between company and employee.

Although crew bosses did not disappear entirely, in some mines they ceased to function as independent subcontractors. The mine companies, especially the larger enterprises, reduced the crew-bosses' authority to that of a salaried foreman, coal grader, or guard and thereby replaced the *nayagashira*'s personal control with company control. Such companies often hired and made contracts directly with their workers but continued to pay a piece wage based on the amount of coal brought to the surface. Intent on encouraging production, they paid cash bonuses as incentives to workers who produced more than an average quota of usable coal per day. To give miners a stake in company operation, discourage absenteeism, and curb the miner's tendency to drift from one job to another, companies also introduced the *katamai*, or the shift-rice system, which allowed miners to buy rice at a discount according to the number of shifts worked. Variations on this scheme provided purchase rights for fixed amounts of rice depending on the miner's seniority

and position within the company.[32] At some mines the company bound
the employee further by paying him in scrip usable only at the company
store or kept store prices low so as not to raise wages. To make
sure that miners would not disappear after payday, companies also
instituted compulsory saving plans. Although mining laws after 1900
mandated that wages be paid at least monthly, this did not prevent the
larger mines from withholding a certain amount from the worker's
wage, which could be drawn upon only under specific conditions.[33]

The companies' measures reflected the common view that miners
were fundamentally incapable of looking after themselves. From the
standpoint of efficiency-minded managers, the pit worker's notoriety
was entirely deserved. Miners were famous for using whatever money
they could lay their hands on for drinking, gambling, and whoring.
At the Ube mine in Yamaguchi, for example, the day-after-payday
absenteeism attributed to drunkenness regularly climbed to 30 percent.
Many believed the miner's live-for-the-moment attitude toward work
and money was as unalterable as the pit worker's supposedly constant
need for liquor.[34] (See fig. 13.) As a testimony to the miners' reputation
for fast but not particularly high living, brothels and drinking houses—
some built with mining company money—were common features of
the mining town.

Social reformers like Kagawa wrote deploringly of yakuza, gamblers,
and prostitutes, who were ever-present in and around mine compounds.
Others, however, tended to see the frontier-like conditions as part of the
cost of coal production. Mikami Tokusaburō noted that the miner's
work was dangerously unpredictable and that his desire to enjoy today
what he might not be able to savor tomorrow should surprise no one.
But even Mikami, who avoided moralistic condemnation of the pit
worker's pleasures, expressed concern over the threat to public health
posed by mining town conditions. Taira in southern Fukushima prefecture, for example, had a total resident population of only 20,000 in
1918 but was home to six brothels within the borders of the township.
Separate pleasure quarters had also grown up just outside of town.
Mikami, however, was less disturbed by the number of brothels than he
was by reports that nine out of ten women who worked in them were
infected with syphilis or some other venereal disease.[35]

Paying the miner in scrip or rice or withholding a portion of his
salary helped the company deal with the miner's casual work ethics and
reduced high rates of employee turnover. But the company store and
shift-rice systems were justified as worker benefits rather than as man-

agement manipulation. As was explained in a Bureau of Mines report, miners often lived in regions distant from large food markets, and as a service to pit workers, the company store served to bring the market to them. To make sure that the miners could keep abreast of rising prices, the mining companies stocked their stores with rice, soy sauce, bean paste, and other basic food products at prices often lower than those on the open market.[36] Rice prices at the Mitsui company store, for example, usually hovered just at the wholesale level. But when wholesale prices rose to thirty-eight sen per shō during the second half of 1918, the company continued to sell grain at twenty-seven sen per shō, the rate before the rise. From the summer of 1918 through the spring of 1920, Mitsui stores consistently maintained rice prices at 45 to 50 percent below the prevailing wholesale price.[37]

Some mining companies, as might be expected, used the monopoly on the company store and the scrip system to take with one hand what they paid with the other. But in the larger zaibatsu operations petty squeezing was not the aim of these measures. Instead, they allowed management to demonstrate concern for miner welfare and keep pit workers on the job. Company and government officials alike believed that miners simply could not be trusted with cash. Although there is evidence that suggests that by 1918 miners were probably about as competent as the general population in managing their money, company policy usually assumed that a miner would spend all the money he had—and often more—on wine, women, and gambling.[38] Management thus saw the company-store system, whereby food could be advanced against wages, as a way to assure that the miner's family would be fed no matter how profligate the main breadwinner. A similar idea stood behind the compulsory saving and shift-rice schemes.

Mitsui Mining's company-store bylaws reminded miners always to beware of wasteful tendencies, to preserve the unadorned simple virtues, and to save, save, save. Such a guiding philosophy nicely served the company's aim of securing a stable work force and justifying low wages. Management did not want to raise pay rates, for obvious economic reasons. But companies also resisted giving the miner more money because cash meant mobility—or from the miner's perspective, independence, if not freedom. Long before the 1918 riots and into the recession of the early 1920s, even major zaibatsu concerns therefore favored policies that provided cheap food through company subsidization rather than simple raises in worker's wages.[39]

No matter what the company's motives were, it is undeniable that the pit worker's lot, particularly at the larger zaibatsu mines, improved increasingly after 1900. Mitsui and other major mining companies moved beyond economic disincentives and opened nurseries, elementary schools, and recreational facilities in an attempt to satisfy workers and thereby maintain a more stable work force.[40] Yet, despite these gains, miners were dissatisfied. Neither the old *naya* system, with its exploiting crew boss, nor the still-evolving system of direct management, typical of zaibatsu operations, met their demands for higher wages and improved working conditions. Appeals for autonomy in negotiation had also been expressed in numerous labor struggles before the 1918 riots. By 1914 the number of mine disputes was increasing, and so were demands for better pay. Wartime inflation, which contributed to protests for higher wages in other industries, encouraged similar movements among miners. The number of disputes in metal and coal mines jumped from five with 1,168 participants in 1915 to sixty-six involving 23,758 miners in 1918.[41] The issues, methods, and course of struggles in Japanese coal mines during 1918 suggest that they were part of an already ongoing movement that would continue after the rice riots.

The 1918 Coalfield Riots

Works such as Yoshikawa Mitsusada's *Iwayuru kome sōdō jiken no kenkyū* present the coalfield riots as the last stage in a series of nationwide disturbances. These disturbances had begun in Toyama and spread "like a contagious disease" (*densen byō-teki*) to major cities and outlying regions throughout central Japan, finally breaking out in the mining areas of southwestern Honshu and northern Kyushu.[42] This chronological description misleads in two respects. Generally, it suggests that rioting, the "contagion," was uniform both in etiology and in symptoms. Specifically, it makes no mention of the numerous mine disputes that occurred before the first Toyama protest. In addition to Meiji and early Taishō disputes, strikes indistinguishable from the ones later called "rice riots" occurred repeatedly in 1917 and 1918, especially in Kyushu mines. On 6 July 1917, for example, fifty miners at the Tsunemi mine in Moji walked off the job, demanding higher wages. They were followed a few weeks later by miners at Mitsubishi's Yoshi-tani pit, who protested low wages by refusing to work.[43] Both of these actions were peaceful. But in May 1918, two months before the first

Toyama shipping boycott, a violent dispute broke out in which sixteen hundred miners refused to enter the pits and attacked company offices at the Taishō Mining Company's Nakazuru operation.[44]

Because the 1918 coalfield "rice riots" differed little from earlier labor protests, it is somewhat arbitrary to set a beginning date for them. Nevertheless, most studies point to the 17 August uprising of miners in Ube village, Yamaguchi prefecture, as the first coal miners' rice riot. Following the Ube disturbance, labor unrest spread throughout northern Kyushu mines. Although individual incidents seldom lasted longer than two or three days and in only a single instance did the restoration of order take as long as a week, sporadic disturbances in southwestern Honshu and northern Kyushu coalfields continued from 17 August until 17 September. During this period authorities reported riots at more than thirty coal mines. Major disturbances recurred in Fukushima, Yamaguchi, Fukuoka, Kumamoto, and Saga prefectures. In smaller work stoppages less than a hundred people might join in the disputes, but police also reported mass rioting involving as many as ten thousand.[45]

Coalfield riots commonly included attacks on mine buildings and sometimes arson. In the Chikuhō coalfield riots, miners hurled dynamite at troops sent to quell the disturbance.[46] Mine company officials' failure to keep negotiation deadlines or management's attempts to delay the implementation of wage raises made destructive protests more likely. When miners resorted to violent methods, prefectural governments mobilized troops to put down or prevent rioting within their jurisdictions. In some cases, however, miner representatives and company officials peacefully settled the workers' grievances.

The miners' demands usually centered on three sets of issues: (1) wages, rice prices, and the company store; (2) working conditions; and (3) employee relations. All three were clearly interrelated under the old or modified *naya* system. Working conditions (for example, poor coal-cart circulation) or employee relations (antagonism between coal graders and miners) had an effect on the size of a miner's wage. Therefore, even though miners appeared most concerned with economic issues, they often presented management with a list of grievances that included appeals for action on seemingly unrelated problems. In the incidents discussed below, the rioters' primary aim was to increase wages by 30 to 50 percent. From economic demands rioters moved to an attack on inequalities in the coal-grading system, the despotic position of foremen as well as the haughty attitude of managerial personnel, and the operation of mandatory savings programs. In other words, the coalfield riots represented a popular indictment of the basic features of the modified crew-boss system.

Lower real wages caused by wartime inflation and high prices for rice added to the miners' frustration with the *naya* system. In Yamaguchi, Fukuoka, and other coal-mining prefectures, newspapers predicted that the cost of a single shō of rice would top 50 sen by late August 1918. With a miner's average day wage ranging between .96 and 1.30 yen (and assuming that the miner and his family required a minimum of one shō of rice daily), the soaring cost of rice meant that from one-third to one-half of daily earnings might be required for this single important food item.[47] In major Jōban mines and those managed by Mitsui, subsidized rice prices and even generous distributions of extra grain were intended to lessen the impact of inflation. Mine companies also attempted to deal with steep consumer costs by instituting minuscule wage increases, cutting prices at distribution centers, and issuing rice-discount coupons. Instead of easing tensions, however, such steps angered miners, who viewed them as mere stopgap measures. As was evident in their wage demands, the miners wanted significantly higher pay, not more rice scrip.

Worker dissatisfaction with token measures can be seen in the dispute at the Okinoyama mines in Ube village, Yamaguchi prefecture. There management's attempts to help miners combat the high cost of living failed to cover even day-to-day increases in rice prices. Although miners had been demanding higher wages since early June 1918, neither the president of the Okinoyama mines nor his staff had responded to the workers' attempts to negotiate. When company representatives at last acknowledged that inflation was creating genuine problems for their workers, they attempted to remedy the situation by issuing 2-sen rice-discount coupons. The move was clearly inadequate, since rice prices jumped by 1 to 2 sen daily during August 1918. Mine workers responded by requesting a 35 percent wage increase to bring day wages from .96 to 1.20 yen. The company ignored this demand and on 10 August authorized yet another distribution of rice coupons, this time allowing for a 3-sen discount off market price. The measure did little to improve the miners' plight. In the ten-day period before management made coupons available, rice prices had risen from 40 to 45 sen.[48] While waiting for the company's palliative measures, the miners had actually lost ground in their struggle to maintain the value of real wages.

At the Mineji no. 2 pit in Fukuoka, miners took issue with company-imposed conditions limiting aid eligibility rather than the amount of help offered. As rice approached the fifty-sen level in August, Mineji's management distributed discount coupons enabling recipients to buy rice at 35 sen per shō. For miners who worked a complete shift, the company made available additional coupons allowing for purchase of a limited amount of rice at 25 sen per shō. At Jōban mines the discount price for rice was a standard feature of the shift-rice system. But only those who worked were eligible for rice at the lower rate. The miner who did not work an assigned shift had to pay retail, a rate nearly double the company's subsidized price. At Mineji there were no acceptable reasons for not working a shift. Genuinely sick or injured workers were denied the twenty-five-sen benefit, just as those were who stayed home because of laziness or hangovers. The company's eligibility restrictions applied also to miners' wives, who were barred from purchasing cheaper grain if their husbands did not work. Even spouses of men recently conscripted for service in Siberia received no special consideration in the discount plan.[49] Mineji workers complained about the unfairness of these conditions in their demands for higher wages. Similarly, when management substituted payment in kind or coupons for higher wages, as they did at the Okinoyama, Shinbara, and other mines, workers protested by going on strike or rioting.

Merely raising wages did not guarantee smooth relations between the mine company and the worker. The size of the pay hike also made a difference. A small increase that did not sufficiently cover the decline in real wages was as ineffective as discount coupons that failed to keep pace with the higher cost of rice. At one colliery in Sage prefecture, for example, management authorized a 10 percent hike in day wages before the onset of rioting. Miners immediately criticized the move as insufficient, since it did not cover higher consumer costs. They responded to the company's action by demonstrating in support of their own demand for a 30 percent wage hike.[50] An identical dispute occurred at the Taku mine, also in Saga, when miners rejected a company offer for a 20 percent pay raise, which fell far short of their demand for a 50 percent hike. In the Ube riots and in labor disputes at Mitsui-owned mines in Fukuoka and Kumamoto, the low level of wage increases offered by the company also contributed to the friction.

Whether miners really expected to receive as much as a doubling of their wages cannot be known with certainty. The large wage demands may have represented a negotiation tactic whereby workers made maximum demands at the outset in anticipation of a later compromise. In some disputes just such a process took place. But the negotiation process did not always go so smoothly. In several major riots, calls for a 30 to 50 percent wage increase were widely supported and did not seem intended merely as an opening position in negotiation. In some cases miners refused to budge from their initial demands and rioted when management offered 10 to 20 percent raises.

The miners' demand that wages sufficiently cover increased consumer costs contributed to their inflexible stand. They had no illusions about the negative impact of inflation, as is shown in a roughly worded and threatening letter to managers of a northern Kyushu pit:

> We make an appeal. At present there are many points of unfairness in the [company's announced] wage increases. To the first-, second-, and third-shift members, old and young, give all of us ten sen more! If we don't get ten sen or more, a family of four cannot make ends meet no matter how you figure it. Please heed this. If you don't a terrible riot will occur.[51]

The letter also indicates the miners' concern over unequal pay levels. Inequality was inherent in the wage system because miners were paid only for what they produced, not for time or energy expended. The government's Fukuoka Mine Office's analysis of the riots acknowledged that the unrest had stemmed not only from low wages but also from unequal pay for equal work. The hardness of the ground, the quantity and quality of coal deposits, the distance from the coal face to the pit entrance—all of these affected the miner's level of income. Although the mine office stopped short of recommending that the existing wage system be abolished, it did note that natural conditions should be considered in adjusting wage policies.[52]

The basis for the recommendations in the report can be seen in the Mineji riots, where workers like Yonekura Inokichi protested the unequal working conditions that reduced real wages. When Yonekura began working as a miner the price of rice mattered little to him. Because mine companies were chronically short of help, finding work at a reasonable rate of pay was easy, especially for young, single workers. In his words, "Eating rice mixed with barley [typical fare of the poor who could not afford polished rice] was for farmers. If you followed your nose to a smokestack, you could have white rice and sake. Only housewives knew the cost of grain."[53] But the good times did not last. The sudden increase in consumer costs in 1917 and 1918 prompted Yonekura and others to organize a petition movement for higher wages at

Mineji. Their protest was not a simple reaction to higher prices. At Mineji the coal seams were of uneven quality, and the miners' wages tended to fluctuate unpredictably. Where a two-man team had formerly been able to bring up five carts of coal, the depletion of deposits by 1918 meant that miners were bringing up more and more unusable shale. Because the company's wage system made no allowances for work-site differences, the crew boss could credit workers like Yone-kura with only two or three cartloads despite the time and labor ex-pended in bringing five loads to the surface. Consequently, Yonekura's day wage fell from 1.30 to .80 yen during the first half of 1918.[54]

As was noted in the Fukuoka Mine Office report, much of the in-equality in the piece-wage system resulted from man-made wage and personnel policies rather than limitations in the natural environment. Some mines reserved special benefits for staff and long-term em-ployees, using seniority bonuses and rice allotments to maintain a reli-able work force. In the riots at Mitsui's Miyaura mine, only 5 percent of the employees were eligible for the company's long-term employee re-ward (*einen kinzoku hyōshō*) and the special bonus it carried. Even before the onset of rioting, miners criticized the benefit as unfair and discriminatory. Once rioting had broken out in mines all over northern Kyushu, a small band of Miyaura miners organized fellow workers and presented Mitsui officials with demands for both a 30 percent wage increase and the abolition of the special award.[55]

Miners advocated regulating prices at the company store and dis-tribution center as yet another way of maintaining real-wage levels. Some worker petitions called for setting rice prices at twenty or twenty-five sen per shō and reducing prices on other goods by as much as 30 percent. Other workers complained of the quality of merchandise and inconvenient operating hours. At the Akasaka mine in Fukuoka, miners claimed that company-provided rice was full of gravel and sold at full price for less than full measure. At the Hōkoku mine, also in Fukuoka, miners requested that the company store's operating hours be extended until 7:30 P.M. In other disputes miners protested the company store's monopoly, demanding that private merchants be granted free access to the mine compound.[56]

In every mine where destructive rioting occurred, rioters vandalized the company store in addition to the mine's general affairs office or branch headquarters. Attacks on stores and distribution centers were carried out to adjust inequalities in wages by leveling store prices and, in some cases, the stores themselves. Miners coerced store managers or clerks to reduce prices for rice and a variety of other goods. If prices were not cut, the miners took what they wanted and left. Sometimes they forced agreement on a "fair price," paid a token amount, and distributed goods to family members and neighbors. In most riots, however, the miners took items for their own use. Even when they paid the "fair price," the amount of money exchanged was so ridiculously low that the rioters' actions amounted to little more than looting.[57]

More important than booty in motivating attacks on the company store was disagreement over company policies that governed its operation. Although ostensibly operated for the miners' benefit, the store symbolized the company's control over workers. Miners often expressed their resentment by destruction rather than theft. (See figs. 14 and 15.) At the Iwaya coal mine, for example, they smashed windows, cases, and shelves. Instead of carrying off goods, they poured out sake and scattered sugar and rice on the roadway. At the Shinbara no. 5 mine in Fukuoka, the miners attacked the company store and threw everything from cider bottles to dried fish into the streets. Rioters also destroyed the fixtures, turned over tubs of bean paste, ruined rolls of cotton cloth, and broke whatever could be broken. In other riots the miners washed their hands and feet in sake or used it as starter fuel to burn store goods. They could, of course, have taken whatever they pleased without wrecking buildings, fixtures, and merchandise. But as miners who took part in destroying the Mineji mine distribution center later explained, they were seeking revenge for being ill-treated, not gain.[58]

One way to improve conditions was to force mine management to make specific changes that would help equalize wage rates. The miners' most frequent demand, presented in written or oral petitions, was for an improvement in coal-box and cart circulation. They also requested the completion of cart systems not yet in operation.[59] Improvements in cart circulation meant that miners could get coal to the surface more quickly, produce more loads in a single day, and conceivably increase earnings. In written petitions miners berated poor management—indicated by sluggish coal movement within the mine—for imposing an unnatural barrier on the individual's or work team's productivity. Miners also criticized shortages of boxes, breakdowns of drills and other equipment, and badly maintained paths and roads within the mine compound.[60] A few petitions even demanded that rules regulating dynamite usage be revised. At one pit laborers summarily asserted that management interfered in actual work and that mining should be left to the miners.[61]

Although workers did not explicitly advocate trade unionism during the coalfield disturbances, their petitions and destruction of company property nevertheless expressed a bitter, if diffuse, resentment of company management. A social and economic gulf separated rank-and-file coal miners from the mining company's supervisors, office staff, and directors. Miners were held in low esteem not only by the general public but also by the owners and directors of the mines. For years after the Meiji Restoration, the employment policies of mine companies treated pit workers as if they were no more than a necessary evil, deserving of only enough to keep them working. In the 1880s Gotō Shōjirō, the Takashima mine concessionaire and erstwhile leader of the Liberty and Popular Rights movement, explained that he delayed paying cash wages to his workers because the miners "are not the kind of people to be looked at in the same light as ordinary mankind. They are animals which know today but not tomorrow; and therefore if they were paid as their works were done, they would have one by one run away."[62] Although conditions within the mines had changed since the 1880s, attitudes similar to Gotō's had not.

The pit workers' menial status contrasted sharply with that of the company staff, which enjoyed better wages, living conditions, and employment security. Equally galling was the company's enforcement of a kind of caste system that enabled staff workers to act as the underground workers' overseers. A Fukuoka Mine Office report indicates that the miners did not readily accept an ascriptive status in which they were regarded as social inferiors best kept at a distance. It adds that the social gulf separating miners from management, which spawned constant resentments, grew not only from material deprivation but also from simple discrimination. Unless the companies bridged the gap dividing the "separate interests" of management and workers, unrest would not end with the rice riots.[63]

During the summer of 1918 miners were reminded of their second-class citizenship by the companies' reluctant attempts to enact remedial measures to check declining real wages. In riots ranging from Yamaguchi to Saga prefecture, pit workers protested company indifference toward their difficult economic situation. They frequently expressed resentment of hypocritical mine officials who profited from the strong market demand for coal while disdaining and maltreating those who actually worked in the pits. During rioting at a Mitsui pit in Fukuoka, an anonymous miner tacked an open letter at the entrance to the compound's post office. The letter presents the miners' perspective on employee relations and suggests the resentments that led many to join the riots:

> Everyone, open wide your eyes and look at the company's actions. Prices have risen fiercely and in truth it is no longer possible for laborers to exist peacefully another day. At times like the present, we sometimes lack even three meals a day. Old men cry for a single drink [of sake] and children cry from hunger. . . . Working hundreds of feet underground, doing an extremely dangerous job, sacrificing our bodies and our lives, for this we receive wages not even sufficient to feed us. . . . Indeed, we are angry. . . . But contrast our condition to that of the gang of company directors. They dress in fine clothes, feast sumptuously, and own splendid cars. They are the very image of contentment and satisfaction. To our unspeakable poverty and tearful entreaties they turn a deaf ear and show but total indifference. Nothing need be said of the inhuman attitude of those [running the company], those that have relied upon our real strength [to work the mines]. [Their attitude is] as cool as water, as cold as ice. The unfeelingness of the company director and the coolness of the manager! If we leave things to such people, in no time at all they will lead us down a path whereby we [will be forced to] eat grass, grind our teeth on tree bark, and finally die. That is all we will gain. [Do we] rely upon the company and those high-collar characters, the managers? Miners, respect yourselves![64]

As is evident in this letter and in other petitions as well, many pit workers complained about the obvious inequalities in wealth that distinguished company staff (*sha'in*) from manual laborers. The separate and superior housing given mine staff members, their higher pay, and even their wives' clothing (described in one petition as rivaling a geisha's) elicited angry comment from the miners. But the issue did not end with these gross differences in remuneration. The miners also complained that pit workers seemed to be needed to keep the coal coming but were given no respect for their work.

Within the mine compound pit workers were expected to be subservient to everyone except other miners. Even the miners' forms of address to company superiors were exceptionally deferential. Custom dictated that rank-and-file miners call supervisors and staff "Mr. Official" (*kan'in-san*). The miners' irritation over the arrogant attitude of bosses and company superiors found its way into several written petitions. Along with demands for a 30 percent pay raise, one document stated that labor bosses (*nayagashira*) must stop using insulting language toward miners. In more general demands at Mitsui's Miyahara mine, miners asked that all supervisors change their attitude (*taido*) toward workers and end their despotic practices. At the Iwaya mine in

Saga prefecture, an improved attitude meant that the company should employ only trustworthy staff members who would treat miners fairly. This included the company's medical personnel, whom the miners criticized as arrogant and unsympathetic in dealing with their health problems.[65]

The miners reserved their greatest anger for the coal graders, foremen, and barracks bosses. Again, feelings toward these men cannot be separated entirely from concerns over wage-related issues. The complaints against graders, for example, arose from the personalized structure of the pay system. Coal grading was hardly an exact science; it relied on an "eyeball" appraisal of coal quality and not merely weight. Those entrusted with evaluating the miner's individual production could potentially decide the worker's income, and this kind of power bred abuses. In petitions presented during the 1918 riots, miners complained that graders and bosses lorded it over pit workers. At some mines supervisory personnel had to be given special gifts of chicken and other goods, or the miners' wives or daughters were forced to work "voluntarily" without pay in the homes of company superiors. All of these indignities had to be suffered if the miner was to remain in the good graces of his superiors.[66]

In some incidents bad relations between workers and supervisors sparked violence. At the Mitsui Manda mine, pit workers suspected unfair coal grading and underweighing of coal boxes. Although company officials brought miners to the weighing station to assure them that their coal was being fairly evaluated, rioting still broke out. The miners involved in this incident, demonstrating their general suspicion of the graders and bosses, refused to accept underweighing as an honest mistake or, perhaps, a misunderstanding on the pit workers' part. Instead, the Manda miners accused graders of deliberately cheating or punishing individual workers. The negative attitude toward graders was not limited to Mitsui mines. In petitions presented in other disputes, miners demanded that the company immediately fire explicitly named graders and foremen.[67] In the Manda rioting the miners also requested that miners be included among the coal graders to assure fairness and impartiality. In the months following the riots, Mitsui officials in fact adopted this recommendation along with several others suggested by pit workers.[68]

It is difficult to separate economic concerns from ones related to worker "dignity" in assessing the impetus behind the riots. As was noted above, in most cases the miners demonstrated decidedly mixed motives. Under the modified *naya* system the miners' economic grievances were often inseparable from perceived inequalities in the management-worker relationship. To contemporary observers, however, the miners' lowly position, rather than rice prices or wages, was seen as the most important cause of the riots. A reporter for the *Fukuoka Nichinichi* observed:

> The present riots have nothing to do with rice prices or wages but represent an emotional issue [*kanjō mondai*]. . . . We can venture to say that the miners have not been driven by necessity to speak out [on the question of] wages and rice prices. On the contrary, [demands for higher pay and so on] are excuses. A common accord between labor and management has long been lacking [and] the situation is like that existing between enemy states. In recent riots, the rice problem can be seen only as a fuse leading to an explosion of daily discontent.[69]

The Pattern of Protest

Many of the summer coalfield disputes started peacefully and never escalated into riots. For example, workers at the Namazuda, Hōkoku, Meinohana, Meiji, and other pits scattered over Kyushu and Honshu participated in essentially nonviolent labor disputes through August and September. Miners did not destroy property in strikes; in riots they did. Yet whether they chose to strike or riot, their demands were fundamentally the same: increase wages, improve mine operation, and provide better treatment.

Once pit workers began to act, protests spread rapidly from mine to mine. Word of mouth and newspaper accounts of nationwide rioting obviously helped expand the coalfield unrest. One miner later recalled that press reports of the Toyama riots encouraged him and fellow miners to organize workers for a 30 percent wage increase at the Mineji mine.[70] Events closer to home also recommended protest. Pit workers saw the effectiveness of strikes at nearby steel mills, zinc works, and shipping docks. Rioting inspired by example was particularly evident in northern Kyushu where coal mines, factories, and arsenals were closely linked in a newly established regional industrial network. In late August, shortly before the miners' protest at Mitsui's Manda coalfield, for example, Mitsui electrical and chemical workers went on strike demanding a 40 percent wage increase. The action's effectiveness became manifest within two days, when management conceded a special allowance and increased incentive pay for plant workers. Encouraged by the factory workers' success, Mitsui's miners immediately made similar demands. The management of the company's coal division, however, was less sympathetic to the miners' petitions, and the wage protest developed into rioting on 4 September.[71]

Coalfield strikes or rioting also spread by direct communication between leaders in different mines. Although leaders of disputes made little attempt to mobilize miners as an occupational group, pit workers attempted to present unified demands within their own company. Workers in different mines under the same management (or in mines under separate management but close to one another) kept in touch to encourage unity in demands and broad-based participation by pit workers. Sympathy strikes were also reported.[72]

The pattern that rioting followed in spreading from one mine to another is fairly clear. But the question of why miners in one dispute carried out peaceful strikes or work slowdowns while those in another rioted deserves additional attention. Part of the explanation is simply that miners who led peaceful wage disputes had little to lose by escalating their protest. By walking off the job and encouraging others to do the same, they had already violated Article 17 of the Peace Preservation Law, which stipulated that workers could not organize for "collective actions concerning conditions of work or remuneration."[73] Miners at the Akasaka mine in Fukuoka who organized a peaceful work slowdown for higher wages were, in fact, later arrested and indicted under the law's provisions.[74] Whether miners who organized to demand higher pay rioted or not, they jeopardized their positions with the company and with the law and could be sure that penalties would be exacted for their acts.

The miners also threatened violence for "rational" reasons. The possibility of a riot gave them leverage in negotiations with company officials. The miners played upon the fears of both company management and local authorities by explicitly threatening violence in petitions and posters. Nevertheless, in most disputes rioting only began when the workers' demands were ignored or when companies failed to meet negotiation deadlines.

Emotion also played a part in transforming a peaceful work stoppage into a riot. In some protests, rioters' actions demonstrated more of the "natural and spontaneous" character (*shizen hassei-teki*) that historians have repeatedly used to describe the nationwide riots. At the Mineji mines in Fukuoka and at the Okinoyama and Misome pits in Ube, where two of the largest riots took place, protest planners clear-

ly did not intend the destructive attacks that followed negotiations
with mine management. But after months of wrangling, frustrations
got out of hand. Miners in Ube complained of repeated attempts by
the company either to ignore their demands or to stall negotiations.
Although Okinoyama workers had presented appeals in June, it was
not until 16 August, when owners learned that workers were organizing potentially violent demonstrations, that the company began to
negotiate seriously. By that time miners were no longer willing to listen
to offers of substantial wage increases. Despite the apparently peaceful
achievement of their basic aims, they attacked mine buildings and
burned down large sections of the company town.[75]

In contrast to the desperate frustration demonstrated by Ube miners,
the mood of the Mineji rioters was almost festive. Not coincidentally,
the outbreak of rioting at Mineji and other mines corresponded with
the advent of Bon (the Buddhist Festival of the Dead). The holiday provided miners with free time for drinking and practicing festival dances,
which helped gather and enliven crowds that protest leaders depended
on in mounting a broad-based protest for higher wages. But the sake-
drenched holiday mood also made crowds difficult to control. At Mineji
rioting appears to have escalated from a brawl between rival youth
gangs to attacks on mine buildings and eventually the sacking of the
company store. Rioting caught the original organizers of the wage dispute completely off guard. Until the clash between the young miners,
the protest had proceeded peacefully, and management seemed to be
seriously considering worker demands. The fact that strike leaders were
not directly responsible for the direction that the protest took did not
help them with the authorities. All were later arrested and several ended
up serving prison terms.

The festive mood at Mineji was evident in other mine riots. Hundreds of miners jammed the narrow streets of the mine compound
shouting "Wassha! Wassha!" as if they might have been taking part in a
matsuri procession rather than attacking buildings, destroying company records, and looting stores.[76] In riots in Yamaguchi and Fukuoka,
miners maintained the festival spirit by setting up refreshment stations
where stolen kegs of sake were opened and all were allowed to drink
their fill. Even in riots where the labor protest was not forgotten in the
midst of revelry, the miners passed around bottles to bolster their spirits
before taking on foremen or managers considered responsible for their
grievances. This curious mood, half festive and half serious, was espe-

cially strong at Mineji. Surrounded by armed troops, men and women gathered to continue their Obon dances defiantly within the mine compound the day after their protest had been unambiguously crushed (see fig. 17).[77]

Organization, Negotiations, and Protest Targets

From eyewitness accounts, trial records, and company histories one can piece together a "typical" pattern in the coalfield protests. Many sources suggest that rioting began when a core group of miners, meeting secretly and without any direct outside encouragement, decided to draw up demands intended to change company policy. The leaders, usually younger male miners, spread word to their fellows by means of handbills or face-to-face meetings in which they encouraged miners to halt work and to convene a mass meeting. The propaganda work usually brought out hundreds of miners to rallies at local shrines, temples, and primary schools or in parks and vacant lots. At these meetings the leaders presented their proposals and solicited opinions from the crowd. In some disputes, the gatherings convened several times on a single day or repeatedly over a two- or three-day period so that leaders could modify petitions, meet with company representatives, and report back to workers on the progress of negotiations. At times leaders also conferred with protest organizers at other mines under the same company management or with representatives from nearby pits.

The miners' demands usually carried a specific deadline for management's response and threatened work stoppages or rioting if mine officials failed to respond punctually. Although the miners occasionally transmitted demands verbally to the mining company, in most cases one of the literate miners was appointed secretary to record each point approved at the mass meetings. In the Mineji protest the organizers of the dispute also required miners to sign their names and affix their seals to petitions to indicate their support. After the demands were approved, a negotiating committee, usually composed of the original planning group, was appointed if one had not already been selected.

Although the leaders' intentions sometimes went awry, the miners planned these protests carefully. At Mineji, for example, the miners who led the protest met repeatedly to discuss the phrasing of their demands and to ponder the possible consequences of their actions. Speculating about what would happen if the proper representative was not selected to approach company management, they chose a middle-aged miner out of fear that one of their own youthful number would not be given a serious hearing. They also decided that if management fired any one of them, they would leave as a group to look for work elsewhere. Those who did not quit would have to provide a day's pay as a parting gift to the workers the company dismissed.[78] At the Iwaya mine in Saga, crowd organizers gave similar assurances. On warning the crowd that many of them were likely to be arrested and imprisoned, one leader proposed that other miners help the family members of those who might later be jailed. Although the crowd heartily approved, it is unclear whether the miners actually made good their promises.[79]

The miners also prepared for attacks within the mine compound. At the Takatori company's Kishima mine, leaders organized the gathering of food and the setting-up of feeding stations so that miners could be provided with boiled rice during the protests. Rioters elsewhere dressed in light clothing, wore straw sandals, and armed themselves with ax handles. In some incidents shock troops led the attacks on company property, using conch shells, whistles, and drum cans as noisemakers to guide the crowd's movements.[80] Leaders urged all miners at a particular pit or workers from several mines under the same management to join the movement for higher wages. To rouse as many miners as possible, they used persuasion and sometimes coercion. At the Okinoyama and Mineji mines, members of organizing groups fanned out among the long rows of barracks-like housing, going from door to door to urge everyone's participation. Those reluctant to join in were not only subjected to group pressure but also threatened with beatings or arson. In the Shaganoo riots, handbills posted outside the community baths and at the entrances to public toilets warned that people who failed to join in the protest for higher wages would be "taken care of." Speakers at one rally even advocated taking hostage anyone who hung back during attacks on the company store. At Ube, where miners worked in ten-man teams headed by a company foreman, rank-and-file pit workers also settled old scores by pushing their supervisors to the forefront of the protest, thereby embarrassing the foremen, who were often disliked for currying favors from management at their work team's expense. Rioters at the Okinomiya pits derided their foremen as the bosses' lapdogs (*sara neburi*) and threatened them with death if they did not stand with their crews.[81]

It seems unlikely that coercive force was actually used. Riot leaders obviously sought to make their movement as unified and broad-based as possible; to have done otherwise would have weakened their negotiating position. Nevertheless, Takahashi Masao, a historian of the Kyushu mining region, attributes the threats of beatings and death to hyperbole characteristic of the miners' rough speech and generally overblown manners. He argues that miners never intended to follow through on their threats.[82] In fact, although incidents of miners intimidating miners were widely reported (especially after the riots when pit workers sought to explain, or perhaps explain away, their behavior), there is no evidence to suggest that miners were coerced or tricked into joining the protests.

After workers had agreed on demands, selected negotiators, and set a general course of action, they approached the company. Miners sometimes took lists of grievances and demands to the foreman for delivery to the appropriate mine official. But in most cases they sent one of their own number to meet with the company-store manager, white-collar staff members, or even the director of the mining company. Once demands had been made, local police intervened on their own initiative or at the behest of mine management. Before rioting at the Ube and Miike mines, police officials appeared at mass meetings, advising caution and offering to serve as mediators. Working with mine foremen, policemen in Ōmuta and Ube convened talks between workers and mine representatives at local police stations.

In some incidents these negotiating sessions defused a potentially explosive confrontation—but not always. One reason for the lack of success was that coalfield rioters, in contrast to rioters elsewhere, saw their protest first and foremost as a labor dispute. From the miners' standpoint, officials or unofficial community leaders outside the mine compound really had no cause to interfere in issues that concerned only pit workers and their employers. Miners at Ube derided local police as "meddlers" who had no grounds for butting into wage negotiations since the protest was against the mining company and not at all a police matter.[83] Ube's police chief, Kitagawa Kashichi, privately agreed with this interpretation. As he noted in his report on the Ube protests to Yamaguchi's prefectural governor:

> The riots here differ from those in other regions. Only a single rice dealership was attacked. Clearly, the riots had little to do with the issue of rice prices. They stand for a demand for higher wages.[84]

Similarly, at the Kaijima Mine Company's Iwaya pit, police were treated as peripheral to the confrontation. Shortly before rioting began at Iwaya, the local police chief and company representatives faced workers at a rally to urge the selection of a bargaining committee and to continue discussions. Miners countered by arguing that they had already put their demands in writing and submitted them to the company. The crowd demanded an on-the-spot public answer to their demands for a 30 percent pay raise and proposed changes in mine operation. When they were again requested to select negotiators, they began to vandalize company property.[85]

As these examples suggest, it was the company's response, not that of the police, that determined whether attacks on mine property and personnel occurred. After rioting had begun (as a result of a breakdown in talks with company management or the escalation of "spontaneous" vandalism against mine property), the miners attacked specific targets. With the notable exception of the bloody Ube riots, they centered on mine property and only minimally involved the community outside the company gates. Rioters most frequently attacked the company store or goods-distribution center, management offices, company residences, guard shacks, and in a few cases police stations located near the mines.

In some incidents miners virtually took over the entire colliery for periods lasting from several hours to one or two days. Since mine officials, guards, and supervisory personnel had in most cases already fled the mines when noisy gatherings threatened to turn riotous, the miners were left to do what they wished until police or troops restored order.

Although miners clearly intended to interrupt operations, they did not attempt to put the companies out of business or even cause a long-term disruption in production. At the Kishima pit miners reportedly shoved carts into the shafts, and at one of the Mitsui mines workers occupied the boiler and fan rooms for a brief period during the peak of unrest. But no permanent damage resulted from either of these exceptional acts. In Mitsui's in-house report on the riots, officials noted damage only to surface structures despite the miners' opportunities to cripple mine operations with dynamite or fire or by flooding mine shafts. Mitsui's direct losses due to property destruction totaled only 6,210 yen, a mere fraction of the losses due to the suspended production of coal.[86] The limited damage to the physical plant is evident in the speed at which work resumed; at most pits, mining resumed within days of riot suppression, if not the day after.

The limited extent of the damage stemmed less from high-minded self-control than from the miners' commonsense approach to the disputes. Their restraint in attacking mine property reflected their overall tactical approach. It was acceptable to interrupt production because this significantly penalized the company by forcing it to lose thousands of yen daily. But putting the mining companies out of business would have cost the miners their own jobs. In destroying company property not critical to production they were able to satisfy their resentments against the company store, manipulative crew bosses, and the arrogant attitude of management. They could also indicate that costs to the company might be higher next time, thus making the company more willing to listen to worker grievances.

The miners' concern with reinforcing their limited demands by attacking property is also evident in the surprising care with which they singled out residences of mine staff members and company owners for retributory attacks. Leaders exhorted the crowd not to disturb private homes, doctors' offices, or the property of those not involved in the mine dispute. Although people who kept to the sidelines were left alone, rioters did not hesitate to attack anyone who seemed to side with mine management. When officials of Mitsui's Fukuoka mines organized, armed, and ordered uniformed local reservists (*zaigō gunjin*) to protect mine property, rioters dealt with them as if they were strikebreakers or the company's private soldiers. They chased off as many reservists as they could and beat those unlucky enough to be caught. Similarly, merchants or others who sided with the company by obstructing the protest or allowing mine staff members to hide in their shops suffered property destruction. In several incidents, police were also attacked when they tried to arrest rioters or refused to release miners detained in local jails.[87]

The company's willingness to negotiate played a large part in determining how much of its property would be destroyed, just as grudges against company staff helped decide who would be harassed. This rule of thumb was at work in attacks that totally destroyed the homes of Watanabe Yusaku, the Okinoyama mine owner, and Nishino Kashiro, an unpopular foreman who directed day-to-day pit operations.[88] In many riots such property destruction seemed largely symbolic. In attacks on the director of the navy's Shinbara mine, in Ube, and elsewhere, the rioters took special glee in destroying the personal effects of the targeted individual. They took bedclothes, kimonos, mosquito nets, and other items out of the house and ceremoniously ripped them to pieces. Crowds yelled "Banzai!" as the mine director's property was thrown into sewer ditches or set afire. Although miners looted household items such as soap, canned goods, and brooms from company stores, they appeared more intent on destroying goods than making off with them. Little, if anything, was stolen during the attacks on the houses of wealthy owners and senior staff members. Attacks on lower-ranking company officials lacked the personal animus that appeared to fire assaults on the houses and belongings of higher officials. Although eighty homes suffered damage in neighborhoods near the Mineji mine, destruction was usually limited to the windows and shutters of staff housing.

Aside from trashing the personal property of mine managers, the miners committed few acts of violence. In many cases, company officials, fearing for their own and their families' safety, had fled to the shelter of sympathetic friends before rioting broke out. Yet in a few incidents such as the Iwaya riots, police and company representatives were both present when the miners began their attack on mine property. The miners merely pushed aside the officials when the rioting began, allowing them to leave the mine unharmed.[89] Even in riots that brought as many as ten thousand miners into the streets, the only injuries attributed to the rioters occurred in confrontations between workers and guards, police, or mobilized soldiers.

Mine takeovers were usually short-lived. Miners lacked long-range plans, and in any case government authorities would not likely have permitted their implementation. This is not to denigrate the significance of either the miners' presentation of detailed demands or their disciplined attempts to force management concessions. But the effectiveness of their acts was obstructed by self-imposed limits as well as ones enforced from outside. Rioting accomplished certain immediate ends. The uprisings effectively protested management policy, and thanks to newspaper reports, the harsh conditions under which miners worked and lived were vividly presented to the larger society as well. But after negotiating, making threats, and attacking company property, the miners appeared at a loss for what to do next. True, management's favorable response to organized protests hinted at the gains possible in future strikes. But in 1918 the miners did not have the necessary unity, organization, planning, or resources to keep the protest alive. As nonunion workers, they lacked a strike fund or other income to enable them to remain long off the job. Aside from hasty, informal agreements between workers, they lacked effective means of dealing with the punishment they expected from management and legal authorities. Even when grievances were shared among several mines, dispute leaders did not call for expanded regional (let alone nationwide) protest. After attacks on homes and personal property, the protests tended to degenerate into looting and public drunkenness. In many mine protests the activism that had moved workers to leave the pits in record numbers quickly turned to passivity as miners waited for the inevitable restoration of company authority.

They usually did not have long to wait. Although the mining industry had tolerated individual and disunified wage protests in the past, the unity evident in the mine riots led company executives once again to see labor problems as problems for the police as well as management. Concern with the enforcement of labor laws was keen in mining towns, where local authorities regarded pit workers as wild, unpredictable, and in need of stern discipline. Therefore, authorities seldom allowed incipient protest to subside of its own accord. Central-government and local officials, fearful that socialists and other carriers of "dangerous thoughts" could agitate miners as they might burakumin or other socially alienated groups, lent urgency to demands that calm be speedily restored. Although fears of a "red" contagion behind the mine riots proved groundless, as they did in protests elsewhere, no one at the time could predict what might happen if the miners were left to their own devices. Nor could officials be sure of what new development might grow from the workers' protest. As postriot statements by politicians and political thinkers make clear, the Russian Revolution created deep fears over the relationship between deceptively minor lapses in labor discipline and a possible reordering of Japan's social and political structure from top to bottom. Home Ministry and police officials thus moved quickly to crush dissent before it took on a more ideological coloring.

Economic considerations added to official concern. Shutting down coal production hurt the mining companies financially. According to reports in the *Fukuoka nichinichi*, the Kurauchi Mining Company lost ten thousand yen each day that rioting halted production.[90] At Mitsui's Fukuoka and Kumamoto pits, operations larger than those of the Kurauchi company production stopped or fell to a fraction of normal levels during the week-long period of sporadic rioting.[91] The mining companies as well as the communities dependent on them faced significant losses unless the riots were suppressed quickly.

Several companies attempted to continue minimal operations while dealing with the miners' labor protest. They relied on hired guards, front-office staff, foremen, and local police to keep production going or at least to project a business-as-usual sangfroid to strikers. But such efforts could not disguise the fact that miners had taken control of the pits. In mining centers like Ōmuta and Ube, where as many as ten thousand people rioted, crowds easily chased off police and hired guards, thus demonstrating the woeful inadequacy of local peace-keepers.

The breakdown of order prompted prefectural governors in Yama-guchi, Fukuoka, Kumamoto, and Saga to order troop mobilization. De-ployments in collieries accounted for one-fourth of the 120 locations nationwide where the regular army was called out. In Kyushu alone, prefectural governors ordered troops to suppress riots in twenty-five locations, nineteen of these in Fukuoka mining districts.[92] The soldiers' presence did not immediately restore order. Armed workers frequently confronted troops guarding mine buildings and jails where other rioters were detained. Pit workers attempted to intimidate soldiers by chanting *"maito, maito"* (dynamite, dynamite) as they clashed with troops. In two or three cases, miners carried off dynamite or actually used explo-sives against mobilized troops.[93] (See fig. 16.) The miners' resistance shocked officers sent to quell the rioting. In explaining why soldiers fired upon rioters at Mineji, a troop commander remarked: "As for soldiers firing upon Japanese rioters (*naichi no bōto*), there is a prece-dent for that in the Ashio dispute. But rioters throwing dynamite at troops? That's simply unheard of, past or present!"[94]

Although the press pandered to the popular imagination by exagger-ating the ferocity of the coalfield uprisings, there is no doubt that rioters did their best to provoke troops sent to quell them. Miners cursed sol-diers, pelted them with coal, and derided them for selling out to the mine owners' interests. They taunted the soldiers by asking how they could defend companies responsible for the terrible conditions within the mines. At Ube the rioters seemed unable to believe that soldiers would actually use their weapons. In noisy confrontations with soldiers stand-ing in protective sentry lines, the miners bared their chests or pulled rifle barrels toward their throats, saying, "You soldiers are Japanese (*dōho*). If you are going to shoot me, shoot here!"[95]

The Ube miners, like those at Mineji, Sochi, and at other pits, were tragically mistaken in believing that the soldiers would not use their guns and bayonets. Six hundred troops clashed repeatedly with miners at Ube in a struggle to regain control of the village. During the first days of unrest the local police chief had foolishly assured the miners that no one would be punished for participating in the disturbance. Not long after, however, patrolmen began arresting rioters. During a tense stand-off between miners and troops in front of the jail, the chief relented and released several prisoners. This move failed to appease the rioters, who believed that many more were still held inside. The company commander, fearing that he might lose control of the situation, finally ordered his men to retreat ten paces and fire a round of blanks at the crowd. Contrary to his expectations, the rioters were emboldened, not frightened, by his bluff. Within twenty minutes they once again had the station under siege. When several miners seemed about to break into the jail from its unguarded side, the troops, who had reloaded with live ammunition, fired into the crowd, killing thirteen and wounding many more. When the miners realized what had happened, they fled in all directions, leaving the dead where they had fallen.[96]

When soldiers used lethal force, rioting ended immediately. Armed miners sometimes fled into nearby hills, not to continue their resistance but to escape arrest. After the bloodletting a sense of shock settled over the mining towns, and rioters, having nowhere else to go, drifted back to the company compound. Once local police and troops had regained the initiative, they acted with speed and thoroughness in rounding up suspects. At Mitsubishi's Ochi mine in Saga prefecture, where soldiers shot or stabbed to death three rioters, concentric rings of sentry lines made escape from the camp impossible. Policemen worked their way through long rows of housing, arresting anyone believed involved in the riots. At Mineji, police made similar sweeps, detaining anyone found with a gun, a Japanese sword, or a knife. They also used the miners' signed petition of protest as a guide for rounding up suspects.[97]

The dragnet style of arrests was arbitrary and wholesale. Anyone faintly suspicious was held for several days while police and special prosecutors sent to investigate the riots determined whether the individual should be held for continued interrogation and indictment. Rioters in Ube were roped together and taken to local theaters, where they were held until they were transferred one by one to a nearby primary school for interrogation by officials from the Yamaguchi regional court. Of the more than 1,800 miners initially detained in Ube, 373 were later indicted for crimes ranging from arson to participation in a public disturbance.[98] It sometimes took months before prosecutors handed down indictments. During this period suspects remained in detention and were questioned repeatedly on their attitudes toward leftist causes. One miner detained for a month at the navy's Shinbara mine later recalled:

> It was a real kangaroo court. They called us socialists and treated us like socialists, always threatening and bullying. We didn't know a single thing about socialists or socialism. After the [initial] interrogation we were taken to the prosecutors for a preliminary hearing. It was just the same. Total nonsense.[99]

According to a Mineji miner, an additional reason for the persistent search for a socialist conspiracy was that interrogators commonly assumed miners were just too stupid to organize a peaceful wage protest.[100]

While prosecutors searched for leftist planners, they also sought to prove that the riots were nothing more than apolitical outbursts in which willful violence and random destruction had been intended from the very beginning. One leader of the Mineji protest had this interpretation pressed upon him repeatedly during lengthy interrogation sessions. His response was a question: would the miners fix their names to a petition if faced with the possibility of later being arrested for rioting? It did him little good: he was finally sentenced to two and a half years at hard labor. Throughout the nation over 5,000 people were found guilty of riot-related crimes. Those arrested in the coalfield disputes constituted nearly 25 percent of this figure.[101]

Postriot Changes in Company Operations and Incipient Unionism

The mining companies arranged their own punishment for dissident workers. At Mitsui mines in Fukuoka and Kumamoto, the company summarily dismissed everyone indicted for rioting, along with their family members. At the Manda pit, management fired not only 118 miners prosecuted after the riots but also 96 of their family members who had taken no part in the protest. To soften the penalty, Mitsui's management provided a small allowance of cash and rice to the families of detainees until suspects were either freed or held over for additional questioning. If indicted, the miner or his dependents received the wages due up to the date riots broke out and the worker's holdings in Mitsui's compulsory saving program. In some cases the company provided train fares for family members to return to their home towns. Miners also reported that managers compiled lists of individuals believed to have led the riots. These lists, which were circulated among company personnel offices, effectively blackballed an unknown number of workers from ever finding a job in the mines again.[102]

In Ube the Okinoyama Mining Company's postriot sanctions were more perfunctory and appeared aimed at getting miners back to work. Following the riots, company owners arranged to feed the group of more than a thousand miners held at local theaters. They also appealed to authorities to release able-bodied workers as soon as possible. Since the seasonal peak period in demand for coal was fast approaching and company representatives were anxiously seeking to restore production levels, they fired—and immediately rehired—all of their workers, regardless of whether they were suspected of rioting. Before returning to work, however, all mine workers were required to sign an oath promising to obey company rules and regulations.[103] Using similar tactics, other mines adopted measures to rid their operations of "bad apples," activists and protest leaders, while attempting to resume or step up stalled production rapidly.

Such short-term steps brought miners peacefully back to work. But the mining companies went beyond them to institute changes in wage and personnel policies. Although no company that was attacked during the riots capitulated to every worker demand, all did increase wages or reduce rice prices. (See fig. 18.) Even the government-operated Shinbara mine compromised with the rioters' demands by agreeing to forward the rioters' petitions to the Ministry of the Navy. In the meantime, Shinbara's management provided miners with rice at twenty-five sen per shō and discounted all company-store goods by 5 percent. At the Mitsui mines the company instituted temporary wage increases and promised workers that pay raises would henceforth be made quarterly instead of twice a year.[104]

Companies also tried to eliminate inequality in wages, upgrade working conditions, and improve management-worker relations. Although the piece-wage system survived the riots, mining companies sought to eliminate the grosser inequalities in pay schemes. At Mitsui, for example, management set up a complicated wage system whereby basic and bonus wages were staggered to compensate for inequalities arising from variations in work sites. The miners also received partial credit for labor expended in bringing up low-grade coal and shale. To deal with man-made inequalities in earnings, Mitsui included rank-and-file miners among their coal graders. Other mining companies improved the systems of coal-box and cart circulation. In response to complaints regarding health care, several companies also hired additional medical personnel and increased cash payments to sick and injured workers.[105]

With these improvements came changes in management-worker relations. In the Fukuoka Mine Office report issued after the riots, government officials warned that the gap between company and miner interests was too broad and had to be narrowed if future unrest was to be avoided. Mine managers appeared to take this advice to heart. Within months, staff members organized capital and labor associations to harmonize human relationships within the company and avoid antagonism between capital and labor. Mutual aid societies, the forerunners of the enterprise union, were established on a company-by-company basis. Bearing names such as Mitsui's "Mutual Love Association" (Kyōaikai) or the Okinoyama company's "Beloved Association" (Shin'-aikai), the associations, as was evident in their bylaws, aimed at improving the miners' material and spiritual lives as well as harmonizing contentious factions within the company. They encouraged miners to save their wages, practice thrift, be hardworking, and bring their grievances to the management-dominated associations.[106]

The miners' protests did not do away with paternalistic practices. At the very least, however, some were turned more to the workers' advantage. Several riot participants later recalled that life in the mines improved after the disturbances. Workers not only received better wages and care but were also treated with more respect by bosses and company officials.[107] Yet the achievement of these aims was purchased at a high price. Not only were twenty miners killed in the riots, but many workers had to serve long prison sentences for joining in the protests (or for failing to convince prosecutors that they had not).

Of more importance to the historical development of Japan's labor movement, the mining companies' strengthening and improvement of paternalistic management practices, which in their unreformed state had led to rioting, helped to retard the development of independent trade unionism within the coal industry. Wage increases and a new attentiveness of management to workers represented more than Pyrrhic victories in the miners' struggle for humane treatment. Nevertheless, the coal miner's freedom to negotiate wages and working conditions independently, to bargain freely rather than as a fictive son or daughter in an inherently unequal filial relationship, was not gained until the post-war period.

It might be argued that such an outcome was foreordained; cultural reasons made industrial paternalism predictable and caused workers to accept membership in "love associations" easily.[108] Some have suggested that what Japanese labor really wanted from management was a combination of security and respect, which could best be provided through the company union. This view finds support in the general weakness of the prewar labor movement. As Stephen Large has noted in his study of unionism during the interwar period, "organized labor in prewar Japan erupted several times, expanded very little, and made practically no progress at all toward the imposition of its objectives."[109] Statistics bear this out. In the 1930s, at the very peak of Japanese labor organization, only about 8 percent of the national work force was represented by unions. Union membership in the mining industry was even less than the national average, attaining a prewar maximum of only 2.4 percent. Moreover, even this small number does not give an adequate sense of how membership was distributed. After the rice riots, more metal miners than coal miners joined unions; membership was high in a few regions, nonexistent in many more.[110]

Yet the weakness of trade or craft unions was not a predictable product of the Japanese "national character." In the coal industry the failure of autonomous unions was clearly the outcome of conscious design rather than the result of cultural determinism. By the autumn of 1918 the leadership of both big business and organized labor recognized that the coalfield "rice riots" represented something either far more threatening or far more hopeful, depending on whether you were a company or a union man, than a mere spontaneous, directionless riot.

Suzuki Bunji, the head of Japan's largest labor association, the Yūaikai, visited mines in northern Kyushu shortly after troops were withdrawn. On 15 September he stopped at Mitsui's Tagawa mine to encourage workers there to form a new Yūaikai branch. Local company officials saw this as an opportunistic attempt to fish in their troubled waters and an impertinence, to which they responded by encouraging hecklers to disrupt the labor leader's rallies. Suzuki soon returned to Tokyo, but his staff continued to push ahead with local organizational efforts in Kyushu collieries. Approximately one year after the riots had been put down, when the Yūaikai was reorganized into the National Federation of Labor Unions (Dai Nihon Rōdō Sōdōmei Yūaikai), the new national organization established a northern Kyushu regional center to coordinate seven lesser branches in Fukuoka.

Union building was making headway among the miners, but not because the mining companies had ceased their resistance to outside organization. In September 1919 the Mitsui company refused Suzuki admission to the Miyanoura pit where miners had invited him to speak. Rank-and-file miners complained that company pressure, often exerted through local police as well as foremen, was intended to discourage them from having anything to do with the Yūaikai. Nor was the "Friendly Society" the only labor association to suffer such harassment. The Rōyūkai, a labor group that competed with the Yūaikai for miner support, also found that its speakers were forbidden to set foot on company property. Even organizing from outside company grounds was difficult. When Yūaikai or Rōyūkai representatives visited mining towns they often discovered that police, town officials, and reservists had been instructed to make the labor organizers' stay unpleasant and short. Workers who attempted to organize from within the company were usually dismissed if found out.

Despite the harassment, the Yūaikai succeeded in establishing a major branch office at Ōmuta in the spring of 1920. Indicative of the importance that the labor federation attached to work among the miners, Kagawa Toyohiko was called upon to give the inaugural address at the new center. In October of the same year, the Yūaikai, in an attempt to forge links with miners throughout the nation, sponsored the Greater Japan Miners Federation (Zen Nihon Kōfu Sōrengō Kai).[111] But the factional disputes frustrating the Yūaikai's struggle for unity and leadership of Japanese industrial workers were also creeping into the coal miners' organizations. By 1927, in the wake of several name changes and reorganizations, the Japan Miner's Union (Nihon Kōfu Kumiai) split into two factions aligned respectively with the Sōdōmei and the Hyōgikai, the two organizations into which the Yūaikai had divided after being rent by socialist and conservative wings.[112]

The Yūaikai had been involved in organizing mine labor before the rice riots, but the level of its activities increased dramatically from late 1918. The change came as part of the Yūaikai leadership's attempt to transform their organization from a moderate "friendly society" into the directorate of nationally federated trade unions. Where Suzuki Bunji saw promise in worker activism, mining companies saw threats and attempted to punish workers sympathetic to the union call. But managers, particularly at the leading zaibatsu mines, also realized that disincentives alone would neither secure the miner's loyalty nor create a reliably stable work force. The companies would have to adopt, albeit selectively, aspects of the very programs that made unions attractive to workers.

Since 1900, when the Meiji government placed direct management control of Japan's ten largest mines in zaibatsu hands, the companies had struggled to find tractable workers willing to take the risks inherent in the miner's life. Mitsui and other companies found part of what they wanted in convict labor, which continued to be used in the mines into the 1930s. But there were not enough prisoners, nor were they sufficiently enthusiastic about the work, to keep coal production in line with industrial demand. A Mitsui directive written in 1900 laid out one of the company's plans to remedy the mining labor shortage by recruiting "farmers unfamiliar with the ways of the world." Kagoshima was cited as a good place to find pure, simple bumpkins who would neither expect much in pay nor run away when faced with harsh working conditions. The Mitsui company requested village and county officials throughout Kyushu to help find farmers whom the company could transform into "model miners."[113] The plan was not a success, and in 1918 company management had not yet hit upon a formula for creating cooperative company-miner relations and maintaining steady profits. If anything, ties between management and rank-and-file workers had grown more rancorous. Economic expansion during the war years, instead of fostering the complacency desired in pit workers, had led miners to realize that their labor was a valuable commodity in short supply. Moreover, the organizers of Japan's incipient unions had begun to suggest methods by which miners could derive a better return for their toil.

Major firms responded to union competition for the loyalty of labor by obscuring the differences between the company's worker-management association and noncompany labor groups. This extended even to the names given to the rash of company groups formed after the rice riots. Between 1919 and 1925, company associations with titles that resembled Suzuki Bunji's Yūaikai, or Friendly Society, included the Miner's Friendly Society (Kaijima Mining's Kōyūkai), the Harmony Society (Mitsubishi Mining's Kyōwakai), the Faith and Harmony Society (Meiji Mining's Shinwakai), and a variety of others.[114]

The similarity of the company associations to "friendly societies" often encompassed policies and programs. From its founding in 1912 and until 1919 (the year that it turned from mutual aid to the goal of genuine federated unionism), the Yūaikai's main efforts had been in bettering the worker's health, education, and welfare. Suzuki Bunji advocated such specific programs as training to cultivate or improve worker skills, the organizing of buying and saving cooperatives, procedures to guarantee on-the-job safety, as well as factory clinics, classes, and child-care facilities. There was little in the Yūaikai's early program to suggest uncompromising conflict between capital and labor. In fact, Suzuki's group, largely because of its moderate image, had even earned the support of the Social Policy Society (Shakai Seisaku Gakkai), a prestigious council of industrialists, bureaucrats, and academics, which since 1896 had actively advised the central government on ways to avoid industrial strife.[115]

The worker associations sponsored by the mining companies included virtually every program introduced in early Yūaikai proposals. Initially, the associations were long on lofty rhetoric and short on materially helpful programs. Although management spoke of promoting a warmer understanding in the family company, concrete programs seldom went beyond the formation of simple savings cooperatives to defray the costs of emergency assistance, injury, or burial.[116] But association benefits were soon expanded to provide health clinics, cooperatives, public crèches, recreational activities, and barbershops.

There was, of course, one salient factor that distinguished these forerunners of the enterprise union (kigyō betsu kumiai) even from the early Yūaikai: the authority to guide the association's program was never in the hands of the workers. In the general directive that established Mitsui Mining's Mutual Love Association (Kyōaikai) in 1919, mining division director Fujioka Jōkichi stressed that the new organization would be based on "labor-capital cooperatism" (Kumiai wa ryōshi kyōchō shugi ni yoru koto).[117] But Dan Takuma, a mining engineer trained at M.I.T. and head of all Mitsui operations in 1919, made clear that his idea of the Mutual Love Association was quite different from the worker-dominated union suggested by Fujioka's use of the term kumiai. Baron Dan wrote:

> This is not a "labor union" (rōdō kumiai). It is rather the product of workers willingly joining together out of a spirit of industrial harmony in an organization for consultation with those who own the enterprise.[118]

Mitsui's management and others that sponsored cooperative associations, curbed the actual working of these groups to conform to the consultative role envisioned by Dan. Their efforts corresponded with corporate attempts to keep alive, or perhaps create anew in an industrial setting, the "traditional" *oyabun-kobun* relationship between management and labor.

In the mining companies' organizational structure, the associations were clearly at the bottom of the pyramid. According to rules governing the Meiji Mining Company's Faith and Harmony Association, established in 1919, the association's central headquarters was the company headquarters; the company president served as chairperson of all associations. Each coal-mining operation had its own branch of the cooperative association, headed by none other than the local mine director. According to association rules, the director should strive to improve management-worker communication, push ahead with the replacement of the old *naya* system, and help plan new educational, welfare, and financial services. A mixed committee made up of miners and managers was to assist the director in his efforts. But only one half of the committee's members would be elected by fellow miners; the other half would be appointed by company management. The Meiji rules resembled those adopted by Mitsui associations.

At Mitsui's northern Kyushu mines, members of the Mutual Love Association did not decide company policy or even minor matters concerned with working conditions. Instead, management used the associations to convince employees of the wisdom of company policy. Although the associations were also charged with ferreting out worker concerns so as to defuse potential conflicts between capital and labor, in general they enhanced a flow of communication from the top down.

The guiding spirit behind the associations much resembled the one behind the Meiji Constitution. The associations' charters were gifts bestowed, if not by an emperor, by the highest company councils. As Dan Takuma pointed out, they were not the product of some Western-style concept of labor autonomy; rather, they suggested that miners should recognize their place in an organic hierarchy in which, ideally, a worker's duties outweighed his rights, and management's care of its charges was more important than profits.

The miners did not readily buy this credo. Their actions during the rice riots indicated that they knew what grieved them (for example, wages and working conditions), even if they lacked the organizational skills or institutional basis necessary to change the situation. Even after the introduction of company-sponsored associations, miners continued to challenge management. The associations were not readily or gratefully accepted as gifts from above; indeed, the company's creation and control of these bodies made them suspect. Particularly galling to miners was the company's requirement that all employees join the groups and that worker complaints be handled only through the local harmony association. Other federated unions, such as the Yūaikai before 1919 and in its various forms thereafter, were not allowed to represent miners at pits that had organized associations. This rule was ignored at the risk of summary dismissal. Given the limitations that associations placed on worker autonomy, perhaps the miners intuitively realized that, from the standpoint of their interests, a "company union" was largely an oxymoron.

To assert that "mutual love" and kindred company groups were less satisfactory to miners than genuine trade unionism is not to deny that these associations improved conditions. Although the working and living environment of many mines was so wretched that almost any change was an improvement, the cooperative associations did provide concrete benefits even in their first years of operation. But miners as well as independent labor organizers were worried that what a mutual love association might provide during flush times or in periods of labor shortage it might take away in times of stringency or industrial slowdown. Workers also recognized the divide-and-conquer strategy inherent in the association's structure. Although a general charter and bylaws governed the working of the cooperative groups, specific agreements reached with employees at one mine or factory did not necessarily apply to other installations under the company's management. Management decided whether and to what extent benefits gained by workers in an individual dispute would be shared with workers in different branches of the company.

Worker discontent with postriot relations with management is evident in a series of work stoppages that broke out in 1919 and culminated in the 1924 Miike strike.[119] The strikes, attempts at union organization, and linkages formed between miners and other workers also indicate that miners had learned to organize better to promote their own interests. For example, the Miike strike, which lasted from May through July 1924, involved six thousand workers, including employees at Mitsui Manufacturing, Mitsui Mines, and Mitsui Zinc Smelting. The Fukuoka chief of police noted that the strike was conducted in an orderly and organized manner. In contrast to the uncoordinated 1918 protests, Miike workers created a formal strike organization that divided its labors into relief, accounting, and information sections. Strikers and their families were even put to work making goods for vending door to door. The sales not only helped maintain strike funds but also provided the public with the strikers' view of the dispute while maintaining morale among idled workers.[120]

With the development of more orderly labor protests came changes in the strikers' aims. In large part, the shift in demands reflected the worsening economic conditions of the post–World War I years. In the Miike strike, for example, workers demanded a 50 percent raise in wages. But one of their main justifications was a series of earlier pay cuts and threats by management to trim wages even further. In labor disputes after 1919 workers increasingly stressed job security, as well as higher pay. The Miike workers were in no way atypical in demanding unemployment benefits along with the doubling of normal wages. Although "lifelong employment" was not a bargaining issue, workers did seek separation allowances in the event of a business downturn and additional compensation for workers whose hours had been cut.

Significantly, they did not see the company's employee association as the agency to secure such benefits for them. During the severe recession of the early 1920s, strikers attempted to save their jobs rather than push only for higher pay. Nevertheless, the need for job security did not translate into worker support of company love associations. Indeed, one of the primary demands from the Joint Miike Strike Headquarters in 1924 was a proposal to abolish the Mitsui's Kyōaikai immediately at all company operations.

The Miike strike eventually ended in compromise. Mitsui agreed to study wage increases, paid some workers one-half the wages that they might have earned had there been no strike, and promised that none of the strikers would be "sacrificed" for walking off the job. But it adamantly refused to disband the Kyōaikai.[121] Mitsui's reluctance to part with the association reflected management's view that such groups served a useful function. But Kyōaikai also continued to exist because management simply did not feel as compelled to capitulate to worker demands in 1924 as it had in 1918.

Much has been written about the traditional malleability of the Japanese worker. The individual worker's support for trade unionism is said to have been halfhearted because of Japanese respect for hierarchy, the desire for individual security that made workers rush to the support of the system of seniority and lifelong employment (*nenkō-joretsu*), and the laborer's shortsighted use-and-discard attitude toward unions. Critics have also pointed to union leaders' lack of respect toward rank-and-file workers. A culturally based love of factional intrigue and fondness for theoretical hairsplitting is said to have frustrated a drive for labor unity and helped to alienate workers from the union's "intellectual" leadership. These reasons partially account for the weakness not only of the labor movement but also of leftist politics in general before and after 1945. Nevertheless, they do not provide a complete explanation.

To understand why miner-organized trade unions never gained significant bargaining strength after their potentially powerful start in 1918, the impact of the post–World War I recession must not be forgotten. By the spring of 1920 the war boom was fast turning to peacetime bust. Unemployment was estimated in March as including fifty thousand industrial workers.[122] Decreased factory production and reduced exports soon resulted in a decline in coal orders; by May 1920 coal prices were plunging and Kyushu mines had begun to dismiss workers.[123]

In contrast to conditions in 1918, the problem for mine management was no longer one of retaining workers but of coping with surplus production and producers. In the postwar economic environment, companies found no profit in continuing incentive bonuses or special allowances for higher output. Worker benefits, which might have been defended by a trade union, were not supported by management-dominated cooperative associations. By 1923 many larger firms retained only a "diligence" (*seikin*) bonus awarded for not having missed a single day of work in a month. Mining companies cut pay raises awarded during the war boom and began penalizing miners for work performances below par, an action that finally prompted the government's Bureau of Mines to intervene to prevent the excessive docking of worker wages.[124]

Mitsui, the first zaibatsu company to inaugurate cooperative associations, was also among the first to cut its surplus workers. On 1 June 1920 the company began eliminating production at selected pits; in August it released 877 mine workers. Mitsui's lead was followed by cutbacks at the Taishō mines (3,400 workers), Furukawa (1,825), and approximately 1,700 from smaller operations. During the opening years of the 1920s, workers lucky enough to retain their jobs were forced to accept pay cuts ranging upward from 15 percent of their pre-recession wages. The Fukuoka Mine Office reported that, because of scores of mine closings, the number of coal miners employed in northern Kyushu had dipped to 201,185, a 26 percent decline from the 1919 level.[125]

Economic hard times shifted the direction of the miners' labor movement just as it was beginning to develop toward trade unionism. Pit workers continued to struggle for what they perceived as their rights. But between 1920 and 1923 they seldom demanded higher wages or shorter working hours. The many disputes that occurred focused instead on the issues of pay cuts, unfair dismissals, and insufficient severance pay. Although the demand for coal began to revive after 1923, the coal miners' interest in unions, or even their nonunion opposition to company policy, did not regain the vigor it had demonstrated before 1920. The coal miner's prewar involvement in union organization revived briefly with the 1924 Miike struggle. But it is estimated that even during that year only 4 percent of Japan's coal miners took part in any labor dispute, a dramatic decline from 1918 when one out of every three participants in labor disputes was a mine worker.[126]

Other industrial workers continued to be involved in labor organization into the 1930s. But coal miners did not. The economic recession following World War I had enabled major Japanese mining companies to reap long-term benefits from what turned out to be short-term misfortune. The market changes also corresponded with a newly developing managerial policy of "industrial rationalization" (*sangyō gōrika*) in larger Japanese industrial firms and the coal-mining industry. This policy stressed the introduction of automatic machinery in factory production, assembly lines, standardization, and higher productivity per worker. Its success was clear by 1930 when miners produced more coal than ever before while expending fewer worker hours.

The mining company's cooperative association had played an important organizational role in creating workers' acceptance of rationalization. After the futile struggles of the early 1920s, coal miners warmed to the company organizations as improvements over the old crew-boss system, a change in attitude that is not difficult to understand in an era when simply having a job was considered lucky. Between 1920 and the mid-1930s, labor disputes at coal mines with over a thousand workers declined in a straight-line manner: in 1919, large zaibatsu operations accounted for one-half of all mine disputes; by 1924, the share fell to one-third; and by 1936 it was zero.[127] The only mines in which protest continued to occur with any statistical significance were ones that continued to rely on the traditional *naya* system.

Conclusion

The coal mine riots in 1918 present a case of resistance to old or reinterpreted versions of paternalistic labor relations. In this light, they appear as another chapter in the uneasy history of relations between pit workers and the owners or managers of mines. The miners' struggle in 1918 differed from ongoing protests elsewhere in the issues involved, the methods and targets of protest, and the implications of the rioters' actions. In the southwestern Honshu and northern Kyushu coalfields, the miners made a primary issue of wages and working conditions and only secondarily, if ever, protested the high cost of rice. Although it can be argued that rioting would not have occurred if rice had been cheaper, this does not account for disputes that long predate the riots, nor does it explain the miners' noneconomic demands. In pressing these demands the coal miners used strikes, labor slowdowns, the presentation of written petitions, and attacks on mine plants and sometimes personnel. They did not take their grievances to the representatives of the larger community outside the mine compound; they made no appeals to village heads or mayors for rice distribution or discount coupons. Instead, they sent their demands and complaints directly to the people in charge of running the mines.

Unlike participants in the more traditional Toyama riots or in rural uprisings, mine workers tended to reject traditional, paternalistic ideas. The miners demanded wages in cash, not in kind. They protested, sometimes violently, management's attempts to pay them in company scrip, discount coupons, or rice. In contrast to participants in other disturbances, who sought care at the hands of officials and community leaders and demanded that rice prices should be set by moral rather than market considerations, the miners seemed indifferent to such issues. They appeared to accept the market economy on its own terms. Rice was just a commodity to be sold—not the staff of life but a product like any other. A market "rationality" rather than moral considerations characterized the miners' dealings with foremen, managers, and company owners. Despite glowing reports of smooth relations between crew bosses and pit workers (such as the one issued by the Japan Bureau of Mines), the coalfield rioters explicitly sought to do away with abuses in the modified *naya* system.

The mining riots, perhaps more than other incidents of popular protest, provide examples that support explanations of the widespread unrest as spontaneous, undisciplined mob activity. In August and September 1918 mine workers did burn buildings, loot stores, and beat foremen. Furthermore, neither riot leaders nor the petitions they submitted to company negotiators mentioned unionization or leftist ideas. The miners expressed little interest in an even remotely ideological labor struggle. But stressing the miners' violent methods and their lack of explicitly leftist aims diverts attention from the similarities between the coalfield riots and labor disputes in other sectors of Japanese industry. As was discussed above, the miners repeatedly demanded better pay, improved working conditions, and a larger voice in deciding mine operation. They usually resorted to violence only after attempts to negotiate these issues with mine officials had broken down. While a Marxist like Katayama Sen could see only the apolitical content of the coalfield riots, a labor leader like Samuel Gompers would likely have endorsed their generally nonsocialistic aim of improving the mine workers' economic welfare.

Of all rioting groups, the coal miners were at once the most fully integrated into the national market economy and the most alienated from mainstream Japanese society. The sprawling zaibatsu mine compounds were new industrial creations. Despite the putative ties of loyalty between bosses (*oyabun*) and followers (*kobun*), the miner's way of life and the conditions in which he worked created demands for economically rational relations between workers and management. In 1918 the miners—virtual social pariahs drifting from job to job, earning their wages by the cartload of coal, acutely conscious of unequal working conditions that reduced their pay—demonstrated little patience with mining companies' manipulative paternalism. But mine owners were always one jump ahead of the workers. Instead of discarding the paternalistic employment system, they consciously modified it to correct the most obvious abuses criticized by rioting miners. This action eventually dampened the miners' enthusiasm for labor protests. The companies' use of "love associations," which played on traditional Japanese concepts of obligation (*giri*) and gratitude (*on*), did much to foster Japan's modern enterprise union system within the coal industry.

SIX

Conclusion

The lower classes [*kasō min*] alone took the initiative in the recent riots. As a result of their extreme acts, their demands have been satisfied. They have become aware of their own strength. They have discovered the value of violence! This discovery poses an extreme threat to the future of our nation. It has created an evil precedent, one that should be eternally feared.

Taiyō, October 1918

Beginning with the women's uprising in Toyama, the masses carried out a tremendous riot to bring down rice prices. Minister of Agriculture and Commerce Nakakōji had labored for a year, yet prices just kept skyrocketing. But the people had merely to stage a three- or four-day movement and foreign rice was sold at half price and domestic rice at one-third off. The strength of "bureaucratic power" versus "the power of the people" has been thoroughly tested by this incident. . . . The masses have clearly realized the political truth that "popular movements are of first importance."

Shin Nippon, September 1918

Public opinion on the meaning and lasting significance of the riots was divided in 1918 and continued to be divided in the decades after the protests. Historians have been more uniform in their views. Western studies have tended to see the protests as full of sound and fury, effecting little change. Japanese scholarship has stressed the failed promise of a mass awakening or, to mix metaphor with cliché, the tragedy of a great historical turning point that did not turn. To understand the significance of the riots, it is useful to examine their aftermath.

By the winter of 1918 rioting had ended and Japan once again appeared at peace. But the wheel had turned, moving political, economic, and social relations in different directions. The changes were, as the riots had been, multifaceted. Some were long-term and enduring, others provided but temporary ameliorations of immediate popular grievances. In the wake of the protests, opportunities for popular political participation expanded, but alongside such liberalization there emerged repressive police laws and rightist popular movements for the protection of the nation's farmers.

By initially crushing the rioters' resistance and by later funneling money and rice to the needy, the state appeared to have quieted the protests. Nevertheless, the government of Terauchi Masatake could not escape political responsibility for the riots. During the massive urban riots, speakers at citizens rallies repeatedly demanded the ouster of Terauchi and his "cronies." Their demands were answered when the prime minister and his nonparty cabinet were forced from office within weeks of the last major uprising. The breakdown of civil order thus played an important role in both the rise of Hara Takashi, the first nonpeer prime minister, and the beginning of cabinets routinely composed of party politicians.

Yamagata Aritomo, one of the few remaining genro in 1918, did not initially support the formation of a cabinet led by Hara. Disdainful of party politics and politicians, he preferred a fellow aristocrat like Saionji Kinmochi or Privy Councillor Kiyoura Keigo, who would continue the policy of government above politics. But even Yamagata grudgingly realized that public opposition to transcendent politics, unequivocally expressed by urban rioters, had to be answered. Although he never demonstrated public enthusiasm for the Seiyūkai leader, Yamagata did not actively oppose Hara's nomination. Hara himself had no doubts about the importance of the riots in changing the immediate direction of Japanese politics. Throughout the protests he had bided his time. Seeing no need to murder a cabinet in the process of committing political suicide, he refrained from personally criticizing the government's economic policies. Although reluctant to step forward as the people's advocate, he was willing to reap the benefits of public opposition to genro-dominated politics. In response to a journalist's comments on his ability to "open Yamagata's eyes," Hara blithely replied, "It was the rice riots. There's no doubt about it. If our party had done anything inflammatory at the time [of the riots], there would have been terrible consequences. Yamagata, too, had come to clearly understand the impotency of bureaucratic politics."[1]

The political significance of the riots as the sole cause of the turn from transcendent governments should not be overstressed. The protests occurred in the context of worldwide campaigns for greater popular rights and of earlier resistance movements within Japan. We probably cannot know to what degree challenges to despotic governments, from the Russian Revolution to the Chinese May Fourth Movement to Indian riots against British colonial domination, contributed to unrest within Japan. We can say that the Japanese press reflected attitudes that suggested that popular action against unjust legal authority, whether elected or imposed, was pardonable civil disobedience. After the riots, Terauchi observed that an international movement for greater democratization and the spread of "dangerous thoughts" contributed to a "permissive" mood within his country.[2] But as this book has argued, the connection between events outside Japan and protests within the country was usually tenuous. There was not a universal driving force or a single ideology behind the rice riots. Terauchi, to whom "dangerous thoughts" was a code word for "socialism," was dead wrong in attributing doctrinaire motives to his rioting countrymen. Those hunting for "red" agitators behind the riots always came up empty-handed. Yet the protests themselves can be seen as symptoms of deeper changes, which had begun before the riots and continued afterward. The transformation altered the public's attitude toward governmental and corporate policies, whether they were explicit (as in the state's legal prohibition of strikes) or implied (as in the gulf separating company profits from worker wages).

The protests resulted in far more than just the replacement of Terauchi by a "commoner" prime minister. Widespread civilian unrest engendered a host of long-lasting changes in central and local government policy. Officials initiated new laws regulating commodity trading, social welfare, police control, and labor relations. Not all of them led to greater social liberalization. Some were plainly repressive, intended to make permanent the "candy and whip" measures that were part of the government's early efforts to quell dissent.

One major postriot reform was the creation of permanent, systematized government measures for providing and distributing rice. Following the riots, the public continued to demand that the central government design a definitive food policy. During the forty-first Diet session, in late 1918, various groups presented 200 petitions demanding that their representatives make Japan self-sufficient in food. An additional 216 petitions specifically demanded the regulation of rice prices.[3] Shortly after taking office Hara abandoned Nakakōji's policy of regulation by emergency fiat, instead backing moves to increase grain supplies by deregulating imports. He also supported the establishment of a central food-supply board to oversee and regulate fluctuations in food reserves.[4] Such measures led to a brief fall in the retail price of rice; wholesale rice prices, which hit 42 yen per koku in August 1918, declined to about 36 yen during September.[5] Although bad weather resulted in record high levels of rice prices during July and August 1919, the rioting did not resume, perhaps because of a dramatic increase in wages in the wake of the protests. By 1919 the growth of real earnings had surpassed the rise in the inflation rate and, along with greater consumer spending power and continuing relief measures, obviously eased the difficult circumstances that had contributed to unrest. The transition from the overheated economy of the war years to the postwar recessionary slowdown of the early 1920s continued to restrain any growth in consumer prices. The wholesale price for a single koku of rice on the Tokyo exchange fell from 52.90 yen in June 1920 to 24.00 yen in December 1920.[6] As the demand for exports dried up, unemployment replaced inflation as the critical economic problem of the day.

Declining consumer prices did not curtail central-government planning against a future absolute scarcity of rice that might create conditions conducive to riots. The government's rice policy aimed at a long-term self-sufficiency in the food supply by increasing Japanese-produced grain reserves while improving the quantity and quality of colonial rice production. In the process, the Seiyūkai majority party began to put the interests of cultivating tenants and urban consumers before that of rural landlords.[7]

Almost immediately after the riots, the Hara government began an ambitious fifteen-year land reclamation plan for the home islands. Before the protests, only 1 percent of the budget of the Ministry of Agriculture and Commerce had gone for the expansion of cultivatable acreage. By 1925 the budgetary proportion had increased to 11 percent. Government programs also encouraged uniform paddy sizes to increase farmer efficiency. Although this idea did not catch on, the state was more successful in its program to help finance the building of additional local rice warehouses. One cause of the riots had been the volatility of market conditions, created when producers or other grain holders simultaneously sold their harvests to central brokers. To prevent radical swings in market prices, check hoarding, and guarantee local supplies in times of shortages or bad harvests, the government helped recreate in modern form the ever-normal granary system. Similar programs—land reclamation, paddy rationalization, and state subsidies for the purchase of chemical fertilizers—were also introduced into Korea and Taiwan to develop the colonies as reserve rice baskets.[8]

246

Postriot changes in colonial policy had far-reaching consequences. In the immediate wake of the riots, ministerial orders directed that imports of sorghum (milo) from Manchuria into Korea be stepped up so that this lower-quality grain could replace rice in the Korean diet and produce an exportable surplus for the home islands. Similarly, in Taiwan the colonial government encouraged the local consumption of sweet potatoes and extended its monopoly control over various agricultural products to ease rice scarcity within Japan. The Ministry of Agriculture and Commerce also initiated its long-term "Rice Production Development Plan" (*Sanmai zōshoku keikaku*), which provided a budget for research and agricultural extension services, investment in irrigation and water-control schemes, and the increased introduction in both of its major colonies of rice strains palatable to the Japanese consumer. Economic historians have suggested that these measures decreased Japan's food independence, depressed domestic agricultural wages, and indirectly contributed to greater Japanese involvement in imperial politics abroad and the rise of fascism at home. The lasting implications of the policy may have had just this impact, but in the short run it achieved what its architects desired: between 1915 and 1935, rice imports from Korea and Taiwan grew from a level equal to 5 percent of Japan's domestic production to a full 20 percent.[9]

To promote long-term planning, a new rice law was promulgated in April 1921, which set a regulation system firmly in place. It included a special budget of 200 million yen for grain-market regulation and created permanent procedures for the state's direct intervention in commodity exchanges. It also enabled government agents to buy up or sell off rice stocks whenever the need arose and it gave officials a free hand in adjusting rice import duties. To check commodity-market speculation and hoarding, the law now obliged grain dealers, middlemen, and warehousers to open their places of business, account ledgers, and other documents to the state's inspectors. Resisters were subject to stiff fines. Although these measures stopped short of mandating the cost of rice, they gave the government a much stronger hand in regulating prices.[10]

After the riots central and local governments, as well as private philanthropic agencies, stepped up social welfare programs. In several major cities political leaders led a drive for rudimentary relief measures. From 1911 until 1917 private spending for regional relief amounted to a paltry 1.4 million yen. In 1918 social welfare expenditures jumped to 12 million yen, increasing to more than 20 million yen by 1924.[11] Local governments also tended to take added responsibility for new relief programs. The riots contributed to the establishment of special divisions within prefectural governments concerned exclusively with social welfare. Osaka prefecture and Osaka city, which before the riots had established welfare agencies, took the lead in upgrading small government sections or subsections into full-fledged divisions. Within a few years of the organization of Osaka city's Social Division, all of Japan's major cities had similar agencies.[12] Urban political leaders also led the establishment of subsidized public markets, housing-assistance offices, worker lunchrooms, and even day-care facilities for working mothers.

The public concept of social welfare had clearly changed following the riots. Traditionally, welfare had been based on charity provided to individuals from the purses of well-off private citizens or the emperor. The taboo associated with socialism caused officials self-consciously to avoid using any term that had "society" as a component part. Tago Ichimin, appointed in 1919 to head the newly formed Social Bureau (Shakai Kyoku), observed:

> From the Meiji period you will not find the term "social service" [*shakai jigyō*] in public documents. Not only that, but at times the government even despised the very word "society" and went to extreme lengths to absolutely avoid its use. In 1909, at the first meeting of the Regional Reform training course, the conference was to use "social betterment" or "social reform" in its title. But many saw such words as offensive and caused them to be replaced with "regional." Considering past practice, for the central government to create a [new department] and name it with a word that was hated like poison surely indicates a startling transformation. . . . Charity, benevolence, and relief—these things have become the work of society itself.[13]

"Social welfare" increasingly worked its way into the state bureaucrat's vocabulary; officials expounded on it in speeches at both local- and central-government gatherings. At a regional conference in 1923, Asari Saburō, Toyama prefecture's director of internal affairs, excoriated *narikin* by name and spoke sympathetically of working people's "demand for recognition of their dignity" (*jinkaku ninshiki o suru*). Along with urging that worker wages be raised to match those in other professions, he counseled against treating laborers as mere machines. The conference keynote speaker did Asari one better. Saitō Tatsuki, a Home Ministry official, extolled the virtues of the Confucian family state and quoted from Kropotkin's *Mutual Aid* in describing a nation's need for a strong social welfare policy.

Saitō also outlined ministry-level programs to realize the state's new welfare mission. Calling for inexpensive life insurance (a Ministry of Commerce goal), the employment and rehabilitation of ex-convicts (Justice), and the stricter enforcement of labor laws (Home), these planned or newly implemented programs would be added to the existing state-supported network of public markets, job introduction offices, and similar services. By good words and better deeds, Saitō asserted, the gap alienating labor from capital would be bridged. Not all of Saitō's plans were put into practice. Indeed, the term "social welfare" was frequently used for cosmetic purposes only. But even this limited currency suggests that social services were increasingly seen as the state's responsibility, which it was expected to support with public funds.[14]

The riots also contributed to a "mass awakening," which resulted in the fullest flowering of "Taishō democracy." The notion that common citizens could resist the state or private enterprise had been seen in earlier labor actions and political protests. Nevertheless, organized mass movements had been largely in abeyance since the 1911 execution of a number of leading activists alleged to have plotted the assassination of the Meiji emperor (the *taigyaku jiken*, or High Treason Incident). The rice riots changed quiescence into activism by sparking renewed confidence in the efficacy of grass-roots organization. Even without conventional or uniform ideological grounding, the rioters' methods altered the political behavior of workers and intellectuals alike.

From 1919 to 1922 new mass-based organizations advocating the rights of factory laborers, farmers, women, and burakumin were formed one after another. Government officials and the public viewed them with a mixture of joy and alarm. Whereas the Home Ministry simultaneously spoke of expanding social welfare and fretted over the evil precedent established by the riots, others saw them as having sliced through the Gordian knot of bureaucratic politics to bring forth the fair prices justly demanded by the Japanese public. As the *Shin Nippon* writers noted, both the state and the public had learned important lessons.

The concrete application of these lessons was not long in coming. Labor unions stepped up their activities, staging major strikes in 1918 for better wages and working conditions at the Nippon Paint factory in Osaka, at Nippon Chisso in Kumamoto, and at the government-managed Tsurumai arsenal.[15] During the years after the riots, workers also struck many zaibatsu and other companies with close ties to the government. Mitsubishi Shipyards, Yawata Steel, and the Ashio mines were but a few of the enterprises that suffered unrest during this period.

In an attempt to distance his organization from the acts of disorderly street protesters, Suzuki Bunji claimed that not a single Yūaikai member had taken part in the riots. But even this advocate of cooperation between labor and management acknowledged the tremendous boost that the nationwide protests had given to expanding workers' rights and achieving the aims of organized labor.[16] A sharp increase in unions paralleled the upsurge in factory protests. From 107 unions in 1918, the number of labor groups increased to 300 with more than 100,000 members in 1921 and reached 457 organizations with 254,000 members by 1925. With the founding of the national Japan Labor Union (Nihon Rōdō Sōdōmei) in 1921, workers abandoned many of the conciliatory methods used in earlier labor disputes and began to put their own interests first. They now demanded the right to collective bargaining and other reforms, including an eight-hour day.[17]

To ease the increasingly sharp confrontations between labor and capital, the Hara government subsidized the private Kyōchōkai (Conciliation Society). Receiving an additional one million yen from private industry, this organization of scholars and bureaucrats was commissioned to study all "social enterprises at home and abroad" in order to create harmonious labor relations in Japan. Kyōchōkai leaders invited Suzuki Bunji to join in their efforts, but the leader of Japan's most important labor group—which had moved after the riots from a policy of harmony with management to one that advocated strikes in defense of workers' rights—declined their gesture of goodwill. In later years the Conciliation Society's research and recommendations contributed greatly to an understanding of the problems plaguing relations between labor and management, but its actions did little to temper the worker-first attitude of labor organizations during the early 1920s.

The rural tenant movement also became more militant and better organized following the riots. Ann Waswo has noted that the new strength of the tenant movement did not necessarily spring from an idealistic concern over "social justice" or a desire to battle the "evils of capitalism." As in the cities, the riots in the countryside revealed the impotency of local authorities faced with a concerted organized protest. It was this pragmatic lesson, not ideology, that tenant farmers applied in their disputes with landlords, with an enthusiasm heretofore unseen.[18] Tenancy disputes jumped from 85 incidents in 1917 to 326 in 1919 and reached almost 2,000 by 1923. Confrontations over rent reductions, unfair evictions, and the alleged irresponsible behavior of absentee landlords continued throughout the 1920s, particularly in central Japan.[19] By 1922 the movement had grown strong enough to support a nationwide organization, the Japan Farmers League, to represent the interests of tenant farmers.[20]

Organized movements for women, for burakumin, and for a general expansion of political rights also accelerated after 1918. All of these movements had existed in some form before, but they had become largely inactive under the weight of bureaucratic politics and restrictive police laws and in the long shadow of the High Treason Incident. The leaders discovered new possibilities for political action in the 1918 protests, in particular the idea that popular movements could effect change in government policy. Thus in 1920 the movement for women's rights, including the expansion of suffrage, was revived. Burakumin who were dissatisfied with the tokenism of the government-sponsored Yūwa Movement took the initiative in demanding equal rights. No longer would they meekly accept second-class citizenship in dirty, disease-ridden ghettos. In 1922 the Suiheisha, the "Association of Levelers" originally founded in 1912, became a nationwide organization. Its manifesto declared that henceforth "burakumin would rely on their own movement" (*tokushu burakumin wa burakumin jishin no kōdō ni yote*) in obtaining "absolute" (*zettai no*) social emancipation and the economic and occupational freedom inherent in it.[21] Many regional Suiheisha leaders had followed a direct course from involvement in the riots to key positions in the reorganized movement for burakumin rights.[22]

The mass groups organized after the riots were generally opposed to a bureaucratic monopolization of politics. Workers, women, and outcaste minorities advocated greater voting rights and the opportunity to participate in Japan's domestic political process. Intellectuals supported their demands from a variety of political positions. From the moderate liberalism of Yoshino Sakuzō and his "Minponshugi" (or "people as the base-ism") to the revolutionary theories of Katayama Sen, intellectuals looked with approval on the "mass awakening." Although political liberals such as Yoshino, Ōyama Ikuo, and Ishibashi Tanzan tempered their support of popular politics with warnings of the dangers of unleashing the terrible power of the masses and seldom if ever joined in unseemly rallies or strikes, their writings lent intellectual respectability to an expansion of political rights.[23] They encouraged the actions of Imai Yoshiyuki, popularly known as the "Doctor of Universal Suffrage," and others like him to enlist mass organizations in the struggle for greater voting rights.[24] In 1925 the movement was rewarded with the passage of the male universal suffrage law. But the victory was incomplete. Along with the expansion of voting rights, the government promulgated the Peace Preservation Law, a measure designed to control mass organizations and political dissenters, specifically socialists and communists.

The middle- and lower-class groups supporting the expansion of suffrage during the early 1920s took a cold attitude toward military affairs. The 1921 Washington Conference on Naval Disarmament, which led to cuts in military spending, enjoyed wide public support. The distaste for the military was also seen in the lack of enthusiasm for Japan's little war in Siberia. During the 1895 Sino-Japanese War and the 1905 Russo-Japanese War, recruits had been given festive send-offs complete with nationalistic speeches and the good wishes of local dignitaries. But the public mood shifted after the riots. Military leaders bemoaned the fact that recruits embarking for Siberia often left from deserted train platforms without a single banzai. In fact, when military men traveled outside their bases they changed their uniforms for mufti to escape civilian hatred.[25] Yamagata Aritomo foresaw in 1918 the possibility of the riots damaging popular support for the military. In a letter to Tokutomi Sohō he wrote:

> Riots have recently broken out because of the [rising] price of rice and have spread to the areas of developing industrial and commercial enterprises. Of course, there are various direct and indirect domestic and foreign causes, but I wonder whether [the Terauchi government] has not erred [in its understanding of general worldwide trends]. It is deeply deplorable that these riots have occurred at a time coinciding with the despatch of troops [to Siberia]. It will not be an easy task to redirect public opinion. For things to come to this pass causes me to be very concerned and anxious about the future of Japan.[26]

His worries proved justified. During the early 1920s the public's attitude toward intervention in the Russian Revolution tended to shift from grumbling acceptance to opposition, contributing to the government's decision to withdraw most Japanese troops in 1922. The public's lack of enthusiasm for military adventures abroad in the 1920s defies simple explanation. But one reason that soldiers were probably never as unpopular as they were following the rice riots is that the public had not forgotten their deployment against civilians.

After nearly a decade of generally progressive social and political change moderated at times by political trade-offs such as the new police law, Taishō democracy began to wither. The multiple causes for its decline have been voluminously discussed elsewhere. Historians stressing domestic reasons for the setbacks of the late 1920s and 1930s have pointed to divisions within mass organizations, an unbridgeable gap between classes, repressive laws, and the timidity of liberal political parties challenged by a resurgent military. Others, seeking to explain the dark decade of the 1930s after the promise of the 1920s, have stressed international factors such as the worldwide economic depression, xenophobic nationalism, and the international acceptability of fascistic movements.

Although there is continuing debate over why democratic trends during the Taishō period were later stifled, there is little doubt that the rice riots significantly accelerated the pace of political and social change during the 1920s and thereafter. Yet the riots had an importance as regional uprisings as well. In general, historians, with good reason, have concentrated on the cumulative, delayed, and indirect effects of the national uprising and have neglected the regional variations found in local protests. The stress on changes that came after the uprisings has also moved attention away from the traditions of protest that facilitated the riots.

Yet there was one widely shared characteristic linking the 1918 protests: a widespread concern with what might be called a "moral economy," which, in varying degrees, informed rioters' actions wherever disputes occurred. In Japan because of a popular tradition stressing the values of economic justice and social fairness, it was considered unacceptable for market manipulation to deprive local residents of their perceived fair share of food or other resources. Once the laws of the moral economy appeared to have been violated—and appearance was often as decisive as an actual infraction—people felt justified in dealing with market profiteers and hoarders in their own manner. The responsibility for maintaining the moral economic order fell upon the shoulders of local political leaders and merchants. Officials who did not rectify market abuses also became the targets of the crowd's version of "justice."

This Japanese notion of a moral economy did not burst upon the scene with the 1918 protests. Protesters praised the *ikki* (traditional uprising) raised by the Toyama women. Urban crowds called out for a Taishō Ōshio Heihachirō, the samurai leader of an uprising in Osaka in 1837, to come forth and lead them. As the popular journalist and editor Ishibashi Tanzan insightfully pointed out shortly after the riots, many of the mass protests bore the markings of a "restoration" (*kangen-teki*) movement mounted in defense of "existence rights" (*seizonken*).[27]

Ishibashi was certainly right in stressing the traditional impetus to protest. Nevertheless, rioters looked to the future as well as to the past. The concerns of city protesters or coal miners had little in common with those expressed by Toyama or rural rioters. Instead of a return to paternalism, urban residents and mine workers demanded what they perceived as their political rights or economic entitlement. Rather than the almost ritualistic give-and-take between protesters and their targets that appeared in traditional disputes, rioters in crowded cities and sprawling mining towns resorted to new forms of protest. They sometimes harked back to past slogans or symbols of popular resistance. But they turned tradition on its head by seeking political and economic rights suitable to the place of the citizen or the worker in a newly emerging urban and industrial society.

Notes

Abbreviations

IKSK	Shihō Keiji Kyoku, ed. *Iwayuru kome sōdō jiken no kenkyū.* 1938 reprint. Tokyo: Tōyō Bunka, 1974.
KSNK	Inoue Kiyoshi and Watanabe Tōru, eds. *Kome sōdō no kenkyū.* 5 vols. Tokyo: Yūhikaku, 1959–1962.
Namerikawa shiryō	Namerikawa Shi Hensan Iin Kai. *Namerikawa-shi shi: shiryō hen.* Namerikawa City: Namerikawa-shi, 1982.
NNA	Asahi Shinbun Sha. *Asahi shinbun ni miru Nihon no ayumi.* 5 vols. Tokyo: Asahi Shinbun Sha, 1975.
Shiryō	Rōdō Undō Shiryō Iin Kai. *Nihon rōdō undō shiryō.* 10 vols. Tokyo: Rōdō Undō Shiryō Kankō, 1959.
SKS	Kita Nihon Shinbun Sha. *Shōgen: kome sōdō.* Toyama City: Kita Nihon Shinbun Sha, 1974.

Introduction

1. Shihō Keiji Kyoku, ed., *Iwayuru kome sōdō jiken no kenkyū.*
2. Hosokawa's almost obsessive interest in the riots seemed to stem as much from happenstance as from conscious design. Although a graduate of the prestigious Law Department of Tokyo Imperial University, Hosokawa differed from Yoshikawa, a fellow Teidai alumnus, in not following what was becoming a well-worn path from the university to the central government bureaucracy. He instead worked awhile for Sumitomo enterprises, drifted from that industrial conglomerate (zaibatsu) to the staff of the Yomiuri newspaper, and returned briefly to the university as a lecturer. But he found his life's work only after taking a post at the Ōhara institute. For details of Hosokawa's career and a collection of his writings, see Hosokawa, *Hosokawa Karoku chosaku shū.*

Volume 1, pp. 293–394, deals specifically with the Toyama and Wakayama rice riots. See also Hosokawa, "'Kome sōdō' to sono go no kokumin-teki seichō," 42–59; and Tsuji, "1918 kome sōdō no kenkyū to Hosokawa shiryō," 1–9.

3. From Katayama's own writings we do know that this Comintern member and longtime exile firmly believed that the 1918 riots were but the first skirmish arising from heretofore hidden, but nonetheless fundamental, contradictions inherent in Japan's emperor system. From his standpoint, understanding the elemental class conflicts behind the riots was essential to understanding Japan's potentially revolutionary future. Katayama wrote three major essays on the riots, including "Saikin no kome sōdō ni tsuite" (1918); "Taisen go ni okeru Nippon kaikyū undō no hihan-teki sōkan" (1931); and "Nippon ni okeru 1918 nen no kome sōdō no jūgo nen ni yosete" (1933). These are included in Katayama, Katayama Sen chosaku shū.

4. Inoue Kiyoshi and Watanabe Tōru, eds., Kome sōdō no kenkyū.

5. Koyama Hitoshi, "Kome sōdō to shakai mondai," 135–36.

6. E. P. Thompson, "The Moral Economy of the English Crowd in the Eighteenth Century," 79.

Chapter 1. The 1918 Nationwide Riots: Mass Protest, Political Parties, and State Response

1. Y. Takenob [sic], ed., Japan Year Book, 1919–20, 302.

2. Richard Smethurst has recently postulated that from 1890 to 1930, rice production increased by nearly 70 percent because of improved farming techniques and the widespread use of chemical fertilizers; see Smethurst, Agricultural Development and Tenancy Disputes in Japan, 1870–1940, 53. Nevertheless, many questions remain unanswered regarding the steady improvement in Japanese economic conditions from the mid-Tokugawa period through the Meiji. The degree of actual economic growth, its uniformity across Japanese society, its benefit for certain groups, its qualitative impact on individual lives— these are but a few of the issues that have produced a lively and continuing debate among scholars of Japan. The opening chapters of Smethurst's work provide a thorough, if partisan, summary of the economic conditions debate.

3. Shinobu, Taishō seiji shi 2 (1951): 541.

4. Ibid., 557. Part of the explanation for higher disease rates recorded nationwide between 1914 and 1918 is that fast-growing and overcrowded cities, where harsh working conditions and inadequate public sanitation led to an increase in contagious diseases, distorted the statistical picture for Japan as a whole. But conditions were not only bad in the cities. In 1900, Japan's infant mortality rate was 110 per 1,000 live births; in 1915 and throughout the war years it had increased until it peaked in 1918 at 190 per 1,000. Toyama prefecture demonstrated the same statistical pattern, except that the infant mortality rate began at 180 infant deaths per 1,000 and reached 252 per 1,000 in 1918. Mortality and disease rates in Iwate, which was less industrialized than rural Toyama, were even higher. Although the causes of higher disease and death rates during the boom years merit a more rigorous discussion than that pre-

sented here, my view is that the growth of Japan's aggregate gross national product did not provide prosperity or better health for citizens generally. See Toyama-ken, *Toyama-ken shi: kindai, tōkei zuhyō*, 353; for a comparison of Toyama and Iwate, see Kokusei In, *Nippon teikoku dai sanjūkyū nen tōkei nenkan*, 51 and 125.

5. Inoue Kiyoshi and Watanabe Tōru, eds., *Kome sōdō no kenkyū* 1 (1959): 51–63. Hereafter cited as *KSNK*. A discussion of "paupers in Western clothes" appeared in the *Shizuoka min'yū shinbun*, 16, 21, and 30 August 1918.

6. Shinobu, *Seiji shi*, 2:556–57.

7. Ibid., 634–35. In some instances, public employees simply quit their jobs to seek more lucrative work elsewhere. In 1918 the governor of Yamaguchi prefecture reported to the central government that a combination of low wages and high food prices was depleting the ranks of the prefecture's police force. See Ogawa Kunihara et al., *Yamaguchi-ken no hyaku nen*, 152.

8. *Ōsaka mainichi shinbun*, 17 June 1917, in *KSNK* 1:57; see also Tokyo Hyaku Nen Shi Iin Kai, *Tokyo hyaku nen shi* 4 (1979): 983.

9. *KSNK* 1:9.

10. Rōdō Undō Shiryō Iin Kai, *Nihon rōdō undō shiryō* 10 (1959): 440–41. Hereafter cited as *Shiryō*. See also Andrew Gordon, *the Evolution of Labor Relations in Japan*, 47–121, passim.

11. Y. Takenob [*sic*], ed., *Japan Year Book, 1917*, 298.

12. Kuwada, "Social Politics and Social Problems: Introductory Remarks," 295.

13. Duus, *Party Rivalry and Political Change in Taishō Japan*, 65.

14. During the Taishō period, Inukai and Ozaki Yukio were known as the two "gods of constitutional government" (*kensei no kami*). For a discussion of the tension between idealism and political necessity in Inukai's career, see Tetsuo Najita, "Inukai Tsuyoshi: Some Dilemmas in Party Development in Pre–World War I Japan," *American Historical Review* 74, no. 2 (December 1968): 492–510.

15. Kawabe, *Press and Politics in Japan*, 143–45.

16. Takenob, ed. *Japan Year Book, 1921–22*, 69.

17. Ibid., 100.

18. Takenob, ed., *Japan Year Book, 1917*, 645.

19. Even those party men most closely allied to Terauchi watched and waited. Hara's diary, for example, reveals his awareness of the weaknesses of Terauchi's policies for rice price control. Yet neither he nor his party recommended substantive remedial measures. They had little political reason to do so; more could be gained by sitting back while the situation worsened for the government in power and enhanced the opposition parties' political position. Hara, *Hara Takashi nikki* 4:430–32.

20. *KSNK* 2:27–28; see also Toyoda, *Hara Takashi no ansatsu to taishū undō bokkō*, 115–117.

21. Takahashi Hozuma, "Terauchi naikaku ki no seiji taisei," 44–46.

22. *Ōsaka asahi shinbun*, 11 August 1918, in Shihō Keiji Kyoku, ed., *Iwayuru kome sōdō jiken no kenkyū*, 438–40. This work, hereafter cited as

IKSK, is a reprint of Special Prosecutor Yoshikawa Mitsusada's 1938 report on the rice riots to Justice Ministry Officials.

23. On the parties' abrupt turnabout from amicable relations with the Terauchi government to attacks on it, Fukuda Tokuzō, a leading economist and legal scholar, noted that the politicians had completely forgotten their former cooperative attitude. He wryly commented that they had also quite suddenly become reform-minded. Before the riots they had extolled the sanctity of free enterprise and the inviolability of property rights. Now they called for government intervention in the marketplace and for welfare programs. Fukuda, "Bōdō ni tai suru tōkyoku no taido," 93–94.

24. Saeki et al., "Kome to sono daiyō tabemono no kenkyū," 99–117. Newspapers and other periodicals also carried articles on how to prepare delicious "foreign rice" (*gaimai* or *Nankin mai*), a product that was popularly considered foul-smelling and inferior to domestic grain. See also Ishibashi, "Gaimai no tabekata," 47.

25. *Kokumin shinbun*, 16 August 1917, in *KSNK* 1:62.

26. *Ōsaka mainichi*, 16 July 1917, in *KSNK* 1:18–19.

27. Ibid., 19.

28. *Tōkyō asahi shinbun*, 8 May 1918, in Asahi Shinbun Sha, *Asahi shinbunni miru Nihon no ayumi* 2:207. Hereafter *NNA*.

29. *KSNK* 1:19.

30. Shinobu, *Seiji shi* 1:562; see also *Tōkyō asahi shinbun*, 27 January 1918.

31. Shōji, *Kome sōdō no kenkyū*, 207.

32. *Tōkyō asahi shinbun*, 8 May 1918, in *NNA* 2:210.

33. *KSNK* 1:31

34. Imai, *Nihon kindai shi* 2:161.

35. Young, *Japan Under the Taisho Tenno*, 90.

36. Kobayashi, *Basic Industries and Social History of Japan, 1914–1918*, 37–45; see also *Tōkyō asahi shinbun*, 29 April 1918, in *NNA* 2:209.

37. *KSNK* 1:25–26. The popular view that zaibatsu trading firms manipulated the national grain supply to increase company profitability probably arose from their extensive involvement in Japan's domestic rice trade. Although Suzuki Shōten, Mitsui Bussan, and similar companies promoted Japanese exports, they also worked closely with the state in regulating imports. One of the trading companies' most important products was grain. In 1919 rice ranked fourth among major commodities traded by Mitsui Bussan and accounted for 7.4 percent of the company's total sales; see Yoshihara, *Sogo Shosha*, 20–22.

38. *Tōkyō asahi shinbun*, 29 April 1918, in *NNA* 2:207.

39. *Kyōto hinode shinbun*, 9 August 1918, in *KSNK* 1:37–38.

40. *KSNK* 1:35–38.

41. Shōji, *Kome sōdō no kenkyū*, 208.

42. Ibid. The Terauchi government also attempted last-minute importation of rice from mainland China. The attempt failed because Chinese officials feared that, despite a bountiful harvest for 1918, sending rice to Japan might spark an increase in banditry or even local rioting. For a detailed discussion of the secret Sino-Japanese rice negotiations, see Baba, "Chūgoku mai yunyū mondai," 1–2.

43. Aoki, *Taishō nōmin sōjō shiryō nenpyō* 2:779.
44. The low figure is found in many general treatments of the riots and in standard reference works. For example, see Toyama and Satō, *Nihon kenkyū nyūmon*. The estimate of 10 million participants is found in Shiota, "The Rice Riots and the [*sic*] Social Problems," 517. Shōji Kichinosuke also estimates that several million joined the protests; see his "Kome sōdō no tenkai katei," 12–16.
45. Matsuo, *Minpon shugi*, 133.
46. *KSNK* 1:108.
47. *KSNK* 5 (1962): 76.
48. *IKSK*, 267–72.
49. Matsuo, "Kyoto chihō no kome sōdō," 123; see also Hijikata, *Hisabetsu buraku no tatakai*, 36–50. For a general account of women in the riots, see *KSNK* 5:288–290.
50. *KSNK* 1:113.
51. Ibid.
52. *KSNK* 1:112.
53. *KSNK* 1:136.
54. Endō and Yoshii, "Kome sōdō to sōgi to gunshuku to," 186–87.
55. *KSNK* 5:79–80.
56. *KSNK* 5:84–86.
57. *KSNK* 3 (1960): 45–46.
58. On the participation of reservists during the riots, the reaction of national leaders to unrest among the ranks, and postriot reorganization of the Reservists Association, see Endō and Yoshii, "Kome sōdō to sōgi to gunshuku to."
59. Among officials responsible for directing the government's tough suppression policy were the minister of justice, Matsumoro Itaru; the vice-minister of justice, Suzuki Kisaburō; and the public prosecutor general, Hiranuma Kiichirō. See Wagatsuma, ed., *Nihon seiji saiban shiroku: Taishō*, 179.
60. *IKSK*, 347.
61. Matsuo, "Kome sōdō chin'atsu no shuppei," 181. Matsuo made a final accounting of the scale of troop mobilization in 1984. For his earlier studies of the military in the rice riots, see Matsuo, *Minpon shugi*, 130; and also Matsuo, "Kome sōdō to guntai," 103–40.
62. Matsuo, *Minpon shugi*, 132.
63. *KSNK* 1:133 and 5:212.
64. Narita, "Toshi minshu sōjō to minpon shugi," 65; *KSNK* 5:152.
65. Wagatsuma, *Saiban shiroku*, 87.
66. Ibid., 183–86.
67. *IKSK*, 432.
68. *KSNK* 5:153–155.
69. *KSNK* 1:142–45. For Nagano relief efforts, see Ōe, "Teikoku shugi kakuritsu ki nōson no mujun," 152; on Fukui, see Suehiro, "Fukui kome sōdō," 46.
70. Kinbara, Samon. "Kome sōdō dankai ni okeru kokumin kyōka no katei," 43.
71. *Osaka asahi shinbun*, 20 August 1918.

72. On the popular rejection of "foreign" rice, see Tōkyō Hyaku Nen Shi Iin Kai, *Tōkyō hyaku nen shi* 4:984.
73. Narita, "Toshi minshu sōjō to minpon shugi," 64.

Chapter 2. Traditional Protest
Along the Toyama Coast

1. Kamiya, "Kome sōdō rokujūnen," 26. That Toyama did not undergo industrial development as early as other prefectures does not deny that it possessed a developed commercial economy. During the Tokugawa period the region included officially designated post-towns (*shuku*) with inns and markets to accommodate official travelers, local residents produced and sold traditional medicines throughout Japan, and small sailing ships took part in coastal trade that supplied Toyama goods to distant cities. Nevertheless, in 1918 rice production was still the cornerstone of the local economy.

2. Toyama-ken, *Toyama-ken shi: kindai, tōkei zuhyō*, 2 and 348–54. One explanation for the higher tuberculosis rate in rural areas is that women workers who had temporarily worked in urban spinning factories carried the disease back to their home villages. See Koyama," Rōdōsha Kaikyū no jōtai," 59.

3. Ibid., 397–98.

4. Nakaniikawa-gun, *Toyama-ken, Nakaniikawa-gun yakushō: shakai kairyō, 1921*. These important but generally uncatalogued materials are held by the Ōhara Shakai Mondai Kenkyūjo in Tokyo. Owing to the destruction of most district office records with the abolition of the county (*gun*) administrative division in the early 1920s, the Ōhara collection provides one of the few sources for understanding how local administration functioned in the Taishō period. For World War I prefectural directives, see Toyama-ken, *Toyama-ken shi: shiryō hen, 7; kindai, 2*, 893–94.

5. *Toyama nippō*, 15 May 1916.

6. Kita Nihon Shinbun Sha, *Shōgen: kome sōdō*, 82. Hereafter cited as *SKS*.

7. Nezu, "Kome sōdō to Shōnai chihō," 38–48.

8. Toyama-ken, *Toyama-ken shi: kindai, tōkei zuhyō*, 97 and 284–85.

9. The Toyama coastal protests more closely resembled the grain riots of eighteenth-century England and France than the uprisings in Japanese cities in 1918. The rioters' concern for maintaining their "right" to locally produced rice and their use of the shipping boycott, or *entrave*, are two similarities common to Japanese and European popular protest. On the purposive nature of popular protest, see Thompson, "The Moral Economy of the English Crowd," 79–136; Tilly, "The Food Riot as a Form of Political Conflict in France," 23–57.

10. Saitō, *Kome sōdō*, 4.

11. Hamada Tsu retired female stevedore and participant in the Toyama riots, personal interview.

12. Toyama-ken, *Toyama-ken shi: tsūshi hen, 5, kindai, 1*, 839.

13. Toyama-ken, *Toyama-ken shi: tsūshi hen, 6, kindai, 2*, 51.

14. Nagoya Chihō Shokugyō Shōkai Jimu Kyoku, *Toyama-ken ka Shimoniikawa-gun shutsugyo dan*, 3. Japan, Ministry of Agriculture and Commerce, *Japan in the Beginning of the Twentieth Century*, 208; Toyama-ken, *Toyama-ken shi: kindai, tōkei zuhyō*, 39; and Toyama-ken, *Toyama-ken shi: tsūshi hen, 6; kindai, 2*, 810–30.

15. Toyama-ken, *Toyama-ken shi: tsūshi hen, 6; kindai, 2*; and Hasegawa and Masujima, "Dai'ichi dankai," 154.

16. Nagoya Chihō Shokugyō Shōkai Jimu Kyoku, *Shutsugyo dan*, 8–9.

17. Kokusei In, *Sanjūkyū nen tōkei*, 145.

18. *SKS*, 7.

19. Hamada Tsu, personal interview.

20. *SKS*, 84.

21. SKS, 84.

22. Kano, *Nihon no rekishi*, 162; see also *SKS*, 150.

23. Nagoya Chihō Shokugyō Shōkai Jimu Kyoku, *Shutsugyo dan*, 3. On the use of the *zen shakin* system in Meiji-period spinning and mining industries, see Okochi, *Labor in Modern Japan*, 11; and Noshiro, "Kome sōdō no omoide," 51.

24. Toyama-ken Shakai Ka, *Toyama-ken ni okeru dekasegi gyofu jijō*, 5.

25. *KSNK* 1:149.

26. Nagoya Chihō Shokugyō Shōkai Jimu Kyoku, *Shutsugyo dan*, 6.

27. Ibid., 5.

28. *SKS*, 81–85.

29. Toyama-ken, *Toyama-ken shi: kindai, tōkei zuhyō*, 292.

30. Saitō, *Kome sōdō*, 4; and Nishino, "Nabewarizuki, 1918 Toyama-wan no kome sōdō," 12.

31. Urada, "1895–1915 nen no Toyama-ken kara no dekasegi jōkyō," 25.

32. Toyama-ken Shakai Ka, *Toyama-ken ni okeru dekasegi gyofu jijō*, 5.

33. Urada, "1895–1915 nen no Toyama-ken kara no dekasegi jōkyō," 4.

34. *KSNK* 1:150.

35. Urada, "1895–1915 nen no Toyama-ken kara no dekasegi jōkyō," 4.

36. Imoto, "Kome sōdō no rokujū shūnen to kan Nihonkai kindaishi no shiten," 23–24.

37. Sakai Sei'ichi, *Toyama-ken no rekishi*, 224.

38. *KSNK* 1:150.

39. Mizuno Hatsu, retired cargo loader and housewife, personal interview conducted by Koshida Yasuo on 5 September 1968, in Namerikawa city.

40. Hamada Tsu, personal interview.

41. Saitō, *Kome sōdō*, 8–9.

42. Namerikawa Shi Hensan Iin Kai, *Namerikawa-shi shi: shiryō hen*, 654. Hereafter cited as *Namerikawa shiryō*. Aichi-ken Gikai Jimu Kyoku, *Aichi-ken gikai shi* 4:1050. In Toyama, as in other places where imported rice was sold at a discount during and after the riots, domestic rice was always more popular than the cheaper, more readily available foreign rice. The strong demand for domestic grain led officials in some areas to require the purchase of one part foreign for every two parts domestic rice at the reduced price. So many of those qualified for relief were able to pay more for Japanese rice that in some

Notes to Pages 43–55

localities officials, to conserve domestic supplies, increased the proportion of foreign rice required.

In a report of the governor of Yamaguchi prefecture concerning discount grain sales in 1918, a local police chief noted that middle-class people were ashamed to be seen even buying foreign or Korean rice. To avoid embarrassment many were reported to have tried to purchase it at night. For Yamaguchi conditions, see Ogawa, *Yamaguchi-ken*, 154.

43. Saitō, *Kome sōdō*, 3.

44. Kamiya, "Kome sōdō no rokujūnen," 24. In Namerikawa, rice prices increased from thirty-one sen to forty-two sen for one shō between 31 July and 7 August.

45. Koshida Yasuo, personal interview.

46. Saitō, *Kome sōdō*, 72.

47. Toyama-ken Keisatsu Shi Iin Kai, *Toyama-ken keisatsu shi* 2:612.

48. Hamada Tsu, personal interview. For an account of Toyama women during the protests, see Matsui, "Suwarikomu Toyama no onnatachi," 143.

49. *SKS*, 113; see also Matsui, "Suwarikomu Toyama no onnatachi," 143.

50. *IKSK*, 272–75. Although Yoshikawa's survey of district courts lists one individual as having been prosecuted for rioting in Toyama, I have found no evidence that the rioter was from the coastal region. The Japan statistical yearbook for 1918 indicates that no one was tried for rioting in Toyama during 1918. See Kokusei In, *Tōkei nenkan*, 442.

51. Hasegawa and Masujima, "Kome sōdō no dai'ichi dankai (kanketsu)," 126. The prelude–peak–pacification interpretation is also found in *KSNK* 1:151–68.

52. Toyama-ken, *Toyama-ken shi: tsūshi hen, 6; kindai*, 2, 383.

53. *SKS*, 10.

54. *KSNK* 1:151.

55. Takai, ed., *Toyama-ken josei shi*, 255. For the police account of the first disturbance, see Toyama-ken Keisatsu Shi Iin Kai, *Keisatsu shi* 2:602.

56. Toyama-ken Keisatsu Shi Iin Kai, *Keisatsu shi* 2:603.

57. *KSNK* 1:151.

58. Aoki, *Taishō nōmin sōjō* 2:209.

59. *KSNK* 1:152.

60. *Toyama nippō*, 3 August 1918, in Fujimori, *Toyama-ken kome sōdō nisshi*, 7.

61. *KSNK* 1:153.

62. Nishino, "Nabewarizuki," 13.

63. *SKS*, 40.

64. Hasegawa and Masujima, "Kanketsu," 115–16.

65. *Ibid.*, 129.

66. Saitō, *Kome sōdō*, 16.

67. Ibid., 16–17.

68. *Namerikawa shiryō*, 630.

69. Saitō, *Kome sōdō*, 18–19.

70. *SKS*, 128.

71. *KSNK* 1:156.

72. Unless otherwise indicated, the account of the protest at Kanagawa's house is based upon Saitō, *Kome sōdō*, 21–24; and *SKS*.

73. Kaji, *Kanagawa Sōzaemon*, 1–33. I am grateful to Imoto Mitsuo for calling my attention to this work.

74. Namerikawa Shi Hensan Iin Kai, *Namerikawa-shi shi: tsūshi hen*, 500.

75. Kaji, *Kanagawa Sōzaemon*, 35.

76. Toyama-ken, *Toyama-ken shi: tsūshi hen*, 6; *kindai*, 2, 55–57. Kanagawa Sōzaemon's story ends sadly. After the 1918 riots he was said to have suffered a mental breakdown brought on by the strain of the incident and by later business reverses. The collapse of rice prices in the 1920s eventually forced the family to sell their land and home. Thereafter most of the family's members moved from Toyama. Sōzaemon died in Namerikawa in 1928. See Kaji, *Kanagawa Sōzaemon*, 37–54. For a detailed account of pre–World War II socialist activities in Toyama and the connections linking local political activists with nationally prominent social reformers and leftists such as Sakai Toshihiko, Arahata Kanson, Yokoyama Gennosuke, and others, see Uchiyama, *Toyama-ken senzen shakai undō shi*.

77. Toyama-ken Keisatsu Shi Iin Kai, *Keisatsu shi* 2:616–20.

78. *SKS*, 123.

79. Nishino, "Nabewarizuki," 24.

80. Saitō, *Kome sōdō*, 31.

81. *SKS*, 133–34.

82. The problem of whether to make arrests at the risk of escalating the protest was faced by police in towns outside Toyama. In Hamada, the scene of the largest protests in Shimane prefecture, the official police report notes that one rioter was arrested and released on the same night. Police testimony later explained that the local chief simply believed that it was foolish to make arrests at the risk of provoking attacks on the station. See Shimane-ken Keisatsu Honbu, *Shimane-ken keisatsu shi*, 659.

83. Toyama-ken, *Toyama-ken shi: kindai, tōkei zuhyō*, 99.

84. *SKS*, 130–31.

85. In Mizuhashi the local police appeared to side with the rioters. Mizuhashi residents who had participated in the riots, when interviewed in 1968 credited police with having discreetly ordered grain dealers to stop shipping. I have found no record substantiating this. Nevertheless, that rioters believed that police tried to end the protests amicably attests to the generally good relations between local people and the police. The role of Toyama police in siding with consumers and, in some cases, opposing merchants who profited from their rational ties with the central market is strikingly similar to the role of constables in food riots in early nineteenth-century England. See Matsui, "Toyama no onnatachi," 145; and, for a discussion of the police role in protecting a "moral" economic order, Wells, "The Revolt of the Southwest, 1800–1801," 743.

86. *KSNK* 1:162 and 175.

87. Harada, *Kinsei toshi no sōjō shi*, 261–84.

88. A distinct pattern of protest can be seen in rural *ikki*. Hugh Borton described numerous Tokugawa uprisings and their characteristic cycle of appeals, property destruction, suppression, harsh punishment and, finally, cor-

rection of official policy or chastisement of officials. Despite this recurring pattern he concluded that all such protests were entirely spontaneous and apolitical. More recent scholarship, particularly Stephen Vlastos's work on Tokugawa peasant protest in Aizu, has begun to analyze the political content of *ikki*. For a contrast of two generations of scholarship of Japanese peasant protest, see Borton, *Peasant Uprisings of the Tokugawa Period*; Vlastos, "Tokugawa Peasant Movements in Fukushima," 181–91; and Burton, "Peasant Struggles in Japan," 135–69.

89. Harada, *Sōjō shi*, 366. Yazaki Takeo notes that in Tokugawa-period riots, officials sometimes tacitly supported popular antimerchant protests. This seems a risky attitude for officials to take because local uprisings could be seen as an indictment of local political administration. In one 1783 protest discussed by Yazaki, rioters not only demanded that local officials ban unlawful grain exports but also called upon them to keep a one-year's reserve rice supply in government storehouses. The demand clearly implied that local political administration needed improvement. See Yazaki, *Social Change and the City in Japan*, 258–64.

90. Sakai, *Rekishi*, 190. The Toyama coastal region was not the only grain-marshaling area with a tradition of *tsudome*. In the 1918 riots the tradition resurfaced in Ochiai, Yubara, and other seaboard towns in Okayama prefecture. These towns experienced unrest before similar incidents broke out in more central prefectural cities. See Hasegawa, "Kome sōdō," 236.

91. On rioting in Himi and Hōshōzu, see Harada, *Sōjō shi*, 78–80.

92. Toyama-ken Shi Hensan Iin Kai, *Toyama-ken no rekishi to bunka*, 282.

93. *KSNK* 1:169–71; see also Toyama-ken, *Toyama-ken shi: tsūshi hen*, 6; *kindai*, 2, 280–86.

94. The number of steamships calling at Fushiki, Toyama's main coastal port, increased from 63 in 1879, the first year for which statistics are available, to 2,156 in 1911. The yen value in rice shipped from Fushiki over this same period grew from 1.5 million yen to 10 million yen, peaking at 14 million yen in 1918 (Toyama-ken, *Toyama-ken shi: kindai, tōkei zuhyō*, 272 and 286).

95. Smith and Wiswell, *The Women of Suye Mura*, xxxvii. On the transformation of Japanese women into "good wives and wise mothers"—and resistance to that process—see Smith, "Making Village Women into 'Good Wives and Wise Mothers' in Prewar Japan."

96. Toyama-ken, *Toyama-ken shi: tsūshi hen, 6; kindai*, 2, 383.

97. Toyama-ken Shi Hensan Iin Kai, *Rekishi to bunka*, 282.

98. *KSNK* 1:172–76. Relief measures adopted in Namerikawa differed little from those implemented in other towns.

99. *Namerikawa shiryō*, 629–631. The following discussion of relief efforts relies on local government documents (including communiqués, surveys, and official reports) between Namerikawa, Nakaniikawa county, and the Toyama prefectural office.

100. Kamiya, *Namerikawa-machi*, 15–16; *KSNK* 1:174.

101. Umehara, "1918 nen no kome sōdō," 82.

102. Ibid.

103. *Namerikawa shiryō*, 645.
104. Umehara, "1918 nen no kome sōdō," 83.
105. Ibid., 86.
106. Toyama-ken Keisatsu Shi Iin Kai, *Keisatsu shi*, 315.
107. Umehara, "1918 nen no kome sōdō," 87.
108. Saitō, *Kome sōdō*, 83–84.
109. Umehara, "1918 nen no kome sōdō," 83.
110. "List of Contributions to the Rice Fund for the Poor, 1918," unpublished document held by the Namerikawa Bunka Center.
111. *Namerikawa shiryō*, 654.
112. Saitō, *Kome sōdō*, 94.
113. Ibid., 101–2.
114. *Namerikawa shiryō*, 646–47.
115. *Takaoka shinpō*, 13 July 1919, in Abe, "Josei to kome sōdō," 224.
116. *Namerikawa shiryō*, 646.
117. Hamada Tsu, personal interview.
118. For accounts of the electric power dispute, tenant protests, and the activities of local socialists, see Namerikawa-shi Shi Hensan Iin Kai, *Namerikawa-shi shi*, 514–34; and Uchiyama, *Toyama-ken senzen shakai undō shi*, 76–143. On the labor movement in Toyama, see Toyama-ken, *Toyama-ken shi: kindai, tōkei zuhyō*, 302–3.
119. Namerikawa-shi Shi Hensan Iin Kai, *Namerikawa-shi shi*, 648–49.
120. *KSNK* 1:75–79.

Chapter 3. The City Riots:
Mass Protest and Taishō Democracy

1. Itō and Akita, "The Yamagata-Tokutomi Correspondence," 421.
2. Uda, "Ōsaka shichū kome sōdō oboegaki," 28; *KSNK* 5:130; and Wagatsuma, *Seiji saiban*, 178, also discusses the home minister's views on the riots. Oyama Ikuo felt that Mizuno's discounting of the Toyama protests was emblematic of attitudes widely shared among bureaucratic politicians and advocates of "transcendent government." See Ōyama, "Kome sōdō no shakai-teki oyobi seiji-teki kōsatsu," 77–92; for his specific comments on Mizuno, see 81.
3. Toyama rioters also seemed to believe that their local protest would not spread beyond their prefecture. Although they did not agree that the issues leading to protest were trifling, those who joined the coastal riots did not imagine that their appeals and demonstrations would culminate in a national uprising. Many seemed ashamed that it did. Years after the Toyama riots, local residents, particularly medicine vendors who roamed the length and breadth of Japan, complained that most people knew Toyama only as the place where the riots started.
4. *KSNK* 5:332.
5. *KSNK* 1:130. On the Terauchi government's passive response to early signs of unrest see Kinbara, *Taishō ki no seitō*, 42.

6. Nagoya-shi, *Taishō, Shōwa Nagoya-shi shi: shakai hen* 8:188.

7. *KSNK* 1:188. During the 1914 Nagoya streetcar riots, newspapers and individual members of the Nagoya City Council convened the citizens' rallies that met on nine occasions. At the meeting on 6 September 1914, fifty thousand residents gathered to demand reduced fares and improved streetcar routing. Rioting brought city officials to accept the public's demands on these issues. See Hashimoto, "Toshika to minshū undō," 328–29.

8. For details of the riots in Tokyo, see Tōkyō Hyaku Nen Shi Iin Kai, *Hyaku nen shi* 4:972–73.

9. *KSNK* 1:188.

10. Aichi-ken Nōchi Shi Hensan Iin Kai, *Aichi-ken nōchi shi*, 466.

11. *IKSK*, 281.

12. Aichi-ken Gikai Jimu Kyoku, *Aichi-ken gikai shi* 4:1041.

13. Nagoya-shi, *Taishō, Shōwa Nagoya-shi shi: shakai-hen* 8:193.

14. Aichi-ken Nōchi Shi Hensan Iin Kai, *Aichi-ken nōchi shi*, 466.

15. *KSNK* 1:227.

16. *KSNK* 1:192.

17. Before troops were called out to restore order in Hyogo prefecture, 1,690 patrolmen were put on emergency duty, a number approximately ten times the normal deployment. Yet, as the fierce rioting in Kobe attests, early and extensive use of local police did not prevent unrest. See Hyōgo-ken Keisatsu Shi Hensan Iin Kai, *Hyōgo-ken keisatsu shi: Meiji-Taishō hen*, 689.

18. *KSNK* 1:193.

19. *KSNK* 1:193.

20. *KSNK* 1:196.

21. Saitō, *Nagoya chihō rōdō undō shi*, 305.

22. Ibid.

23. *IKSK*, 288.

24. Aichi-ken Keisatsu Shi Iin Kai, *Aichi-ken keisatsu shi* 2:654. One eyewitness account of the rioting around Komeya-chō states that policemen did indeed wrap their weapons in cloth. But in the heat of battle, when it appeared that the crowd would overwhelm the police, patrolmen quickly unwound the wrappings and used their weapons to full effect. It is estimated that police and troops killed fifteen rioters during the city protests. Figures for nonlethal casualties are not available.

25. Aichi-ken Gikai Jimu Kyoku, *Aichi-ken gikai shi*, 1041.

26. *IKSK*, 288.

27. *KSNK* 1:199–200.

28. Aichi-ken Keisatsu Shi Iin Kai, *Aichi-ken keisatsu shi* 2:645.

29. Ibid., 641. Small-scale Tokyo rice retailers also closed their shops because of shortages. In Nara city, however, police intervened and ordered rice dealers to remain open regardless of the amount of stock on hand. They believed that closing the shops would only worsen distribution and add to popular anxieties over possible shortages. For Tokyo, see *KSNK* 3:281. The situation in Nara is discussed in Nara-ken Keisatsu Shi Iin Kai, *Nara-ken keisatsu shi: Meiji-Taishō hen*, 649.

30. Aichi-ken Gikai Jimu Kyoku, *Aichi-ken gikai shi*, 1043.

31. Ibid.

32. Saitō, *Undō shi*, 306–7.

33. *KSNK* 1:203. See also Yamada, *Nagoya shikai shi*, 1463. Concerning similar relief measures taken in the midst of rioting in Tokyo, see Tokyo Hyaku Nen Shi Iin Kai, *Tōkyō hyaku nen shi* 4:985.

34. Saitō, *Undō shi*, 307–8.

35. Aichi-ken Keisatsu Shi Iin Kai, *Aichi-ken keisatsu shi*, 642.

36. *KSNK* 1:203.

37. *KSNK* 1:205–7.

38. Nagoya-shi, *Taishō, Shōwa Nagoya-shi shi: shakai hen*, 8:195–96.

39. The Bon holiday fell on 13 through 16 August according to the Western calendar, on 19 through 22 August on the lunar. Tanabata, the seventh day of the seventh lunar month, fell on 13 August in 1918. For one instance in which the Bon revelers turned to riot, see Hyōgo-ken Keisatsu Shi Hensan Iin Kai, *Hyōgo-ken keisatsu shi*, 689. Uda Tadashi, the son of an Osaka rice merchant, recalled that although the rioters' mood was sometimes lighthearted (*matsuri sawagi no yō na kanji*), rice dealers did not share in the gaiety. But even in the rice-trading district, the danger of accidental fire spreading to engulf an entire neighborhood was feared more than the threat of physical assault or theft. One Osaka rice-store owner was not even intimidated by fire. When confronted by rioters who threatened to burn his store to the ground, he snapped, "If you're going to do it, just go ahead. I've got fire insurance and will even make a little money." See Uda, "Kome sōdō oboegaki," 30–31, and *KSNK* 2:70.

40. *KSNK* 3:301. See also Wagatsuma, *Saiban shiroku*, 180, and Uda, "Kome sōdō oboegaki," 29.

41. Aichi-ken Keisatsu Shi Iin Kai, *Aichi-ken keisatsu shi*, 643–44.

42. Morinaga, *Zoku shidan saiban*, 82.

43. *KSNK* 2:60. Incidents of looting in Tokyo are described in Tōkyō Hyaku Nen Shi Iin Kai, *Tōkyō hyaku nen shi* 4:977. In Hyogo some rioters demanded discount sales of beer and sake as well as rice. See Hyōgo-ken Keisatsu Shi Hensan Iin Kai, *Hyōgō-ken keisatsu shi*, 688.

44. Nagoya-shi, *Taishō, Shōwa Nagoya-shi shi: shakai hen* 8:193, and Itō, *Aichi-ken minshū undō no rekishi*, 165.

45. Adachi, "Kōbe no 'kome sōdō' to shakai shugisha, sono hoka," 2–3.

46. Hashimoto Tetsuya has generally correlated the type of protest to population size and, secondarily, to the city's particular industrial and commercial make-up. My research only partially bears out Hashimoto's conclusions. Although the level of urban industrialization was important in helping shape protesters' aims, particularly in cities with large communities of traditional craftsmen and small-scale traders, population size alone does not entirely explain the type of protest that occurred. See Hashimoto, "Toshika to minshū undō," 333–34.

47. *KSNK* 3:279.

48. Soeda, *Enka no Meiji Taishō shi*, 210–13.

49. Aichi-ken Gikai Jimu Kyoku, *Aichi-ken gikai shi*, 1036.

50. *KSNK* 1:183 and 3:3; Tōkyō Hyaku Nen Shi Hensan Iin Kai, *Tōkyō*

hyaku nen shi 4:970. This work discusses the rising cost of living during 1917 and 1918 and also provides sample budgets for city residents, pp. 981 and 982.

51. Aichi-ken Gikai Jimu Kyoku, *Aichi-ken gikai shi*, 1036.

52. *KSNK* 1:186.

53. Aichi-ken Gikai Jimu Kyoku, *Aichi-ken gikai shi*, 1037.

54. Ibid. See also Aichi-ken Nōchi Shi Hensan Iin Kai, *Aichi-ken nōchi shi*, 466, and Tōkyō Hyaku Nen Shi Iin Kai, *Tōkyō hyaku nen shi* 4:982.

55. *IKSK*, 278–79.

56. Okado, *Nagoya shiwa*, 122.

57. Tilly, "Popular Disorders in Nineteenth-Century Germany," 5.

58. Amano, "Goken undō kome sōdō to minshū no hatten, 1," 60–65. The compilers of the *Tōkyō hyaku nen shi* attribute attacks on private businesses during the Tokyo rice riots as a result of rioters having been prevented from making their protests directly to the central government. They suggest that private firms served as scapegoats for protesters to vent their wrath against Terauchi's policies. This seems entirely plausible given the close connection between cabinet ministers and leaders of major Japanese trading firms. The well-publicized assistance extended by Gotō Shinpei to Suzuki Shōten's Kaneko Naokichi may explain why Suzuki companies, including subsidiaries, were attacked throughout the nation during the urban riots. See Tōkyō Hyaku Nen Shi Iin Kai, *Tōkyō hyaku nen shi* 4:973.

59. Adachi, "Zentei," 17–18.

60. Narita, "Toshi minshū sōjō to minpon shugi," 45–52.

61. For Osaka, see Koyama, *Taishō ki no kenryoku to minshū*, 51; for Tokyo, see Yazaki, *Social Change and the City*, 451. After the riots new laws were passed to protect city dwellers living in rental housing. See Takenob, *Japan Year Book, 1921–22*, 64.

62. Abe, *Hyōgo kome sōdō*, 66.

63. Adachi, "Zentei," 18.

64. In Kansai generally, forty-three rental agencies or housing landlords reported attacks against their property during the rice riots. Yoshimura, "Kansai ni okeru kome sōdō," 7.

65. Aichi-ken Keisatsu Shi Iin Kai, *Aichi-ken keisatsu shi*, 638.

66. *KSNK* 1:198.

67. Abe, *Hyōgo kome sōdō*, 60. Rioters in Kobe also ransacked the Mikado Hotel, which the Suzuki company had recently purchased and redecorated. See Hyōgo-ken Keisatsu Shi Iin Kai, *Hyōgo-ken keisatsu shi*, 684.

68. Besides attacking the grain exchange and rice wholesalers, Tokyo rioters also vandalized brokerage firms, the stock exchange, banks, newspaper offices, brothels and restaurants in the Yoshiwara district, Ginza shops, and expensive private residences. See Tōkyō Hyaku Nen Shi Iin Kai, *Tōkyō hyaku nen shi* 4:974–77.

69. *KSNK* 1:194.

70. *KSNK* 2:31–32.

71. *KSNK* 1:194.

72. *KSNK* 1:198.

73. Tōkyō Hyaku Nen Shi Iin Kai, *Tōkyō hyaku nen shi*, 973–80.

74. *KSNK* 1:198–99.

75. *IKSK* 287–288.

76. *KSNK* 1:200.

77. *KSNK* 1:205.

78. Okamoto, *The Japanese Oligarchy and the Russo-Japanese War*, 196–223; see also Narita, "Toshi minshū sōjō to minpon shugi," 39–41.

79. Okado, *Nagoya shiwa*, 118.

80. Inumaru and Nakamura, *Nihon kindai shi 2: Ni sshin, Nichiro Sensō kara kome sōdō made*, 147–59. For accounts of rioting resulting from the Taishō political crisis and the Siemens scandal, see also Kawabe, *The Press and Politics in Japan*, 138–44.

81. Okamoto, "The Emperor and the Crowd," 258–73. Although Okamoto discusses only the 1905 Hibiya riots, he suggests several features that appear common to Taishō urban uprisings generally. His description of the Hibiya protests as a "church and king" riot, albeit one that implicitly threatened the oligarchic political order, seems also applicable to the 1918 city rice riots.

82. *KSNK* 1:194–98.

83. Takeda, "Yosai," 24–25. If only to maintain a superficial facade of social stability, justice officials, whether in twentieth-century Japan or earlier in European countries, found it essential to treat enforcers of the "just price" as criminals regardless of the criminality of their actions. Such actions do not necessarily mean that even the police believed that those arrested were the actual perpetrators of crimes. On the necessity for local authorities to define the crowd's fixing of popular prices as theft in late-eighteenth-century English food riots, see Charlesworth and Randall, "Morals, Markets and the English Crowd," 209–10.

84. *KSNK* 1:252–63.

85. Wagatsuma, *Saiban shiroku*, 179.

86. Matsuo, "Kyōto chihō no kome sōdō," 132–35.

87. Taeuber, "Urbanization and Population Change in the Development of Modern Japan," 8.

88. For the argument that rapid urbanization, characterized by an influx of rural population into the cities and the disintegration of traditional values, leads to explosive political conditions within cities, see Philip Hauser, "The Social, Economic and Technological Problems of Rapid Urbanization," 199–217.

89. *KSNK* 3:86–100.

90. For some aspects of the acculturation of country people to city life, see Kornhauser, *Urban Japan: Its Foundations and Growth*, and Howton, "Cities, Slums, and Acculturation Process in Developing Countries." On the adaptation of long-term Japanese city residents to new changes in the metropolis, see Robert J. Smith, "Pre-Industrial Urbanism in Japan," 241–57.

91. Yamazaki's account and a capsule biography appear in Itō, *Aichi-ken minshū undō*, 165–66; *KSNK* 1:190–91; and Aichi-ken Keisatsu Shi Hensan Iin Kai, *Aichi-ken keisatsu shi* 2:638.

92. *KSNK* 1:190.

93. A sketch of Yamazaki's wartime activities and career in the Diet through 1947 is given in Shūgi In, ed., *Kokkai taikan*, 321–22 and 527.

94. For an account of the activities of Yamamoto Kenzō, a twenty-four-year-old workshop machinist who followed a path similar to Yamazaki's in becoming involved in leftist politics, see Morinaga, *Zoku shidan saiban*, 85; and *KSNK* 3:288 and 320. Yamamoto spoke before a crowd for the first time at the Hibiya Park citizens' meeting in Tokyo, an action that resulted in a prison term of six months at hard labor. Following his release he continued active in the labor movement and finally became a member of the executive committee of the Japan Communist Party. He was later active in the Comintern and died in exile in the Soviet Union during the 1930s. Neither he nor Yamazaki had been involved in labor organization or leftist politics before the riots.

95. Inoue Kiyoshi, Watanabe Tōru, and the Kyoto University research team compiled and the rioters' profiles, using four police and district court sources: "Conduct Survey Record," "Police Survey," "Records of Preliminary Examination," and "Prosecutor's Record." Unfortunately, the original compilation of such information was not carried out throughout the nation, but depended on the initiative of local court officials. The brief surveys do, however, include a statement of the suspects' employment history, family background, previous arrest record, income, and the defendant's own estimation of his economic level. See *KSNK* 2:153–59.

96. Yazaki, *Social Change and the City*, 382.

97. Ibid., 410.

98. Adachi, "Kōbe no 'kome sōdō,'" 16.

99. Japan, Rōdō Shō, *Tōkei kara mita waga kuni no rōdō sōgi*, 454–55.

100. Matsuo, *Minpon shugi*, 133–34.

101. Hongō, Abe, et al., "Zadankai: kome sōdō no koro," 9, and Abe, *Hyōgo kome sōdō ki*, 47.

102. *KSNK* 1:187.

103. *KSNK* 1:113.

104. *IKSK*, 352–54.

105. *KSNK* 1:111–13.

106. Watanabe, "Buraku kaihō undō," 185.

107. *KSNK* 1:112.

108. Abe, *Hyōgo kome sōdō*, 92. Arbitrary police actions against burakumin were clearly demonstrated in rioting at the Sumiyoshi settlement in Osaka. When rioting broke out near the burakumin ghetto, the neighborhood Buddhist youth association (Bukkyō Seinen Dan) autonomously organized patrols to discourage Sumiyoshi people from becoming involved. After rioting had been suppressed, police swept through the buraku and arrested youth association volunteers for *leading* the uprising. See Sumida, "Kome sōdō ni okeru Sumiyoshi buraku no ugoki," 43–52.

109. *KSNK* 2:22–23. See also Matsuo, "Kyōto chihō no kome sōdō," 120, and Adachi, "Kōbe no 'kome sōdō,'" 8.

110. *KSNK* 1:113. On the burakumin involvement in the Okayama riots see Sakamoto, "Okayama no kome sōdō to burakumin," 59–60.

111. Aichi-ken Keisatsu Shi Iin Kai, *Aichi-ken keisatsu shi*, 641.

112. Adachi, "Kōbe no kome sōdō," 3–4.

113. *IKSK*, 456–57.

114. *KSNK*, 3:187.

115. *KSNK* 1:114.

116. Itō, *Aichi-ken minshū undō*, 165.

117. Tilly, "The Chaos of the Living City," 99.

118. Hongō, Abe, et al., "Zadankai," 7.

119. Takeda, "Yosai," 21–22.

120. *IKSK*, 113 and 265–67. For *sōshi* involvement in rioting in Fukushima city, see Kōriyama-shi, *Kōriyama-shi shi: kindai* 2:118–21.

121. *KSNK* 1:229–30.

122. Ibid.

123. Aichi-ken Gikai Jimu Kyoku, *Aichi-ken gikai shi*, 1055; see also Nagoya Shikai Jimu Kyoku, *Nagoya shikai shi* 3:1431–37; and *KSNK* 1: 230.

124. *KSNK* 1:231.

125. The central government instituted both the Sake Brewing Tax and Tobacco Monopoly laws in 1896 which prohibited the making of rice wine or growing of tobacco for personal consumption. In 1905 it also promulgated the Salt Monopoly Law. Taxes on these basic items provided an important source of state revenue. Ogura, *Can Japanese Agriculture Survive?* 399.

126. Ibid., 195.

127. Saitō, *Undō shi*, 318.

128. Ibid., 320.

129. Takenob, *Japan Year Book, 1921–22*, 530.

130. Ibid., 531.

131. *IKSK*, 478–79. For the change in social welfare in Tokyo and at the central-government level following the riots, see Tōkyō Hyaku Nen Shi Iin Kai, *Tōkyō hyaku nen shi* 4:214–15, and Taira, "Public Assistance in Japan," 97. For the shift in regional policies, see Uda, Takasawa, and Furukawa, *Shakai fukushi no rekishi*, 213.

132. *KSNK* 5:301.

133. Quoted in Kinbara, *Taishōki no seitō*, 95–96.

134. Ōyama, "Kome sōdō no shakai teki oyobi seiji teki no kōsatsu," 81–83; and Fukuda, "Bōdō ni tai suru tōkyoku no taido," 92–94.

135. Nagoya-shi, *Taishō, Shōwa Nagoya-shi shi: shisei hen*, 10, 6:311; see also *KSNK* 1:194.

136. What happened over seventy years ago in Japan, where rioting over food costs led to a reorganization of national leadership, has recent parallels. One example is widespread rioting in Burma, which brought down the government of General Sein Lwin. For a report on the protests there, which demonstrate several similarities to what occurred in Japanese cities in 1918, see "Uprising in Burma: The Old Regime Under Seige." Popular protests in Poland during the 1970s and 1980s, ostensibly about the high cost of living but with political implications for the ruling regime, also provide an allusive comparison for the Japanese city riots in 1918.

Chapter 4. The Rural Riots:
Consumer Protests and Tenant-Landlord Riots

1. As used here, "rural" refers to communities of less than 30,000 administratively defined by the central government in 1918 as "towns" (machi) and "villages" (mura). These settlements generally conform to the simple definition of the differences between rural and urban noted by Thomas O. Wilkerson: "The crucial distinction between rural and urban populations is essentially the labor force concentration in agriculture or other extractive pursuits for the rural population as against a concentration in non-extractive activities for the urban" Urbanization of Japanese Labor, 5). Admittedly, some "rural" towns were well on their way to becoming regional industrial cities by 1918.

The terms "landlord" and "tenant" refer respectively to landowners, who received a significant share of their income in land rents, and to cultivators, who paid a significant amount of their harvest to landowners. There was, of course, a constellation of broad and fine distinctions within the individual landlord or tenant category. As is discussed below, many of these arose from regional differences, landholding patterns, control of harvest, access to markets, and fictive kinship relations.

2. Kyōchōkai, Saikin no shakai undō, 280.

3. Nishida, "Nōmin undō no hatten to jinushi sei," 141–81, passim.

4. KSNK 1:90.

5. The primary sources for the Furuichi riots are included in Watanabe, "Ōsaka-fu Furuichi-machi no kome sōdō," 89–104; and KSNK 2:91–108. Unless otherwise noted, background information for the town and the county, as well as the general account of the Furuichi protest, is based on Watanabe's study.

6. KSNK 2:96.

7. According to the trial records for disturbances in Shizuoka, one protest leader convinced local residents to join the protest by arguing that "to accept relief rice, even for our children's and grandchildren's sake, is shameful. Let's reject that sort of thing and demand that rice be sold at a reasonable price." See Suzuki, "Kome sōdō ki no toshi to nōson," 27.

8. The Fujidera, Minami Kudara, Mozu, and similar rural riots are discussed in KSNK 2:115–16, 121, 130–33, 140.

9. Abe, Hyōgo kome sōdō, 165.

10. Matsuo, "Kyōto chihō no kome sōdō, 128.

11. Yoshimura, "Kansai ni okeru kome sōdō, 16.

12. Ibid., 39.

13. Matsuo, "Kyōto chihō no kome sōdō, 127; for an account of a similar struggle against a village headman in a buraku settlement, see Sakamoto, "Okayama no kome sōdō to burakumin," 54.

14. Before the outbreak of rioting in Ōhama in Aichi prefecture, local residents called for a "sacrifice group" (gisei dan) to move against local grain dealers. In rioting in Ehime and Hyogo prefectures, residents attempted to prevent prosecution by claiming that the people who were arrested had not acted differently from residents in general and by urging local officials to appeal to the

police for leniency toward suspects. In some cases, the targets of attacks declined to press charges, thereby refusing to cooperate with prosecutors. On the Aichi riots, see Aichi-ken Gikai Jimu Kyoku, *Aichi-ken gikai shi* 4:1048; on Ehime, Kyōto Daigaku Jinbungaku Kenkyūjo, "Keisatsu no mita kome sōdō (1)," 40; and for Hyogo, *KSNK* 3:57–58.

15. Yoshimura, "Kansai ni okeru kome sōdō," 38.

16. Abe, *Hyōgo kome sōdō*, 223; see also Matsuo, "Kyōto chihō no kome sōdō," 133–34.

17. *KSNK* 2:131–33.

18. Matsuo, "Kyōto chihō no kome sōdō, 126–28; see also *KSNK* 2:121; and Yoshimura, "Kansai ni okeru kome sōdō," 45.

19. Smethurst, *A Social Basis for Prewar Militarism*, 146.

20. *KSNK* 5:79.

21. *KSNK* 5:84.

22. Endō and Yoshii, "Kome sōdō to sōgi to gunshuku," 182–84.

23. Fukutake, *Rural Society in Japan*, 102. Membership in reservists' organizations was voluntary until 1937. The sense that the organization was as much a local as a national group is suggested by the high rural membership rates (80 percent in the 1920s) in the associations. See Smethurst, *A Social Basis for Prewar Militarism*, 17–20.

24. Matsuo, "Kyōto chihō no kome sōdō," 139.

25. Koyama, "Gun gyōsei to chōson no dōkō," 27.

26. Unless otherwise indicated, the following description of Hōryūji and the account of the rioting there is based on a collection of village data, statistics, and court records in Teruoka, *Jinushi sei.*

27. On the rice-inspection system and its implications for tenant-landlord relations in various Japanese rural regions, see Nishida, "Nōmin undō," 144–47.

28. Teruoka, *Jinushi sei*, 103 and 105.

29. For Morita's background, role in the riots, and later involvement in village politics, see ibid., 178 and 229–31.

30. See tables in ibid., 109 and 103.

31. Ibid., 171–72. The decline of landlords in Nara prefecture, including Hōryūji, is detailed in Takenaga, "Nichiro sengo—ryō taisen kikan ki no jinushi," 169–78.

32. For multiple examples of tenant-landlord disputes during the rice riots, see Yoshimura, "Kansai ni okeru kome sōdō," 39–41; Aoki, *Nōmin sōjō shiryō* 2:763; Nōshōmu Shō Nōmu Kyoku, *Kosaku sankō shiryō*, 158–59; Nōmin Undō Shi Kenkyū Kai, *Nihon nōmin undō shi*, 267; and *KSNK*, 3:377. The incidents examined in these sources are not exhaustive.

33. Nōshōmu Shō, *Kosaku sankō shiryō*, 94.

34. Nezu, "Shōnai chihō," 41.

35. Yamagata-ken, *Yamagata-ken shi: shiryō hen kingendai shiryō*, 2, 50–56 and 62–63. Hara Takashi, who happened to be in Iwate just after the peak of rioting, noted in his diary similar efforts taken in Morioka city to avert rioting: "August 19, 1918. The mayor of Morioka, Mr. Kitada, came to see me, saying that he heard some rumors that riots might spread to Morioka. He suc-

ceeded in lowering the price of rice to 30 *sen* a quart (*shō*) [*sic*] and was continuing to look for other means of lowering the price. The city received a little over 5,000 yen as its share of the Imperial donation. The mayor wanted to build up additional relief funds and asked for a donation. I immediately gave him 300 yen. The mayor said that he was confident of receiving 20,000 yen." Quoted in Lu, ed., *Sources of Japanese History* 2:110.

36. Nezu, "Shōnai chihō," 42.

37. Shōji, *Kindai chihō minshū undō shi, ka,* 103 and 236–37; see also Kōriyama-shi, *Kōriyama-shi shi* 2:113. Three instances of rioting were also reported in Miyagi, Fukushima's immediate neighbor to the north. Protests there were limited to Sendai city and two nearby towns. See *KSNK* 4:347–58.

38. Waswo, *Japanese Landlords*, 95.

39. Kyōchōkai, *Saikin no shakai undō*, 380.

40. Lemarchand, "Comparative Political Clientelism," 8–9.

41. Weingrod, "Patrons, Patronage, and Political Parties," 379.

42. Bennett and Ishino, *Paternalism in the Japanese Economy*, 245.

43. Johnson, "Patronage and Privilege," 202.

44. Dore, *Land Reform*, 6.

45. Ibid., 46.

46. The authors of the monograph detailing the Honma's efforts to increase productivity did not see that allowing the benefits of greater productivity to go to tenants was landlord largess. They instead asked why the "parasitical landlords" did not reduce rents. To me this seems to be an ahistorical question. See Takeuchi, ed., *Tōhoku nōson no shakai hendō*, 288.

47. Another richly suggestive saying from Iwate is "There is no rest for masters or beggars." Shinjō Village, *Shinjō: The Chronicle of a Japanese Village*, 232–33.

48. Dore, *Land Reform*, 45–46.

49. Ibid., 41.

50. Ibid., 33.

51. Johnson, "Patronage and Privilege," 205.

52. Dore, *Land Reform*, 44.

53. Johnson, "Patronage and Privilege," 203.

54. Tōkyō Teikoku Daigaku Nōgakubu Nōseigaku Kenkyū Shitsu, *Shōnai tenjo*. A village study, even one that focuses on a network of local buraku, is analysis at the micro-level. Conditions in Tōgō nevertheless appear comparable to those in other Tōhoku districts. Of course, Fukushima prefecture, with its factory towns and mines in Fukushima city, Taira, and Kōriyama, was more industrialized than the other six *ken* that constitute the region and therefore exceptional. For a macro-level analysis of the entire Tōhoku region, see Teikoku Nōkai, *Tōhoku chihō nōson*.

55. Tōkyō Teikoku Daigaku Nōgakubu Nōseigaku Kenkyū Shitsu, *Shōnai tenjo*, 37–48.

56. On the history of *sangyō kumiai*, see Ogura, *Can Japanese Agriculture Survive?* 265–68.

57. Okado, "Dai'ichiji taisen go no nōson shinkō mondai to sho seiryoku," 40.

58. Teikoku Nōkai, *Tōhoku chihō nōson*, 253.

59. Tokyo Teikoku Daigaku Nōgakubu Nōseigaku Kenkyū Shitsu, *Shōnai tenjo*, 253.

60. Ibid., 232–33.

61. Nōshōmushō Nōmu Kyoku, *Taishō kunen do nōgyō sōkyo* (1935), reproduced in Nishida, "Nōmin undō, 164.

62. Tōkyō Teikoku Daigaku Nōgakubu Nōseigaku Kenkyū Shitsu, *Shōnai tenjo*, 84–85.

63. Ibid., 32.

64. Ibid., 88.

65. Nezu, "Shōnai chihō," 42.

66. Ibid., 45.

67. Tilly, "The Food Riot as a Form of Political Conflict in France," 23.

68. Ibid.

69. Rose, "Eighteenth-Century Price Riots and Public Policy in England," 279.

70. Matsuo, "Kyōto chihō no kome sōdō," 118; see also Watanabe, "Ōsaka-fu Furuichi-machi no kome sōdō," 90.

71. Shōji, *Kindai chihō minshū undō shi, ka*, 99; see also Teruoka, "Japanese Capitalism and Its Agricultural Problems—Culminating in the Rice Riots," 485–92.

72. Shōji, *Kindai chihō minshū undō shi, ka*, 99.

73. Waswo, *Japanese Landlords*, 66.

74. Ibid., 4.

75. Dore, *Land Reform in Japan*, 16.

76. Shōji, *Kindai chihō minshū undō shi, ka*, 105.

77. *Hinode shinbun*, 3 September 1918, in Matsuo, "Kyōtō chihō no kome sōdō," 118.

78. Nōmin Undō Shi Kenkyū Kai, *Nihon nōmin undō shi*, 274–75.

79. Yamamoto, *Shinbun to minshū*, 192.

Chapter 5. The Coalfield Riots:
Riot as Labor Dispute

1. Japan, Bureau of Mines, *Taishō ku nen honpō kōgyō sūsei*, 36; Japan, Imperial Bureau of Mines, *Mining Industry in Japan*, 52; Kokusei In, *Sanjūkyū nen tōkei nenkan*, 155; see also Yoshihara, *Sogo Shosha*, 17–37.

2. Kokusei In, *Sanjūkyū nen tōkei nenkan*, 155.

3. Ribert Martin Vesy Collick, "Labour and Trade Unionism in the Japanese Coal Mining Industry," 31; Japan, Bureau of Mines, *Kōgyō sūsei*, 36; Yoshihara, *Sogo Shosha*, 29–36; Takenob, *Japan Year Book, 1919–1920*, 557. On Mitsui Mining's aggressive acquisition of smaller collieries, see Ichihara, "Dai'ichiji taisen ni itaru Hokutan keiei," 135–56.

4. Japan, Imperial Bureau of Mines, *Mining Industry*, 54; Yazaki, *Social Change and the City in Japan*, 386.

5. Okochi, *Labor in Modern Japan*, 37.

6. Kagawa, "Chikuhō tanden no rōdō mondai, jō," 50; Hane, *Peasants, Rebels, and Outcastes*, 229.

7. Japan, Bureau of Mines, *Kōgyō sūsei*, 205.

8. Ibid., 209–10.

9. *Shiryō* 10:174–75 and 404–5.

10. Japan, Bureau of Mines, *Kōgyō sūsei*, 185. The use of family labor in Japanese coal pits resembled that in French mines in the late nineteenth century; see Reid, "Industrial Paternalism: Discourse and Practice in Nineteenth-Century French Mining and Metallurgy," 583 and 596–97; on pay advances to married workers, see Takenob, *Japan Year Book, 1913*, 313.

11. Hane, *Peasants, Rebels, and Outcastes*, 235.

12. In 1928, the problem of unequal wages appeared solved when women were legally banned from underground work. Despite the ban, women still found pit work at middling and smaller companies that illegally continued the practice. The work restriction weakened their bargaining position, however, because hiring them became an illegal favor, one that stifled complaints about low wages with the threat of dismissal. In 1933 the government allowed married women to work underground again. They continued to do so until a 1946 law blocked anyone but men from entering the pits and postwar custom made mining an exclusively male calling. See ibid., 233–35.

13. *Shiryō* 10:594; 3:176–77.

14. Inumaru and Nakamura, *Nihon kindai shi, 2: Nisshin, Nichiro Sensō kara kome sōdō made*, 62–63.

15. Kagawa, "Chikuhō tanden, ka," 51; Japan, Bureau of Mines, *Kōgyō sūsei*, 215–16.

16. Japan, Bureau of Mines, *Mining in Japan, Past and Present*, 40; Collick, "Coal-mining Industry," 80–87.

17. Inumaru and Nakamura, *Kindai shi*, 63.

18. Collick, "Coal-mining Industry," 220–22.

19. Shindō, *Ōmuta no kindai shi*, 70.

20. *Shiryō* 10:442–47; see aso Kinbara, *Jiyū to handō no chōryū*, 153.

21. *Shiryō* 10:442–47.

22. Japan, Bureau of Mines, *Mining Past and Present*, 44; Hane, *Peasants, Rebels, and Outcastes*, 229.

23. Collick, "Coal-mining Industry," 24.

24. Mikami, *Tankōfu no seikatsu*, 32.

25. Sōseki, *The Miner*, 15. For similar British attitudes toward miners, and conditions in the "modern" coal pits of England in the 1930s, see Orwell, *The Road to Wigan Pier*.

26. Japan, Bureau of Mines, *Mining Past and Present*, 44.

27. A Kyōchōkai survey of coal miners after the 1918 riots noted the following reasons for quitting a particular mine: (1) wage-related grievances, including low pay and dangerous working conditions; (2) relations with other miners; and (3) family concerns. The report noted that although the work was fairly simple, a miner who continued in the pits for ten years could expect to develop black lung. On labor turnover rates, see Collick, "Coal-mining Industry," 133. In his 1918 study of the Chikuhō coal fields, Kagawa Toyohiko

reported an annual worker turnover rate of 140 percent. See Kagawa, "Chiku-hō tanden no rōdō mondai, jō," 36.

28. See Shindō, *Chikuhō no onna kōfutachi*, 94.

29. Mikami, *Tankōfu*, 16–27. The labor procurer and general *nayaga-shira* system in late-Meiji-period copper mines are described in Sōseki's, *The Miner*.

30. Collick, "Coal-mining Industry," 59–60; Hane, *Peasants, Rebels, and Outcastes*, 230.

31. Yoshimura, "Kome sōdō to tankō chingin seido," 50.

32. Collick, "Coal-mining Industry," 136–37.

33. *Shiryō* 3:591. A few zaibatsu operations offered to double the balance accumulated in compulsory savings plans for each five-year period that the miner worked. See Takenob, *Japan Year Book, 1913*, 312.

34. The notion that sake served as the miner's lifeblood continued strong in the 1940s. For example, during the war years officials provided miners with special allotments of rice wine, a drink that was strictly rationed and generally not available to the wider population. For a discussion of the miner's daily life, see Yamaguchi-ken Kyōiku Iin Kai, *Yamaguchi tanden no minzoku*, 113 and passim.

35. Mikami, *Tankōfu*, 149.

36. Japan, Bureau of Mines, *Kōgyō sūsei*, 43.

37. Yoshimura, *Nihon tankō shi*, 229.

38. A contrasting opinion is given by Mikami Tokusaburō. He found that approximately 500 of 2,000 miners in the Jōban mine which he investigated in 1918 maintained postal savings accounts and also participated in the company's compulsory savings plan. A few had even saved enough to open a small restaurant or shop and escape the pits for good. See Mikami, *Tankōfu*, 102.

39. Yoshimura, *Nihon tankō shi*, 226.

40. Collick, "Coal-mining Industry," 131.

41. *Shiryō* 10:442.

42. *IKSK*, 3. Yoshikawa airs his view of the contagious character of the riots on p. 306.

43. Takahashi, ed., *Nihon kindaika to Kyūshū*, 361.

44. *KSNK* 4:369.

45. Takano, *Kome sōdō ki*, 115.

46. Nagasue, *Chikuhō: sekitan to chiiki shi*, 144.

47. *KSNK* 4:95–96. Day wages in Kyushu coalfields were estimated at 1.30 yen. See Takahashi, *Nihon kindaika to Kyushu*, 387.

48. Takano, *Kome sōdō ki*, 88.

49. Yonekura, "Mineji tankō no kome sōdō," 150.

50. *KSNK* 4:537–39.

51. *Shiryō* 3:598.

52. Ibid. 3:590.

53. Yonekura, "Mineji tankō," 149.

54. Ibid., 150.

55. Takahashi, *Nihon kindaika to Kyūshū*, 376–77.

56. *KSNK* 4:406, 431, 538.

57. Takahashi, *Nihon kindaika to Kyūshū*, 382; see also Takano, *Kome sōdō ki*, 64.

58. *KSNK* 4:540; 412; Takahashi, *Nihon kindaika to Kyūshū*, 382; Yonekura, "Mineji tankō," 153.

59. Yoshimura, "Tankō chingin," 49; see also *Shiryō* 3:581; and *KSNK* 4:419 and 537.

60. *KSNK* 4:405–19.

61. *KSNK* 4:537; see also *Shiryō* 3:598. Apart from wage-related demands, miners in several disputes requested that the work day be divided into three instead of two shifts, that housing rents be reduced, and that the company dispense medicines free of charge. Aside from these, the miners' grievances over noneconomic issues centered on the ill-treatment received at the hands of mine bosses and company management. For noneconomic demands, see Yoshimura, "Tankō chingin," 49; and *KSNK* 4:541.

62. Collick, "Coal-mining Industry," 39–40.

63. *Shiryō* 3:590.

64. Ibid. 3: 598–99.

65. Yonekura, "*Mineji tankō*, 154; *KSNK* 4:531.

66. Takahashi, *Nihon kindaika to Kyūshū*, 380–81; and Hayashi, *Chikuhō kome sōdō ki*, 29.

67. *Shiryō* 3:596; *KSNK* 4:542; Yonekura, "Mineji tankō," 49.

68. Mitsui Bunkō, *Mitsui jigyō shi*, 2:429–30; see also *Shiryō* 3:603.

69. Takahashi, *Nihon kindaika to Kyūshū*, 380–81.

70. Yonekura, "Mineji tankō," 150.

71. *KSNK* 4:371–73; Takahashi, *Nihon kindaika to Kyūshū*, 379–80.

72. *KSNK* 4:390; see also Takahashi, *Nihon kindaika to Kyūshū*, 384; and Takano, *Kome sōdō ki*, 35–37.

73. Ayusawa, *A History of Labor in Modern Japan*, 71–72.

74. *KSNK* 4:428 and 430–31.

75. Takano, *Kome sōdō ki*, 63–69; see also Kuroha, *Guntai no kataru Nihon no kindai shi*, 153–56.

76. Yonekura, "Mineji tankō," 152–57.

77. One explanation given in 1918 for the popularity of festivals in the mining areas, not only during periods of riot but the year around, was that the *matsuri* symbolically rejected the superior-inferior relations that normally governed human relations in the camps. According to one Taishō journalist who temporarily became a miner, during the Obon dances, "capitalists and workers are equal before the gods" (*Kami no mae ni wa shihonka mo rōdōsha mo byōdō de aru*). See Mikami, *Tankōfu*, 145.

78. Yonekura, "Mineji tankō," 151.

79. *KSNK* 4:538.

80. *KSNK* 4:542; Takano, *Kome sōdō ki*, 65.

81. Takano, *Kome sōdō ki*, 50.

82. Takahashi, *Nihon kindaika to Kyūshū*, 378.

83. Takano, *Kome sōdō ki*, 41–42 and 101; Takahashi, *Nihon kindaika to Kyūshū*, 378; and *KSNK* 4:416 and 428.

84. Asahi Shinbun Sha Ube-Shi Kyoku, *Ube tankō shiwa*, 189.

85. *KSNK* 4:539.

86. *KSNK* 4:540; see also *Shiryō* 3:599–600.

87. Takano, *Kome sōdō ki*, 60; *Shiryō* 3:597; Takano, *Niikawa kara Ube*, 94.

88. Takano, *Kome sōdō ki*, 60–62.

89. *KSNK* 4:406; 359 and 539; Takano, *Kome sōdō ki*, 86.

90. *KSNK* 4:395.

91. *Shiryō* 3:601.

92. Takahashi, *Nihon kindaika to Kyūshū*, 369–70.

93. *KSNK* 4:392; see also Takano, *Kome sōdō ki*, 84.

94. *KSNK* 3:393.

95. Takano, *Kome sōdō ki*, 81.

96. Ibid., 72–83.

97. *KSNK* 4:548; Yonekura, "Mineji tankō," 155.

98. *KSNK* 5:141.

99. Noshiro, "Kome sōdō no omoide," 47.

100. Hayashi, *Chikuhō kome sōdō ki*, 178.

101. Yonekura, "Mineji tankō," 156; Takahashi, *Nihon kindaika to Kyūshū*, 386.

102. *Shiryō* 3:602–5; on blackballing, see Hayashi, *Chikuhō kome sōdō ki*, 264–65.

103. *KSNK* 4:122.

104. *Shiryō* 3:581; Takahashi, *Nihon kindaika to Kyūshū*, 387.

105. Mitsui Bunkō, *Jigyōshi*, 429–30; see also Takahashi, *Nihon kindaika to Kyūshū*, 380; Yoshimura, "Tankō chingin," 53; and *Shiryō* 3:581 and 601–3.

106. Mitsui Bunkō, *Jigyōshi*, 434–36; also Takano, *Niikawa kara Ube*, 104; and Takenob, *Japan Year Book, 1919–1920*, 297. Cooperative associations had existed before 1918, but the number and activities of these groups expanded dramatically after World War I. Both before and after the war, management used these groups in a variety of enterprises. On the role of Mitsubishi Shipbuilding's "Three Smiles Association" (Sanshōkai) in management-worker relations, see Nishinarita, "Dai'ichiji taisen chū, go no zaibatsu-kei zōsen kigyō no rōshi kankei," 26–49.

107. Noshiro, "Kome sōdō no ōmoide," 47.

108. At most mines, the miners had no say in whether they would or would not join the associations. At Ube, for example, membership was compulsory in the Okinomiya mines. See Asahi Shinbun Sha Ube Shikyoku, *Ube tankō shiwa*, 194.

109. Large, *Organized Workers and Socialist Politics in Interwar Japan*, 11.

110. Collick, "Coal-mining Industry," 203–4.

111. Koga, ed., *Kita Kyūshū chihō shakai rōdō shi nenpyō*, 173–93.

112. Collick, "Coal-mining Industry," 206.

113. Shindō, *Ōmuta no kindai shi*, 61–62.

114. Nagasue, *Chikuhō*, 146–51; see also Koga, ed., *Kita Kyūshū*, 209.

115. Large, *Organized Workers*, 17–18.

116. Nagasue, *Chikuhō*, 146.

117. Shindō, *Ōmuta no kindai shi*, 70.
118. Ibid., 71.
119. For a detailed chronology of ongoing labor unrest in the coalfields between 1919 and 1924, see Koga, ed., *Kita Kyūshū*, 173–228. For developments at Ube mines during this same period (including Sōdōmei efforts to organize miners, company efforts to bolster its association and support the Hotoku-kai, or "Return of Virtue Association," and strikes), see Asahi Shinbun Sha Ube Shikyoku, *Ube tankō shiwa*, 194–97.
120. Nagasue, *Chikuhō*, 72–73; Koga, ed., *Kita Kyūshū* 225–27. Raising strike funds was always a problem, one that workers had to solve creatively in the absence of any strong union federation. See Collick, "Coal-mining Industry," 243–44.
121. Koga, ed., *Kita Kyūshū*, 225–27.
122. Scalapino, *The Early Japanese Labor Movement*, 99.
123. Koga, ed., *Kita Kyūshū*, 189.
124. Kyōchōkai, *Saikin shakai undō*, 115–16.
125. Ibid., 187–213, passim.
126. Collick, "Coal-mining Industry," 249.
127. Ibid., 256.

Chapter 6. Conclusion

1. Hotta, "Taishō kōki no seiji," 258.
2. *KSNK* 5:226–28.
3. Suzuki, *Kome: jiyū to tōsei*, 37–38.
4. *IKSK*, 472.
5. Kyōchōkai, *Saikin shakai undō*, 692.
6. Takenob, *Japan Year Book, 1921–22*, 383.
7. Ann Waswo discusses several laws that benefited cultivators, including the 1924 Tenancy Conciliation Law and the 1926 Regulations for the Establishment of Owner-Cultivators, in "The Transformation of Rural Society, 1900–1950."
8. Omameuda, "1920 nendai ni okeru shokuryō seisaku no tenkai," 54–56.
9. Hayami and Ruttan, "Korean Rice, Taiwan Rice, and Japanese Agricultural Stagnation," 570.
10. Suzuki, *Kome: jiyū to tōsei*, 36–39.
11. Kyōchōkai, Saikin *shakai undō*, 694.
12. *IKSK*, 478–79. Regarding the change in social welfare in Tokyo and at the central government level following the riots, see Tōkyō Hyaku Nen Shi Iin Kai, *Tokyo hyaku nen shi* 4:214–15; and Taira, "Public Assistance in Japan," 97. For the shift in regional policies, see Uda, Takasawa, and Furukawa, *Shakai fukushi no rekishi*, 213; and Koyama, "Kome sōdō to shakai mondai," 138.
13. For expressions of concern over social welfare made by central and local government officials, see Toyama-ken Naimu Bu, *Ishikawa-Toyama ryōken*, 1–29.

14. Toyama-ken Naimu Bu, *Ishikawa-Toyama ryōken*, 7–13. From 1919 through the early 1920s, the Diet promulgated numerous social welfare laws, established research committees, and supported the relief efforts of private organizations. Local governments did the same. National legislation included the Tuberculosis Prevention Law, Trachoma Law, Insane Asylum Law, Employment Introduction Law, and Housing Law. In 1919 the central government began offering low-interest loans to social welfare organizations and, in 1920, created the Social Bureau (Shakai Kyoku) within the Home Ministry. For a comprehensive discussion of public and private social welfare organizations, see Shakai Fukushi Chōsa Kenkyu Kai, *Senzen Nihon no shakai jigyō chōsa*, 641–85, passim.

15. Kyōchōkai, *Saikin shakai undō*, 694.

16. Suzuki Bunji, "Kome sōdō to Yūaikai," 186–88; see also Suzuki, *Rōdō undō nijū nen*, 163–69.

17. *Shiryō* 10:424; see also Duus, *Party Rivalry*, 126–27, and Uda, Takasawa, and Furukawa, *Shakai fukushi*, 214.

18. Waswo, "The Origins of Tenant Unrest," 277.

19. Nōmin Undō Shi Kenkyū Kai, *Nōmin undō shi*, 273.

20. Matsuo, "The Development of Democracy in Japan," 629.

21. Watanabe, "Buraku kaihō undō," 189. The change in direction of the buraku movement is also discussed in Kyōchōkai, *Shakai undō*, 694.

22. Kurokawa Midori, "Kome sōdō to Suiheisha," 180; and Sakamoto, "Okayama no kome sōdō to burakumin," 61.

23. For the immediate reactions of Watanabe Tetsuzō, Ōyama Ikuo, Fukuda Tokuzō, and Yoshino Sakuzō to the riots, see *Chūō kōron*, September 1918, pp. 69–98. Yoshino was particularly concerned about the fearful potential inherent in uncontrolled mass protest. Nevertheless, he and his associates in the Rimeikai, organized after the 1918 riots, continued to advocate popular participation in the nation's politics. Tokyo Imperial University students took a similar stand following the establishment of the Shinjinkai.

24. Matsuo, "Development of Democracy," 628.

25. Ibid., 630.

26. Itō and Akita, "The Yamagata-Tokutomi Correspondence," 421.

27. Ishibashi, "Sōjō no seiji igi," in *Ishibashi Tanzan zenshū* 2:78. Fukuda Tokuzō shared Ishibashi's view that the modern rice riot resembled the traditional subsistence crisis in being motivated by the rioters' "right of extreme need." See Fukuda, "Bōdō ni tai suru tōkyoku no taido," 93.

Bibliography

Interviews

Hamada Ken'ichi. Personal interview. Namerikawa, Japan, 15 April 1982.

Hamada Tsu. Personal interview. Namerikawa, Japan, 15 April 1982.

Ise Takahashi. Personal interview. Namerikawa, Japan, 16 April 1982.

Kaneko Tadao. Personal interview. Namerikawa, Japan, 12 April 1982.

Koshida Yasuo. Personal interview. Namerikawa, Japan, 14 April 1982.

Nakamata Isamu. Personal interview. Uozu, Japan, 15 April 1982.

Ochiai Shigenobu. Personal interview. Kobe, Japan, 8 September 1982.

Takeda Hōichi. Personal interview. Kobe, Japan, 9 September 1982.

Tsunezawa Isamu. Personal interview, Namerikawa, Japan, 13 April 1982.

Manuscript Collections

Nagoya City Library, Tsurumai Branch. Aichi-ken kōhō. Unpublished prefectural documents, including decrees, ordinances, and orders for rice. Nagoya, Japan.

Namerikawa Bunka Center. Document collection for the Namerikawa city history. Namerikawa, Japan.

Ōhara Shakai Mondai Kenkyūjo. The Hosokawa collection of rice riot research materials and local government records. Tokyo, Japan.

Works Cited

Abe Makoto. "Hyōgo-ken ka no kome sōdō" [Rice riots in Hyogo prefecture]. *Hyōgo shigaku*, no. 50 (September 1968).

———. *Hyōgo kome sōdō ki* [A record of the Hyogo riots]. Tokyo: Shin Nihon Shinsho, 1969.

Abe Tsunehisa. "Josei to kome sōdō" [Women and rice riots]. In *Joseitachi no kindai*, Kindai Josei Shi Kenkyū Kai. Tokyo: Kashiwa Shobō, 1978.

———. "Meiji nijūsan nen kome sōdō no tenkai katei—Niigata-ken o chūshin ni" [The transitional process of the 1897 Rice Riots—focusing on Niigata prefecture]. *Niigata shigaku* 9 (October 1974).

Abrahamian, E. "The Crowd in Iranian Politics, 1905–1953." *Past and Present*, no. 41 (December 1968).

Adachi Masa'aki. "Kobe no 'kome sōdō' to shakai shugisha, sono hoka" [The Kobe "rice riots," socialists, and other issues]. *Rekishi to Kōbe* 8 (August 1968).

———. "Kome sōdō (Kōbe no) zentei" [The (Kobe) rice riots: premises]. *Rekishi to Kōbe* 2 (August 1964).

Adas, Michael. "'Moral Economy' or 'Contest State'? Elite Demands and the Origins of Peasant Protest in Southeast Asia." *Journal of Social History* 13, no. 4 (Summer 1980).

Aichi-ken Gikai Jimu Kyoku. *Aichi-ken gikai shi* [History of the Aichi prefecture assembly]. 4 vols. Nagoya: Aichi-ken Gikai, 1966.

Aichi-ken Keisatsu Shi Hensan Iin Kai. *Aichi-ken keisatsu shi* [History of the Aichi prefecture police]. 2 vols. Nagoya: Aichi-ken, 1973.

Aichi-ken Nōchi Shi Hensan Iin Kai. *Aichi-ken nōchi shi* [Aichi prefecture agricultural history]. Nagoya: Aichi-ken, 1957.

Amano Takurō. "Goken undō kome sōdō to minshū undō no hatten, 1" [The Constitution Protection Movement and the development of mass movements, 1]. *Rekishi hyōron*, no. 149 (January 1963).

———. Goken undō kome sōdō to minshū undō no hatten, 2" [The Constitution Protection Movement and the development of mass movements, 2]. *Rekishi hyōron*, no. 151 (March 1963).

———. "Kome sōdō to kyōiku" [The rice riots and education]. *Buraku mondai kenkyū* 12 (1962).

Andō Yoshio, ed. *Kindai Nihon keizai shi yōran* [A survey of modern Japan's economic history]. Tokyo: Tōkyō Daigaku Shuppan Kai, 1981.

Aoki Kōji. *Hyakushō ikki no nenji-teki kenkyū* [Chronological research on peasant uprisings]. Tokyo: Gannandō, 1966.

———. *Taishō nōmin sōjō shiryō nenpyō* [Chronology of Taishō farmers' riots]. 3 vols. Tokyo: Gannandō, 1977.

Arnold, David. "Looting, Grain Riots and Government Policy in South India, 1918." *Past and Present*, no. 84 (August 1979).

Asahi Shinbun Sha. *Asahi shinbun ni miru Nihon no ayumi* [Japan's course as seen from the *Asahi shinbun*]. 5 vols. Tokyo: Asahi Shinbun Sha, 1975.

Asahi Shinbun Sha Ube-shi Kyoku. *Ube tankō shiwa* [Historical tales of the Ube mines]. Fukuoka City: Asahi Shinbun Sha Ube-shi Kyoku, 1981.

Ayusawa, Iwao. *A History of Labor in Modern Japan*. Honolulu: East-West Center Press, 1966.

Baba Akira. "Chūgoku mai yunyū mondai: beika chōsetsu kara sansen gun iji e" [The problem of importing Chinese rice: from rice price regulation to support of the military's involvement in war]. *Nihon rekishi* 407, no. 4 (April 1982).

Bartlett, Thomas. "An End to Moral Economy: The Irish Militia Disturbances of 1793." *Past and Present*, no. 99 (May 1983).

Bendix, Reinhardt, and Seymour Martin Lipset, eds. *Class, Status, and Power: A Reader in Social Stratification*. New York: Free Press, 1953.

Bennett, John W., and Iwao Ishino. *Paternalism in the Japanese Economy: Anthropological Studies of Oyabun-Kobun Patterns*. Minneapolis: University of Minnesota Press, 1963.

Bernstein, Gail Lee. *Japanese Marxist: A Portrait of Kawakami Hajime*. Cambridge: Harvard University Press, 1976.

Bienen, Henry. *Violence and Social Change: A Review of Current Literature*. Chicago: University of Chicago Press, 1968.

Booth, Alan. "Food Riots in the North-West of England, 1790–1801." *Past and Present*, no. 77 (November 1977).

Borton, Hugh. *Peasant Uprisings of the Tokugawa Period*. 1938 Reprint. New York: Paragon Books, 1968.

Bowen, Roger. "Rice Roots Democracy and Popular Rebellion in Japan." *Journal of Peasant Studies*, no. 1 (October 1978).

Burton, W. Donald. "Peasant Struggle in Japan." *Journal of Peasant Studies*, no. 2 (January 1978).

Charlesworth, Andrew, and Andrian J. Randall. "Morals, Markets, and the English Crowd." *Past and Present*, no. 114 (February 1987).

Coats, A. W. "Contrary Moralities: Plebs, Paternalists, and Political Economists." *Past and Present*, no. 54 (February 1972).

Cobb, R. C. *The Police and the People: French Popular Protest, 1784–1820*. London: Oxford University Press, 1970.

Collick, Ribert Martin Vesy. "Labour and Trade Unionism in the Japanese Coal-mining Industry." Ph.D. diss., Oxford University, 1976.

Daimon Ichijū. *Bukka teikō shi* [History of resistance to consumer prices]. Tokyo: Sanseidō, 1968.

———. *Bukka no hyaku nen* [A hundred-year history of consumer prices]. Tokyo: Hayakawa Shobō, 1967.

Davies, Natalie Zemon. "The Reasons of Misrule: Youth Groups and Charivaris in Sixteenth-Century France." *Past and Present*, no. 50 (February 1971).

de Roover, Raymond. "The Concept of the Just Price: Theory and Economic Policy." *Journal of Economic History*, no. 18 (1958).

Dohi Noritaka. *Edo no komeya* [Edo rice merchants]. Tokyo: Yoshikawa, 1981.

Dore, Ronald, ed. *Aspects of Social Change in Japan*. Princeton: Princeton University Press, 1967.

———. *Land Reform in Japan*. London: Oxford University Press, 1959.

Duus, Peter. *Party Rivalry and Political Change in Taishō Japan*. Cambridge: Harvard University Press, 1968.

Endō Yoshinobu and Yoshii Ken'ichi. "Kome sōdō to sōgi to gunshuku to: Taishō demokurashii ka ni minshū sei o tou" [Rice riots, disputes, and demilitarization: questioning the character of the masses during the Taishō democracy period]. *Gendaishi* (September 1978).

Fujimori Hisao. *Toyama-ken kome sōdō nisshi* [A chronology of the Toyama prefecture rice riots]. Toyama City: Toyama Kenritsu Toshokan, 1968.

Fujino Yutaka, Tokunaga Takashi, and Kurokawa Midori. *Kome sōdō to hisabetsu buraku* [The rice riots and discriminated-against buraku]. Tokyo: Yūzankaku, 1986.

Fukuda Tokuzō. "Bōdō ni tai suru tōkyoku no taido" [The authorities' attitude toward rioting]. *Chūō kōron*, no. 361 (September 1918).

Fukuoka-ken Keisatsu Hensan Iin Kai. *Fukuoka-ken keisatsu shi: Meiji, Taishō hen* [Fukuoka prefecture police history: Meiji, Taishō]. Fukuoka City: Fukuoka-ken Keisatsu Hensan Iin Kai, 1978.

Fukutake, Tadashi. *Rural Society in Japan*. Translated by the Staff of the Japan Interpreter. Tokyo: University of Tokyo Press, 1980.

Geertz, Clifford. "Ideology as a Cultural System." In *Ideology and Discontent*, ed. David E. Apter. New York: The Free Press, 1964.

Genovese, Elizabeth Fox. "The Many Faces of the Moral Economy: A Contribution to a Debate." *Past and Present*, no. 50 (February 1973).

Gilje, Paul A. "The Baltimore Riots of 1812 and the Breakdown of the Anglo-American Mob Tradition." *Journal of Social History* 13, no. 4 (Summer 1980).

Gluck, Carol. *Japan's Modern Myths: Ideology in the Late Meiji Period*. Princeton: Princeton University Press, 1985.

———. "The People in History: Recent Trends in Japanese Historiography." *Journal of Asian Studies* 38, no. 1 (November 1978).

Gordon, Andrew. *The Evolution of Labor Relations in Japan: Heavy Industry, 1853–1956.* Cambridge: Harvard University Press, 1985.

Hanada Katsuji. "Kōfu no natsu—Ube tankō no kome sōdō" [The summer of the coal miner: The Ube mine rice riot]. *Minshū bungaku,* no. 35 (October 1968).

Hane, Mikiso. *Peasants, Rebels, and Outcastes: The Underside of Modern Japan.* New York: Pantheon, 1982.

Hara Atsushi. "Kome sōdō (Kōbe chihō) no hanashi" [Talks on the rice riots (Kobe region)]. *Shinsō,* no. 6 (1946).

Hara Takashi. *Hara Takashi nikki* [The diary of Hara Takashi]. 6 vols. Ed. Hara Kei'ichirō. Tokyo: Fukumura Shobō, 1965.

Harada, Shuichi. *Labor Conditions in Japan.* New York: Columbia University Press, 1928.

Harada Tomohiko. *Kinsei toshi no sōjō shi* [History of rioting in early modern cities]. Tokyo: Shinbun Kaku Shuppan, 1982.

Harari, Ehud. *The Politics of Labor Legislation in Japan: National-International Interaction.* Berkeley and Los Angeles: University of California Press, 1973.

Hasegawa Hiroshi. "Kome sōdō" [The rice riots]. In *Nihon shihon shi no nyūmon,* 3, ed. Arisawa Hiromi et al. Tokyo: Nihon Hyōron Sha, 1958.

Hasegawa Hiroshi and Masujima Kō. "Kome sōdō no dai'ichi dankai: Toyama-ken ka genchi chōsa o chūshin toshite" [The first stage of the rice riots: focusing on field investigations in Toyama prefecture]. *Shakai rōdō kenkyū,* no. 1 (January 1954).

———. "Kome sōdō no dai'ichi dankai (kanketsu): Toyama-ken ka genchi chōsa o chūshin toshite" [The first stage of the rice riots: focusing on field investigations in Toyama prefecture (Conclusion)]. *Shakai rōdō kenkyū,* no. 2 (November 1954).

Hashimoto Tetsuya. "Kanazawa kome sōdō to saiban kiroku" [The trial record of the Kanazawa rice riot]. *Kanazawa Daigaku Keizai Gakubu ronshū* 2, no. 1 (October 1981).

———. "The Lower Socio-Economic Classes and Mass Riots in a Provincial City." *The United Nations University Project on Technology Transfer, Transformation, and Development: The Japan Experience.* Tokyo: The United Nations University, 1981.

———. "Toshika to minshū undō" [Urbanization and mass movements]. In *Nihon rekishi, 17; kindai,* 4. Iwanami Kōza. Tokyo: Iwanami Shoten, 1976.

Hauser, Philip. "The Social, Economic, and Technological Problems of Rapid Urbanization." In *Industrialization and Society,* ed. Bert Hoselitz and Wilbert Moore. The Hague: Mouton for UNESCO, 1963.

Havens, Thomas R. H. *Farm and Nation in Modern Japan: Agrarian National-ism, 1870–1940.* Princeton: Princeton University Press, 1974.

Hayami, Yujiro, and V. W. Ruttan. "Korean Rice, Taiwan Rice, and Japanese Agricultural Stagnation: An Economic Consequence of Colonialism." *Quarterly Journal of Economics* 84 (November 1970).

Hayashi Eidai. *Chikuhō kome sōdō ki* [An account of the Chikuhō region rice riots]. Tokyo: Aki Shobō, 1986.

Hayashi Hirofumi. "Hara naikaku ki ni okeru rōdō undō taisaku kōsō" [The formulation of labor policy during the period of the Hara cabinet]. *Hitotsu-bashi ronsō* 88, no. 3 (September 1982).

Hijikata Tetsu. *Hisabetsu buraku no tatakai* [The struggle of the discriminated-against buraku]. Tokyo: Shinsen Sha, 1972.

Hirata Toshio. "Kome sōdō no gen dankai" [The present stage of the rice riots]. *Rekishi hyōron*, no. 216 (August 1968).

Hirazawa Kazushichi. "Kōzan kōfu bōdō no shinri" [The psychology of the rioting miners]. *Rōdō oyobi sangyō*, no. 5 (May 1919).

Hobsbawm, E. J. *Primitive Rebels: Studies in Archaic Forms of Social Move-ment in the Nineteenth and Twentieth Centuries.* New York: W. W. Nor-ton, 1959.

Holton, Robert J. "The Crowd in History: Some Problems of Method." *Social History* 3, no. 2 (May 1978).

Hōmū Sho, Kōan Chōsa Chō. *Nairan: sōjō nado no bōdō jiken shūroku* [Civil unrest: a collected record on rioting and other uprisings]. Tokyo: Hōmū Shō, 1952.

Hongō Kiyoshi, Abe Makoto, et al. "Zadankai: kome sōdō no koro" [Round-table discussion: at the time of the riots]. *Hyōgo shigaku*, no. 28 (December 1961).

Hosoda Itarō. "Omoide Kure-shi Yoshiura-machi no kome sōdō" [Recollec-tions: the rice riot in Yoshiura, Kure City]. *Rōdō nōmin undō*, no. 29 (Au-gust 1968).

Hosokawa Karoku. *Hosokawa Karoku chosaku shū* [The collected writings of Hosokawa Karoku]. 3 vols. Tokyo: Riron Sha, 1973.

———. "'Kome sōdō' to sono go no kokumin-teki seichō" [Nationalist growth after the "rice riots"]. *Sekai hyōron*, no. 9 (September 1946).

———. "Taishō nana nen kome sōdō shiryō: Toyama-ken, Wakayama-ken" [1918 rice riot research materials: Toyama prefecture and Wakayama pre-fecture]. *Ōhara Shakai Mondai Kenkyūjo zasshi* 9, nos. 1, 2, 3 (1932–33).

Hotta Akio. "Taishō kōki no seiji" [The politics of the late-Taishō period]. In *Taishō ki no kenryoku to minshū*, ed. Koyama Hitoshi. Tokyo: Hōritsu Bunka Sha, 1980.

Howton, F. William. "Cities, Slums, and the Acculturative Process in Developing Countries." In *Urbanism, Urbanization, and Change: Comparative Perspectives*, ed. Paul Meadows and Ephraim H. Mizruchi. Reading, Mass.: Addison-Wesley, 1969.

Hyōgo-ken Keisatsu Shi Hensan Iin Kai. *Hyōgo-ken keisatsu shi: Meiji-Taishō hen* [Hyogo prefecture police history: Meiji–Taishō]. Kobe: Hyōgo-ken Keisatsu Shi Hensan Iin Kai, 1972.

Ichihara Hiroshi. "Dai'ichiji taisen ni itaru Hokutan keiei" [The management of the Hokutan Collier during World War I]. *Hitotsubashi ronsō* 90, no. 3 (September 1983).

Ii, Kei. [Kondō, Eizō.] "Rice Riot: The Struggles of the People in Recent Japan." *Shakai shugi kenkyū*, October 1921.

Imai Sei'ichi. *Nihon kindai shi* [Japan's modern history]. 2 vols. Tokyo: Iwanami Shoten, 1977.

Imoto Mitsuo. "Kome sōdō no rokujū shūnen to kan Nihonkai kindai shi no shiten" [The sixtieth year of the rice riots, from the perspective of the modern history of the Sea of Japan region]. *Kindaishi kenkyū*, no. 2. (1982).

———. "Nihon kindai kome sōdō no fukugō sei to Chōsen, Chūgoku ni okeru rendō" [The dual nature of the modern Japanese rice riots and linkages with Korea and China]. *Rekishi hyōron*, no. 459 (July 1988).

Inami-machi Shi Hensan Iin Kai. *Inami-machi shi* [History of Inami township]. 2 vols. Toyama City: Inami-machi, 1970.

Inoue Kiyoshi and Ōtani Tsutomu. *Gekiga minshū shi: kome sōdō Kōbe Kawasaki Mitsubishi Zōsenjo dai sōgi made* [People's history illustrated: from the rice riots to the Great Kawasaki Mitsubishi Shipbuilding strike] Tokyo: Jiritsu Shobō, 1981.

Inoue Kiyoshi and Watanabe Tōru, eds. *Kome sōdō no kenkyū* [Rice riots research]. 5 vols. Tokyo: Yūhikaku, 1959–1962.

Inumaru Giichi and Nakamura Shintarō. *Nihon kindai shi, 2: Nisshin, Nichiro Sensō kara kome sōdō made* [Japan's modern history, 2: from the Sino-Japanese and Russo-Japanese wars to the rice riots]. Tokyo: Shin Nihon Shuppan Sha, 1975.

Ishibashi Tanzan. "Gaimai no tabekata" [The way to eat foreign rice]. *Tōyō keizai shinpō*, October 1918.

———. "Sōjō no seiji igi" [Rioting's political significance]. In *Ishibashi Tanzan zenshū*, ed. Ishibashi Tanzan Zenshū Hensan Iin Kai. 14 vols. Tokyo: Tōyō Keizai Shinpō Sha, 1970–1971.

Ishida Yoshikazu. *Nihon gyomin shi* [A history of Japanese fishermen]. Tokyo: San'ichi Shobō, 1978.

Itō Ei'ichi. *Aichi-ken minshū undō no rekishi* [History of mass movements in Aichi prefecture]. Nagoya: Sōgen Sha, 1980.

Itō, Takashi, and George Akita. "The Yamagata-Tokutomi Correspondence: Press and Politics in Meiji–Taishō Japan." *Monumenta Nipponica* 36, no. 4 (Winter 1981).

Itoya Toshio and Inaoka Susumu. *Nihon no sōran hyaku nen* [Japan's turbulent century]. 2 vols. Tokyo: Gendai Hyōron Sha, 1969.

Iwakura Seiji. *Kūki ga nakunaru hi* [The day the air disappeared]. Tokyo: Shin Nihon Shuppan Sha, 1969.

Japan, Bureau of Mines. *Mining in Japan, Past and Present*. Tokyo: Bureau of Mines, 1909.

———. *Taishō ku nen honpō kōgyō sūsei* [Industrial trends in mainland Japan, 1920]. Tokyo: Bureau of Mines, 1921. This publication is in both Japanese and in English.

Japan, Imperial Bureau of Mines. *Mining Industry in Japan*. Tokyo: Bureau of Mines, 1915.

Japan, Ministry of Agriculture and Commerce. *Japan in the Beginning of the Twentieth Century*. Tokyo: Ministry of Agriculture and Commerce, 1904.

Japan, Nōrin Shō. *Nōrin Shō ruinen tōkei sho: 1868–1953* [Ministry of Agriculture statistics for successive years, 1868–1953]. Tokyo: Nōrin Shō, 1955.

Japan, Rōdō Shō. *Tōkei kara mita waga kuni no rōdō sōgi* [Japanese labor disputes as seen from statistics]. Tokyo: Rōdō Shō, 1951.

Johnson, Linda. "Patronage and Privilege: The Politics of Provincial Capitalism in Tokugawa Japan." Ph.D. diss., Stanford University, 1983.

"The Journal of Assistant Town Secretary Kido, 1912." Unpublished document, Namerikawa Bunka Center.

Kagawa Toyohiko. "Chikuhō tanden no rōdō mondai, jō" [Labor problems in the Chikuhō coalfields, 1]. *Kyūsai kenkyū* 6, no.9 (September 1918).

———. "Chikuhō tanden no rōdō mondai, ka" [Labor problems in the Chikuhō coalfields, 2]. *Kyūsai kenkyū* 6, no. 10 (October 1918).

Kaji Ryōsaku, ed. *Kanagawa Sōzaemon shi tsuito shi* [Mr. Kanagawa Sōzaemon: a memorial]. Tokyo: privately published, 1941.

Kamiya Nobuo. "Kome sōdō no joseitachi: ugokizume no shōgai" [Women of the rice riots: continuing lives]. *Uozu shidan*, March 1985.

———. "Kome sōdō rokujū nen: sono gen'in ni tsuite" [The sixtieth year since the rice riots: on the origins of the protest]. *Kyōdo no bunka*, 1979.

———. *Namerikawa-machi ni okeru minpon shugi no tenkai* [The development of limited democracy in Namerikawa township]. Uozu City: privately published, 1986.

Kano Masanori. *Nihon no rekishi: Taishō demokurashii* [Japanese history: Taishō democracy]. Tokyo: Shōgaku Kan, 1976.

Katayama Sen. *Katayama Sen chosaku shū* [The collected works of Katayama Sen]. 3 vols. Tokyo: Kawade Shobō, 1960.

———. "Saikin no kome sōdō ni tsuite—hitori no Nihonjin no setsumei" [On the recent rice riots—one Japanese person's explanation]. *Zen'ei,* no. 107 (August 1955).

Kawabe, Kisaburō. *The Press and Politics in Japan: A Study of the Relation Between the Newspaper and the Political Development of Modern Japan.* Chicago: University of Chicago Press, 1920.

Kawai Masaki. "'Kome sōdō' shin shiryō shōkai: Taishō nana nen hachigatsu beika sōjō shōhō, Toyohashi kenpeitai" [An introduction to new materials on the "rice riots": the detailed report of the August 1918 rice price riots, Toyohashi military police]. *Rōdō undō shi kenkyū,* no. 41 (November 1965).

Kawato Hiroshi. "Senzen Nihon no shokuryō beika seisaku: Hara naikaku o chūshin ni" [Prewar Japan's food supply and rice price policy: centered on the Hāra cabinet]. *Matsuyama Shōdai ronshū* 38, nos. 5–6 (February 1988).

Kelly, William W. *Deference and Defiance in Nineteenth-Century Japan.* Princeton: Princeton University Press, 1985.

Kiernan, V. G. "Patterns of Protest in English History." In *Direct Action and Democratic Politics,* ed. G. R. Benewick and T. Smith. London: George Allen and Unwin, 1972.

Kinbara Samon. "Kome sōdō dankai ni okeru kokumin kyōka no katei" [The process of national education at the stage of the rice riots]. *Bunka to kyōiku* 7, no. 2 (1958).

———. "Kome sōdō o meguru shishō-teki dōkō" [Intellectual trends related to the rice riots]. *Nihon rekishi,* no. 135 (September 1959).

———, ed. Nihon minshū no rekishi, 7: jiyū to handō no chōryū [History of Japanese masses, 7: currents of freedom and reaction]. Tokyo: Sanseidō, 1975.

———. *Taishō ki no seitō to kokumin* [Taishō-period political parties and citizens]. Tokyo: Hanawa Shobō, 1973.

Kinbara Samon and Iwakura Seiji. "Kome sōdō to takumashiki joseitachi" [Rice riots and stalwart women]. *Bunka hyōron* 10, no. 198 (October 1977).

Kita Nihon Shinbun Sha. *Shōgen: kome sōdō* [Testimony: the rice riots]. Toyama City: Kita Nihon Shinbun Sha, 1974.

Kobayashi, Ushisaburo. *The Basic Industries and Social History of Japan.* New Haven: Yale University Press, 1930.

Koga Ryōichi, ed. *Kita Kyūshū chihō shakai rōdō shi nenpyō* [A chronology of social and labor movements in the northern Kyushu region]. Fukuoka City: Nishi Nihon Shinbun Sha, 1980.

Kokusei In. *Nippon teikoku dai sanjūkyū nen tōkei nenkan* [The thirty-ninth annual statistical yearbook of Imperial Japan]. Tokyo: Kokusei In, 1921.

Kome Sōdō Shi Kenkyū Kai, Hokuriku Shibu. "Kome sōdō no hizuke shūsei to *Kome sōdō no kenkyū, Hosokawa Shiryō* no genkai" [Correcting the dates of the rice riots: the limits of *Rice Riot Research* and the *Hosokawa Materials*]. *Rekishi hyōron,* no. 459 (July 1988).

Kōmoto Masanori. "Kome sōdō tōji ni okeru Tokuyama-machi no taisaku shiryō" [Materials on remedial policies in Tokuyama township at the time of the rice riots]. *Yamaguchi-ken chihō shi kenkyū,* no. 19 (1968).

Kōriyama-shi. *Kōriyama-shi shi: Kindai* [Kōriyama City history: modern period]. 2 vols. Kōriyama: Kōriyama-shi, 1971.

Kornhauser, David. *Urban Japan: Its Foundations and Growth.* New York: Longman, 1976.

Koyama Hitoshi. "Gun gyōsei to chōson no dōkō" [County administration and trends in towns and villages]. In *Taishō ki no kenryoku to minshū,* Koyama Hitoshi. Tokyo: Hōritsu Bunka Sha, 1980.

———. "Kome sōdō to shakai mondai: kindai Nihon no tenkan ki" [Rice riots and social problems: modern Japan's turning point]. In *Kindai Nihon no kangaekata,* Yamaguchi Kōsaku and Koyama Hitoshi. Kyoto City: Hōritsu Bunka Sha, 1985.

———. "Rōdōsha kaikyū no jōtai" [Conditions of the laboring class]. In *Kindai Nihon no kangaekata,* Yamaguchi Kōsaku and Koyama Hitoshi. Kyoto City: Horitsu Bunka Sha, 1985.

Kuroha Kiyotaka. *Guntai no kataru Nihon no kindai shi* [A military account of Japan's modern history]. Tokyo: Soshiete, 1980.

Kurokawa Midori. "Kome sōdō to Suiheisha undō no keisei: Mie-ken no baai" [The rice riots and the formation of the Suiheisha movement: the case of Mie prefecture]. In *Kome sōdō to hisabetsu buraku,* ed. Fujino Yutaka, Tokunaga Takashi, and Kurokawa Midori. Tokyo: Yūzankaku, 1986.

Kusano Shigeru. "Toyama-ken ni okeru Meiji sanjū nen kome sōdō ni tsuite" [On the 1897 rice riots in Toyama prefecture]. *Nihonshi kenkyū,* no. 33 (March 1957).

Kuwada, Kumazō. "Social Politics and Social Problems: Introductory Remarks." In *Japan Year Book, 1917.* Tokyo: Japan Year Book Office, 1917.

Kyōchōkai. *Saikin no shakai undō* [The recent social movement]. Tokyo: Kyōchōkai, 1929.

Kyōtō Daigaku Jinbungaku Kenkyūjo. "Keisatsu no mita kome sōdō" [The rice riots as seen by the police]. *Rekishigaku kenkyū,* no. 180 (1955).

Large, Stephen S. *Organized Workers and Socialist Politics in Interwar Japan.* London: Cambridge University Press, 1981.

Lemarchand, René. "Comparative Political Clientelism: Structure, Process and Optic." *Political Clientelism, Patronage and Development*, ed. S. N. Eisenstadt and René Lemarchand. Beverly Hills: Sage Publications, 1981.

Lewis, Michael. "1918 nen Nagoya no sōjō" [The 1918 Nagoya riots]. *Rekishi hyōron*, no. 461 (September 1988).

Lu, David John, ed. *Sources of Japanese History*, vol. 2. New York: McGraw-Hill, 1974.

McGown, Valerie. "Paternalism: A Definition." *Social Analysis*, nos. 5–6 (December 1980).

MacPherson, W. J. *The Economic Development of Japan, c. 1868–1941*. London: MacMillan Education, 1987.

Margadant, Ted W. *French Peasants in Revolt: The Insurrection of 1851*. Princeton: Princeton University Press, 1979.

Masujima Kō, Kinbara Samon, and Umeda Kinji. "Kome sōdō o megutte—'Meiji hyaku nen' ka 'kome sōdō gojū nen ka'" [On the rice riots—the "Meiji Centennial" or the "Fiftieth Anniversary of the Rice Riots"?]. *Rekishi hyōron*, no. 216 (August 1968).

Matsui Chiya. "Suwarikomu Toyama no onnatachi" [The Toyama women who sat in]. *Rōdō undō shi kenkyū*, no. 48 (1968).

Matsumoto Hiroshi. "Taishō ki ni okeru jinushi no beikoku hanbai ni tsuite" [On landlord rice marketing during the Taishō period]. *Hitotsubashi ronsō* 60, no. 2 (May 1968).

Matsumoto, Shigeru. *Motoori Norinaga, 1730–1801*. Cambridge: Harvard University Press, 1970.

Matsuo, Takayoshi. "The Development of Democracy in Japan—Taishō Democracy: Its Flowering and Breakdown." *Developing Economies*, no. 4 (December 1966).

———. "Kome sōdō" [Rice riot]. *Buraku*, no. 3 (March 1957).

———. "Kome sōdō chin'atsu no shuppei kibo" [The scale of troop mobilization in suppression of the rice riots]. *Shirin* 71, no. 1 (January 1988).

———. "Kome sōdō kenkyū no ayumi" [The course of rice riot research]. *Rekishigaku kenkyū*, no, 209 (1957).

———. "Kome sōdō to guntai" [Rice riots and the military]. *Jinbun gakuhō* 13 (1960).

———. "Kyōto chihō no kome sōdō" [The Kobe region rice riots]. *Jinbun gakuhō* 6 (1956).

———. *Minpon shugi no chōryū* [Undercurrents of limited democracy]. Tokyo: Bun'eidō, 1970.

———. *Taishō demokurashii no kenkyū*. [Research on Taishō democracy]. Tokyo: Aoki Shoten, 1966.

Mayeda, S. "Rice Riots in Japan." *Japan Magazine*, October 1918.

Mikami Tokusaburō. *Tankōfu no seikatsu* [The lives of coal miners]. Tokyo: Kōgaku Shoin, 1920.

Mitani Taichirō. *Taishō demokurashii ron* [Treatise on Taishō democracy]. Tokyo: Chūō Kōron Sha, 1974.

Mitchell, Richard H. *Thought Control in Prewar Japan*. Ithaca: Cornell University Press, 1976.

Mitsui Bunkō. *Mitsui jigyō shi* [History of Mitsui industry]. 3 vols. Tokyo: Mitsui Bunkō, 1980.

Miyachi Masato. *Nichiro sengo seiji shi no kenkyū: Teikoku shugi keiseiki no toshi to nōson* [Research on political history during the post–Russo-Japanese War period: city and village in the formative period of imperialism] Tokyo: Tōkyō Daigaku Shuppan Kai, 1973.

Moore, Barrington, Jr. *Injustice: The Social Base of Obedience and Revolt*. New York: M. E. Sharpe, 1978.

Morinaga Eisaburō. *Zoku shidan saiban* [Historic trials, continued]. Tokyo: Nihon Hyōron Sha, 1969.

Moulton, Harold Glenn. *Japan: An Economic and Financial Appraisal*. 1931 Reprint. New York: A.M.S. Press, 1969.

Muroboshi Takanobu. "Mizuno naishō no chii to shisei no hihan" [A criticism of Home Minister Mizuno's position and posture]. *Shin kōron* (September 1918).

Nagano Noboru. "Saga chiiki ni okeru kome sōdō" [Rice riots in the Saga region]. *Saga Daigaku keizai ronsō* 10, no. 3 (March 1978).

Nagano-ken. *Nagano-ken seishi* [A political history of Nagano prefecture]. 2 vols. Nagano City: Nagano-ken, 1972.

Nagasue Toshio. *Chikuhō: sekitan to chieki shi* [Chikuhō: coal and the region's history]. Tokyo: NHK Books, 1973.

Nagoya Chihō Shokugyō Shōkai Jimu Kyoku. *Toyama-ken ka Shimoniikawa-gun shutsugyo dan* [Maritime fishing groups in Shimoniikawa county, Toyama prefecture]. Toyama City: n.p., 1924.

Nagoya-shi. *Taishō, Shōwa Nagoya-shi shi* [Nagoya City history, the Taishō and Shōwa periods]. 10 vols. Nagoya: Nagoya-shi 1954.

Nagoya Shikai Jimu Kyoku. *Nagoya shikai shi* [History of the Nagoya city council]. 3 vols. Nagoya: Aichi-ken Gikai Shi Hensan Iin Kai, 1941.

Najita, Tetsuo. "Inukai Tsuyoshi: Some Dilemmas in Party Development in Pre–World War I Japan." *American Historical Review* 74, no. 2 (December 1968).

Nakaniikawa-gun. *Toyama-ken Nakaniikawa-gun yakusho: shakai kairyō* [Nakaniikawa county office, Toyama prefecture: social improvement].

1921. Unpublished documents, Ōhara Shakai Mondai Kenkyūjo document collection.

Namerikawa-machi Yakuba. *Namerikawa-machi shi* [History of Namerikawa township]. Namerikawa-machi: Namerikawa-machi Yakuba, 1913.

Namerikawa Shi Hensan Iin Kai. *Namerikawa-shi shi: shiryō hen* [History of Namerikawa City: research materials]. Namerikawa City: Namerikawa-shi, 1982.

―――. *Namerikawa-shi shi: tsūshi hen* [History of Namerikawa City: general history]. Namerikawa City: Namerikawa-shi, 1985.

Namerikawa-shi Kyōiku Iin Kai. *Kyōdo no ayumi* [Strolls through local history]. Namerikawa City: Namerikawa-shi Kyōiku Iin Kai, 1971.

Nara-ken Keisatsu Shi Iin Kai. *Nara-ken keisatsu shi: Meiji-Taisho hen* [Nara prefecture police history: Meiji–Taishō]. Nara City: Nara-ken Keisatsu Shi Iin kai, 1977.

Narita Ryūichi. "Toshi minshū sōjō to minpon shugi" [Urban masses and limited democracy]. In vol. 3, *Kindai Nihon no sōgō to teikō*, ed. Kano Masanori and Yui Masaomi. Tokyo: Nihon Hyōron Sha, 1982.

Natsume Sōseki. *The Miner*. Translated with an afterword by Jay Rubin. Tokyo: Charles E. Tuttle, 1988.

Natsumeda Tokichi. "Kome sōdō no konseki" [Rice riots past and present]. *Kokumin keizai zasshi*, no. 4 (October 1918).

Nezu Masashi. "Kome sōdō to Shōnai chihō" [Rice riots and the Shōnai region]. *Rekishigaku kenkyū* 2, no. 273 (1963).

Nihon Kindai Shi Kenkyū Kai. *Gakuhō Nihon kindai no rekishi* [Illustrated history of modern Japan]. Tokyo: Sanseidō, 1980.

Nihon Shokuryō Kyōkai. *Senzen ni okeru rekidai naikaku no beikoku shokuryō gyōsei* [The rice and food administration of successive prewar cabinets]. 4 vols. Tokyo: Iwanami Shoten, 1977–1978.

Nishida Yoshiaki. "Nōmin undō no hatten to jinushi sei" [The development of the farmer's movement and the landlord system]. In *Nihon rekishi, 1; kindai, 5*, Iwanami Kōza. Tokyo: Iwanami Shoten, 1975.

Nishinarita Yutaka. "Dai'ichiji taisen chū, go no zaibatsu-kei zōsen kigyō no rōshi kankei" [Labor relations in the zaibatsu-linked shipbuilding industry during and after World War I]. *Hitotsubashi ronsō* 90, no. 3 (September 1983).

Nishino Tokiyoshi. "Nabewarizuki: 1918 nen Toyama wan no kome sōdō" [Months that break the rice bowl: the 1918 Toyama Bay rice riots]. *Minshū bungaku*, no. 35 (September 1968).

Nōmin Undō Shi Kenkyū Kai. *Nihon nōmin undō shi* [History of the Japanese farmers' movement]. Tokyo: Tōyō Keizai Shinpō Sha, 1961.

Noshiro Kunio. "Kome sōdō no omoide" [Recollections of the rice riots]. *Shin sekai*, no. 36 (July 1950).

Nōshōmu Shō Kōzan Kyoku. *Kōgyō hōrei* [Mining industry laws and ordinances]. Tokyo: Nōshōmu Shō Kōzan Kyoku, 1919.

Nōshōmu Shō Nōmu Kyoku. *Kosaku sankō shiryō, kosaku sōgi ni kan suru chōsa* [Tenancy reference materials, surveys concerning tenancy disputes]. Tokyo: Nōmu Kyoku, 1922.

Nōshōmu Shō Rinji Gaimai Kanri Bu. *Gaikoku mai no an'nai* [Information on foreign rice]. Ōhara Shakai Kenkyūjo, packet A for Yamaguchi-ken, Toyoura-gun Yakusho, May–July 1918.

Oakeshott, Michael. *On History and Other Essays*. New Jersey: Barnes and Noble, 1983.

Ōe Shinobu. "Teikoku shugi kakuritsu ki nōson no mujun" [Agrarian contradictions during the period of imperialism's establishment]. In *Nihon fashizmu no keisei to nōson*, ed. Ōe Shinobu. Tokyo: Azekura Shobō, 1978.

Ogawa Kunihara et al. *Yamaguchi-ken no hyaku nen* [Yamaguchi prefecture: one hundred years]. Tokyo: Yamakawa Shuppan, 1983.

Ogura, Takekazu. *Agrarian Problems and Agricultural Policy in Japan: A Historical Sketch*. Tokyo: The Institute of Asian Economic Affairs, 1967.

———. *Can Japanese Agriculture Survive?: A Historical Analysis*. Tokyo: Agricultural Policy Research Center, 1979.

Okado Buhei. *Nagoya shiwa* [Nagoya chronicles]. Nagoya: Sōgen Sha, 1968.

Okado Masakatsu. "Dai'ichiji taisen go no nōson shinkō mondai to sho seiryoku" [Rural village development problems and various influences in the post–World War I period]. *Hitotsubashi ronsō* 89, no. 5 (May 1983).

Okamoto, Shumpei. "The Emperor and the Crowd: The Historical Significance of the Hibiya Riot." In *Conflict in Modern Japan: The Neglected Tradition*, ed. Tetsuo Najita and J. Victor Koschmann. Princeton: Princeton University Press, 1982.

———. *The Japanese Oligarchy and the Russo-Japanese War*. New York: Columbia University Press, 1970.

Okochi, Kazuo. *Labor in Modern Japan*. Tokyo: Science Council of Japan, 1958.

Omameuda Minoru. "1920 nendai ni okeru shokuryō seisaku no tenkai: kome sōdō go zōsan to Beikoku hō" [Development of food-supply policy in the 1920s: post–rice-riot-production increase and the Rice Law]. *Shigaku zasshi* 91, no. 9 (September 1982).

Onodera Itsuya. "Amagazaki-shi no kome sōdō ni okeru chin'atsu seisaku" [The suppression policy in the Amagazaki city rice riots]. *Chiiki shi kenkyū* 5, no. 3 (March 1976).

————. "Kome sōdō ki ni okeru Amagazaki-shi no kyūsai seisaku" [Relief policy during the period of the rice riots in Amagazaki city]. *Chiiki shi kenkyū* 5, no. 1 (July 1975).

Orwell, George. *The Road to Wigan Pier*. Middlesex: Penguin Books, 1962.

Ōyama Ikuo. "Kome sōdō no shakai-teki oyobi seiji-teki kōsatsu" [Social and political considerations of the rice riots]. *Chūō kōron*, no. 361 (September 1918).

Popkin, Samuel L. *The Rational Peasant: The Political Economy of Rural Change in Vietnam*. Berkeley and Los Angeles: University of California Press, 1978.

Powell, John Duncan. "Peasant Society and Clientelist Politics." *American Political Science Review* 64 (June 1970).

Reddy, William M. "The Textile Trade and the Language of the Crowd at Rouen, 1752–1871." *Past and Present*, no. 74 (February 1977).

Reid, Donald. "Industrial Paternalism: Discourse and Practice in Nineteenth-Century French Mining and Metallurgy." *Comparative Studies in Society and History* 27, no. 4 (October 1985).

Rōdō Undō Shi Kenkyū Kai. *Kome sōdō gojū nen* [Rice riots' fiftieth year]. Special issue of *Rōdō undō shi kenkyū*, 1968.

Rōdō Undō Shiryō Iin Kai. *Nihon rōdō undō shiryō* [Research materials on the Japanese labor movement]. 10 vols. Tokyo: Rōdō Undō Shiryō Kankō, 1959.

Rose, R. B. "Eighteenth Century Price Riots and Public Policy in England." *International Review of Social History* 6, no. 21 (1961).

Rude, George. *The Crowd in History: A Study of Popular Disturbances in France and England, 1730–1848*. New York: Wiley, 1964.

————. *Ideology and Popular Protest*. New York: Pantheon, 1980.

Saeki Tadasu et al. "Kome to sono daiyō tabemono no kenkyū" [Research on rice and rice substitutes]. *Chūō kōron*, no. 361 (September 1918).

Saitō Isamu. *Nagoya chihō rōdō undō shi* [The history of the labor movement in the Nagoya region]. Nagoya: Fūbai Sha, 1969.

Saitō Yaichirō. *Kome sōdō* [Rice riot]. Namerikawa City: Saitō Yaichirō Ichō Kankō Kai, 1976.

Sakai Sei'ichi. *Toyama-ken no rekishi* [Toyama prefecture history]. Tokyo: Yamakawa Shuppan Kai, 1970.

Sakai Tadasu and Shimizu Isao, eds. *Kindai manga, 5: Taishō zenki no manga* [Modern cartoons, 5: early-Taishō cartoons]. Tokyo: Chikuma Shobō, 1985.

Sakamoto Chūji. "Okayama no kome sōdō to burakumin no yakuwari o megutte" [Concerning the role of burakumin in the Okayama rice riots]. *Rekishi hyōron*, no. 459 (July 1988).

Scalapino, Robert A. *Democracy and the Party Movement in Prewar Japan: The Failure of the First Attempt.* Berkeley and Los Angeles: University of California Press, 1962.

——. *The Early Japanese Labor Movement: Labor and Politics in a Developing Society.* Berkeley: Institute of East Asian Studies 1983.

Scott, James C. *The Moral Economy of the Peasant.* New Haven: Yale University Press, 1976.

——. "Patron-Client Politics and Political Change in Southeast Asia." *American Political Science Review* 66 (1972).

Shakai Fukushi Chōsa Kenkyūkai. *Senzen Nihon no shakai jigyō chōsa* [A survey of social work in prewar Japan]. Tokyo: Keisō Shobō, 1983.

Shanin, Teodor., ed. *Peasants and Peasant Societies.* Oxford: Basil Blackwell, 1987.

Shelton, Walter J. *English Hunger and Industrial Disorder.* London: Macmillan, 1973.

Shibata Masami. "Kome sōdō tōji no nōson—tōkei sho o riyō shite" [Villages at the time of the rice riots—making use of statistical collections]. *Hyōgo shigaku,* no. 48 (November 1967).

Shihō Keiji Kyoku, ed. *Iwayuru kome sōdō jiken no kenkyū* [Research on the so-called riot incidents]. 1938 Reprint. Tokyo: Tōyō Bunka, 1974.

Shimane-ken Keisatsu Honbu. *Shimane-ken keisatsu shi* [Shimane prefecture police history]. Shimane: Shimane-ken Keisatsu Honbu, 1978.

Shindō Toyoo. *Chikuhō no onna kōfutachi* [Chikuhō women miners]. Tokyo: Buraku Mondai Kenkyūjo Shuppan Bu, 1974.

——. *Ōmuta no kindai shi* [Ōmuta's modern history]. Ōmuta: Ōmuta Kyōiku o Kangaeru Kai, 1977.

Shinjō Village. *Shinjō: The Chronicle of a Japanese Village.* Translated with an introduction by Keith Brown. Pittsburgh: University of Pittsburg Press, 1979.

Shinobu Seizaburō. *Taishō seiji shi* [Taishō political history]. 4 vols. Tokyo: Kawade Shobō, 1951–1952.

Shiota Shōbei "Kome sōdō to gendai" [The rice riots and the present day]. In *Kome sōdō no gojū nen.* Special issue of *Rōdō undō shi kenkyū,* 1968.

——. "The Rice Riots and the [*sic*] Social Problems." *Developing Economies* 6, no. 4 (December 1966).

Shizuoka min'yū shinbun [Shizuoka min'yū newspaper]. 16, 21, and 30 August 1918.

Shōji Kichinosuke. *Kindai chihō minshū undō shi, 2* [Modern history of regional popular movements, 2]. 2 vols. Tokyo: Azekura Shobō, 1978.

——. *Kome sōdō no kenkyū* [Rice riot research]. Tokyo: Mirai Sha, 1957.

————. "Kome sōdō no tenkai katei" [Rice riot development process]. *Rekishi hyōron*, no. 58 (August 1954).

Shoshan, Boaz. "Grain Riots and the 'Moral Economy': Cairo, 1350–1517." *Journal of Interdisciplinary History* 10, no. 3 (Winter 1980).

Shūgi In, ed., *Kokkai taikan* [National Diet chronicle]. Tokyo: Sangyō Keizai Sha, 1954.

Silberman, Bernard S., and H. D. Harootunian, eds. *Japan in Crisis: Essays on Taishō Democracy*. Princeton: Princeton University Press, 1974.

Skocpol, Theda, ed. *Vision and Method in Historical Sociology*. Cambridge: Cambridge University Press, 1984.

Smethurst, Richard J. *Agricultural Development and Tenancy Disputes in Japan, 1870–1940*. Princeton: Princeton University Press, 1986.

————. *A Social Basis for Prewar Militarism: The Army and the Rural Community*. Berkeley and Los Angeles: University of California Press, 1974.

Smith, Adam. *An Inquiry into the Nature and Causes of the Wealth of Nations*. New York: Modern Library, 1937.

Smith, Robert J. "Making Village Women into 'Good Wives and Wise Mothers' in Prewar Japan." *Journal of Family History* 8, no. 1 (Spring 1983).

————. "Pre-industrial Urbanism in Japan: A Consideration of Multiple Traditions in a Feudal Society." *Economic Development and Cultural Change* 9, no. 1, part 2 (October 1960).

Smith, Robert J., and Ella Lury Wiswell. *The Women of Suye Mura*. Chicago: University of Chicago Press, 1982.

Smith, Thomas C. "The Right to Benevolence: Dignity and Japanese Workers, 1890–1920." *Comparative Studies in Society and History* 26, no. 4 (October 1984).

Soeda Tomomichi. *Enka no Meiji Taishō shi* [A popular-ballad history of Meiji–Taishō Japan]. Tokyo: Tōsui Shobō, 1982.

Steiner, Kurt. *Local Government in Japan*. Stanford: Stanford University Press, 1965.

Suehiro Yōwa. "Fukui kome sōdō no chiiki henkaku" [Regional change in the Fukui rice riots]. *Rekishi hyōron*, no. 459 (July 1988).

Sugihata Takahiro. "Kome sōdō to kosaku sōgi—Ishikawa-ken Hakui-gun Shiga-machi no baai" [Rice riots and tenancy disputes—the case of Shiga township, Hakui county, Ishikawa prefecture]. *Hokuriku shigaku*, no. 23 (December 1974).

Sumida Toshio. "Kome sōdō ni okeru Sumiyoshi buraku no ugoki" [The movement of the Sumiyoshi buraku during the rice riots]. *Buraku*, no. 13 (1961).

Suzuki Bunji. "Kome sōdō to Yūaikai" [The rice riots and the Yūaikai]. *Rōdō oyobi sangyō* 7, no. 10 (October 1918).

————. *Rōdō undō nijū nen* [Twenty years in the labor movement]. Tokyo: Seibun Sha, 1931.

Suzuki Masayuki. "Nichiro sengo no nōson mondai no tenkai" [The development of agrarian problems in the post–Russo-Japanese War period]. Special issue of *Rekishigaku kenkyū*, December 1974.

————. "Taishō ki nōmin seiji shisō no issoku men (ka)" [An aspect of Taishō-period agrarian political thought, 2]. *Nihon shi kenkyū*, no. 174 (February 1977).

————. "Taishō ki nōmin seiji shisō no issoku men (ka)" [An aspect of Taishō-period agrarian political thought, 2]. *Nihon shi kenkyū*, no. 174 (February 1977).

Suzuki Motosuke. "Kome sōdō ki no toshi to nōson" [City and village during the rice riot period]. *Shizuoka-ken kindai shi kenkyū*, no. 10 (October 1980).

Suzuki Naoji. *Kome: jiyū to tōsei no rekishi* [Rice: a history of freedom and control]. Tokyo: Nihon Keizai Shinbun Sha, 1974.

Taeuber, Irene B. "Urbanization and Population Change in the Development of Modern Japan." *Economic Development and Cultural Change* 9, no. 1, part 2 (October 1960).

Taguchi Shōichirō. "Kome sōdō to Akita-ken" [The rice riots and Akita prefecture]. *Akita kindaishi kenkyū*, no. 11 (November 1960).

Taira, Kōji. *Economic Development and the Labor Market in Japan*. New York: Columbia University Press, 1970.

————. "Public Assistance in Japan." *Journal of Asian Studies* 27, no. 1 (November 1967).

Takahashi Hozuma. "Terauchi naikaku ki no seiji taisei [The political posture of the Terauchi cabinet]. *Shirin* 67, no. 3 (May 1984).

————. "Terauchi naikaku seiritsu ki no seiji jōkyō" [Political conditions at the time of the Terauchi cabinet's formation]. *Nihon rekishi* 434 (July 1984).

Takahashi, Masao. *Modern Japanese Economy Since the Meiji Restoration*. Tokyo: University of Tokyo Press, 1967.

————, ed. *Nihon kindaika to Kyūshū* [Japan's modernization and Kyushu]. Tokyo: Fukuoka Yunesuko Kyōkai, 1972.

Takai Susumu, ed. *Toyama-ken josei shi* [Toyama prefecture, women's history]. Toyama City: Katsura Shobō, 1982.

Takano Yoshisuke. *Kome sōdō ki* [A record of the rice riots]. Ube City: Kome Sōdō Yonjū Shūnen Kinen Kankō Kai, 1959.

————. *Niikawa kara Ube* [From Niikawa to Ube]. Ube City: n.p. 1953.

Takeda Hōichi. "Shōsetsu *Kuroi kome* no yosai" [Additional material from the novel *Black Rice*]. *Rekishi to Kōbe* 8 (August 1968).

Takenaga Mitsuo. "Nichiro sengo—ryō taisen kikan ki no jinushi-kosaku kankei to nōmin undō" [Landlord-tenant relations from the Russo-Japanese War to the interwar period]. *Nihonshi Kenkyū*, no. 233 (March 1981).

Takenob, Y. *Japan Year Book, 1913*. Tokyo: Japan Year Book Office, 1914.

———. *Japan Year Book, 1917*. Tokyo: Japan Year Book Office, 1918.

———. *Japan Year Book, 1919–20*. Tokyo: Japan Year Book Office, 1920.

———. *Japan Year Book, 1921–22*. Tokyo: Japan Year Book Office, 1922.

Takeuchi Toshimi, ed. *Tōhoku nōson no shakai hendō: shin shūdan no ikusei to sonraku taisei* [The social transformation of Tōhoku villages: the cultivation of new organizations and village conditions]. Tokyo: Tōkyō Daigaku Shuppan Kai, 1963.

Tamura Masao, Tamagawa Nobuaki, and Imoto Mitsuo. *Ima yomigaeru kome sōdō* [Reviving the rice riots today]. Tokyo: Shinkō Shuppan Kai, 1988.

Tanuma Hajime. "Kome sōdō shakai undō no tenkai [Rice riots and social movement development]." In *Nihon rekishi: gendai, 2*. Iwanami Kōza. Tokyo: Iwanami Shoten, 1963.

Teikoku Nōkai. *Tōhoku chihō nōson ni kan suru chōsa* [Investigations concerning Tōhoku region villages]. Tokyo: Teikoku Nōkai, 1933.

Teruoka Shūzō. "Japanese Capitalism and Its Agricultural Problems— Culminating in the Rice Riots." *Developing Economies* 4, no. 4 (December 1966).

———. *Jinushi sei to kome sōdō* [The Landlord system and the rice riots]. Tokyo: Nōrin Shō Nōgyō Kenkyūjo, 1958.

———. *Nihon nōgyō mondai no tenkai* [The development of Japanese agrarian problems]. Tokyo: Tōkyō Daigaku Shuppan Kai, 1970.

Thompson, E. P. "Eighteenth-century English Society: Class Struggle Without Class?" *Social History* 3, no. 2 (May 1978).

———. "The Moral Economy of the English Crowd in the Eighteenth Century." *Past and Present*, no. 50 (February 1971).

Tilly, Charles. "The Chaos of the Living City." In *Violence as Politics*, ed. Herbert Hirsch and David C. Perry. New York: Harper and Row, 1969.

———. "Collective Violence in European Perspective." In *Violence in America: Historical Perspectives, A Report to the National Commission on the Causes and Prevention of Violence, 1964*, ed. Ted Gurr. New York: New American Library, 1969.

———. "Food Supply and Public Order in Modern Europe." In *The Formation of National States in Western Europe*, ed. Charles Tilly. Princeton: Princeton University Press, 1975.

Tilly, Charles, Louise Tilly, and Richard Tilly. *The Rebellious Century, 1830–1930*. Cambridge: Harvard University Press, 1975.

Tilly, Louise A. "The Food Riot as a Form of Political Conflict in France." *Journal of Interdisciplinary History* 2, no. 1 (Summer 1971).

Tilly, Richard. "Popular Disorders in Nineteenth-Century Germany: A Preliminary Survey." *Journal of Social History* 1 (Fall 1970).

Tōbata Sei'ichi. "Nihon nōgyō hatten no ninaite" [Those responsible for Japan's agricultural development]. In *Nihon nōgyō hattatsu shi*, Nihon Nōgyō Hattatsu Shi Chōsa Kai. Tokyo: Chūō Kōron Sha, 1978.

Tōkyō Hyaku Nen Shi Iin Kai. *Tōkyō hyaku nen shi* [A centenary history of Tokyo]. 6 vols. Tokyo: Tokyo Metropolitan Government, 1972–1980.

Tōkyō Teikoku Daigaku Nōgakubu Nōseigaku Kenkyū Shitsu. *Shōnai Tenjo no nōgyō nōson oyobi seikatsu* [Agricultural and village life in Tenjo, Shōnai region]. Tokyo: Iwanami Shoten, 1936.

Totten, George O. "Labor and Agrarian Disputes in Japan Following World War I." *Economic Development and Cultural Change* 9, no. 1, part 2 (October 1960).

Toyama-ken. *Toyama-ken seishi* [Toyama prefecture political history]. 5 vols. Toyama City: Toyama-ken, 1944.

———. *Toyama-ken shi: kindai, tōkei zuhyō* [Toyama prefecture history: modern period, statistics and tables]. Toyama City: Toyama-ken, 1983.

———. *Toyama-ken shi: shiryō hen, 7; kindai, 2* [Toyama prefecture history: materials, 7; modern period, 2]. Toyama City: Toyama-ken, 1983.

———. *Toyama-ken shi: tsūshi hen, 5; kindai, 1* [Toyama prefecture history: general history, 5; modern period, 1] Toyama City: Toyama-ken, 1981.

———. *Toyama-ken shi: tsūshi hen, 6; kindai, 2* [Toyama prefecture history: general history, 6; modern period, 2] Toyama City: Toyama-ken, 1984.

Toyama-ken Keisatsu Shi Iin Kai. *Toyama-ken keisatsu shi* [Toyama prefecture police history]. 2 vols. Toyama City: Toyama-ken Keisatsu Honbu, 1965.

Toyama-ken, Naimu Bu. *Ishikawa-Toyama ryōken rengō shakai jigyō kōshūkai kōgi roku* [Record of lectures of the Joint Ishikawa-Toyama Prefectural Social Work Training Course]. Toyama: Toyama Naimu Bu, 1923.

Toyama-ken Shakai Ka. *Toyama-ken ni okeru dekasegi gyofu jijō* [The condition of Toyama prefecture's emigrant fishermen]. Toyama City: Toyama-ken Shakai Ka, 1930.

Toyama-ken Shi Hensan Iin Kai. *Toyama-ken no rekishi to bunka* [Toyama prefecture's history and culture]. Toyama City: Toyama-ken, 1968.

Toyama Shigeki and Satō Shin'ichi. *Nihonshi kenkyū nyūmon* [An introduction to Japanese historical research]. Tokyo: Tōkyō Daigaku Shuppan Kai, 1962.

Toyoda Jō. *Hara Takashi no ansatsu to taishū undō bokkō* [The assassination of Hara Takashi and the sudden rise of mass movements]. Tokyo: Kōdansha, 1984.

Tsuchiya, Keizo. *Productivity and Technological Progress in Japanese Agriculture.* Tokyo: University of Tokyo Press, 1976.

Tsuji Takashi. "1918 kome sōdō no kenkyū to Hosokawa shiryō" [Research on the 1918 rice riots and the Hosokawa materials]. *Kome sōdō tsūshin,* no. 3 (May 1985).

————. Kumagaya-machi no kome sōdō—iwayuru 'fuon' no ugoki ni tai suru shihai kaikyū no taiō" [The Kumagaya township rice riots—the ruling class's countermeasures toward the movement of so-called unrest]. *Saitama rōdō undō shi kenkyū,* no. 13 (September 1981).

Tsuruhara Kazukichi. *Taishō demokurashii ni okeru seiji to minshū* [Politics and the people in Taishō democracy]. Tokyo: Chūō Kōron Sha, 1961.

Uchiyama Hiromasa. *Toyama-ken senzen shakai undō shi* [History of the Toyama prefecture's prewar social movement]. Toyama City: Toyama-ken Senzen Shakai Undō Shi Kankō Kai, 1983.

Uda Kikue, Takasawa Takeshi, and Furukawa Kōjun. *Shakai fukushi no rekishi: seisaku to undō no tenkai* [A history of social welfare: the developments of movements and policies]. Tokyo: Yūhikaku, 1977.

Uda Tadashi. "Osaka shichū kome sōdō oboegaki" [A memoir of the Osaka city rice riots]. *Rekishi to Kōbe* 3 (October 1964).

Umeda Kinji. "1918 kome sōdō no rekishi-teki igi" [The historical significance of the 1918 rice riots]. *Rekishi hyōron,* no. 216 (August 1968).

————. "'Seizon ken' o shucho shite" [Advocating "existence rights"]. In *Nihon minshū no rekishi, 7: jiyū to handō no chōryū,* ed. Kinbara Samon. Tokyo: Sanseidō, 1975.

————. "Taishō nana nen kome sōdō no hyōka—Tsuruhara Kazukichi ikō *Taishō demokurashii ni okeru seiji to minshū* ni tsuite" [An evaluation of the 1918 rice riots—on the late Tsuruhara Kazukichi's work *Politics and the People in Taishō Democracy*]. *Shikan,* nos. 63–64 (October 1961).

Umehara Taka'aki. "1918 nen no kome sōdō: Namerikawa-machi ni okeru zengo sochi ni tsuite" [The 1918 rice riots: on relief measures in Namerikawa township]. *Toyama Daigaku kiyō Keizai Gakubu ronshū,* no. 3 (March 1954).

"Uprising in Burma: The Old Regime Under Siege." *New York Times.* 12 August 1988.

Urada Shōkichi. "1895–1915 nen no Toyama-ken kara no dekasegi kōjō" [Emigrant female factory workers from Toyama, 1895–1915]. *Kantori,* no. 3 (November 1979).

Vlastos, Stephen. *Peasant Protests and Uprisings in Tokugawa Japan.* Berkeley and Los Angeles: University of California Press, 1986.

————. "Tokugawa Peasant Movements in Fukushima: Conflict and Peasant Mobilization." Ph.D. diss., University of California at Berkeley, 1977.

Wagatsuma Sakae, ed. *Nihon seiji saiban shiroku: Taishō* [The historical record of Japanese political trials: Taishō period]. Tokyo: Dai'ichi Hōki Shuppan, 1969.

Walter, John. "Grain Riots and Popular Attitudes to the Law: Maldon and the Crisis of 1629." In *An Ungovernable People: The English and Their Law in the Seventeenth and Eighteenth Centuries*, ed. John Brewer and John Styles. New Brunswick, N.J.: Rutgers University Press, 1980.

Walthall, Anne. *Social Protest and Popular Culture in Eighteenth-Century Japan*. Tucson: Published for the Association for Asian Studies by the University of Arizona Press, 1986.

Waswo, Ann. *Japanese Landlords: The Decline of a Rural Elite*. Berkeley and Los Angeles: University of California Press, 1977.

———. "The Origins of Tenant Unrest." In *Japan in Crisis: Essays on Taishō Democracy*, ed. Bernard S. Silberman and H. D. Harootunian. Princeton: Princeton University Press, 1974.

———. "The Transformation of Rural Society, 1900–1950." Volume 6 of *The Cambridge History of Japan*, Forthcoming.

Watanabe Tetsuzō. "Hachigatsu bōdō to *Binbō monogatari*" [The August riots and *Binbo Monogatari*]. *Chūō kōron*, no. 361 (September 1918).

———. "Keizai jō yori mitaru kome sōdō" [The rice riots as seen from the perspective of economic conditions]. *Shin kōron* (September 1918).

Watanabe Tōru. "Buraku kaihō undō" [The buraku liberation movement]. In *Nihon rekishi, 18; kindai, 5*. Iwanami Kōza. Tokyo: Iwanami Shoten, 1975.

———. "Ōsaka-fu Furuichi-machi no kome sōdō" [The rice riots in Furuichi township, Osaka prefecture]. *Jinbun gakuhō* 7 (1957).

Weingrod, Alex. "Patrons, Patronage, and Political Parties." *Comparative Studies in History and Society* 10, no. 7 (June 1968).

Wells, Roger. "The Revolt of the Southwest, 1800–1801: A Study in English Popular Protest." *Social History*, no. 6 (October 1977).

Wilkinson, Thomas O. *The Urbanization of Japanese Labor, 1868–1955*. Amherst: University of Massachusetts Press, 1965.

Williams, Dale Edward. "Were 'Hunger' Rioters Really Hungry." *Past and Present*, no. 71 (May 1976).

Wong, R. Bin. "Food Riots in the Qing Dynasty." *Journal of Asian Studies* 41, no. 4 (August 1982).

Yamagata-ken. *Yamagata-ken shi: shiryō hen, 20; kin-gendai shiryō, 2* [Yamagata prefecture history: materials, 20; modern-contemporary history materials, 2]. Yamagata City: Yamagata-ken, 1971.

Yamaguchi Kōsaku and Koyama Hitoshi. *Kindai Nihon no kangaekata* [Ways of thought in modern Japan]. Kyoto City: Hōritsu Bunka Sha, 1985.

Yamaguchi-ken Kyōiku Iin Kai. *Yamaguchi tanden no minzoku* [The folkways of Yamaguchi coalfield miners]. Yamaguchi City: Yamaguchi-ken Kyōiku Iin Kai, 1970.

Yamamoto Sakubei. *Chikuhō tankō emaki* [The Chikuhō Coal Mine painted scroll]. Fukuoka City: Ashi Shobō, 1985.

Yamamoto Taketoshi. *Shinbun to minshū* [Newspapers and the people]. Tokyo: Kinokuniya, 1978.

Yamamoto Yoshihiko. "Shizuoka ni okeru kome sōdō: kome sōdō ki Fukuroi chihō no ichi danmen" [The Shizuoka prefecture rice riots: an aspect of the Fukuroi region during the rice-riot period]. *Shizuoka-ken kindaishi kenkyū*, no. 4 (October 1980).

Yazaki, Takeo. *Social Change and the City in Japan*. Tokyo: Japan Publications, 1968.

Yonekura Inokichi. "Mineji tankō no kome sōdō" [The Mineji Coal Mine rice riot]. In *Kome sōdō no gojū nen*. Special issue of *Rōdō undō shi kenkyū*, 1968.

Yoshihara, Kunio. *Sogo Shosha: The Vanguard of the Japanese Economy*. Oxford: Oxford University Press, 1982.

Yoshimura Takuo. "Kome sōdō to tankō chingin seido" [The rice riots and the coal mine wage system]. *Sangyō rōdō kenkyū johō*, no. 23 (January 1961).

———. *Nihon tankō shi shichū* [A personal appraisal of Japan's coal mining history]. Tokyo: Ochanomizu Shobō, 1984.

Yoshimura Tsutomu. "Kansai ni okeru kome sōdō" [The Kansai rice riots]. *Keizaigaku zasshi* 34, nos. 5–6 (June 1956).

Yoshino Sakuzo. "Kome sōdō ni tai suru kōsatsu" [An examination of the rice riots]. *Chūō kōron*, no. 361 (September 1918).

Young, A. Morgan. *Japan Under the Taisho Tenno, 1912–1926*. London: George Allen and Unwin, 1928.

Zimmermann, Ekkert. *Political Violence, Crises, and Revolutions: Theories and Research*. Boston: G. K. Hall, 1983.

Index

Compositor: Asco Trade Typesetting Ltd., Hong Kong
Text: 10/13 Sabon
Display: Sabon
Printer: Edwards Brothers, Inc.
Binder: Edwards Brothers, Inc.